Yuji Kaku

It feels like volume 1 came out only
a few days ago, but here's volume 2
already. Everything goes by so fast.
The sense of time surrounding weekly
serializations has me so disoriented.

Yuji Kaku debuted as a mangaka in 2009 with the one-shot
"Omoide Zeikan" (Memory Customs), which won honorable mention in
the 14th *Jump SQ* Comic Grand Prix. He went on to write several other
one-shots before beginning his first series, *Fantasma*, which
ran in *Jump SQ* from 2013 to 2014. His second series, *Hell's Paradise:
Jigokuraku*, ran from 2018 to 2021 on Jump+ and received an anime
adaptation. *Ayashimon* is his third title and started its
serialization in *Weekly Shonen Jump* in November 2021.

AYASHIMON

Volume 2
SHONEN JUMP Edition

Story and Art by
Yuji Kaku

TRANSLATION Adrienne Beck
LETTERING Brandon Bovia
DESIGN Shawn Carrico
WEEKLY SHONEN JUMP EDITOR Rae First
GRAPHIC NOVEL EDITOR Andrew Kuhre Bartosh

Published by VIZ Media, LLC
P.O. Box 77010
San Francisco, CA 94107

10 9 8 7 6 5 4 3 2 1
First Printing, June 2023

viz.com

AYASHIMON

2

Aren't We Family?

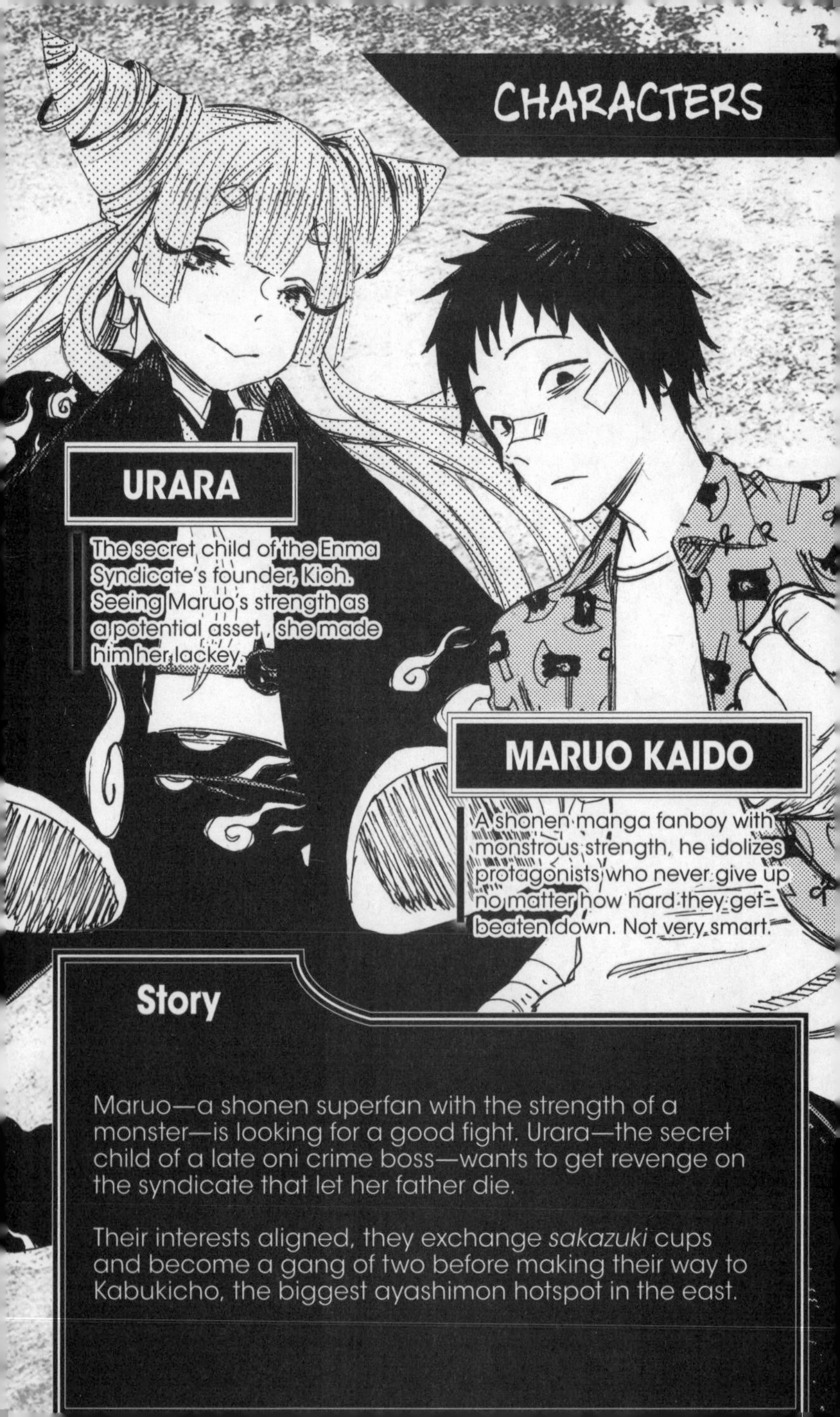

CHARACTERS

URARA

The secret child of the Enma Syndicate's founder, Kioh. Seeing Maruo's strength as a potential asset, she made him her lackey.

MARUO KAIDO

A shonen manga fanboy with monstrous strength, he idolizes protagonists who never give up no matter how hard they get beaten down. Not very smart.

Story

Maruo—a shonen superfan with the strength of a monster—is looking for a good fight. Urara—the secret child of a late oni crime boss—wants to get revenge on the syndicate that let her father die.

Their interests aligned, they exchange *sakazuki* cups and become a gang of two before making their way to Kabukicho, the biggest ayashimon hotspot in the east.

DOPPO AKARI

The second chairman of the Enma Syndicate. He is notoriously vicious and dangerous.

TEN

A yokai from out in the sticks. He joined Urara's gang after being saved by Maruo.

HASHIHIME

A member of the Enma Syndicate. She acted as Urara's caretaker and remains loyal to her.

Kabukicho's Underworld

Following Kioh's death two years ago, the underworld's major players split into four factions.

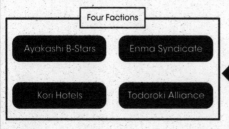

Four Factions

Ayakashi B-Stars

Enma Syndicate

Kori Hotels

Todoroki Alliance

Watches

Cabinet Office, Public Safety

Onmyo Bureau

RITUAL DUEL

A one-on-one fight between ayashimon. It takes place inside a barrier created by the beating of *tsuzumi* drums. The stakes are set using *kotodama* vows, making the results binding.

AYASHIMON

Yokai who have taken on physical form. Most rely on money to build their bodies. If an ayashimon's body is destroyed, it takes them 99 years to revive.

AYASHIMON

2

Aren't We Family?

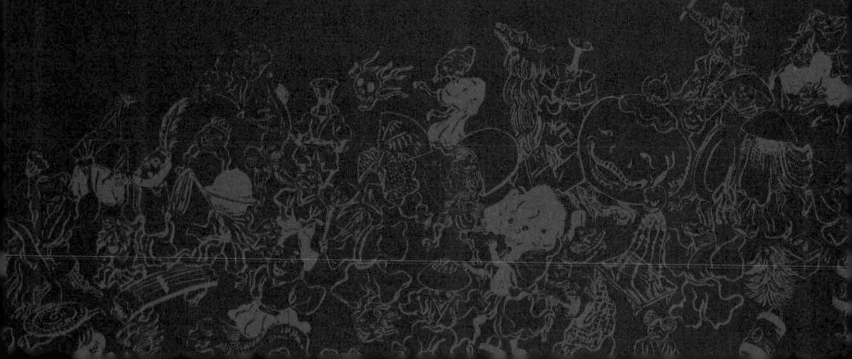

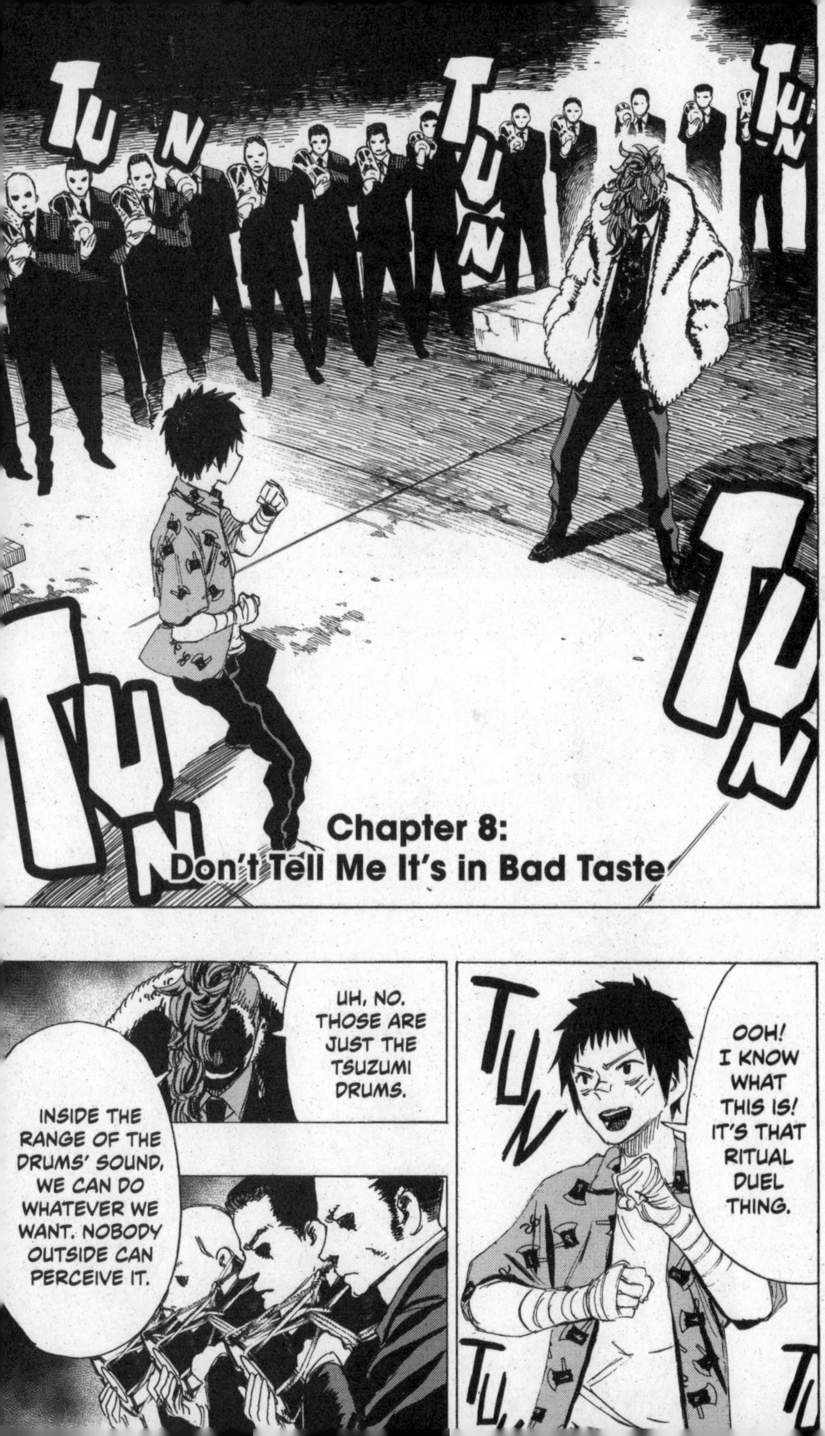
TUN
TUN
TUN
TUN
TUN
TUN
Chapter 8:
Don't Tell Me It's in Bad Taste
TUN
OOH! I KNOW WHAT THIS IS! IT'S THAT RITUAL DUEL THING.
TU..
UH, NO. THOSE ARE JUST THE TSUZUMI DRUMS.
INSIDE THE RANGE OF THE DRUMS' SOUND, WE CAN DO WHATEVER WE WANT. NOBODY OUTSIDE CAN PERCEIVE IT.

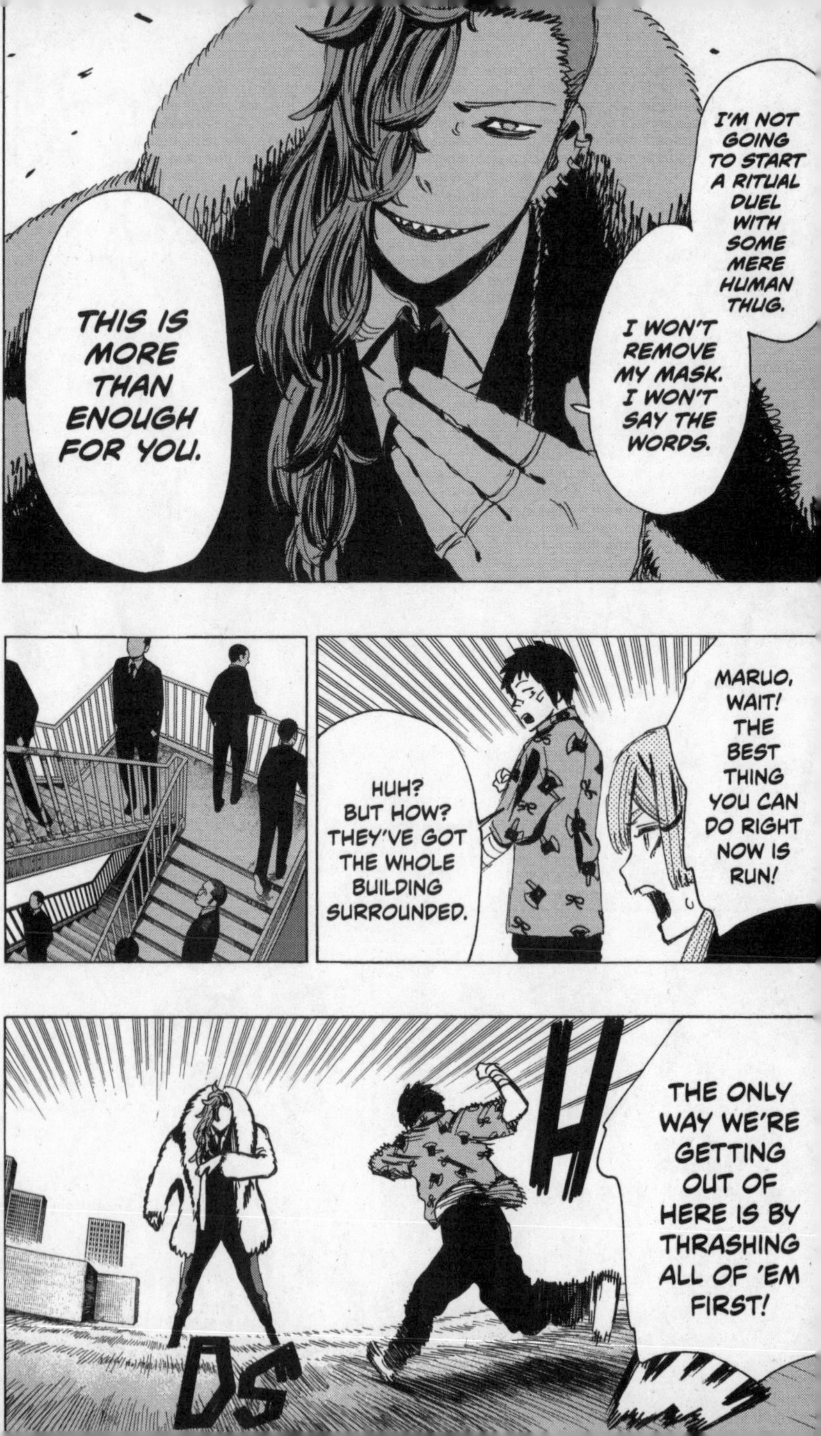
I'M NOT GOING TO START A RITUAL DUEL WITH SOME MERE HUMAN THUG.
I WON'T REMOVE MY MASK. I WON'T SAY THE WORDS.
THIS IS MORE THAN ENOUGH FOR YOU.
MARUO, WAIT! THE BEST THING YOU CAN DO RIGHT NOW IS RUN!
HUH? BUT HOW? THEY'VE GOT THE WHOLE BUILDING SURROUNDED.
THE ONLY WAY WE'RE GETTING OUT OF HERE IS BY THRASHING ALL OF 'EM FIRST!

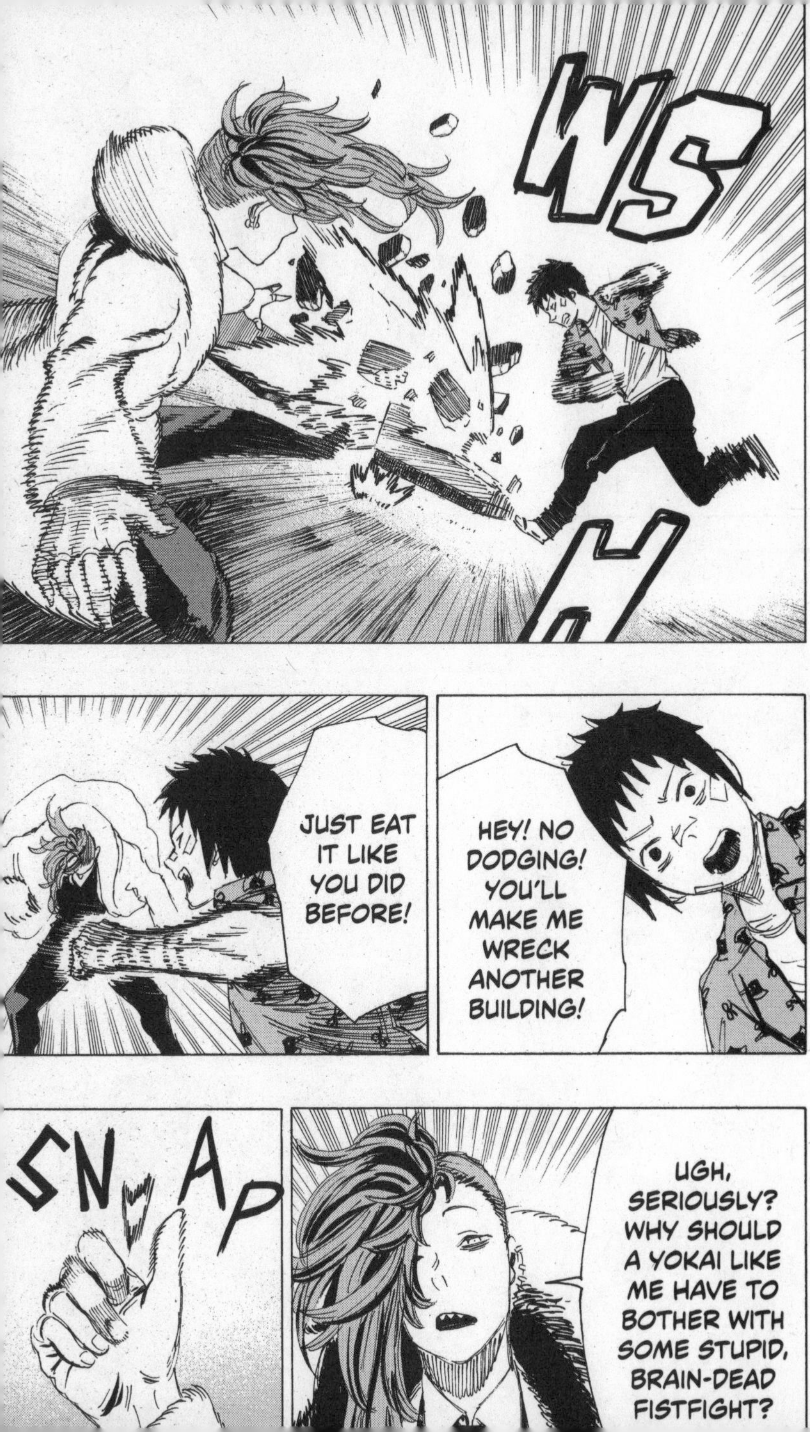
HEY! NO DODGING! YOU'LL MAKE ME WRECK ANOTHER BUILDING!
JUST EAT IT LIKE YOU DID BEFORE!
UGH, SERIOUSLY? WHY SHOULD A YOKAI LIKE ME HAVE TO BOTHER WITH SOME STUPID, BRAIN-DEAD FISTFIGHT?
SNAP

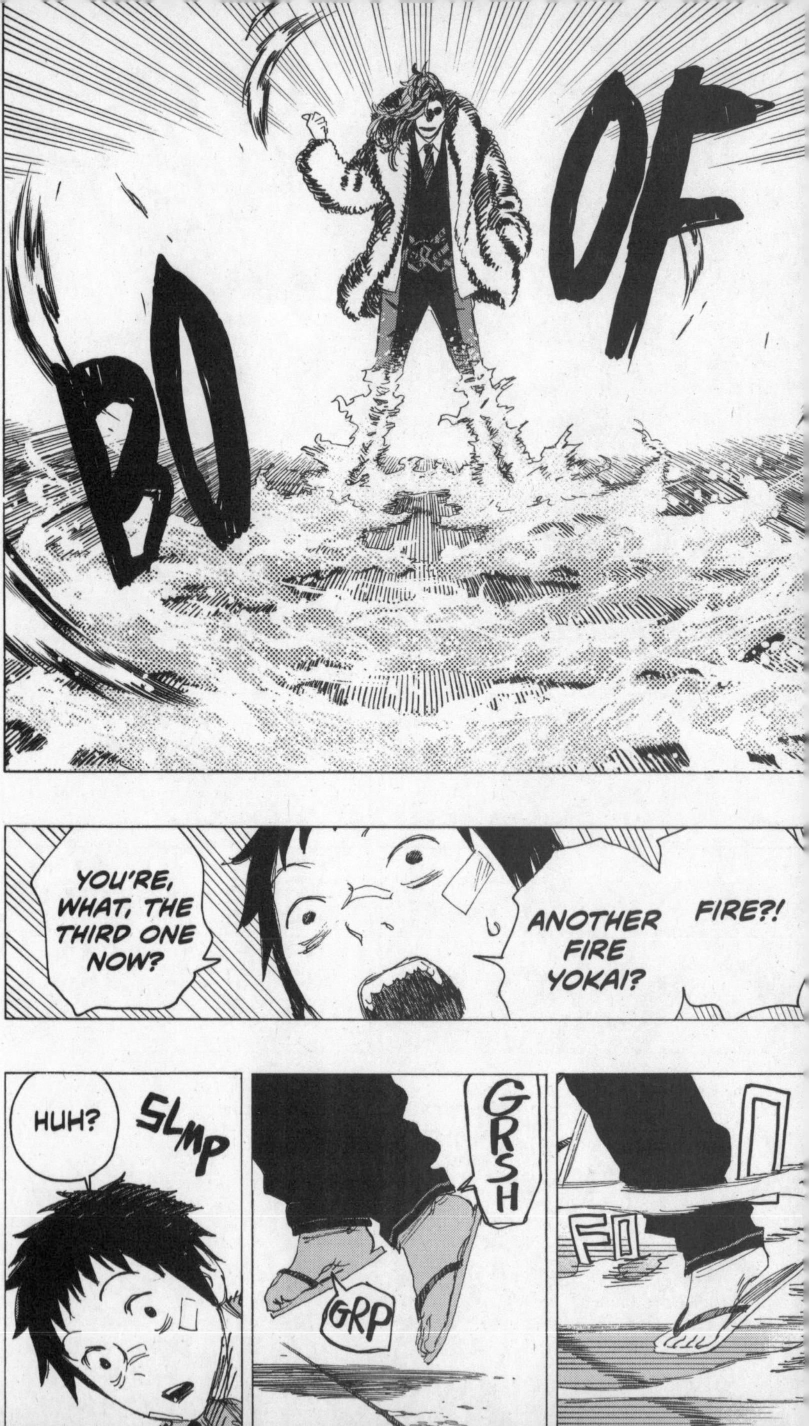
BOOF
FIRE?!
ANOTHER FIRE YOKAI?
YOU'RE, WHAT, THE THIRD ONE NOW?
FOO
GRSH
GRP
SLMP
HUH?

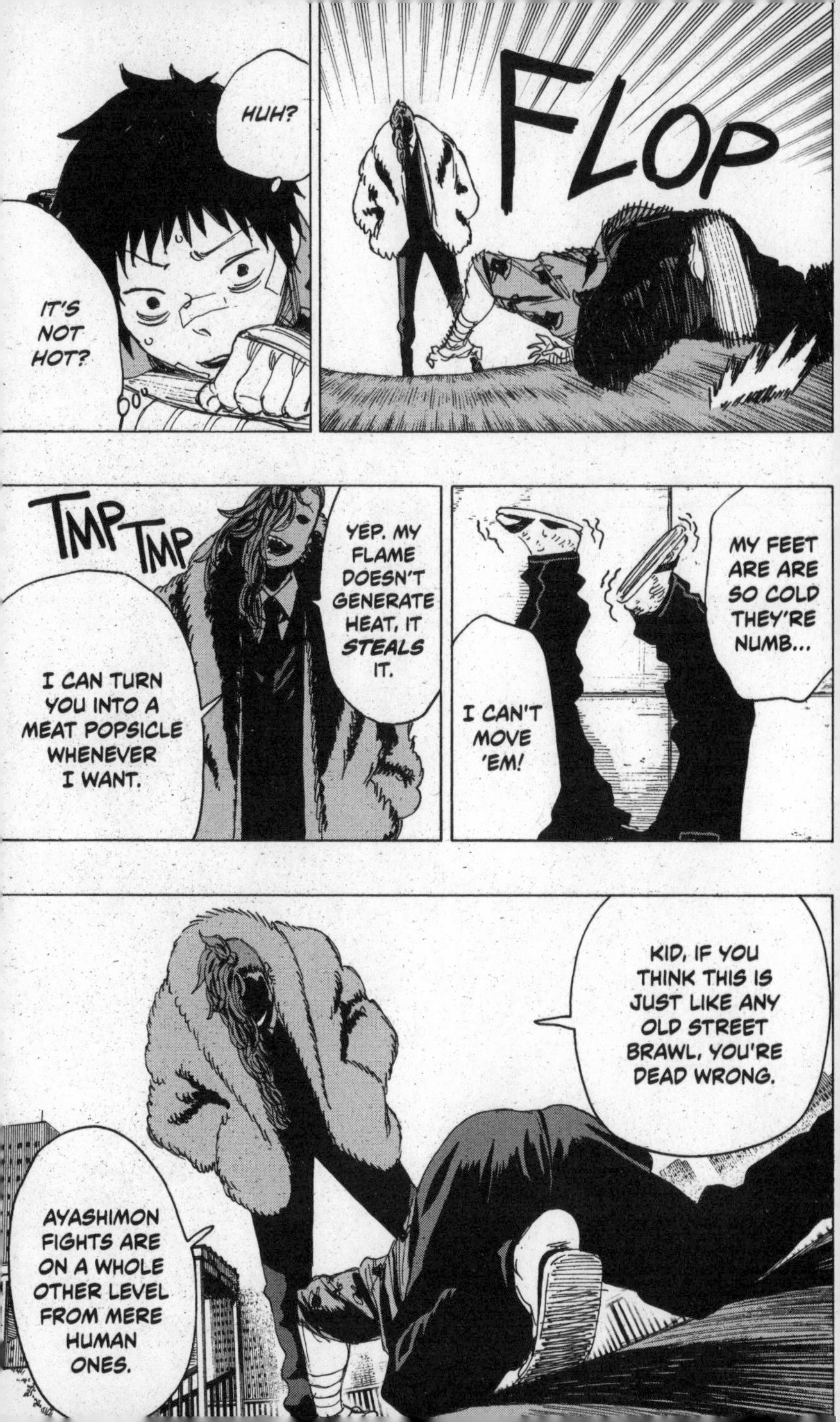
FLOP
HUH?
IT'S NOT HOT?
MY FEET ARE ARE SO COLD THEY'RE NUMB...
I CAN'T MOVE 'EM!
TMP TMP
YEP. MY FLAME DOESN'T GENERATE HEAT, IT *STEALS* IT.
I CAN TURN YOU INTO A MEAT POPSICLE WHENEVER I WANT.
KID, IF YOU THINK THIS IS JUST LIKE ANY OLD STREET BRAWL, YOU'RE DEAD WRONG.
AYASHIMON FIGHTS ARE ON A WHOLE OTHER LEVEL FROM MERE HUMAN ONES.

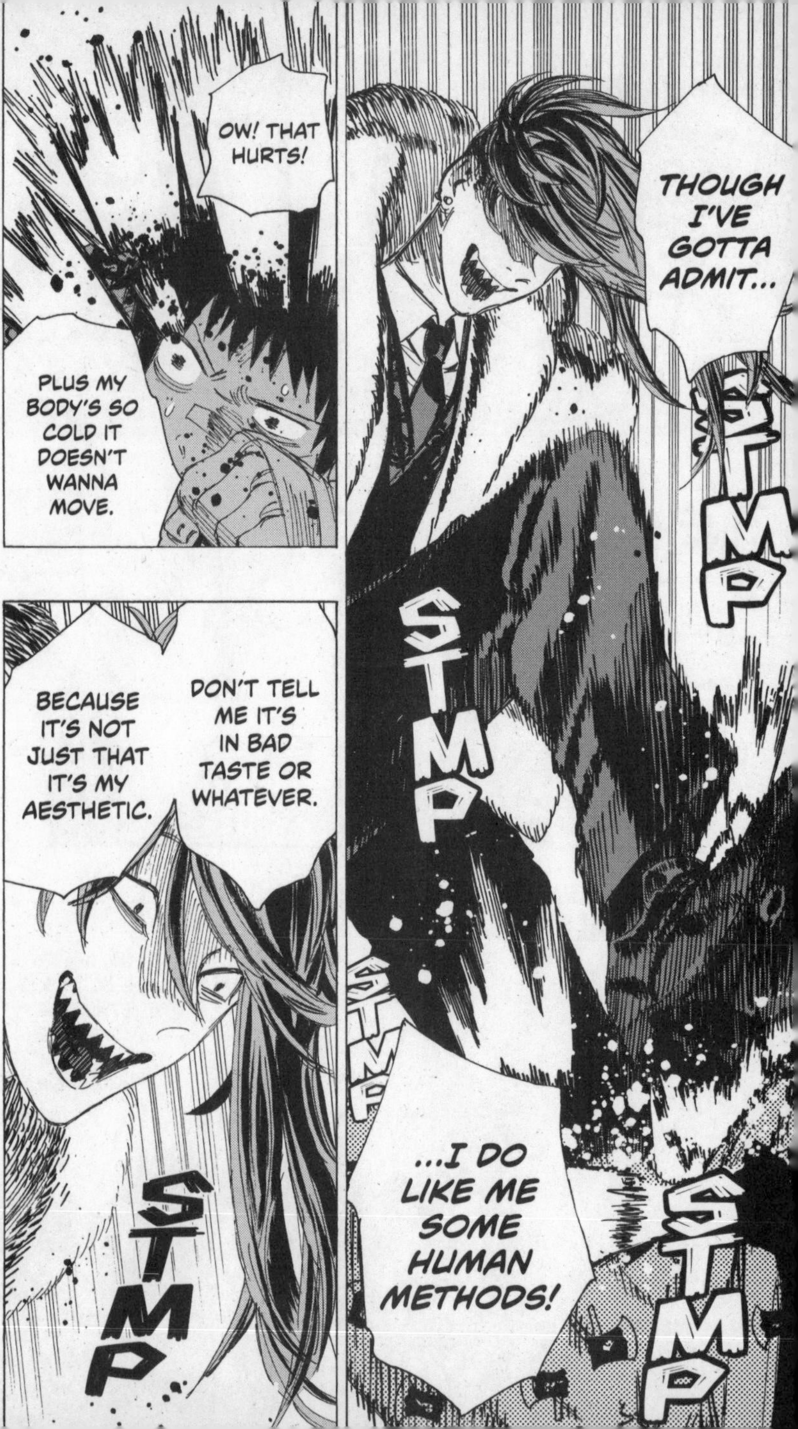
THOUGH I'VE GOTTA ADMIT...
STMP
STMP
STMP
...I DO LIKE ME SOME HUMAN METHODS!
STMP
OW! THAT HURTS!
PLUS MY BODY'S SO COLD IT DOESN'T WANNA MOVE.
DON'T TELL ME IT'S IN BAD TASTE OR WHATEVER.
BECAUSE IT'S NOT JUST THAT IT'S MY AESTHETIC.
STMP

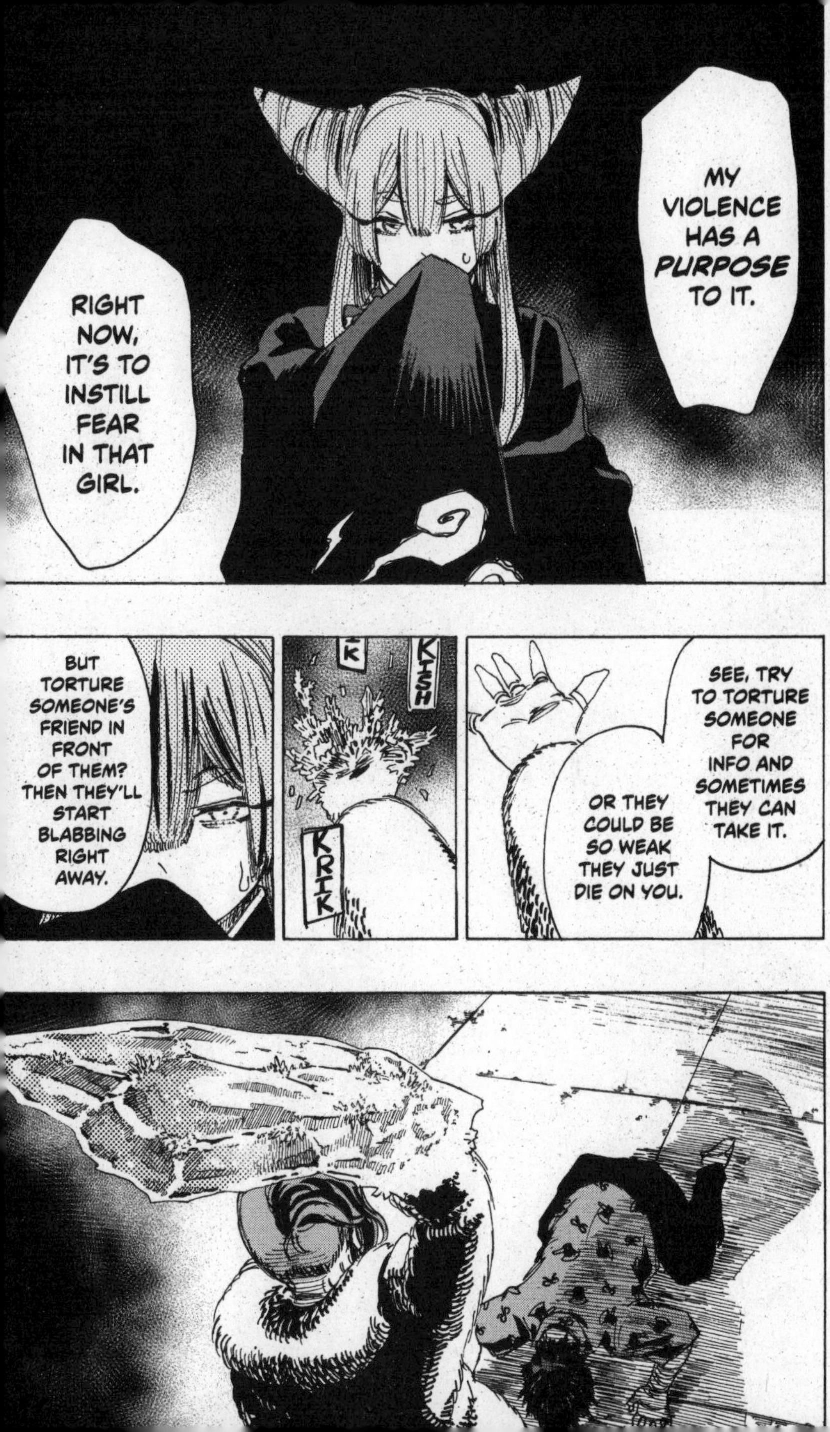
MY VIOLENCE HAS A *PURPOSE* TO IT.
RIGHT NOW, IT'S TO INSTILL FEAR IN THAT GIRL.
SEE, TRY TO TORTURE SOMEONE FOR INFO AND SOMETIMES THEY CAN TAKE IT.
OR THEY COULD BE SO WEAK THEY JUST DIE ON YOU.
KISH
KRIK
BUT TORTURE SOMEONE'S FRIEND IN FRONT OF THEM? THEN THEY'LL START BLABBING RIGHT AWAY.

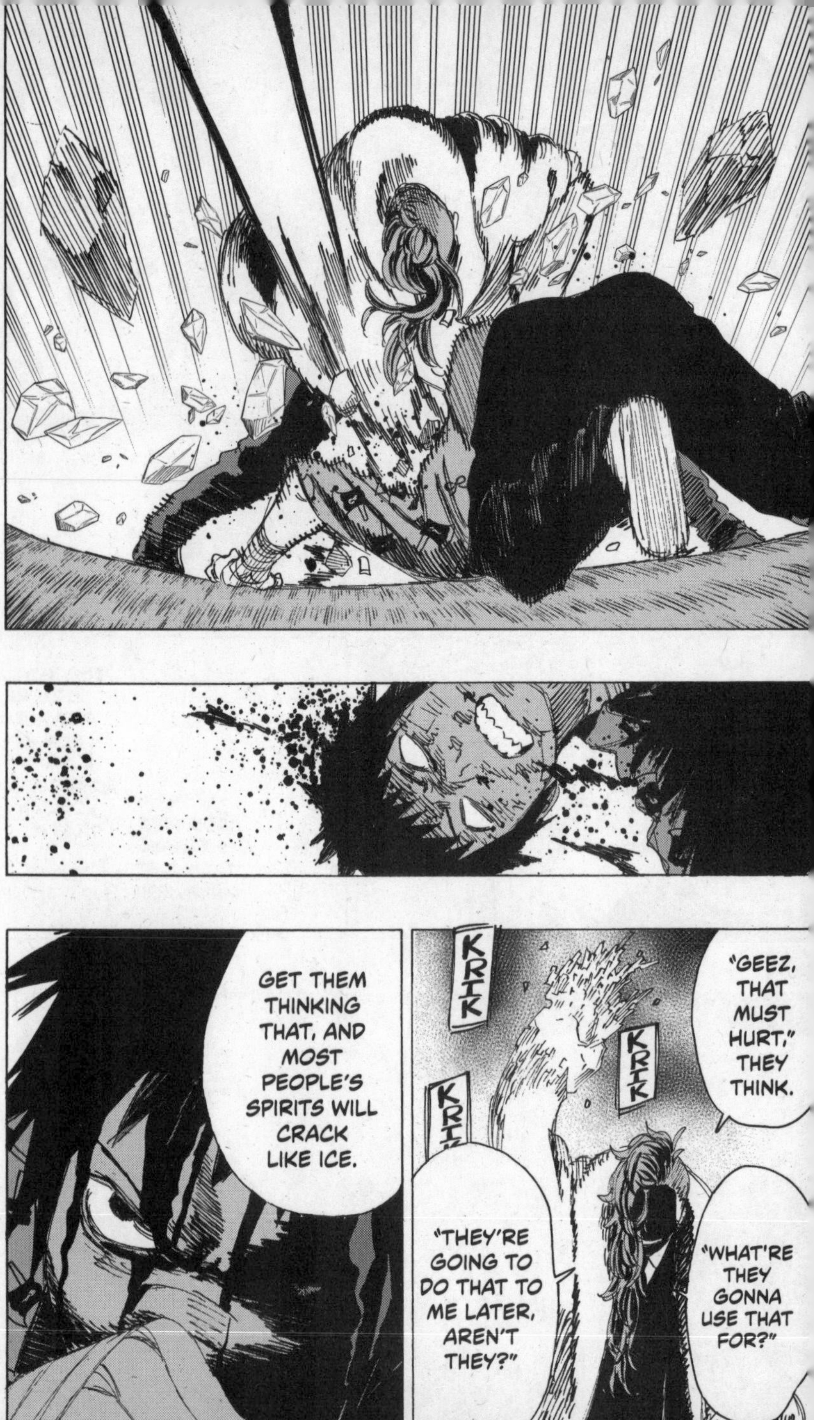
"GEEZ, THAT MUST HURT," THEY THINK.
KRIK
KRIK
KRIK
"WHAT'RE THEY GONNA USE THAT FOR?"
"THEY'RE GOING TO DO THAT TO ME LATER, AREN'T THEY?"
GET THEM THINKING THAT, AND MOST PEOPLE'S SPIRITS WILL CRACK LIKE ICE.

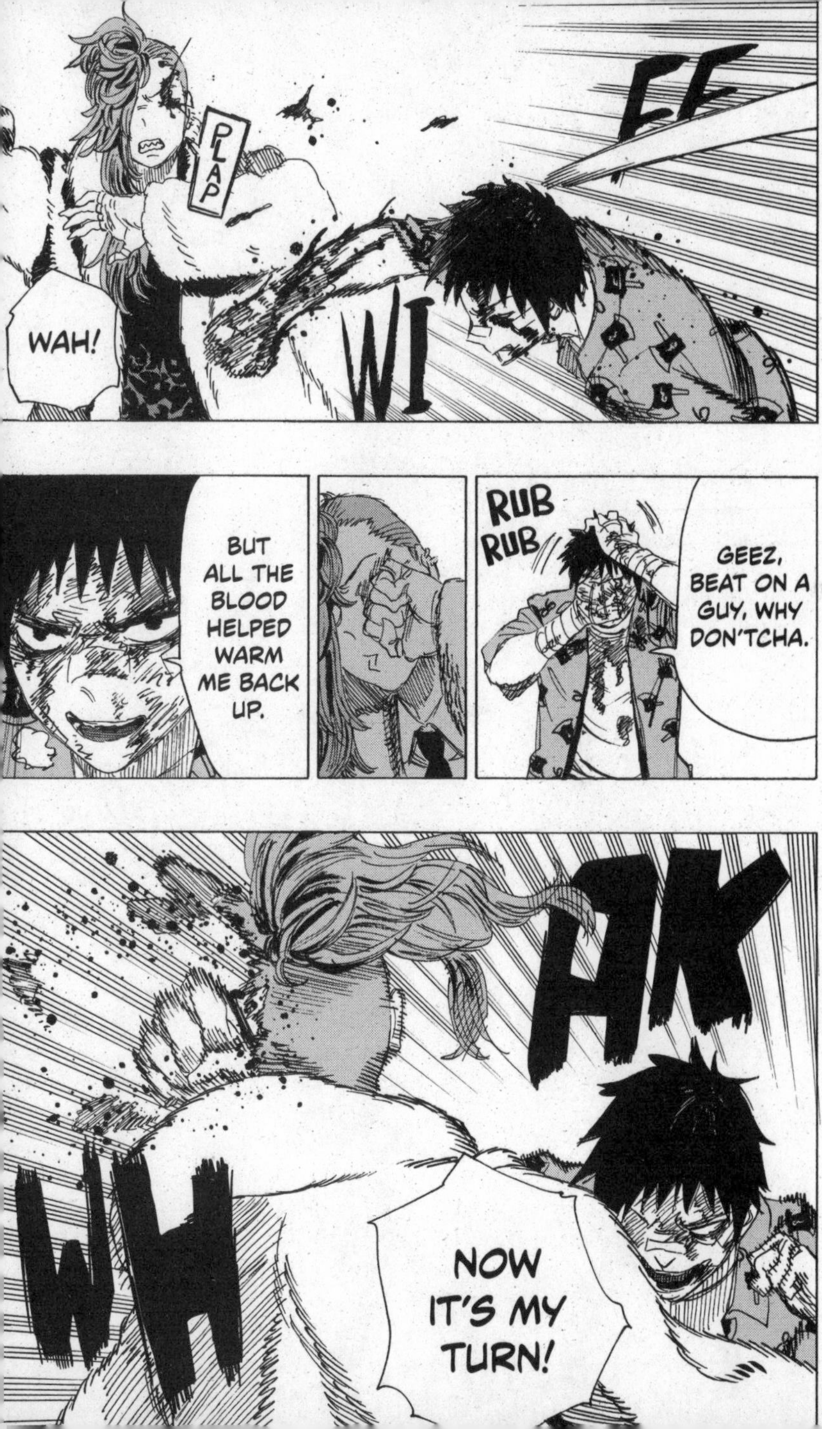
FF
PLAP
WI
WAH!
RUB RUB
GEEZ, BEAT ON A GUY, WHY DON'TCHA.
BUT ALL THE BLOOD HELPED WARM ME BACK UP.
AK
NOW IT'S MY TURN!
WH

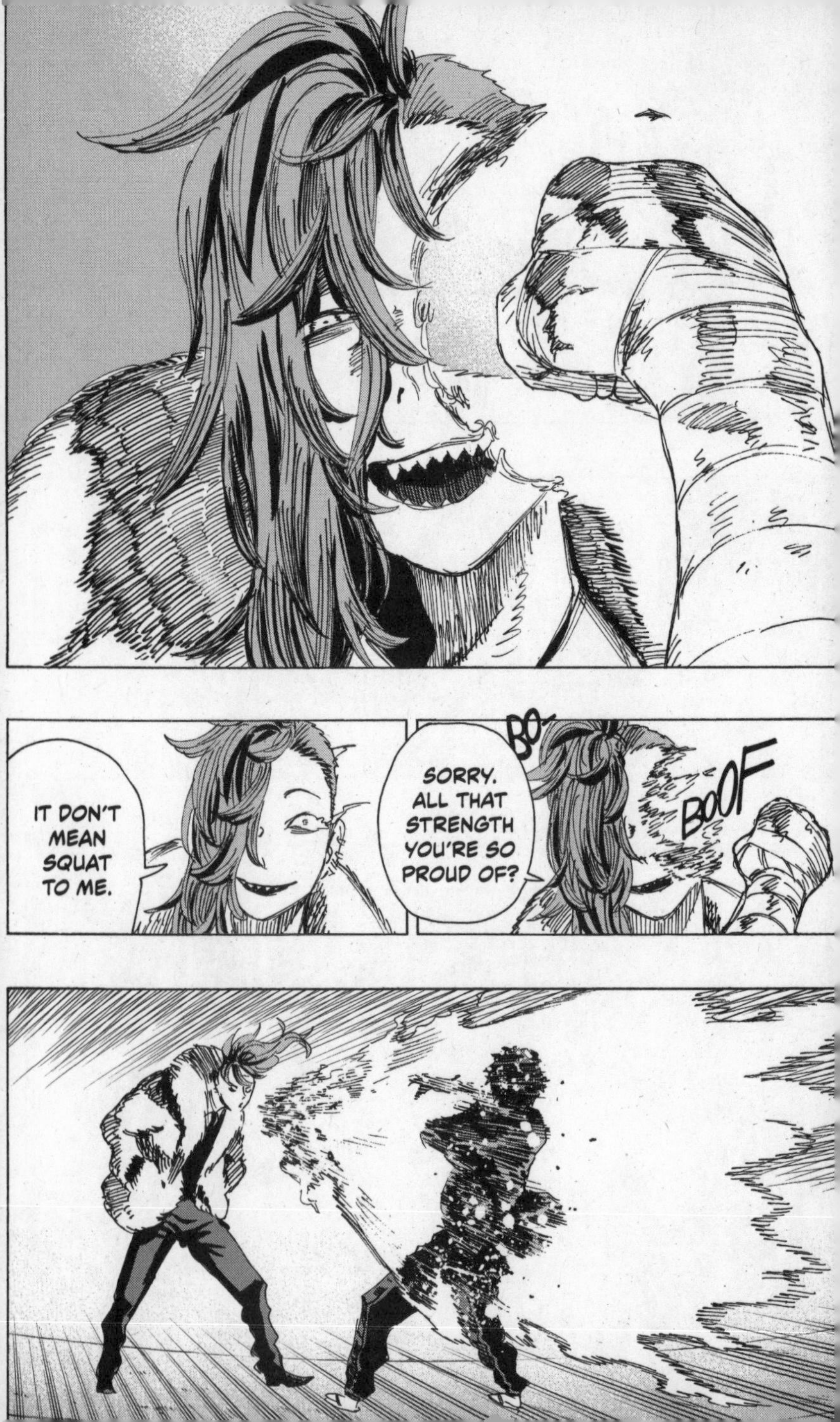
SORRY. ALL THAT STRENGTH YOU'RE SO PROUD OF?
BO-
BOOF
IT DON'T MEAN SQUAT TO ME.

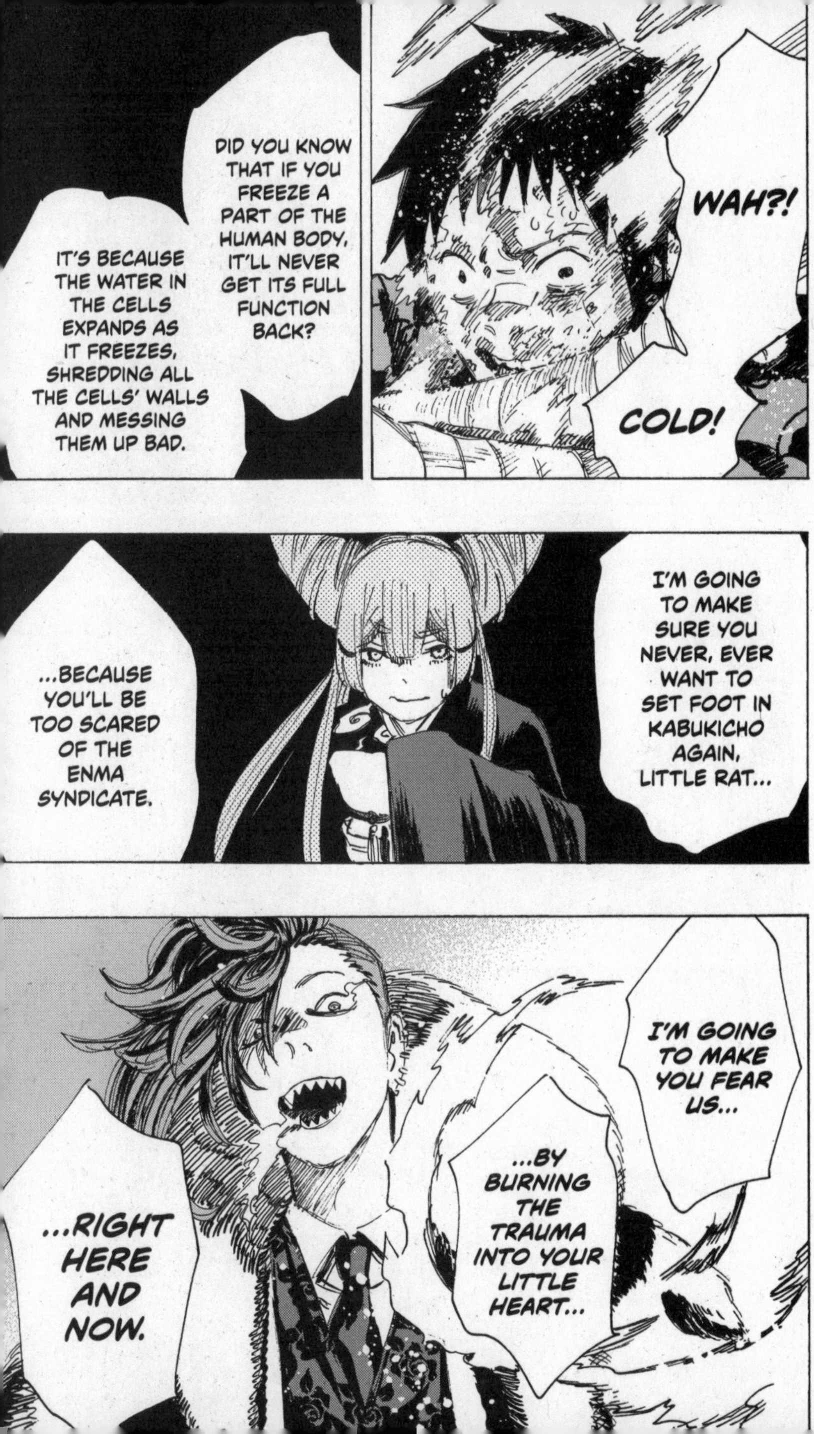
WAH?!
COLD!
DID YOU KNOW THAT IF YOU FREEZE A PART OF THE HUMAN BODY, IT'LL NEVER GET ITS FULL FUNCTION BACK?
IT'S BECAUSE THE WATER IN THE CELLS EXPANDS AS IT FREEZES, SHREDDING ALL THE CELLS' WALLS AND MESSING THEM UP BAD.
I'M GOING TO MAKE SURE YOU NEVER, EVER WANT TO SET FOOT IN KABUKICHO AGAIN, LITTLE RAT...
...BECAUSE YOU'LL BE TOO SCARED OF THE ENMA SYNDICATE.
I'M GOING TO MAKE YOU FEAR US...
...BY BURNING THE TRAUMA INTO YOUR LITTLE HEART...
...RIGHT HERE AND NOW.

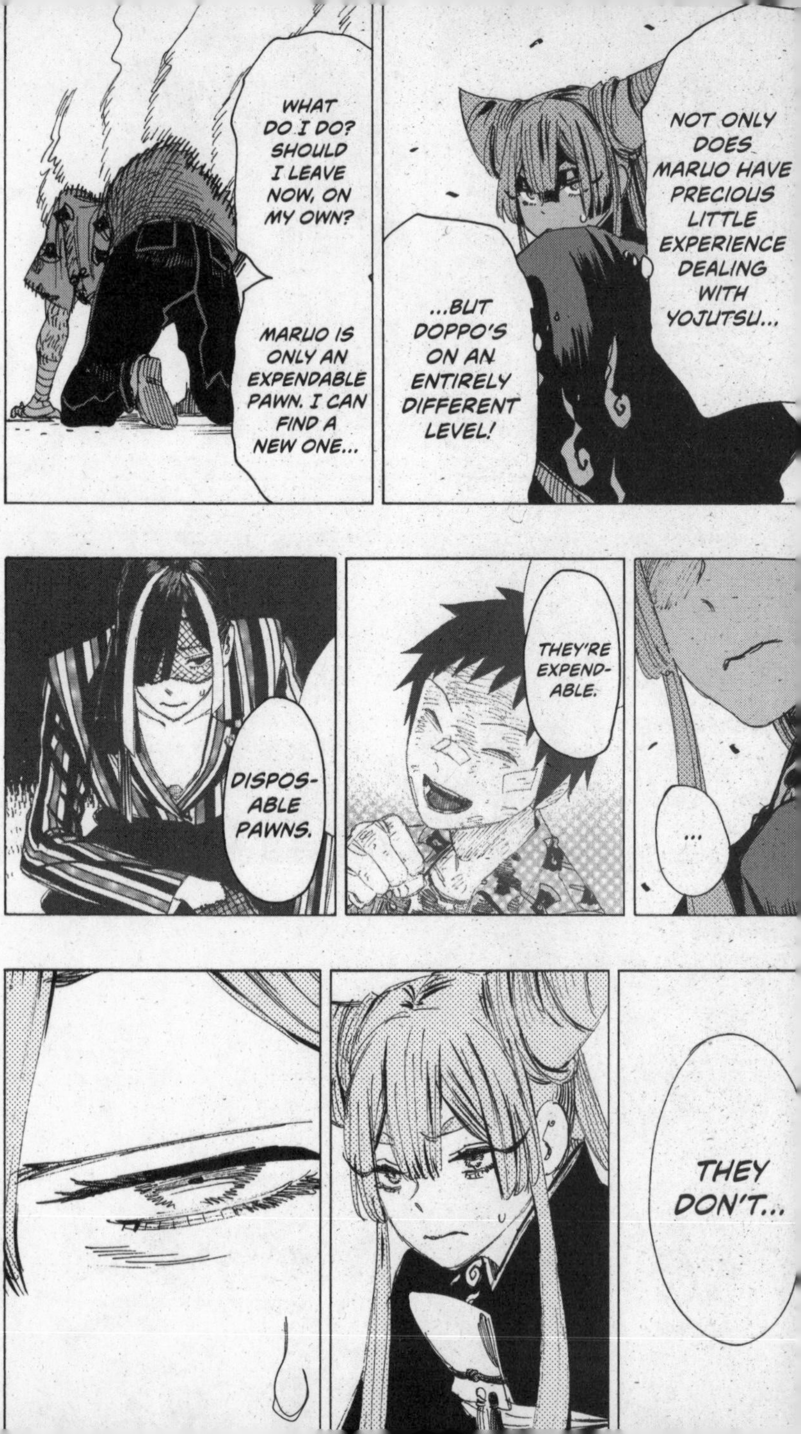
NOT ONLY DOES MARUO HAVE PRECIOUS LITTLE EXPERIENCE DEALING WITH YOJUTSU...
...BUT DOPPO'S ON AN ENTIRELY DIFFERENT LEVEL!
WHAT DO I DO? SHOULD I LEAVE NOW, ON MY OWN?
MARUO IS ONLY AN EXPENDABLE PAWN. I CAN FIND A NEW ONE...
...
THEY'RE EXPEND-ABLE.
DISPOS-ABLE PAWNS.
THEY DON'T...

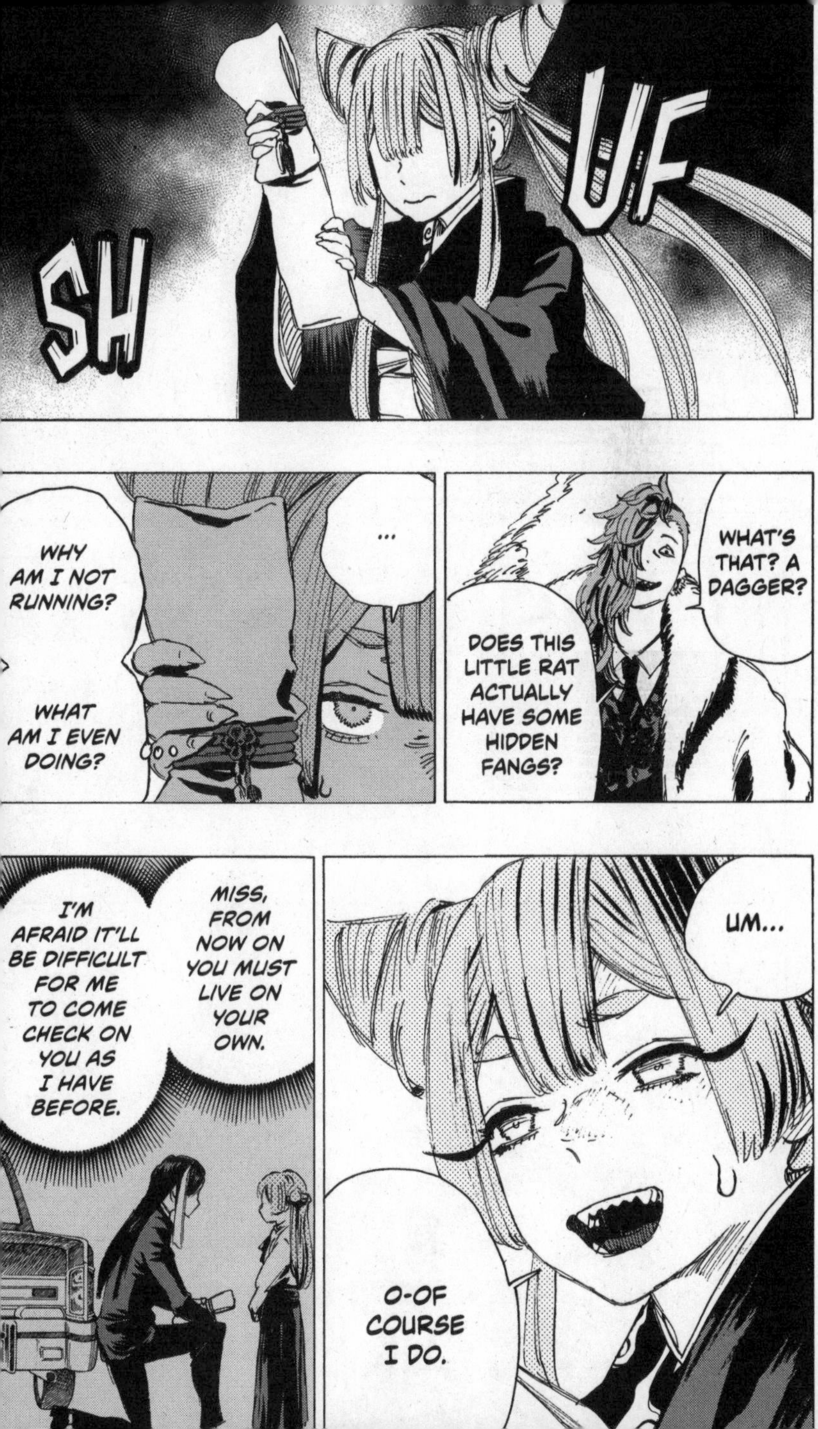
SH
UF
WHAT'S THAT? A DAGGER?
DOES THIS LITTLE RAT ACTUALLY HAVE SOME HIDDEN FANGS?
...
WHY AM I NOT RUNNING?
WHAT AM I EVEN DOING?
UM...
O-OF COURSE I DO.
MISS, FROM NOW ON YOU MUST LIVE ON YOUR OWN.
I'M AFRAID IT'LL BE DIFFICULT FOR ME TO COME CHECK ON YOU AS I HAVE BEFORE.

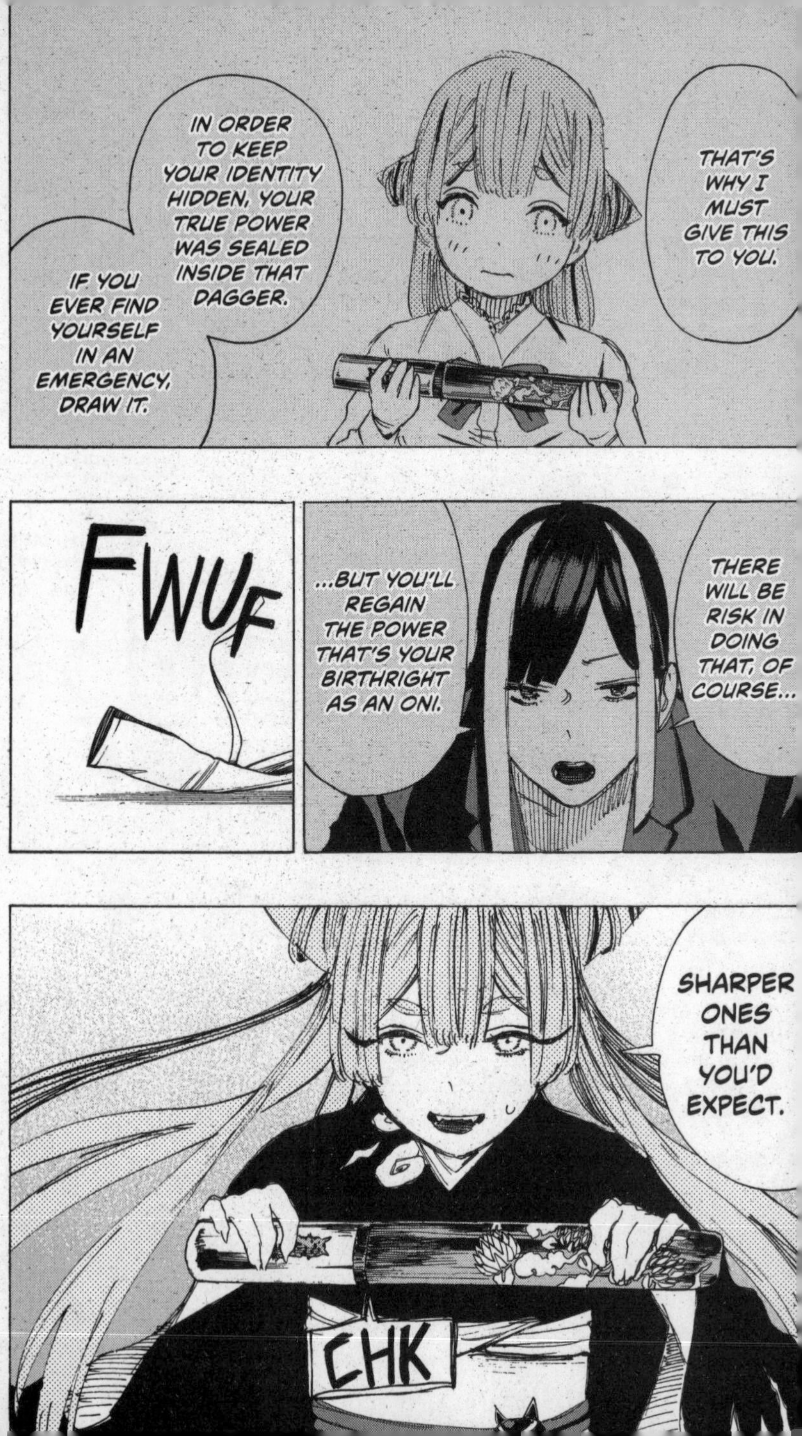
THAT'S WHY I MUST GIVE THIS TO YOU.
IN ORDER TO KEEP YOUR IDENTITY HIDDEN, YOUR TRUE POWER WAS SEALED INSIDE THAT DAGGER.
IF YOU EVER FIND YOURSELF IN AN EMERGENCY, DRAW IT.
THERE WILL BE RISK IN DOING THAT, OF COURSE...
...BUT YOU'LL REGAIN THE POWER THAT'S YOUR BIRTHRIGHT AS AN ONI.
FWUF
SHARPER ONES THAN YOU'D EXPECT.
CHK

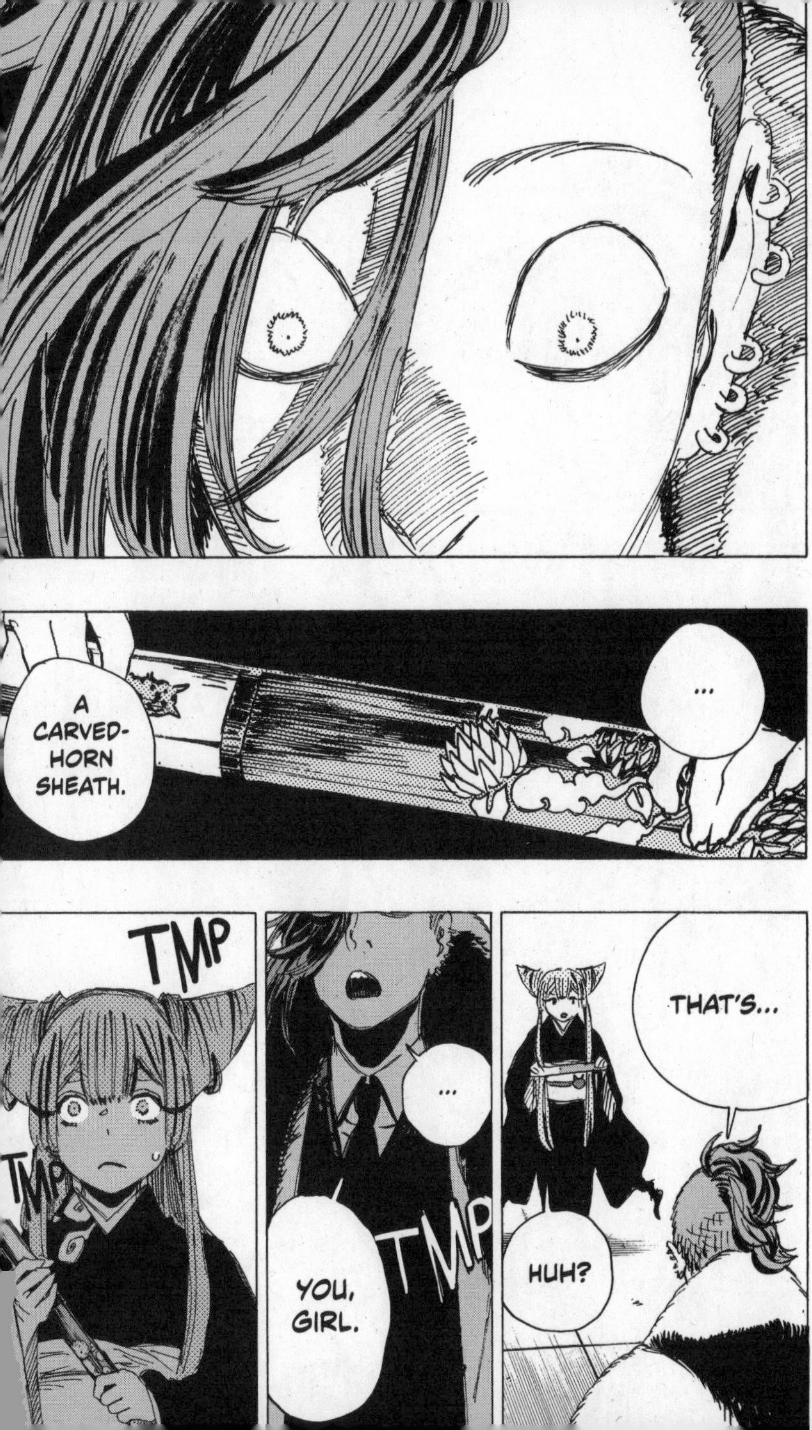
...
A CARVED-HORN SHEATH.
THAT'S...
HUH?
...
TMP
YOU, GIRL.
TMP
TMP

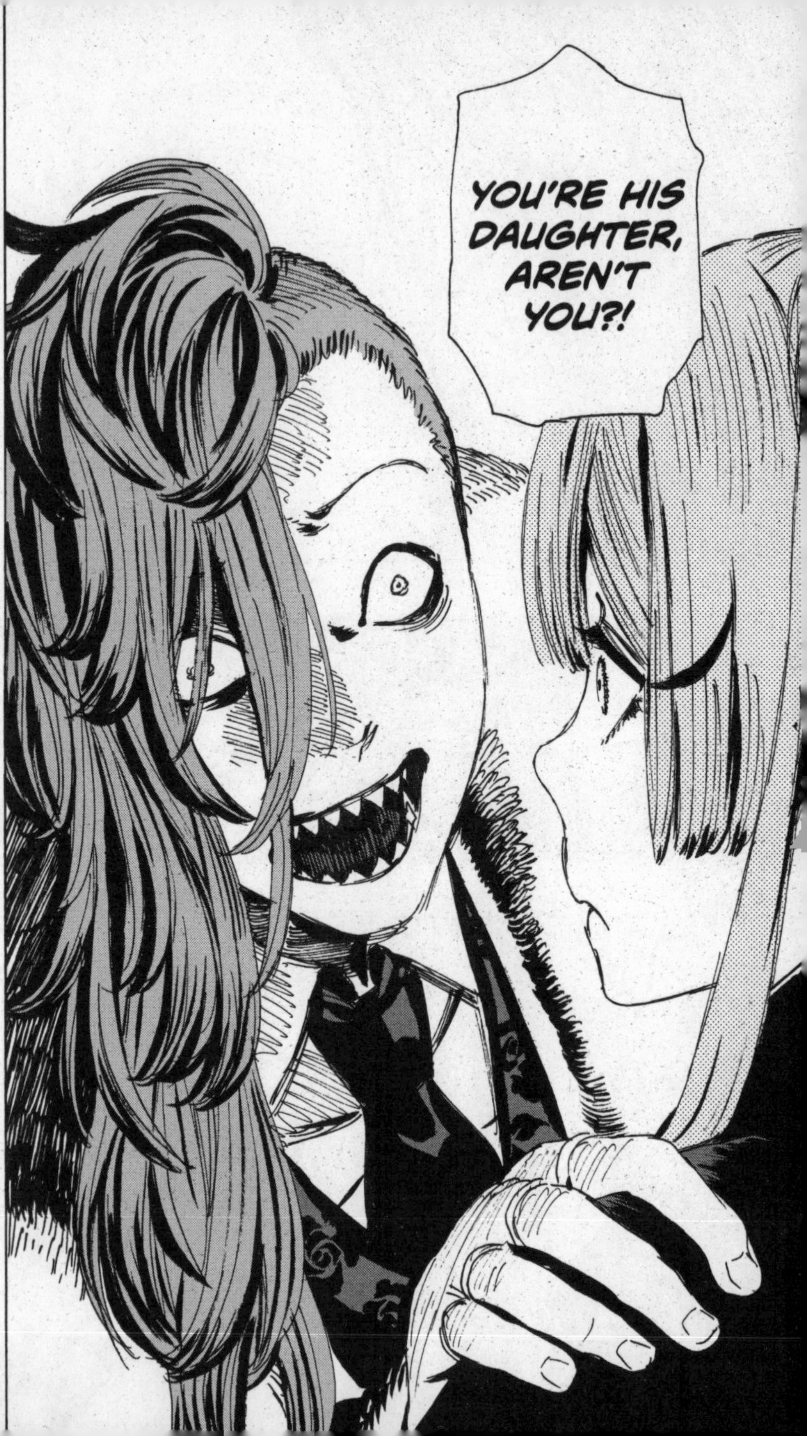
YOU'RE HIS DAUGHTER, AREN'T YOU?!

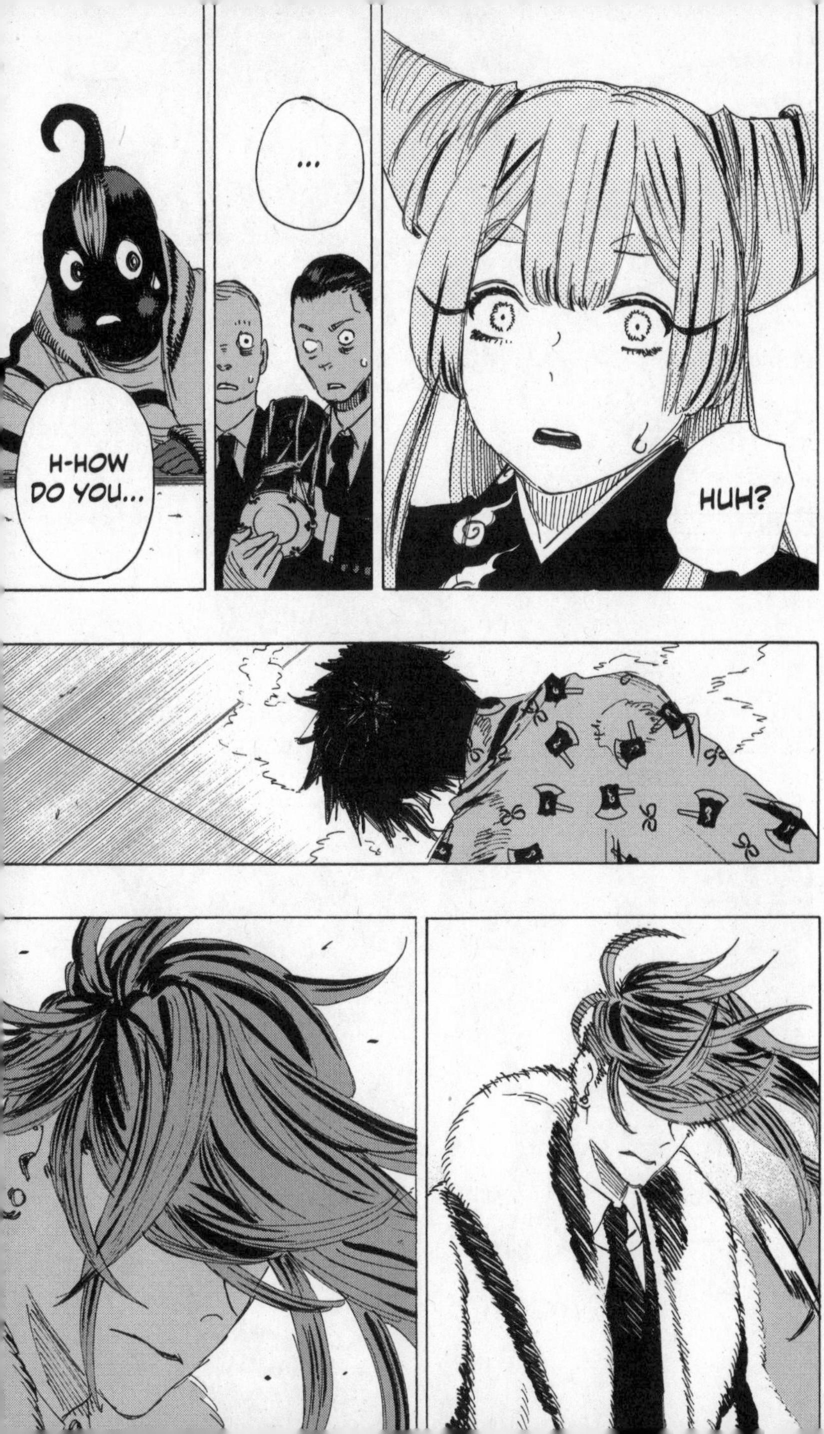
HUH?
...
H-HOW DO YOU...

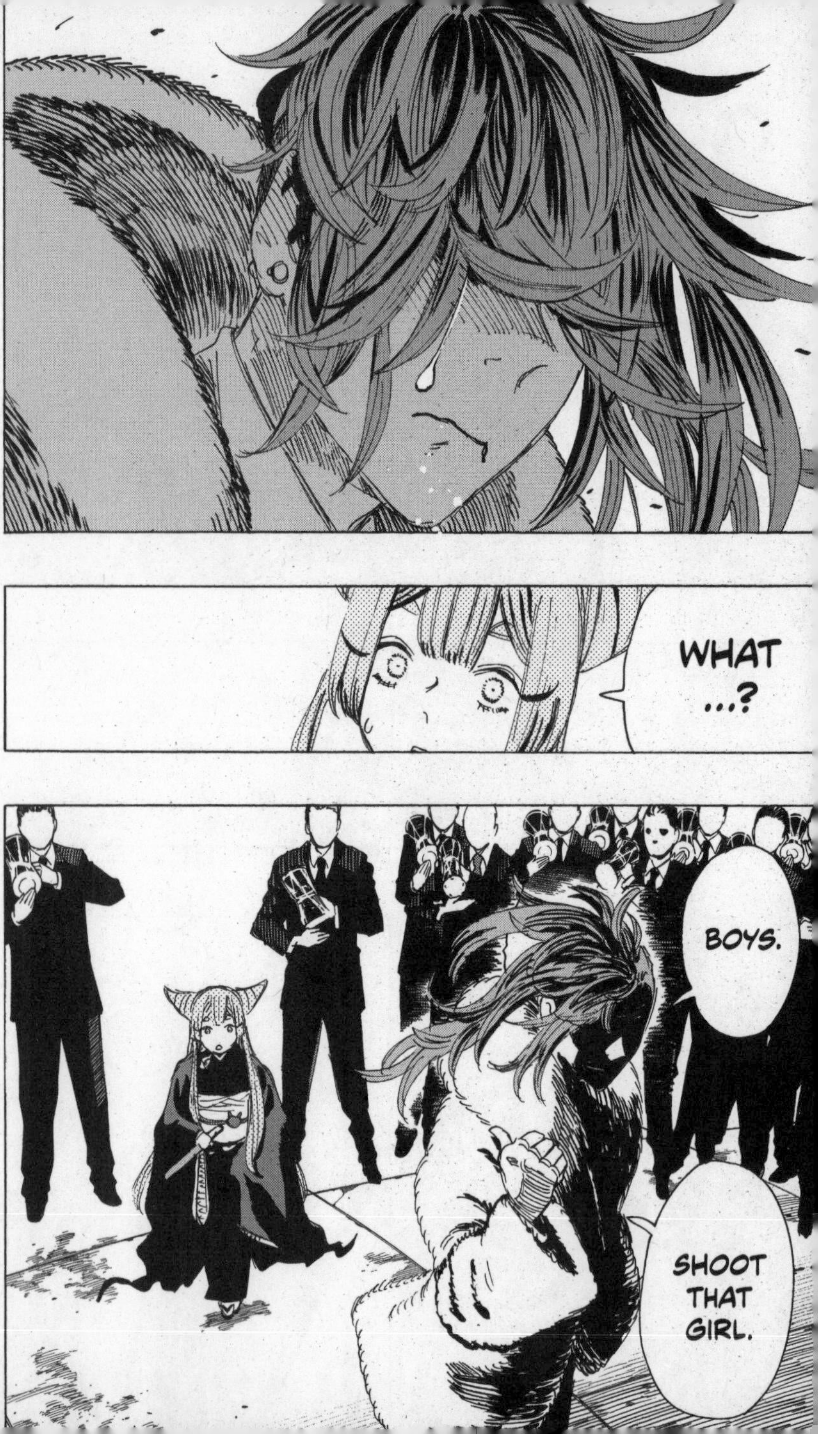
WHAT ...?
BOYS.
SHOOT THAT GIRL.

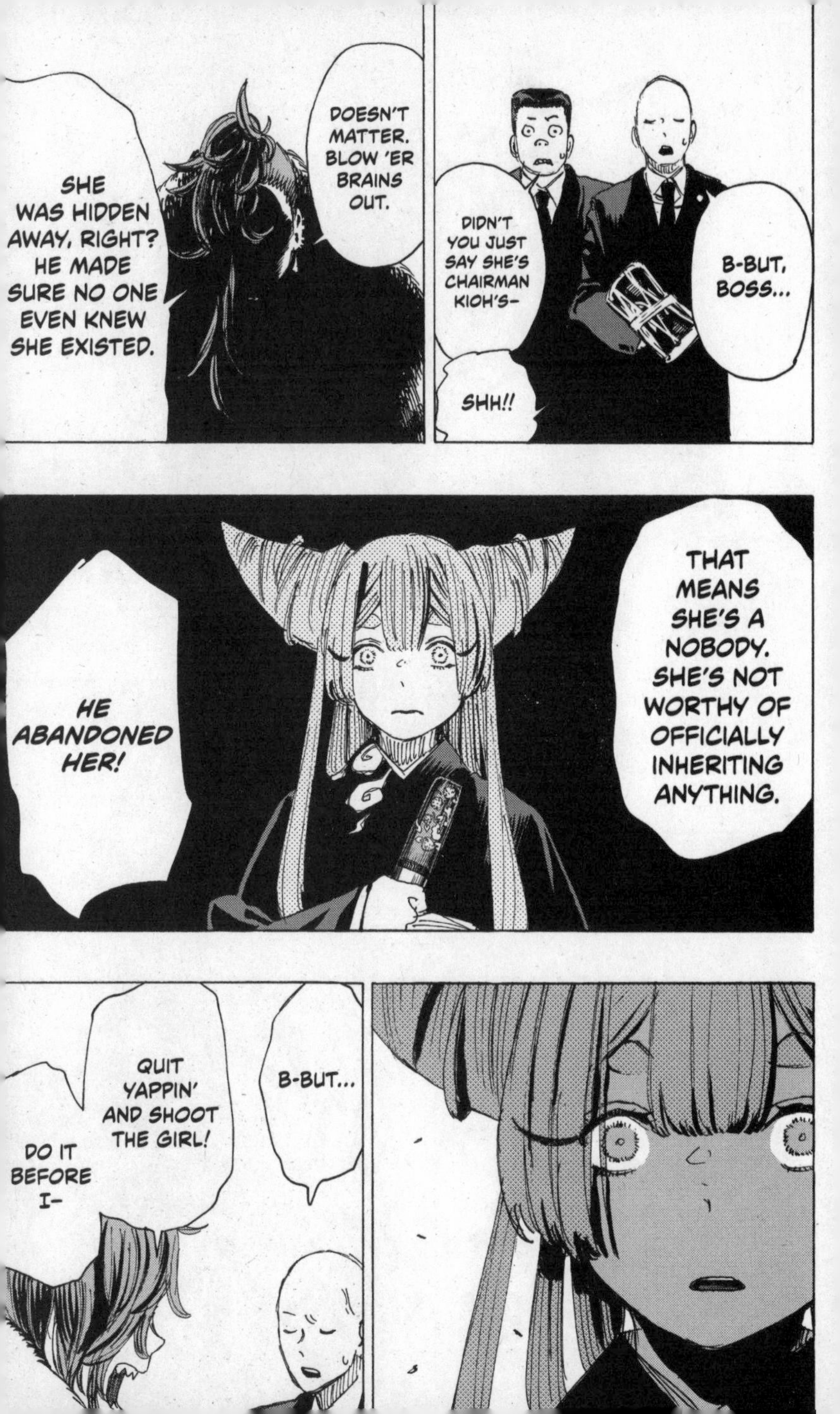
B-BUT, BOSS...
DIDN'T YOU JUST SAY SHE'S CHAIRMAN KIOH'S-
SHH!!
DOESN'T MATTER. BLOW 'ER BRAINS OUT.
SHE WAS HIDDEN AWAY, RIGHT? HE MADE SURE NO ONE EVEN KNEW SHE EXISTED.
THAT MEANS SHE'S A NOBODY. SHE'S NOT WORTHY OF OFFICIALLY INHERITING ANYTHING.
HE ABANDONED HER!
B-BUT...
QUIT YAPPIN' AND SHOOT THE GIRL!
DO IT BEFORE I-

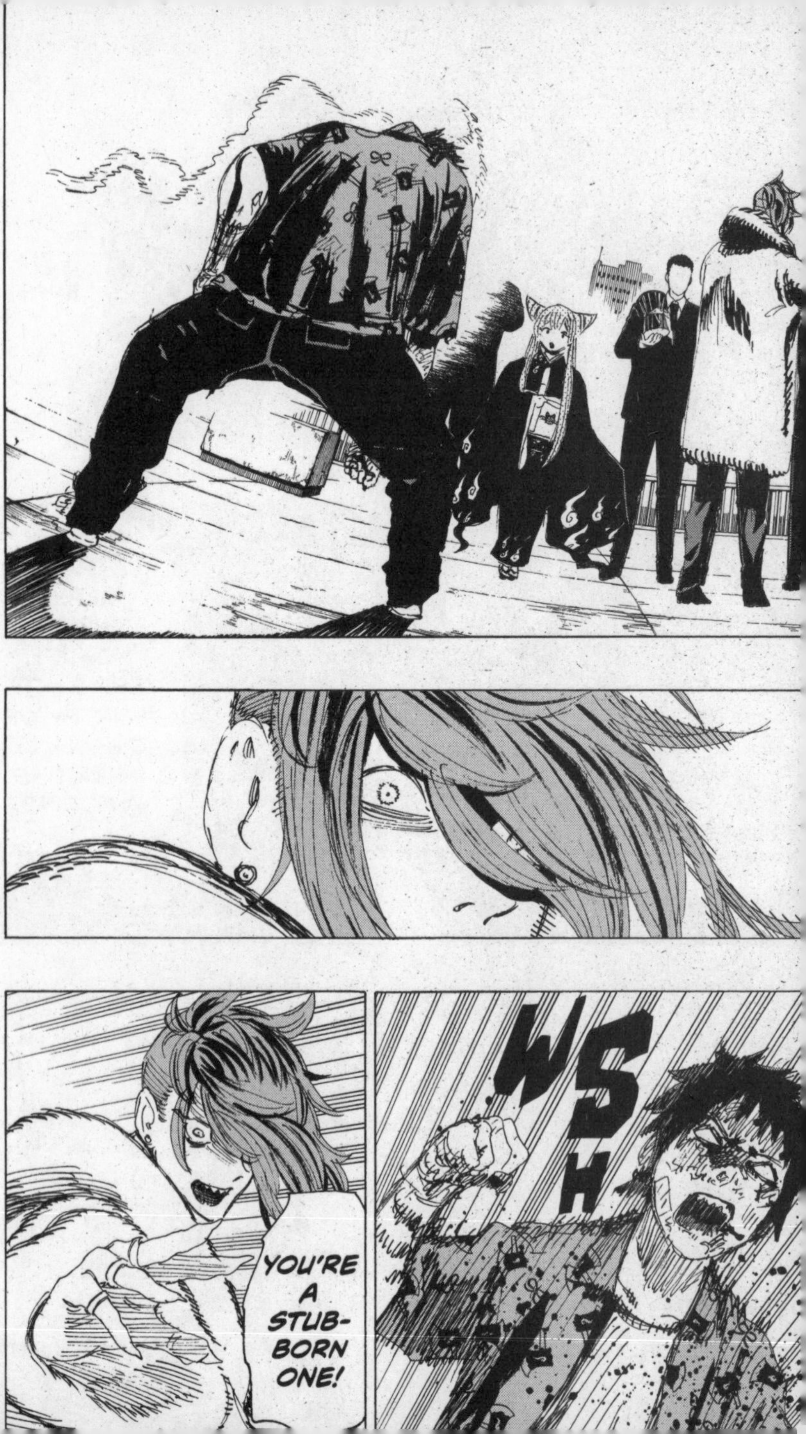
WSH
YOU'RE A STUB-BORN ONE!

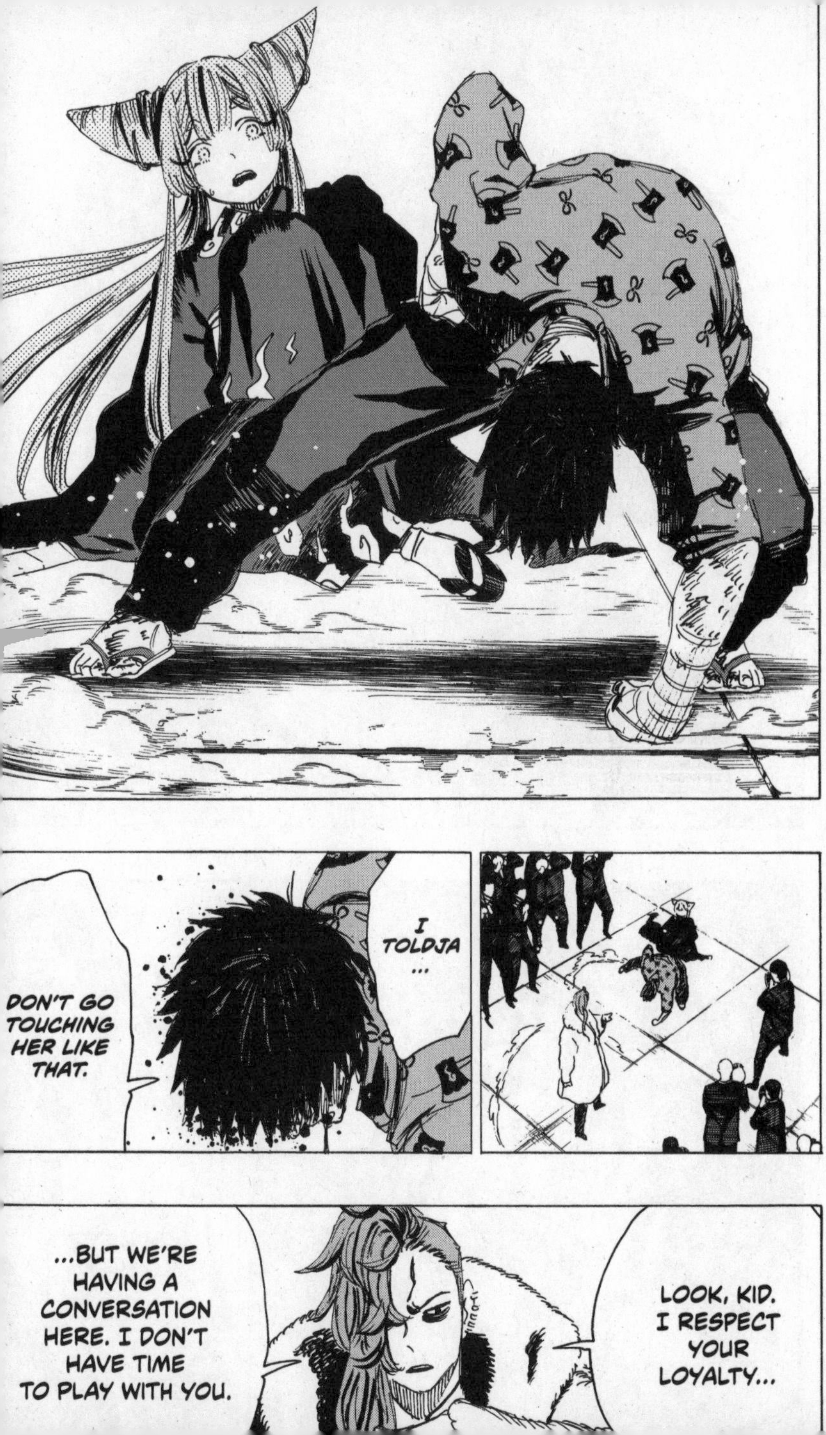
I TOLDJA ...
DON'T GO TOUCHING HER LIKE THAT.
LOOK, KID. I RESPECT YOUR LOYALTY...
...BUT WE'RE HAVING A CONVERSATION HERE. I DON'T HAVE TIME TO PLAY WITH YOU.

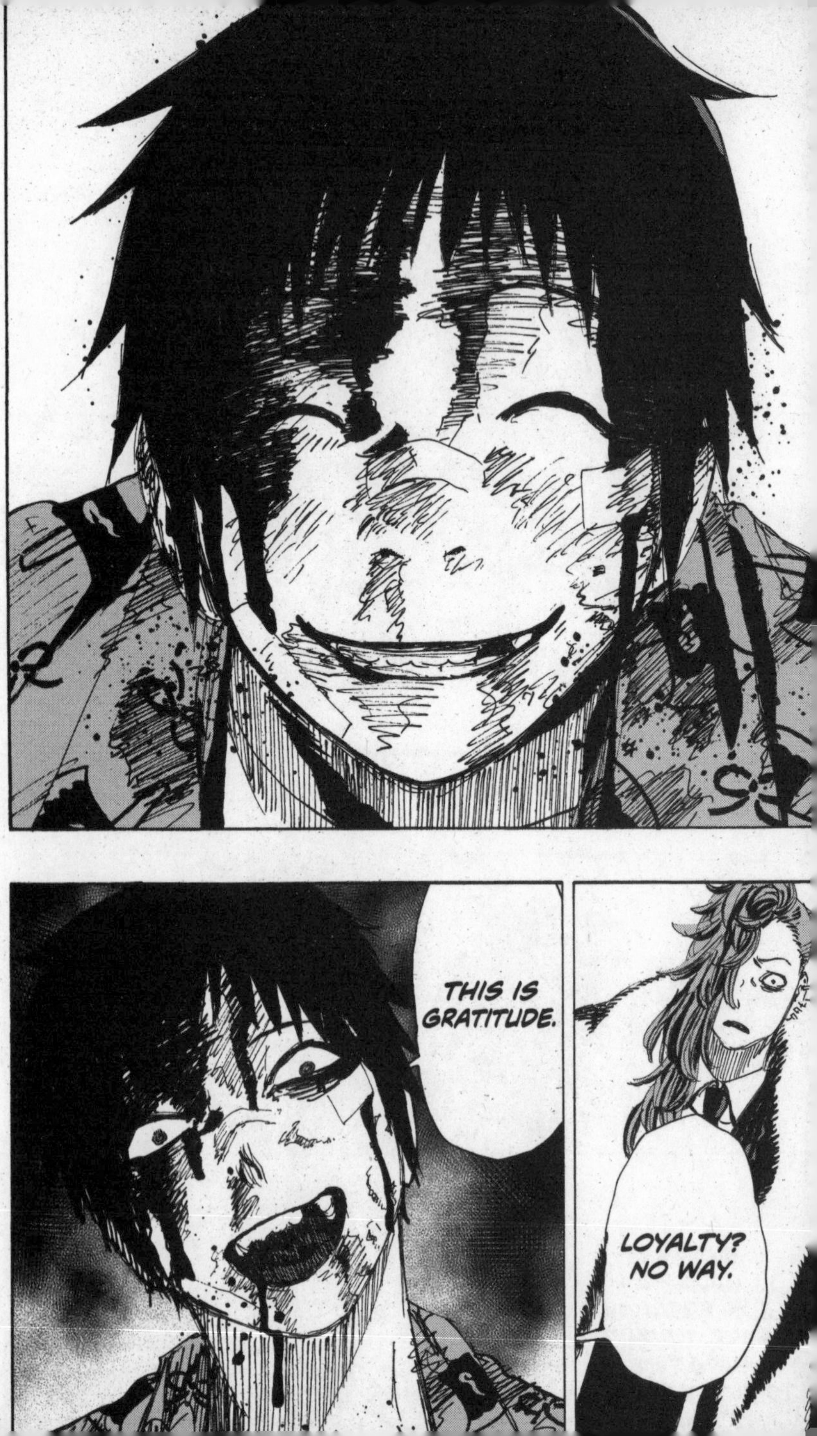
LOYALTY? NO WAY.
THIS IS GRATITUDE.

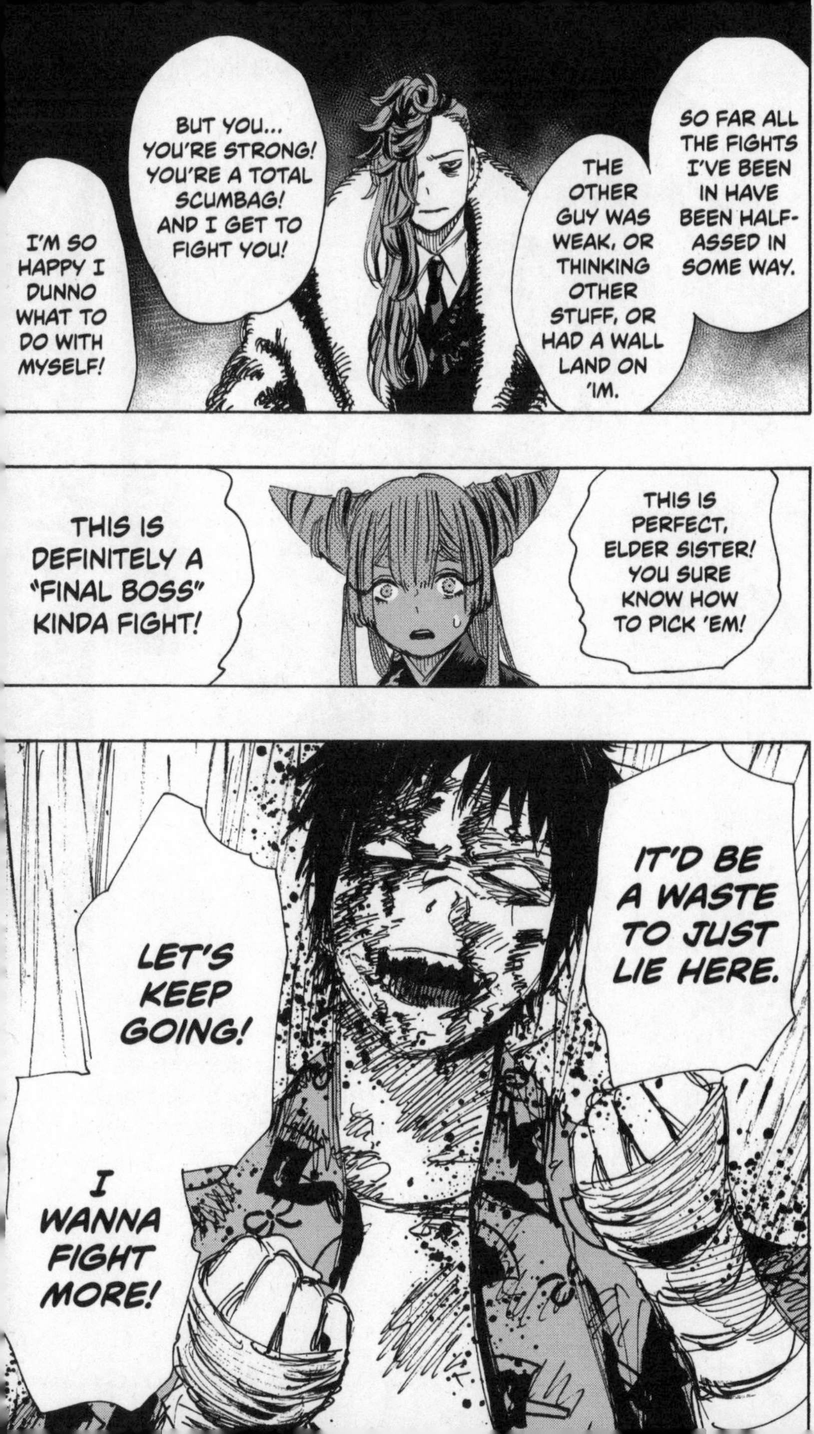
SO FAR ALL THE FIGHTS I'VE BEEN IN HAVE BEEN HALF-ASSED IN SOME WAY.
THE OTHER GUY WAS WEAK, OR THINKING OTHER STUFF, OR HAD A WALL LAND ON 'IM.
BUT YOU... YOU'RE STRONG! YOU'RE A TOTAL SCUMBAG! AND I GET TO FIGHT YOU!
I'M SO HAPPY I DUNNO WHAT TO DO WITH MYSELF!
THIS IS PERFECT, ELDER SISTER! YOU SURE KNOW HOW TO PICK 'EM!
THIS IS DEFINITELY A "FINAL BOSS" KINDA FIGHT!
IT'D BE A WASTE TO JUST LIE HERE.
LET'S KEEP GOING!
I WANNA FIGHT MORE!

KABUKICHO MONSTER MANUAL

Ten (Tenzurushi)

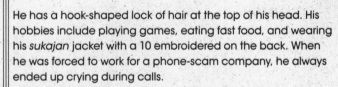

He has a hook-shaped lock of hair at the top of his head. His hobbies include playing games, eating fast food, and wearing his *sukajan* jacket with a 10 embroidered on the back. When he was forced to work for a phone-scam company, he always ended up crying during calls.

Unsurprisingly, he never managed to scam anyone and had the worst sales record in the company.

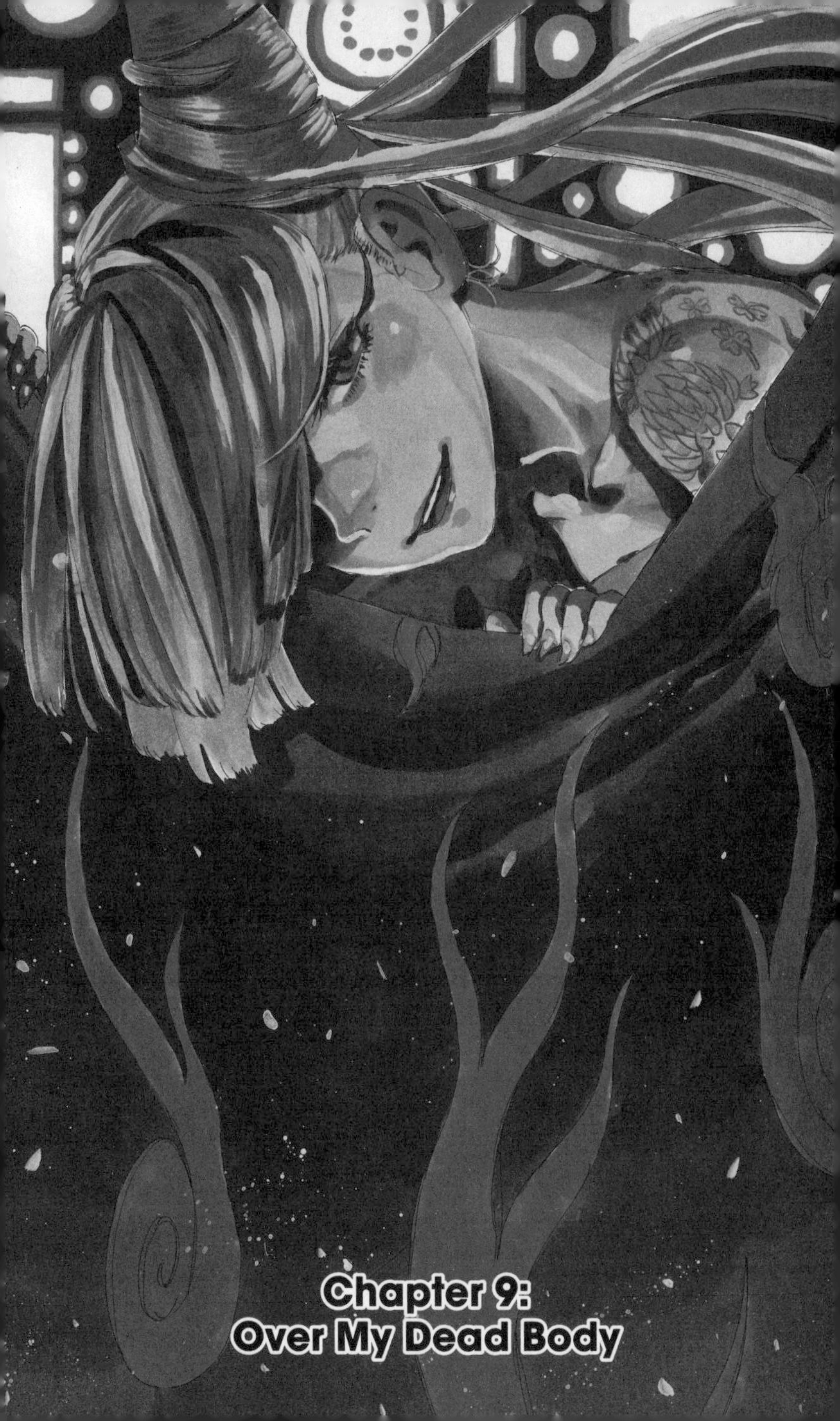
Chapter 9:
Over My Dead Body

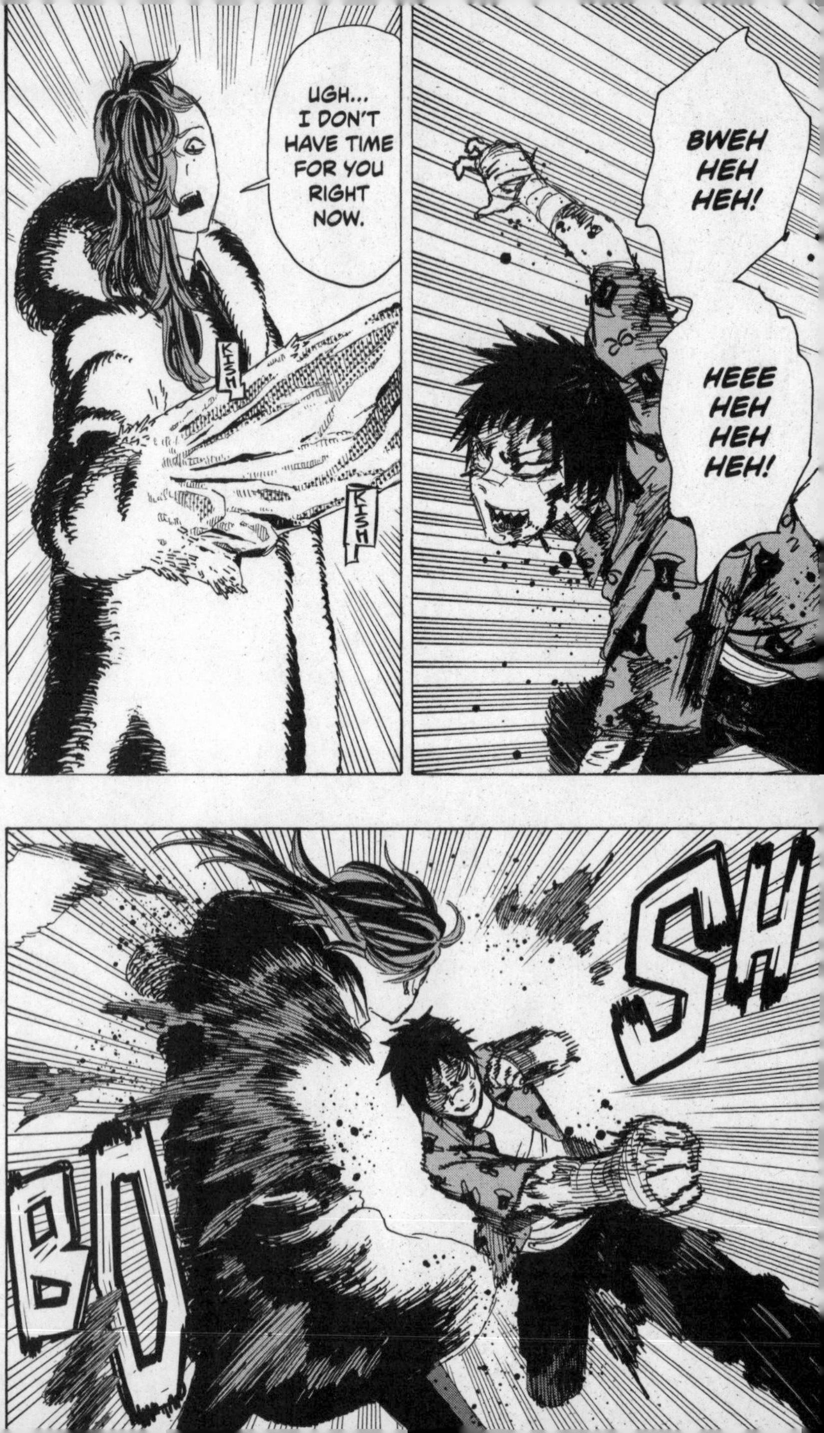
BWEH HEH HEH!
HEEE HEH HEH HEH!
UGH... I DON'T HAVE TIME FOR YOU RIGHT NOW.
KISH
KISH
SH

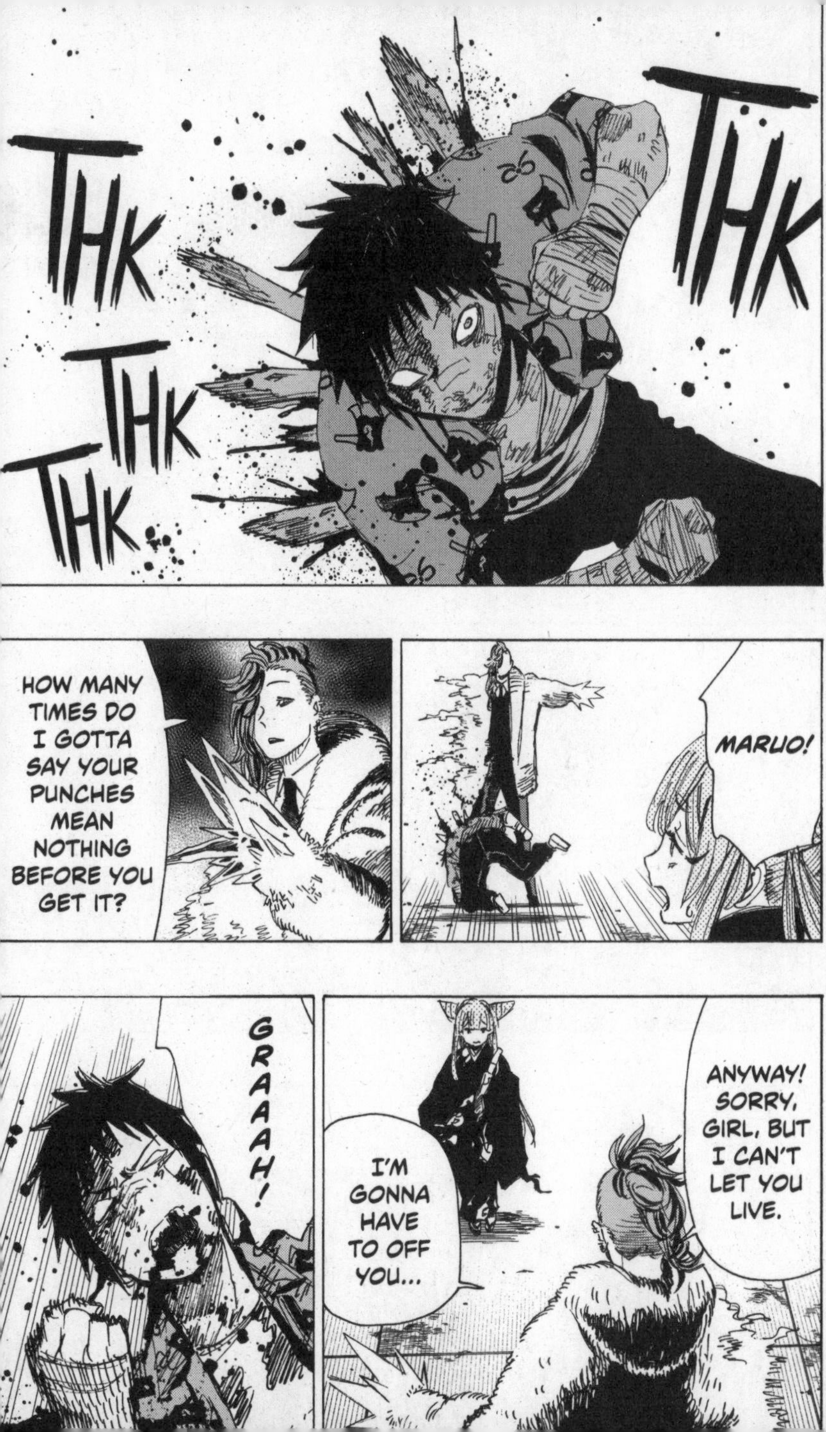
THK
THK
THK
THK
MARUO!
HOW MANY TIMES DO I GOTTA SAY YOUR PUNCHES MEAN NOTHING BEFORE YOU GET IT?
ANYWAY! SORRY, GIRL, BUT I CAN'T LET YOU LIVE.
I'M GONNA HAVE TO OFF YOU...
GRAAAAH!

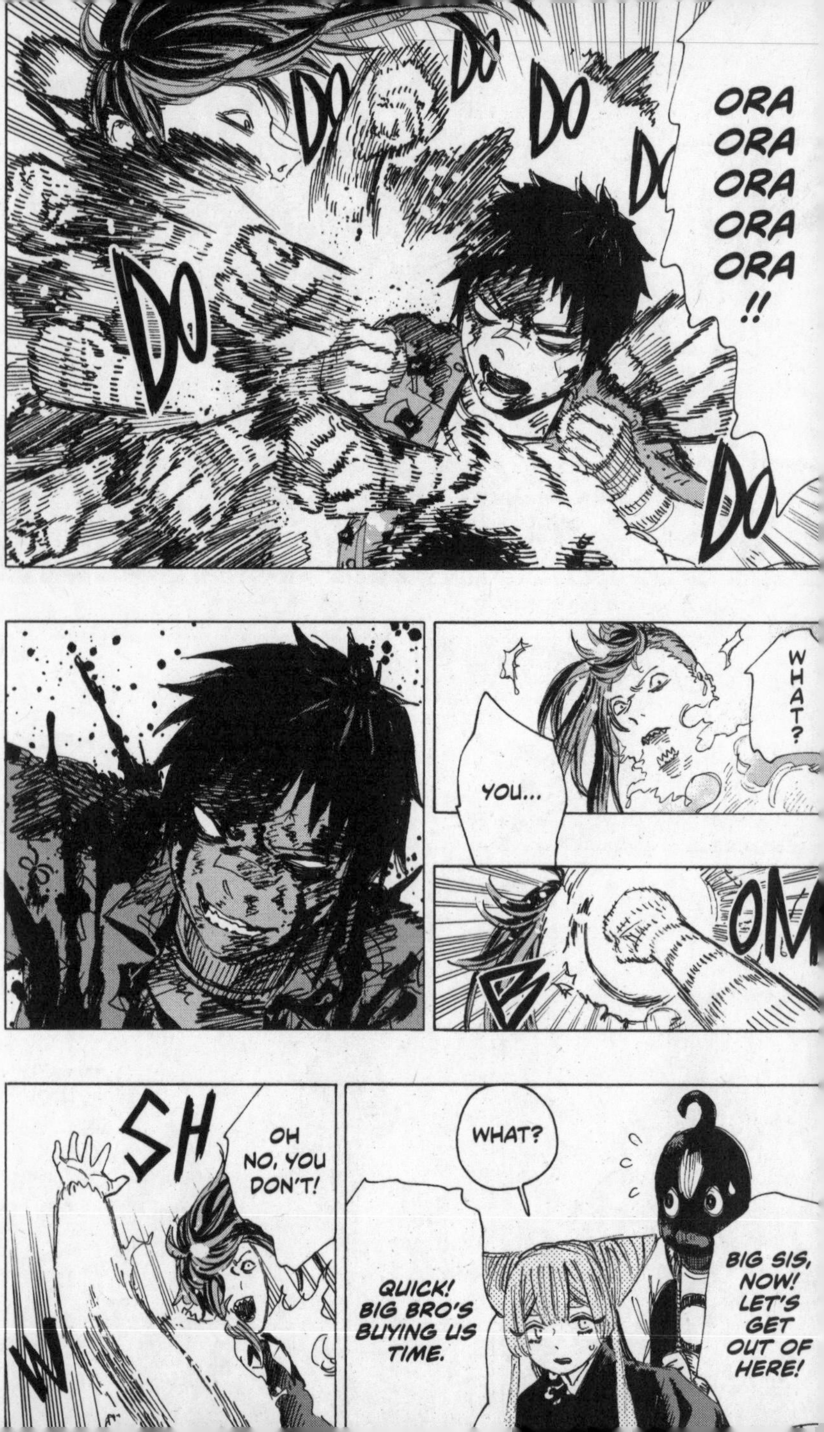
ORA ORA ORA ORA ORA !!
DO
DO
DO
DO
DO
DO
WHAT?
YOU...
OM
BIG SIS, NOW! LET'S GET OUT OF HERE!
WHAT?
QUICK! BIG BRO'S BUYING US TIME.
OH NO, YOU DON'T!
SH

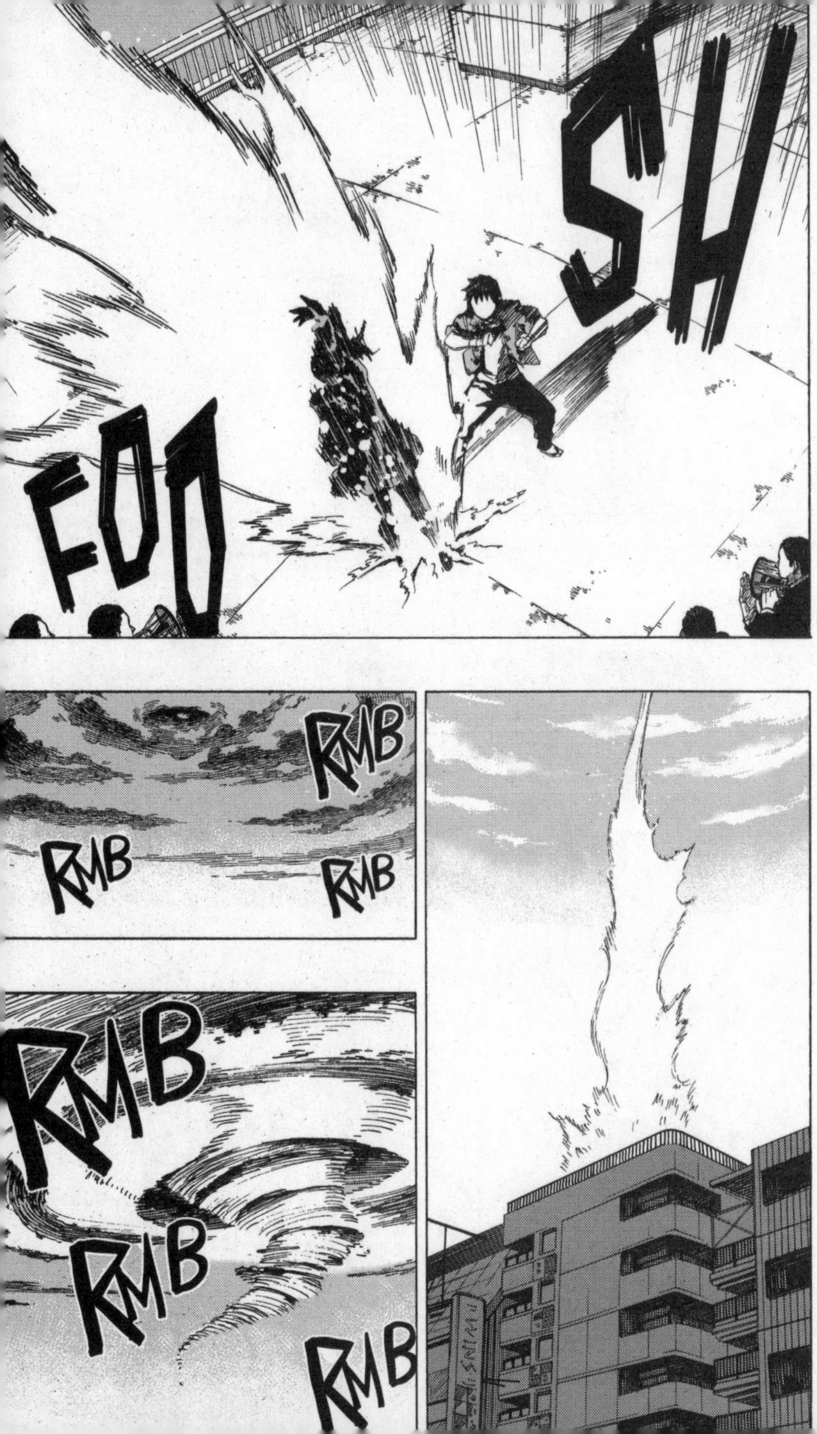
SH
FOO
RMB
RMB
RMB
RMB
RMB
RMB

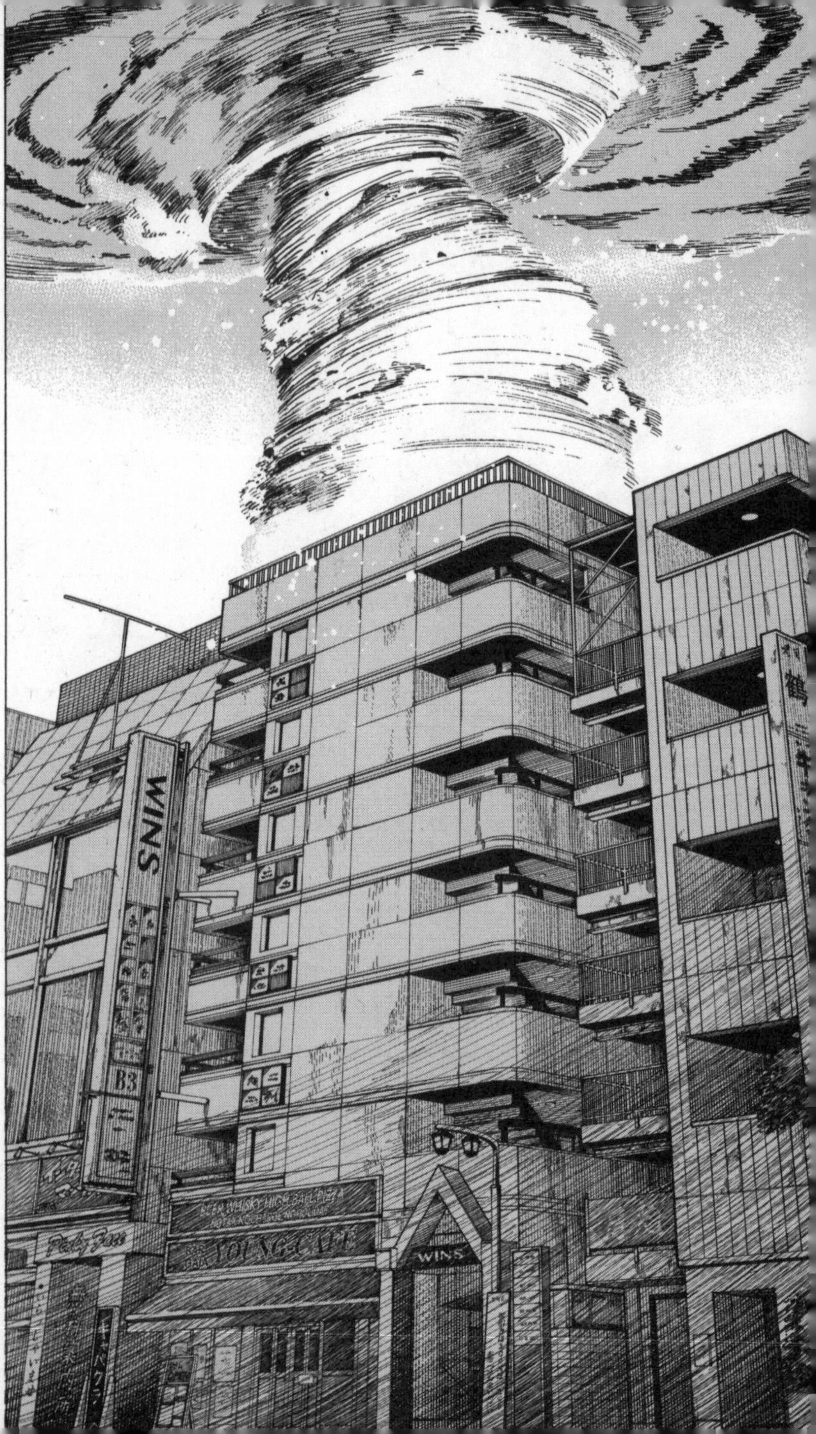

WINS
B3
YOUNG-CAFE
WINS

HWOO

TUN TUN

YEEEEEK! A B-B-BLIZZARD?!

ST

!

MP

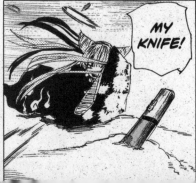

MY KNIFE!

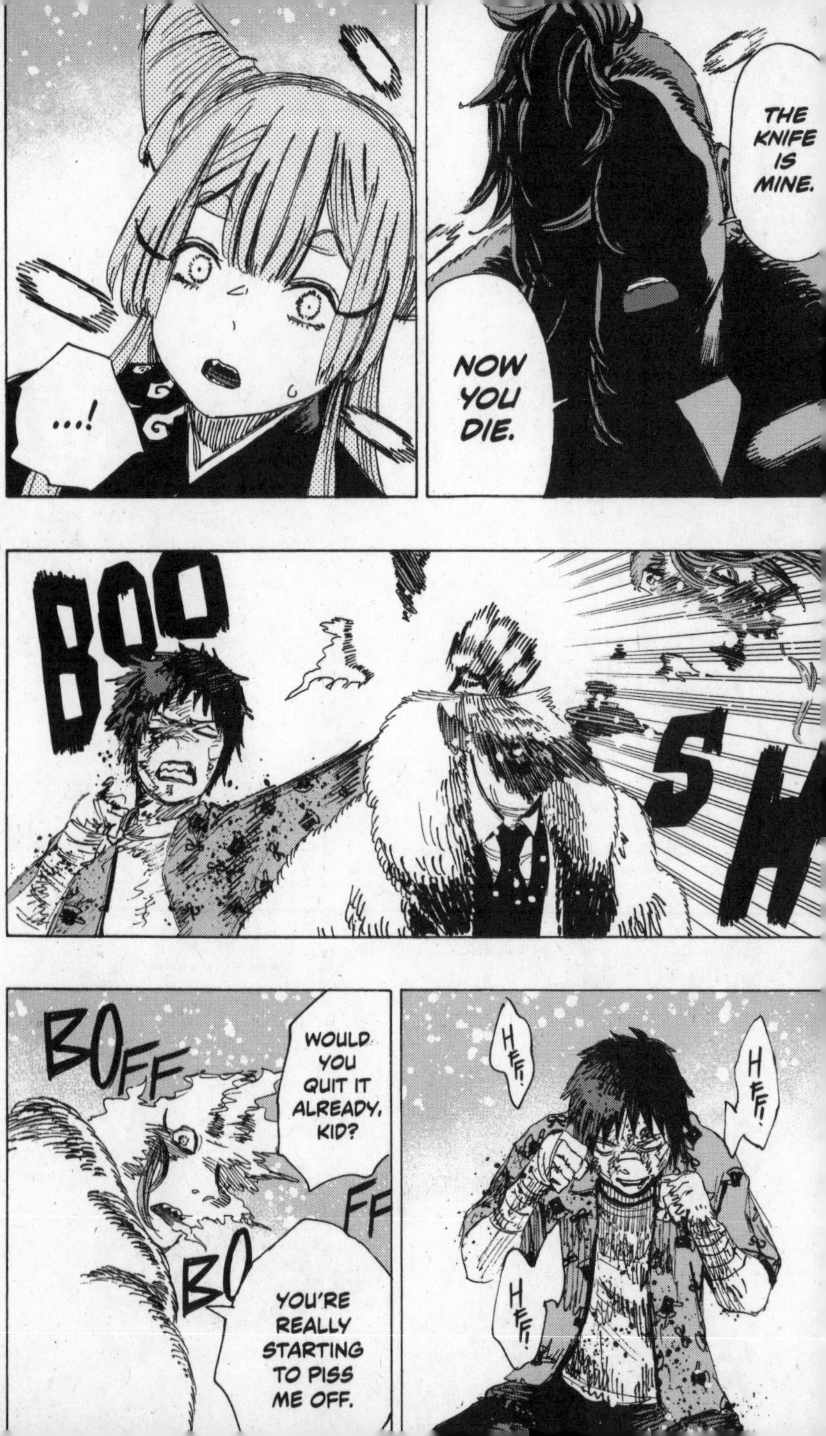
THE KNIFE IS MINE.
NOW YOU DIE.
...!
BOO
SH
HFF!
HFF!
HFF!
BOFF
WOULD YOU QUIT IT ALREADY, KID?
FF
BO
YOU'RE REALLY STARTING TO PISS ME OFF.

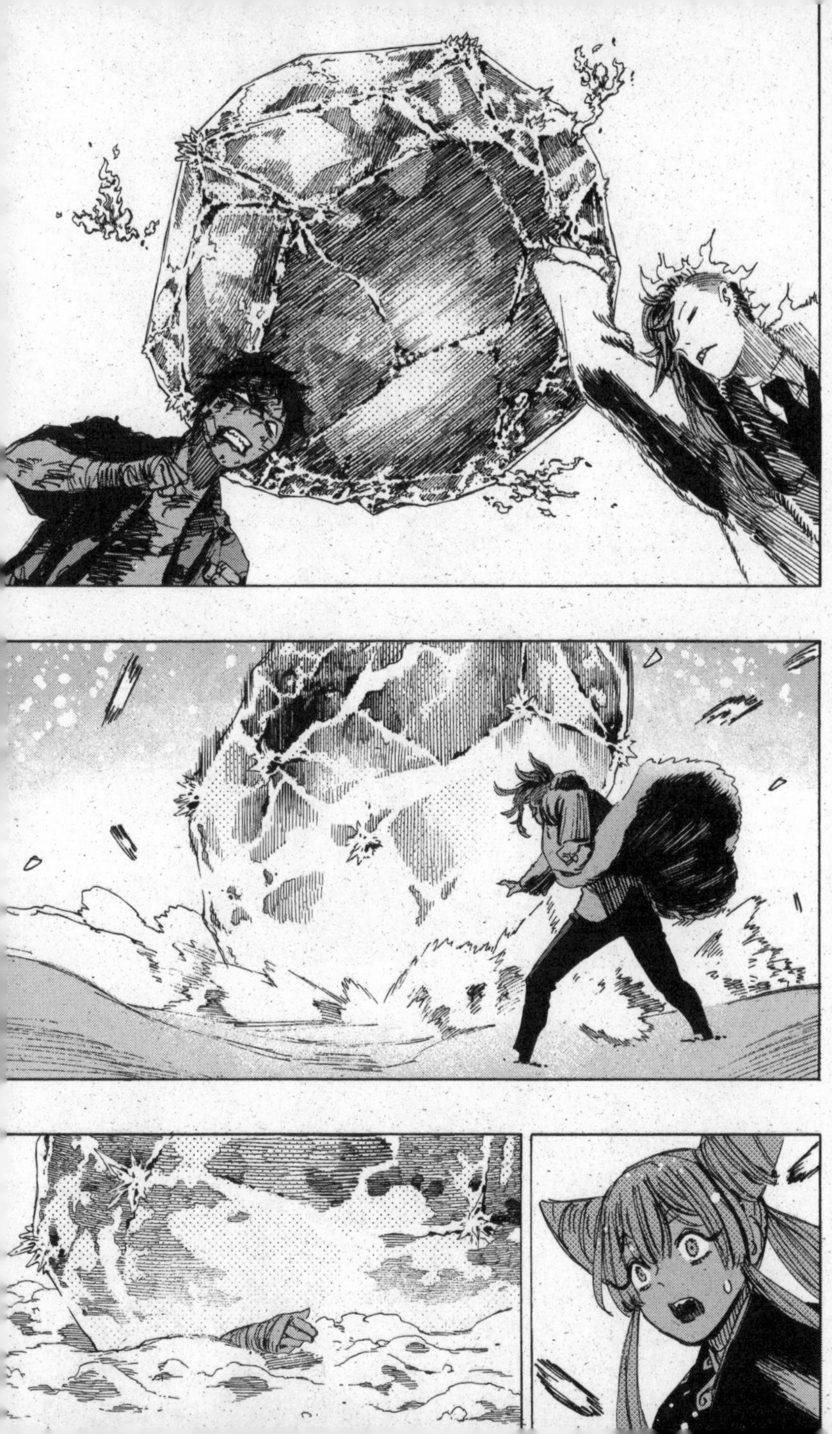

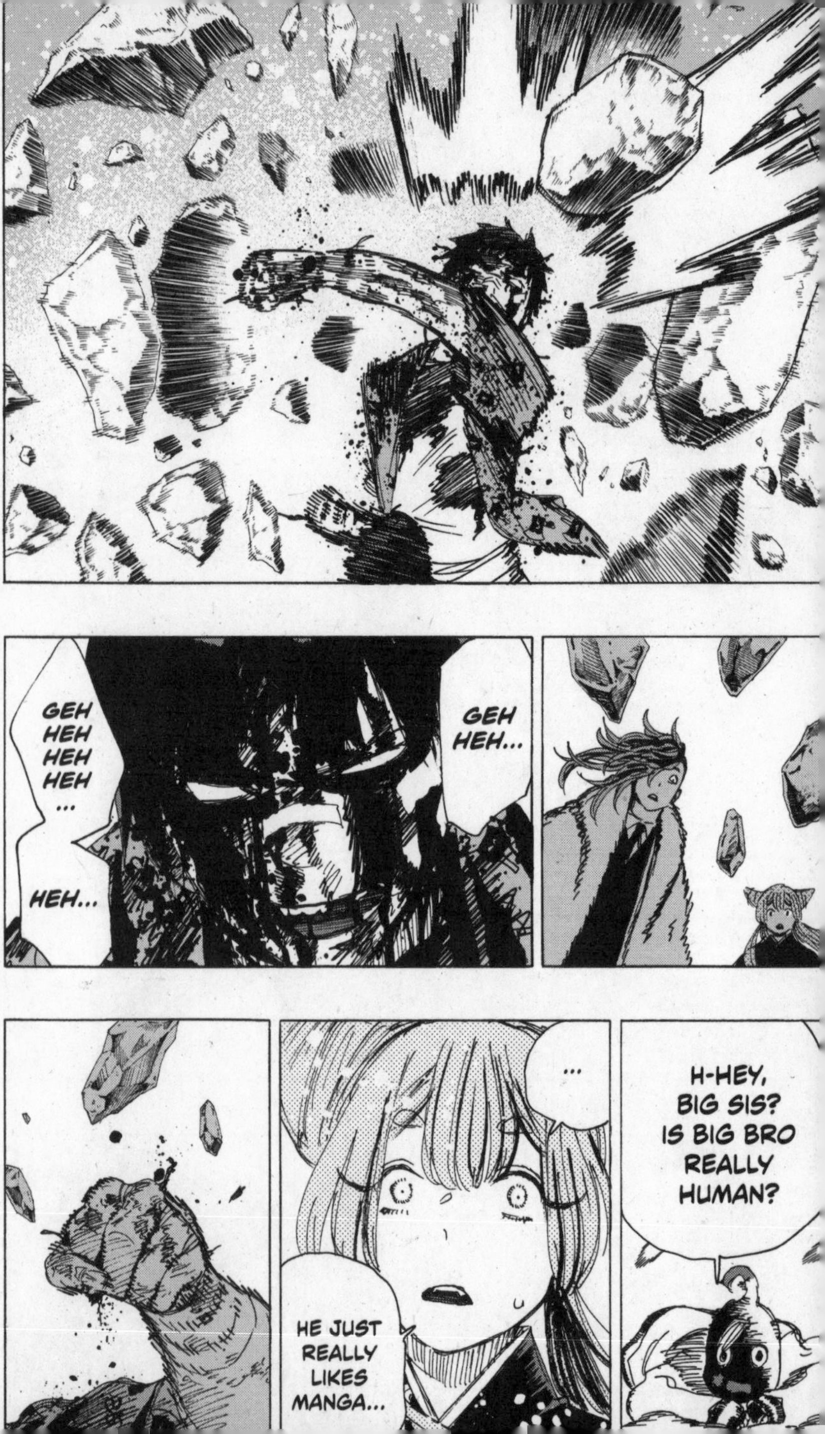
GEH HEH...
GEH HEH HEH HEH ...
HEH...
H-HEY, BIG SIS? IS BIG BRO REALLY HUMAN?
...
HE JUST REALLY LIKES MANGA...

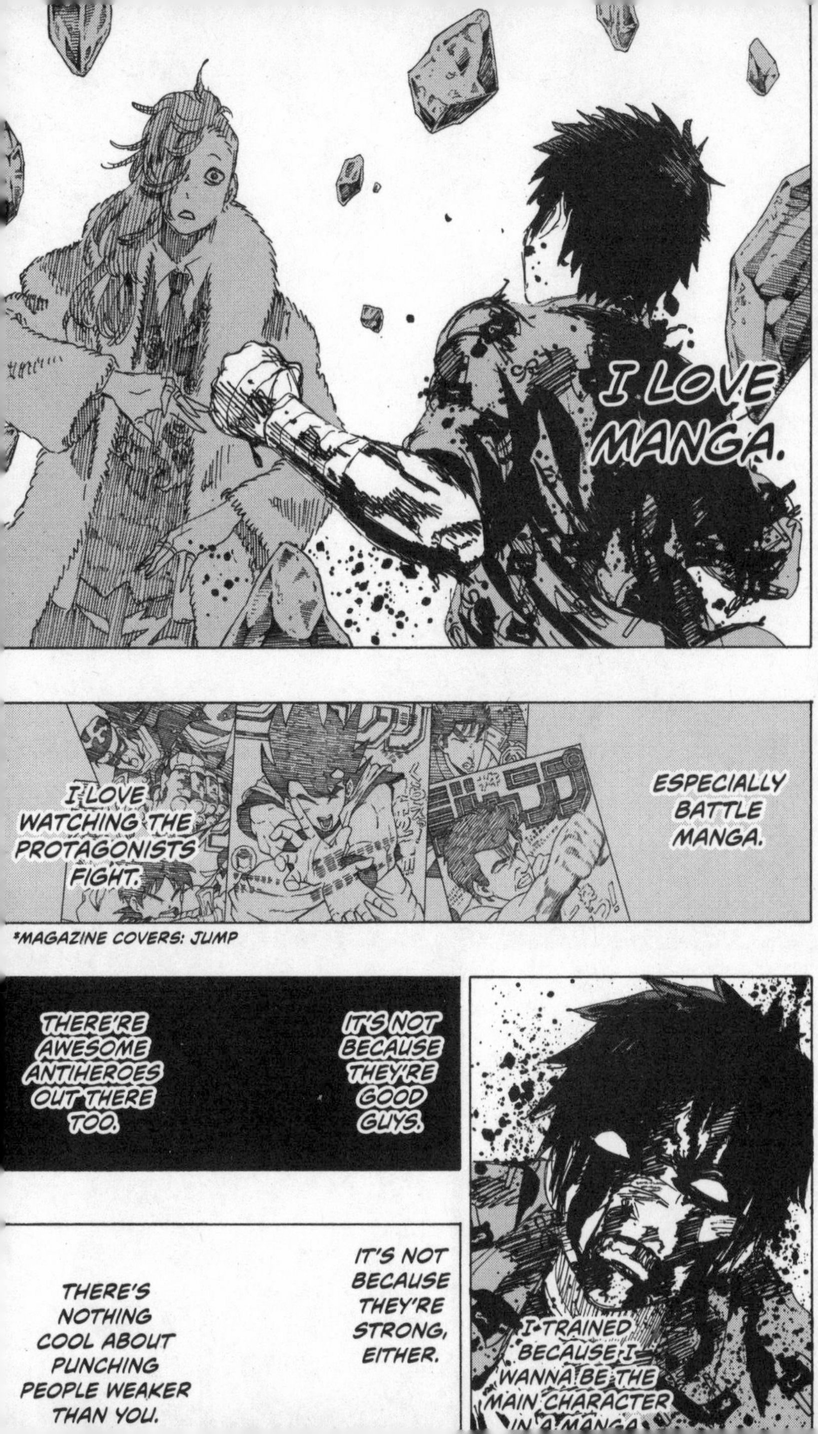
I LOVE MANGA.
ESPECIALLY BATTLE MANGA.
I LOVE WATCHING THE PROTAGONISTS FIGHT.
I TRAINED BECAUSE I WANNA BE THE MAIN CHARACTER IN A MANGA.
IT'S NOT BECAUSE THEY'RE GOOD GUYS.
THERE'RE AWESOME ANTIHEROES OUT THERE TOO.
IT'S NOT BECAUSE THEY'RE STRONG, EITHER.
THERE'S NOTHING COOL ABOUT PUNCHING PEOPLE WEAKER THAN YOU.

*MAGAZINE COVERS: JUMP

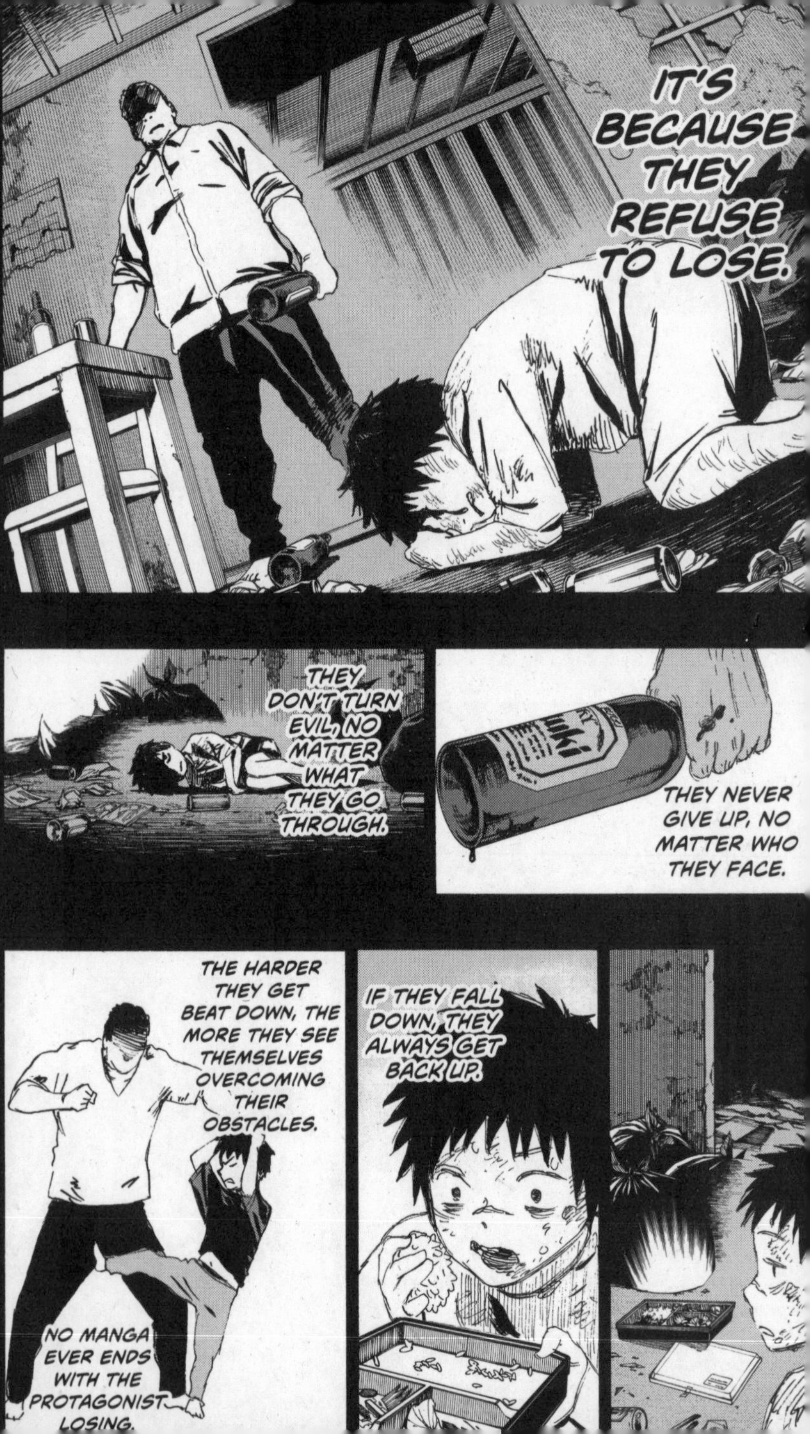
IT'S BECAUSE THEY REFUSE TO LOSE.
THEY NEVER GIVE UP, NO MATTER WHO THEY FACE.
THEY DON'T TURN EVIL, NO MATTER WHAT THEY GO THROUGH.
IF THEY FALL DOWN, THEY ALWAYS GET BACK UP.
THE HARDER THEY GET BEAT DOWN, THE MORE THEY SEE THEMSELVES OVERCOMING THEIR OBSTACLES.
NO MANGA EVER ENDS WITH THE PROTAGONIST LOSING.

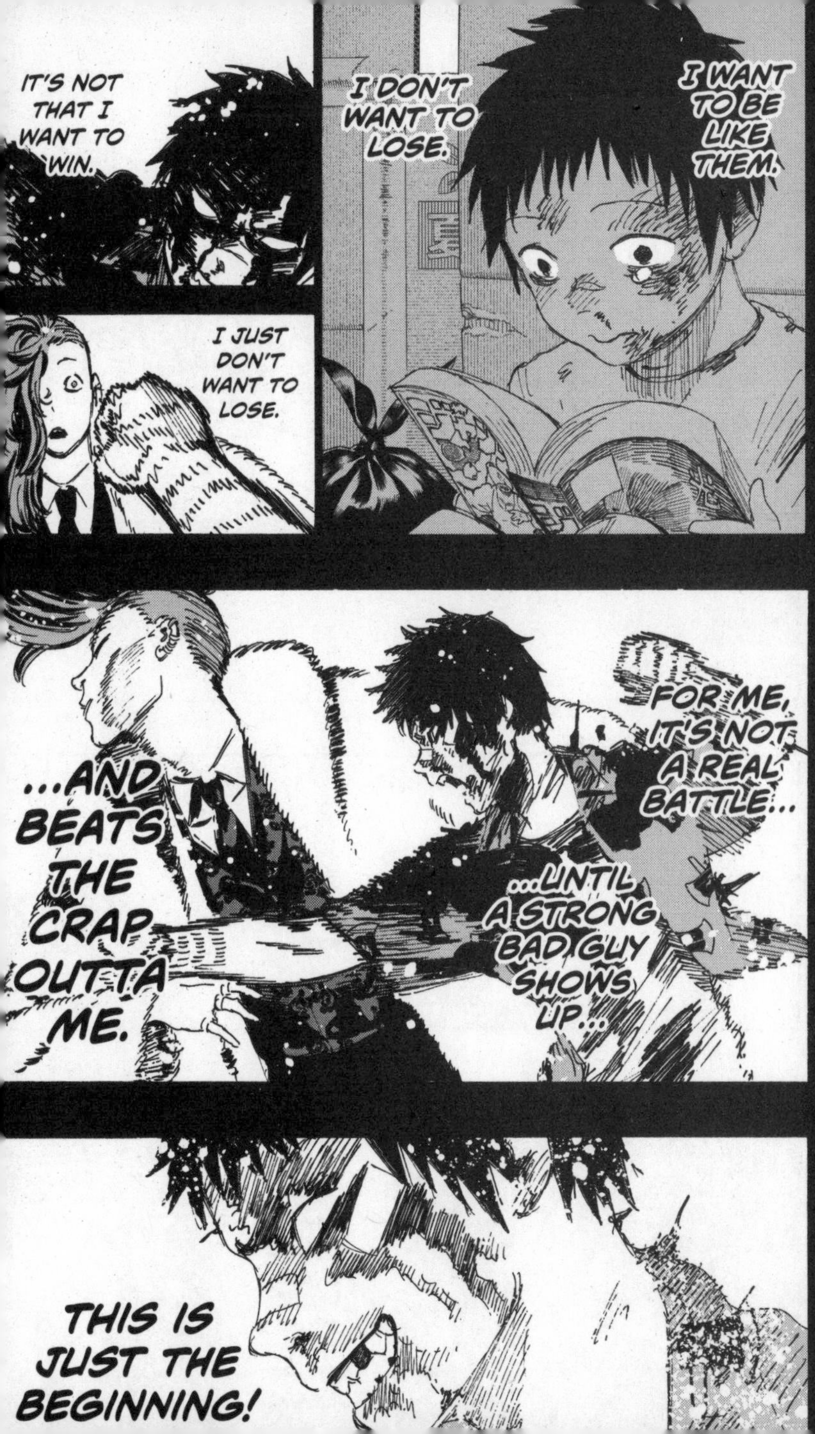
I WANT TO BE LIKE THEM.
I DON'T WANT TO LOSE.
IT'S NOT THAT I WANT TO WIN.
I JUST DON'T WANT TO LOSE.
FOR ME, IT'S NOT A REAL BATTLE...
...UNTIL A STRONG BAD GUY SHOWS UP...
...AND BEATS THE CRAP OUTTA ME.
THIS IS JUST THE BEGINNING!

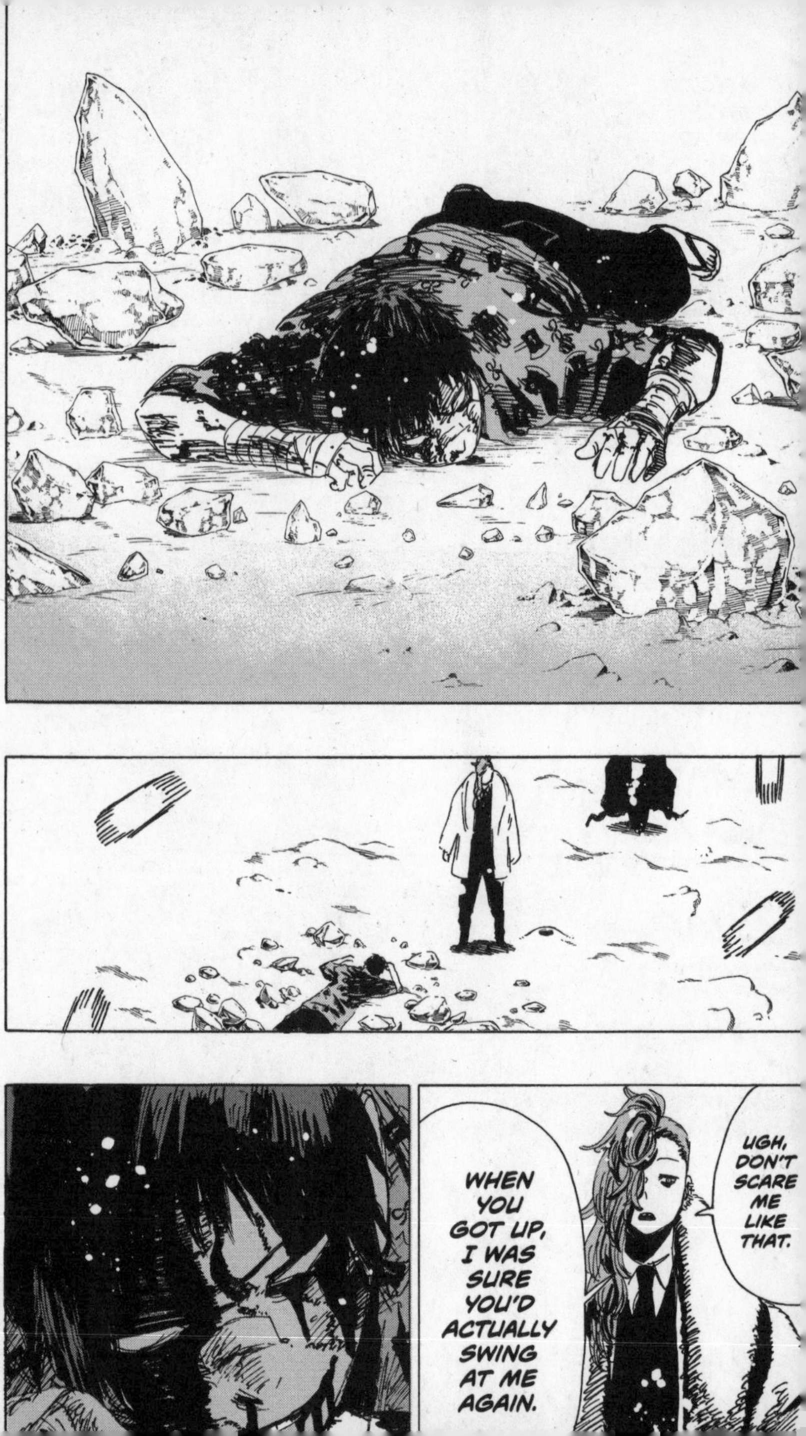
UGH, DON'T SCARE ME LIKE THAT.
WHEN YOU GOT UP, I WAS SURE YOU'D ACTUALLY SWING AT ME AGAIN.

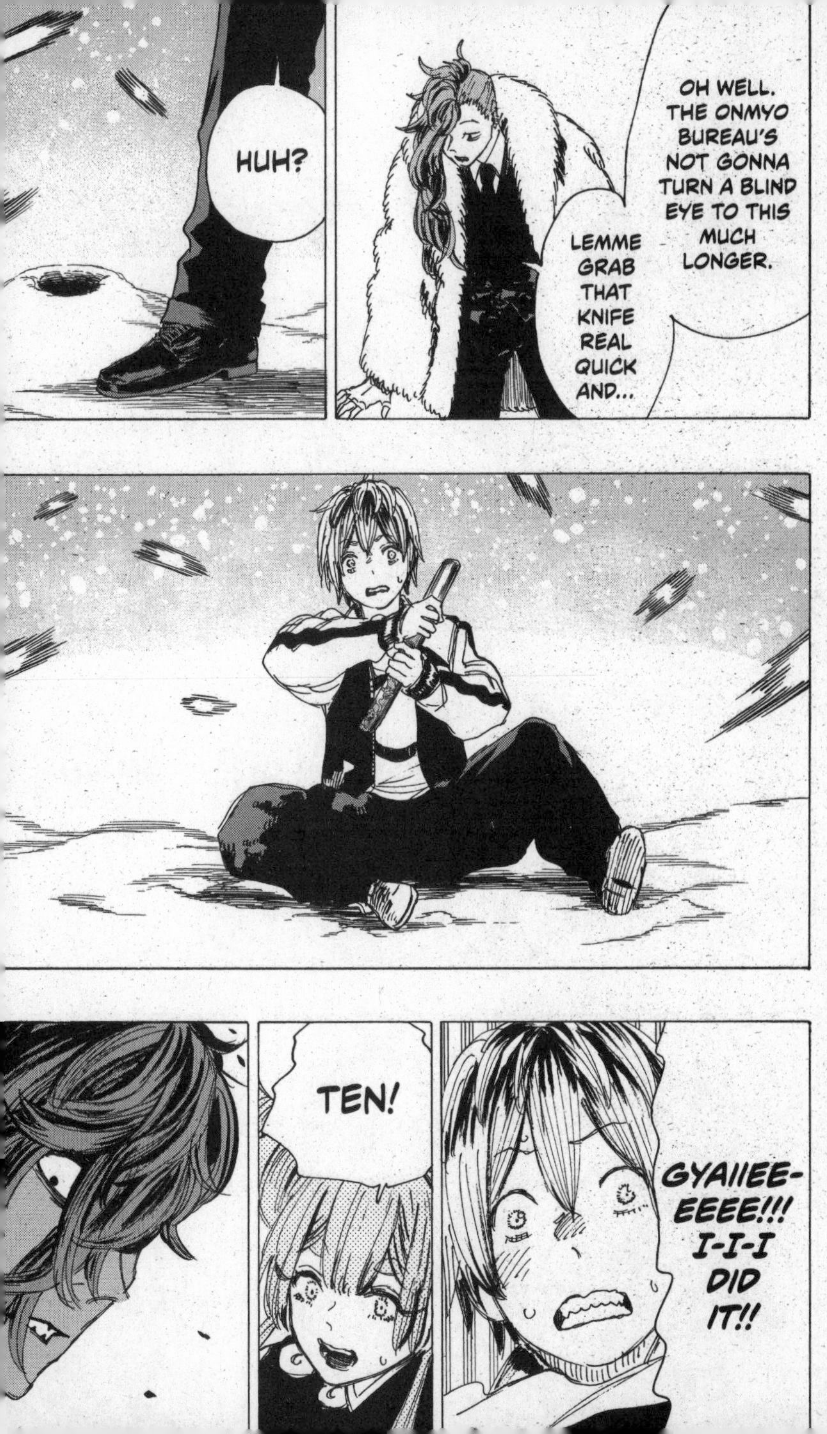
OH WELL. THE ONMYO BUREAU'S NOT GONNA TURN A BLIND EYE TO THIS MUCH LONGER.
LEMME GRAB THAT KNIFE REAL QUICK AND...
HUH?
GYAIIEE-EEEE!!! I-I-I DID IT!!
TEN!

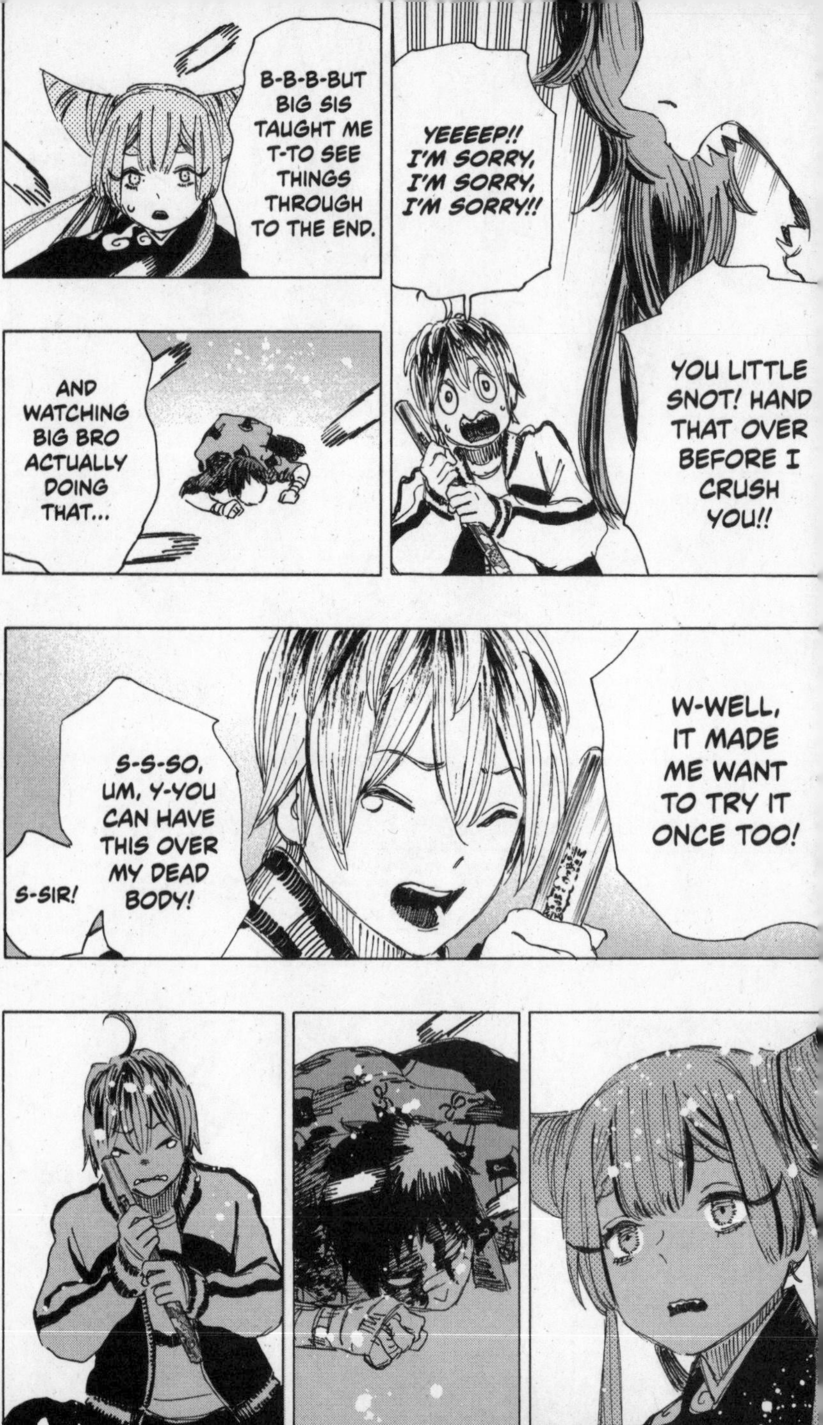
YOU LITTLE SNOT! HAND THAT OVER BEFORE I CRUSH YOU!!
YEEEEP!! I'M SORRY, I'M SORRY, I'M SORRY!!
B-B-B-BUT BIG SIS TAUGHT ME T-TO SEE THINGS THROUGH TO THE END.
AND WATCHING BIG BRO ACTUALLY DOING THAT...
W-WELL, IT MADE ME WANT TO TRY IT ONCE TOO!
S-S-SO, UM, Y-YOU CAN HAVE THIS OVER MY DEAD BODY!
S-SIR!

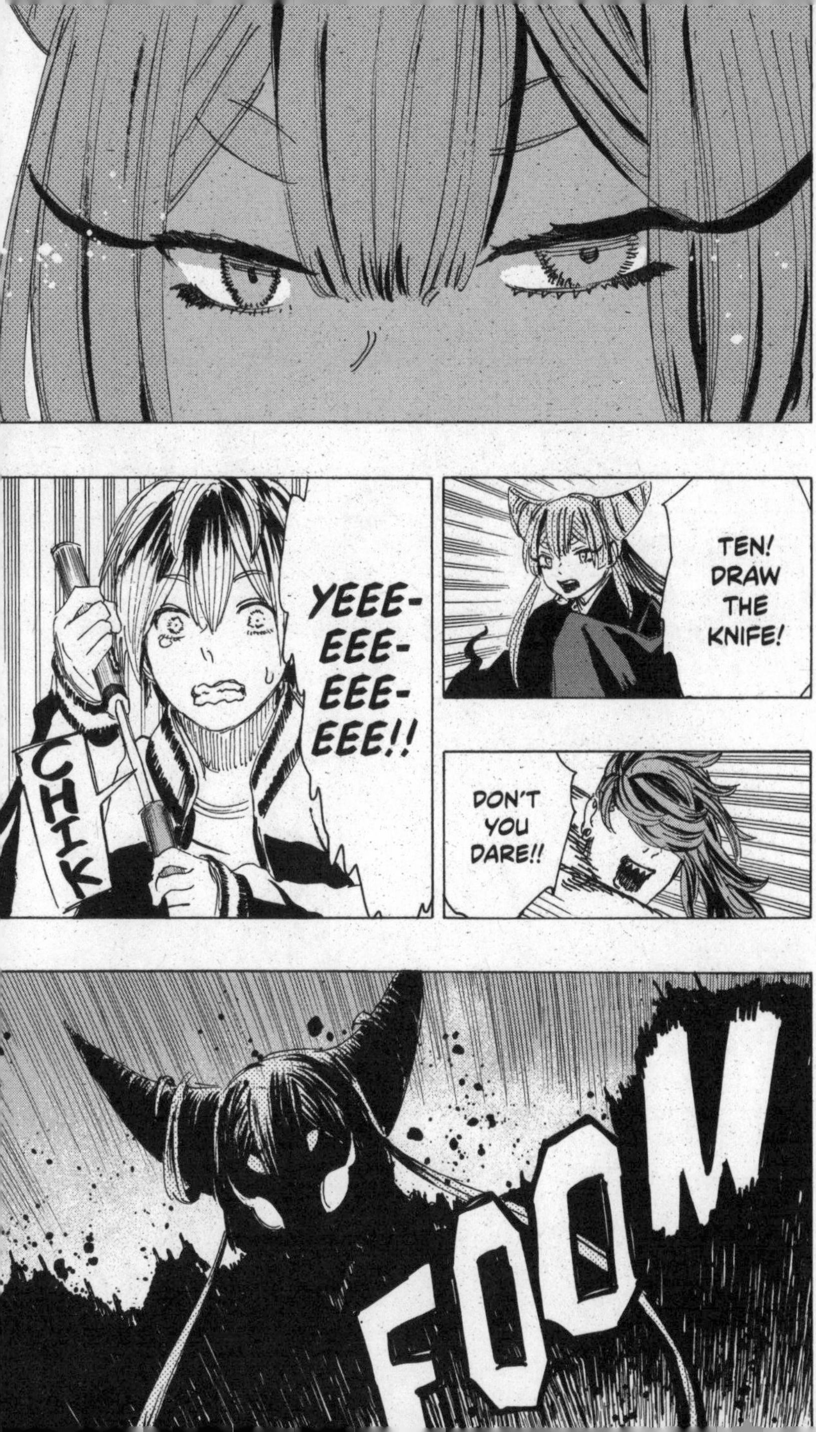
TEN! DRAW THE KNIFE!
DON'T YOU DARE!!
YEEE-EEE-EEE-EEE!!
CHIK
FOOM

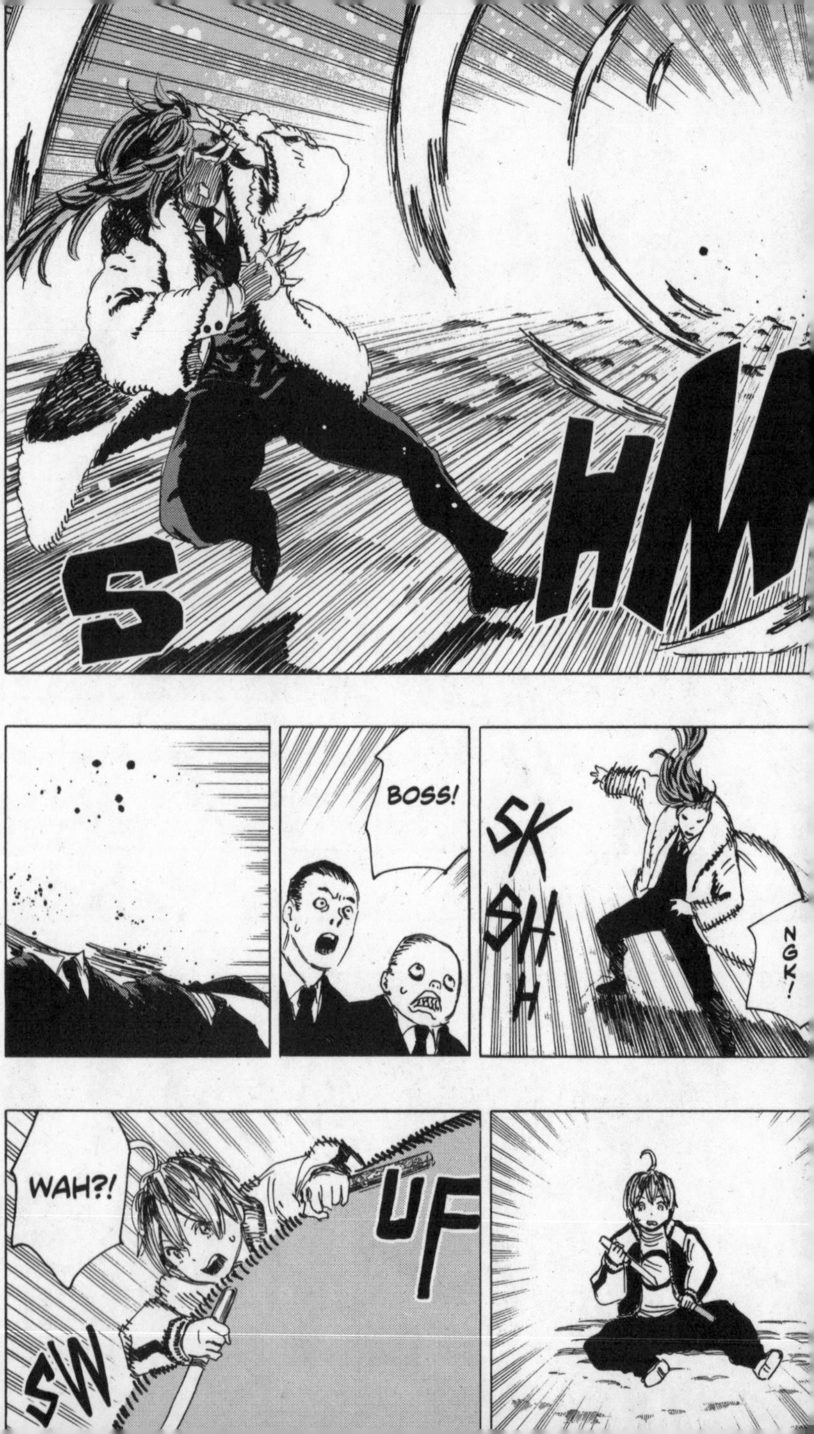
SHW
SK SH H H
NGK!
BOSS!
WAH?!
UF
SW

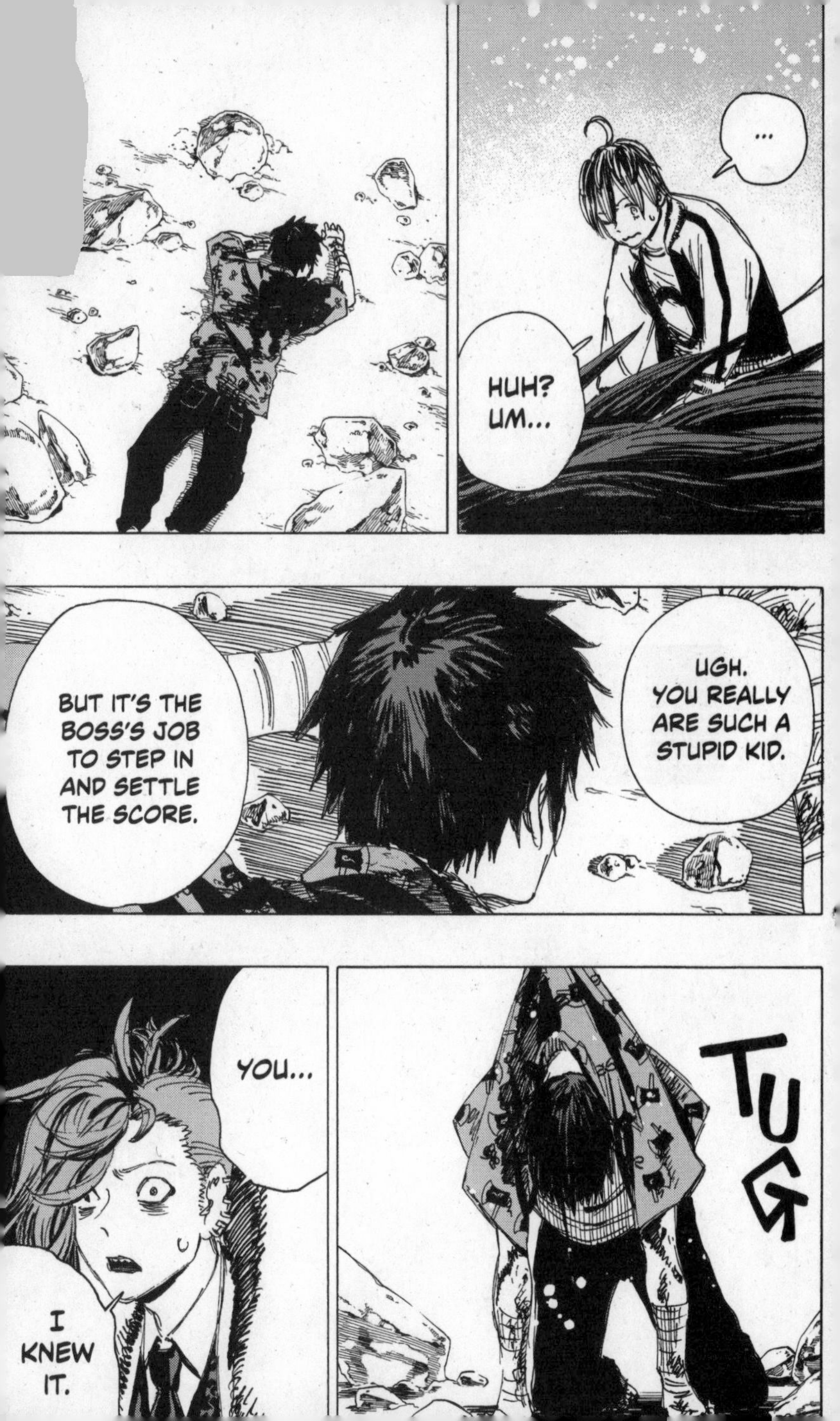
...
HUH? UM...
UGH. YOU REALLY ARE SUCH A STUPID KID.
BUT IT'S THE BOSS'S JOB TO STEP IN AND SETTLE THE SCORE.
TUG
YOU...
I KNEW IT.

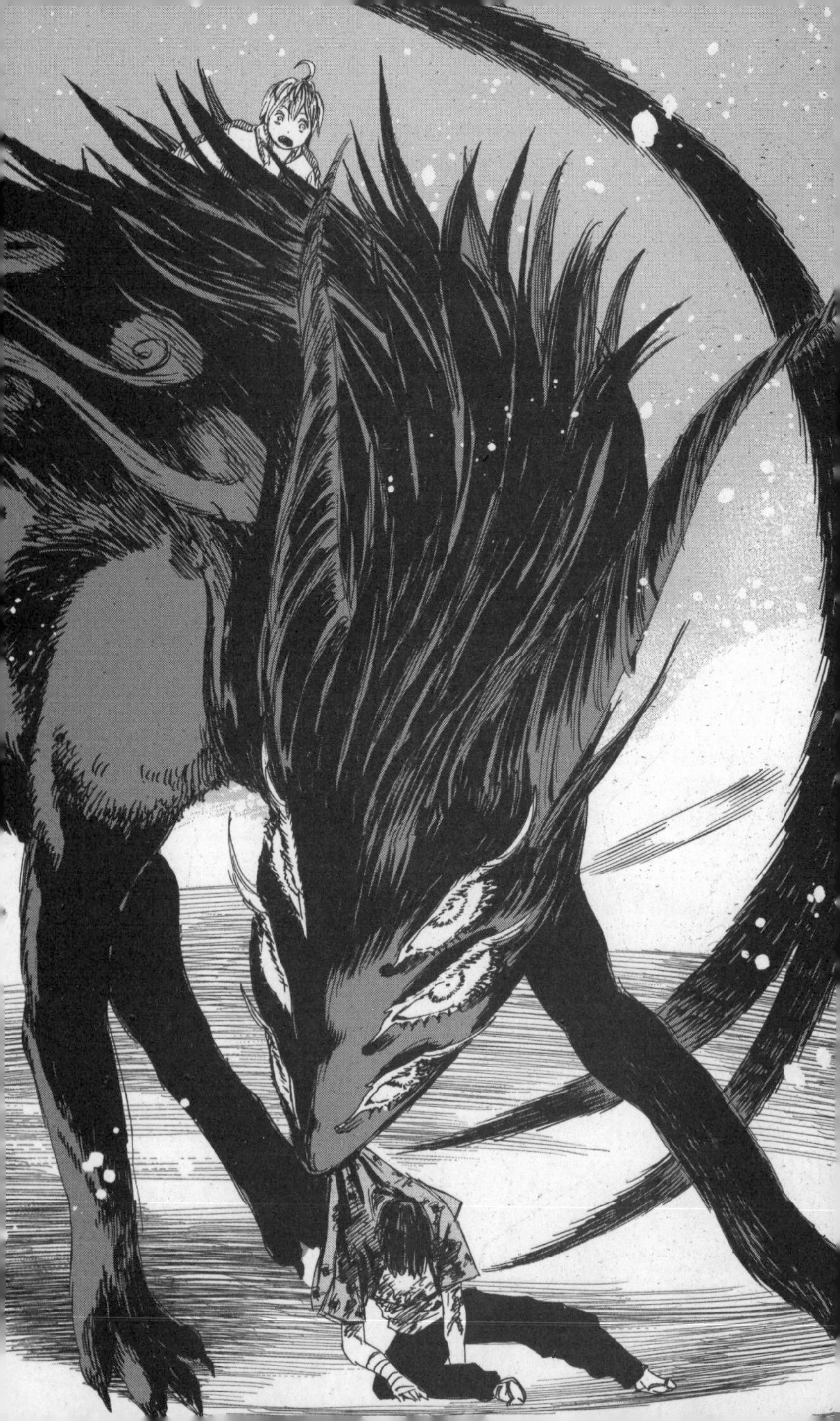

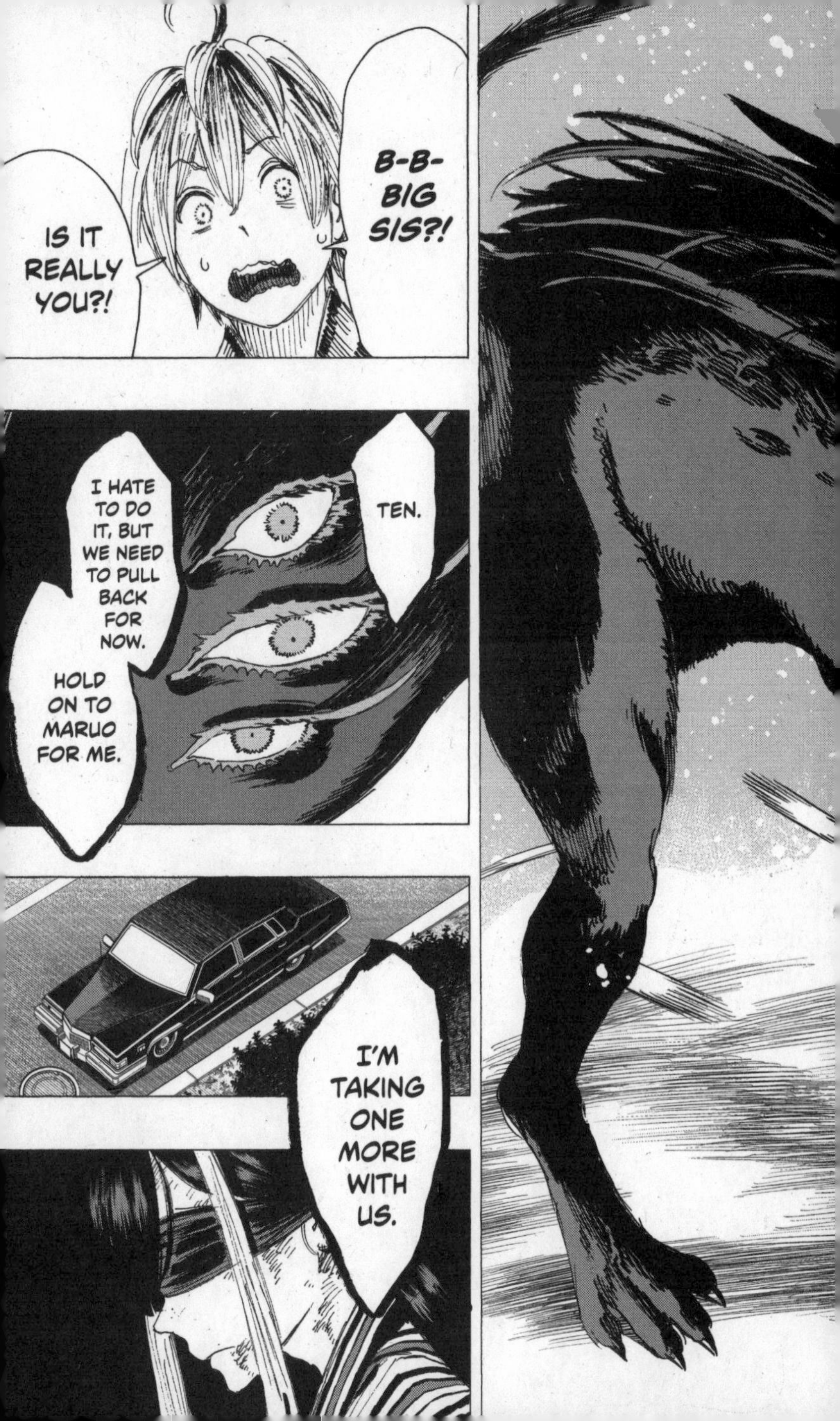
B-B-BIG SIS?!
IS IT REALLY YOU?!
TEN.
I HATE TO DO IT, BUT WE NEED TO PULL BACK FOR NOW.
HOLD ON TO MARUO FOR ME.
I'M TAKING ONE MORE WITH US.

AYASHIMON

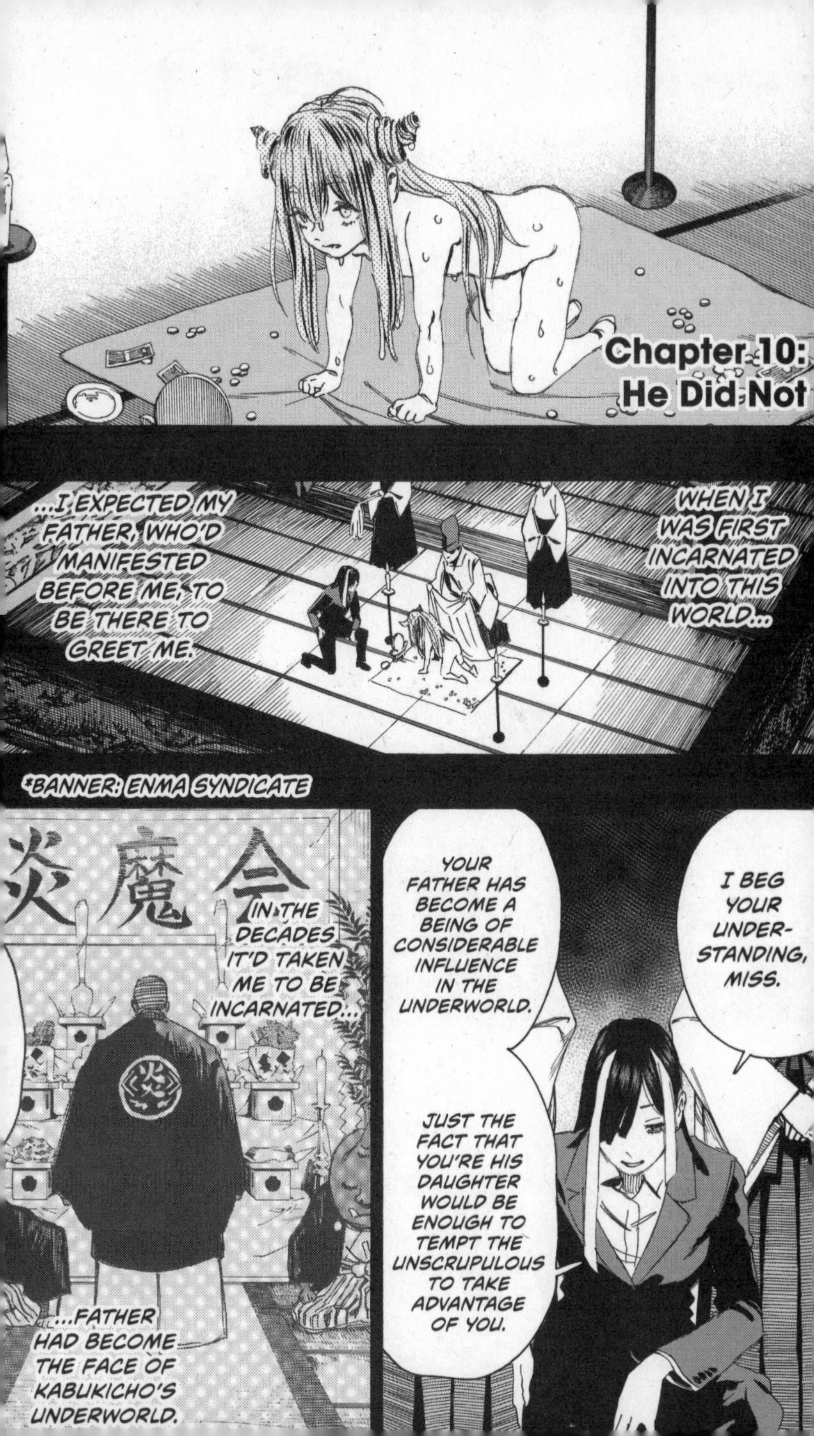

Chapter 10:
He Did Not
WHEN I WAS FIRST INCARNATED INTO THIS WORLD...
...I EXPECTED MY FATHER, WHO'D MANIFESTED BEFORE ME, TO BE THERE TO GREET ME.
*BANNER: ENMA SYNDICATE
I BEG YOUR UNDER-STANDING, MISS.
YOUR FATHER HAS BECOME A BEING OF CONSIDERABLE INFLUENCE IN THE UNDERWORLD.
JUST THE FACT THAT YOU'RE HIS DAUGHTER WOULD BE ENOUGH TO TEMPT THE UNSCRUPULOUS TO TAKE ADVANTAGE OF YOU.
炎魔会
IN THE DECADES IT'D TAKEN ME TO BE INCARNATED...
...FATHER HAD BECOME THE FACE OF KABUKICHO'S UNDERWORLD.

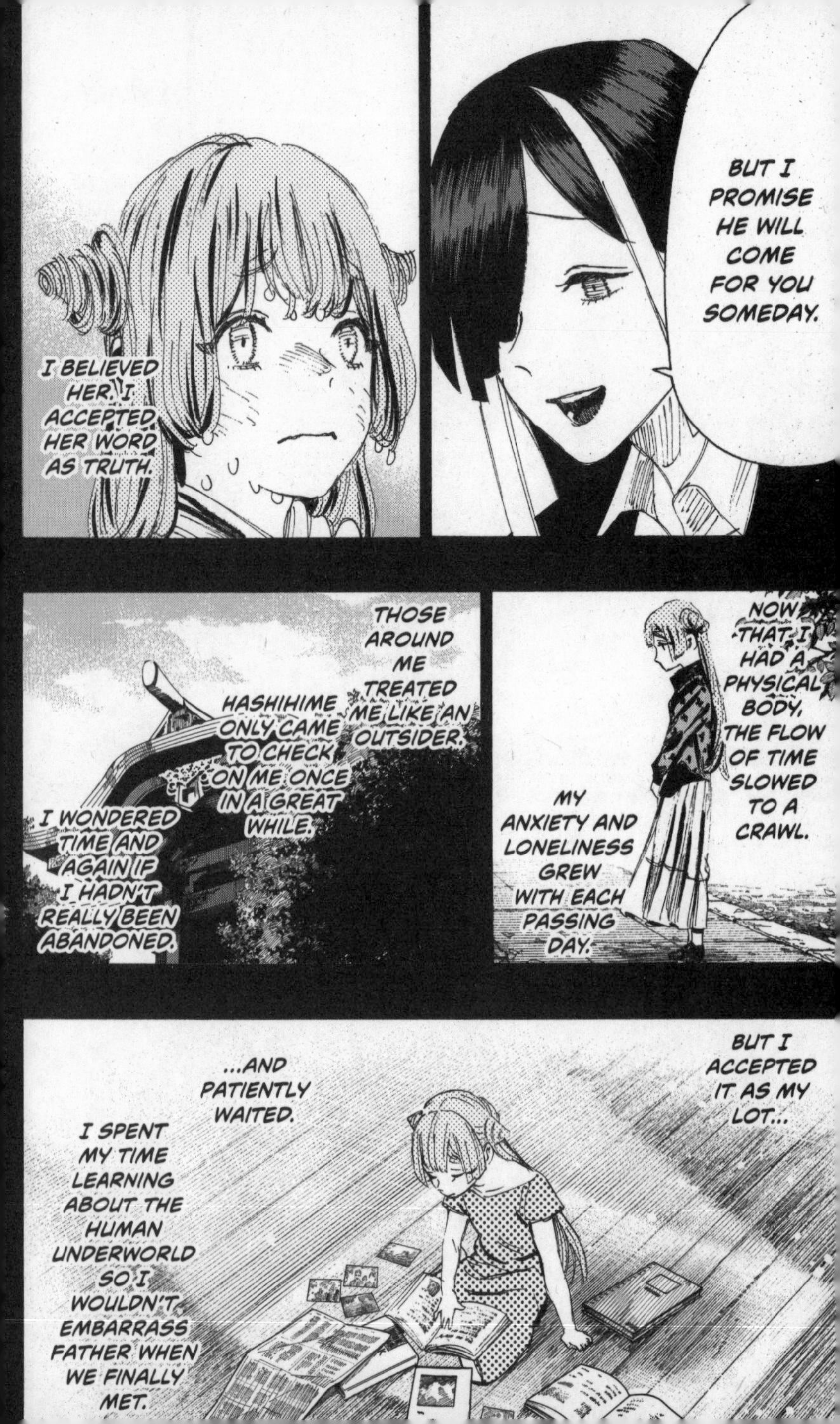
BUT I PROMISE HE WILL COME FOR YOU SOMEDAY.
I BELIEVED HER. I ACCEPTED HER WORD AS TRUTH.
NOW THAT I HAD A PHYSICAL BODY, THE FLOW OF TIME SLOWED TO A CRAWL.
MY ANXIETY AND LONELINESS GREW WITH EACH PASSING DAY.
THOSE AROUND ME TREATED ME LIKE AN OUTSIDER.
HASHIHIME ONLY CAME TO CHECK ON ME ONCE IN A GREAT WHILE.
I WONDERED TIME AND AGAIN IF I HADN'T REALLY BEEN ABANDONED.
BUT I ACCEPTED IT AS MY LOT...
...AND PATIENTLY WAITED.
I SPENT MY TIME LEARNING ABOUT THE HUMAN UNDERWORLD SO I WOULDN'T EMBARRASS FATHER WHEN WE FINALLY MET.

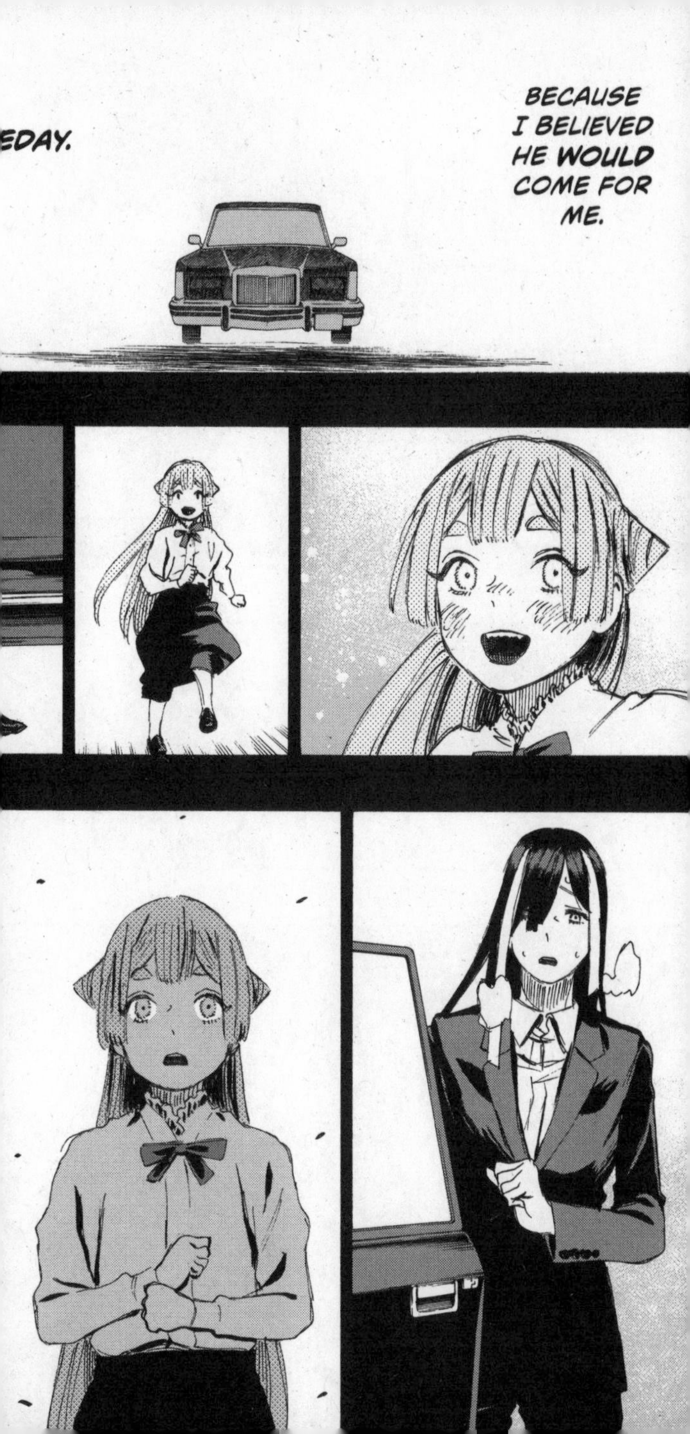

BECAUSE I BELIEVED HE WOULD COME FOR ME.
EDAY.

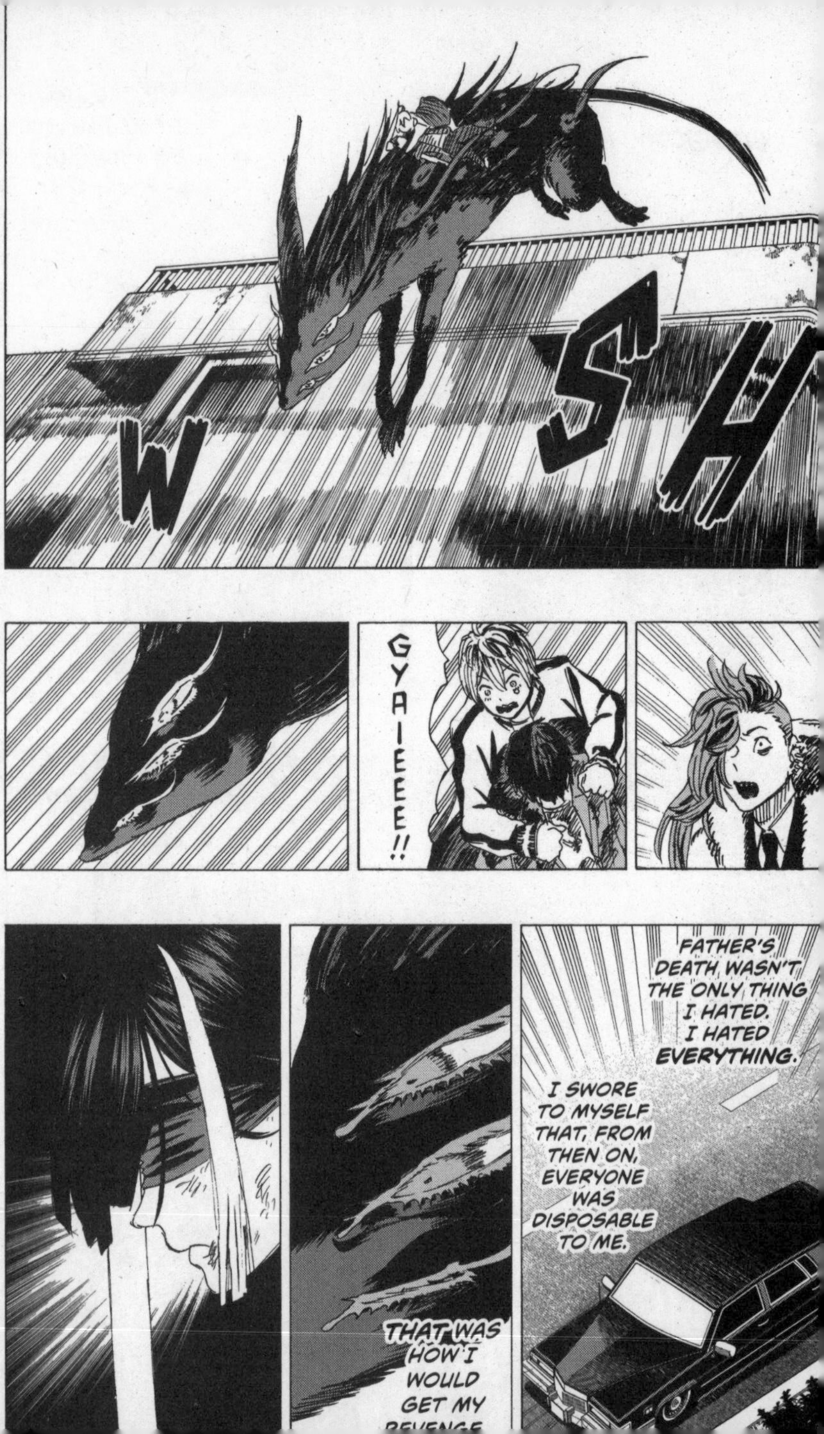

W
SH
GYAIEEEE!!
FATHER'S DEATH WASN'T THE ONLY THING I HATED. I HATED **EVERYTHING.**
I SWORE TO MYSELF THAT, FROM THEN ON, EVERYONE WAS DISPOSABLE TO ME.
THAT WAS HOW I WOULD GET MY

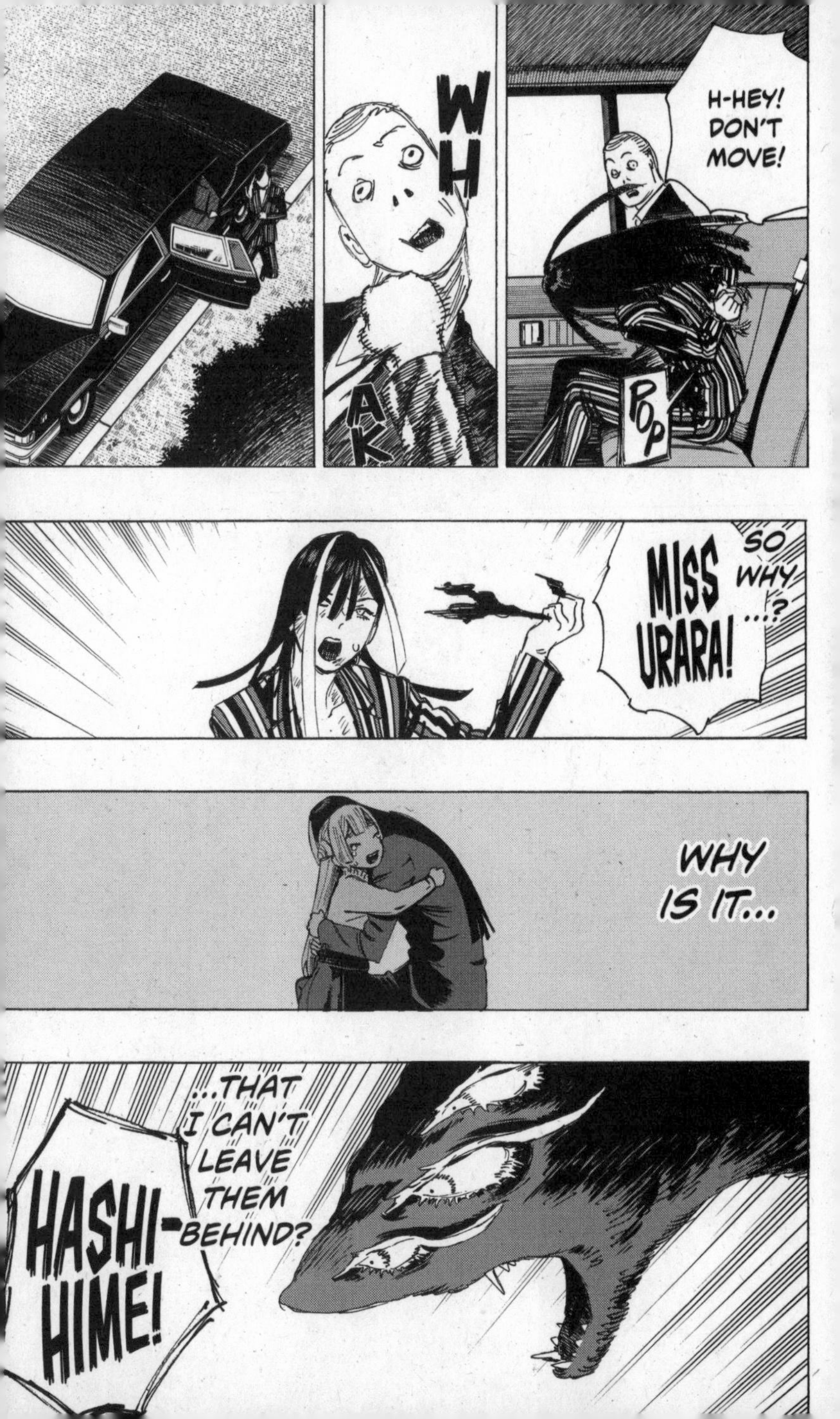
H-HEY! DON'T MOVE!
POP
WHAK
SO WHY...?
MISS URARA!
WHY IS IT...
...THAT I CAN'T LEAVE THEM BEHIND?
HASHI-HIME!

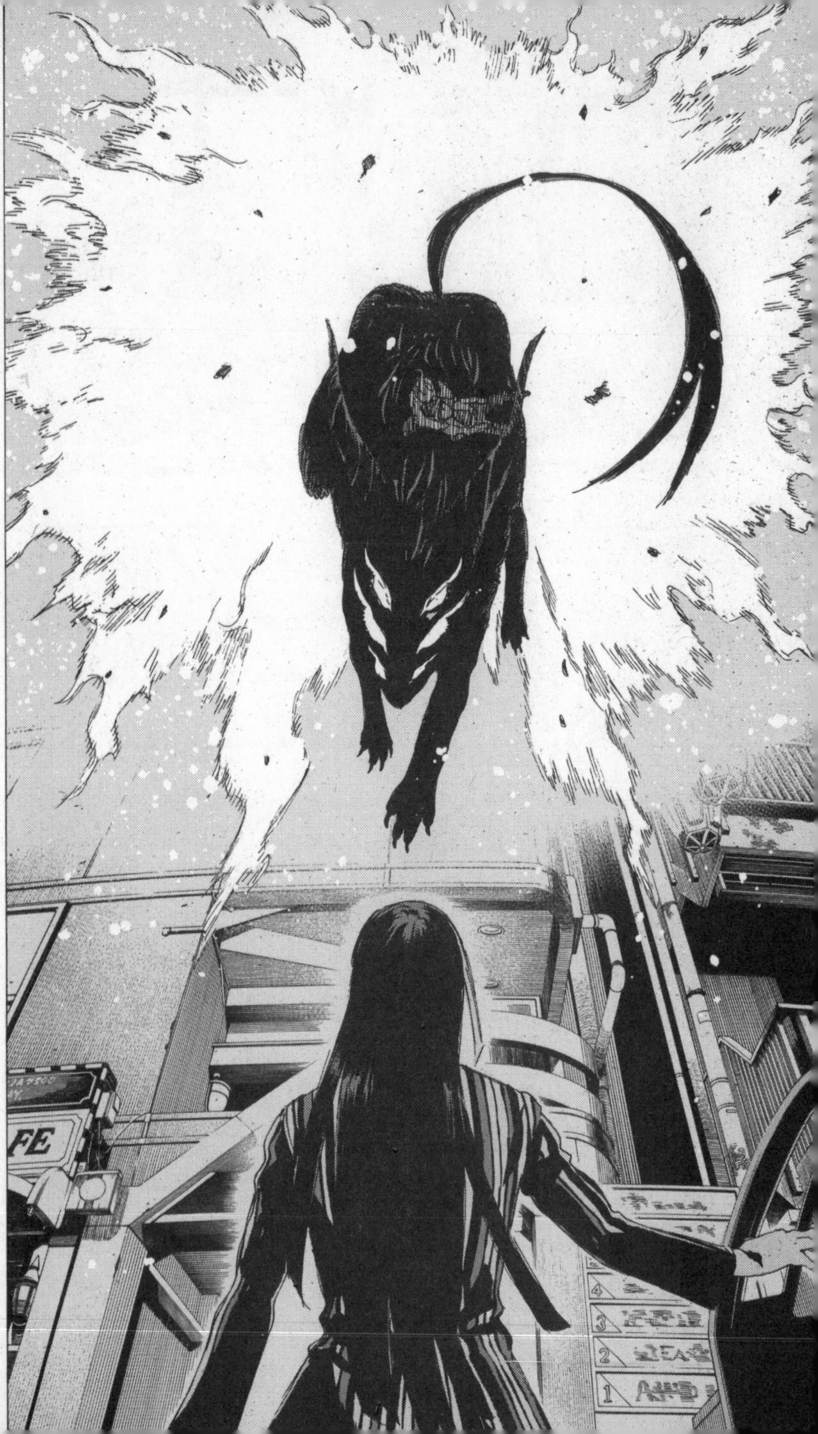
FE

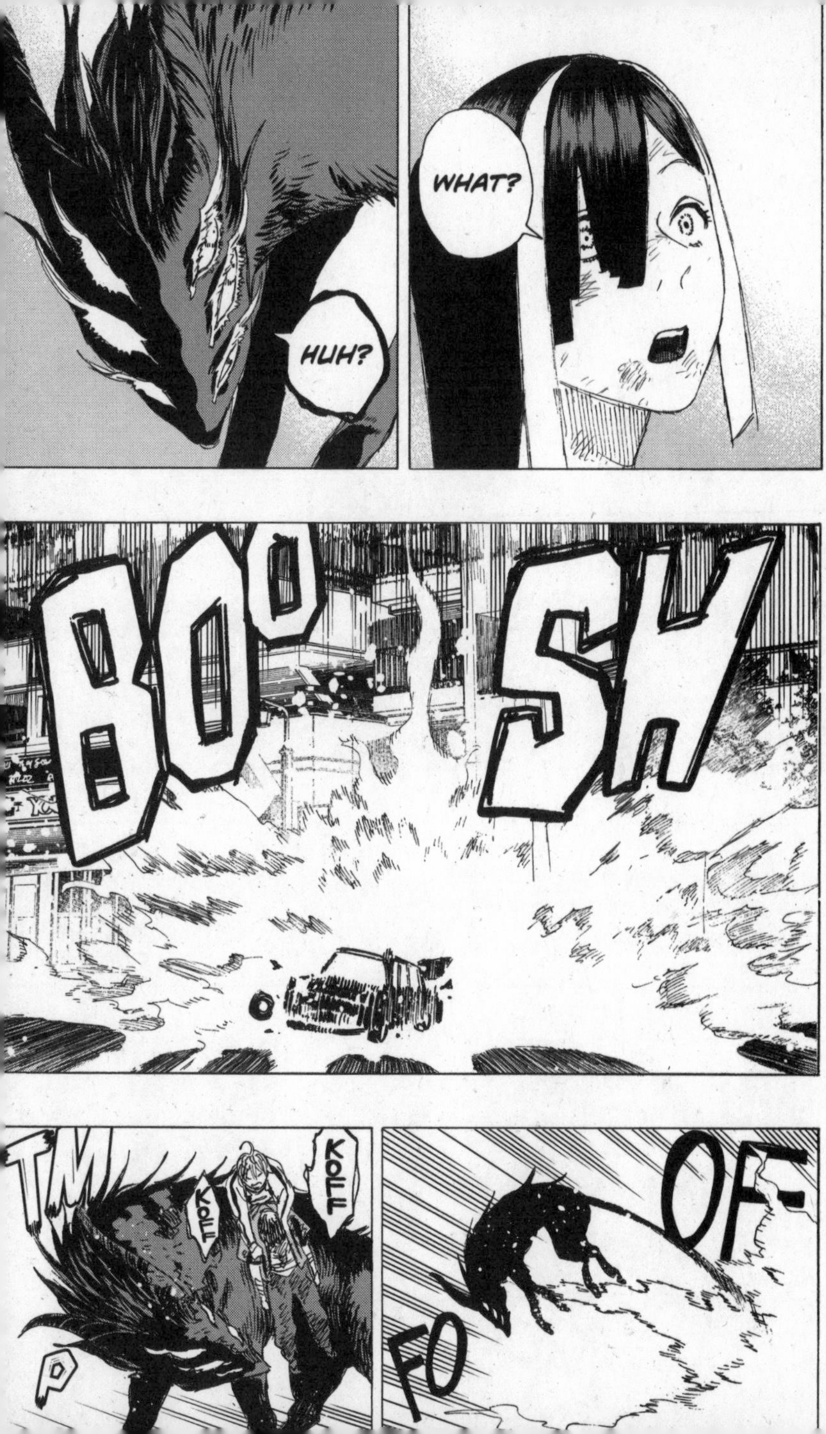
WHAT?
HUH?
BOOSH
OFF-
FO
KOFF
KOFF
TM
P

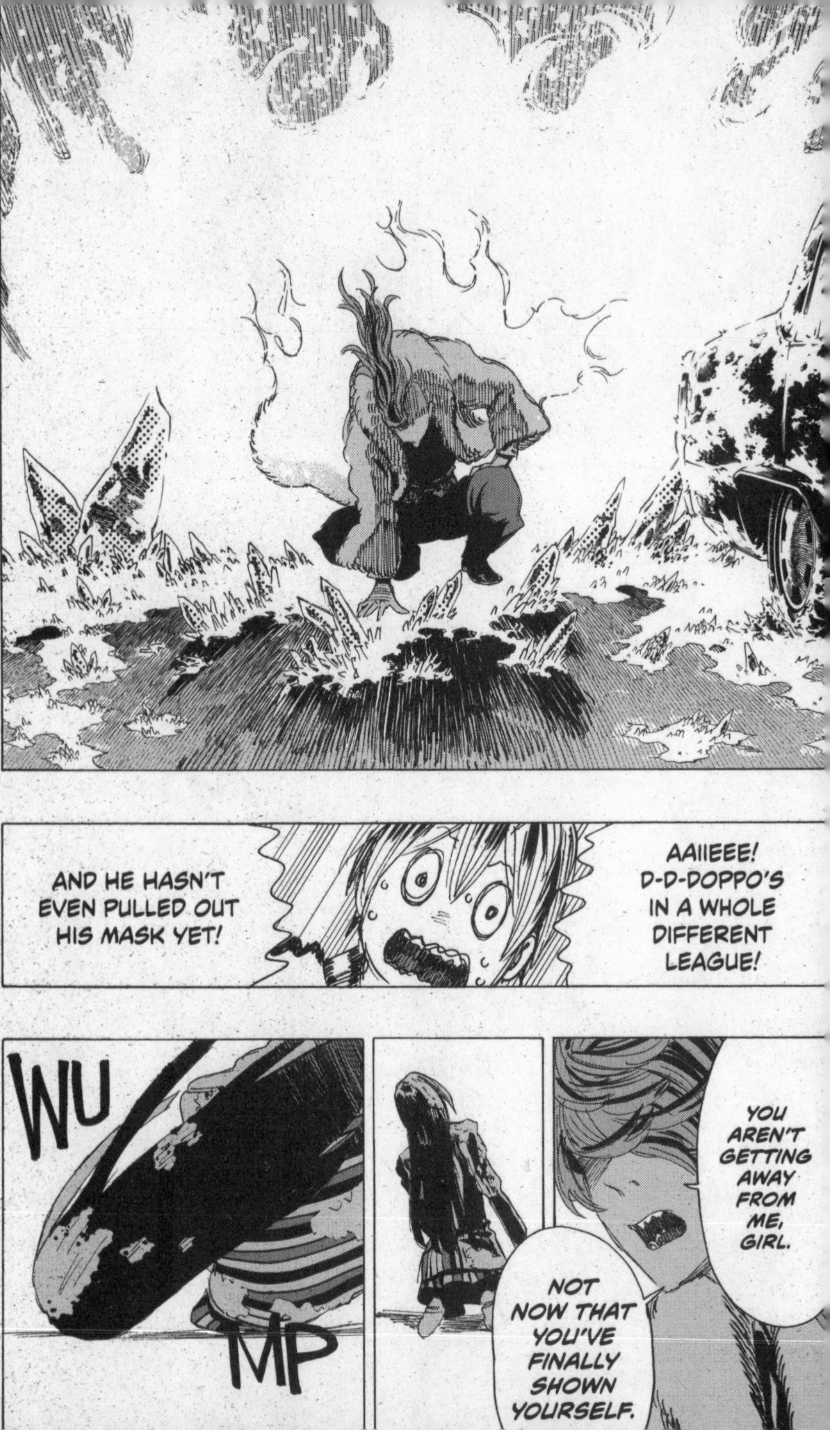
AAIIEEE! D-D-DOPPO'S IN A WHOLE DIFFERENT LEAGUE!
AND HE HASN'T EVEN PULLED OUT HIS MASK YET!
YOU AREN'T GETTING AWAY FROM ME, GIRL.
NOT NOW THAT YOU'VE FINALLY SHOWN YOURSELF.
WUMP

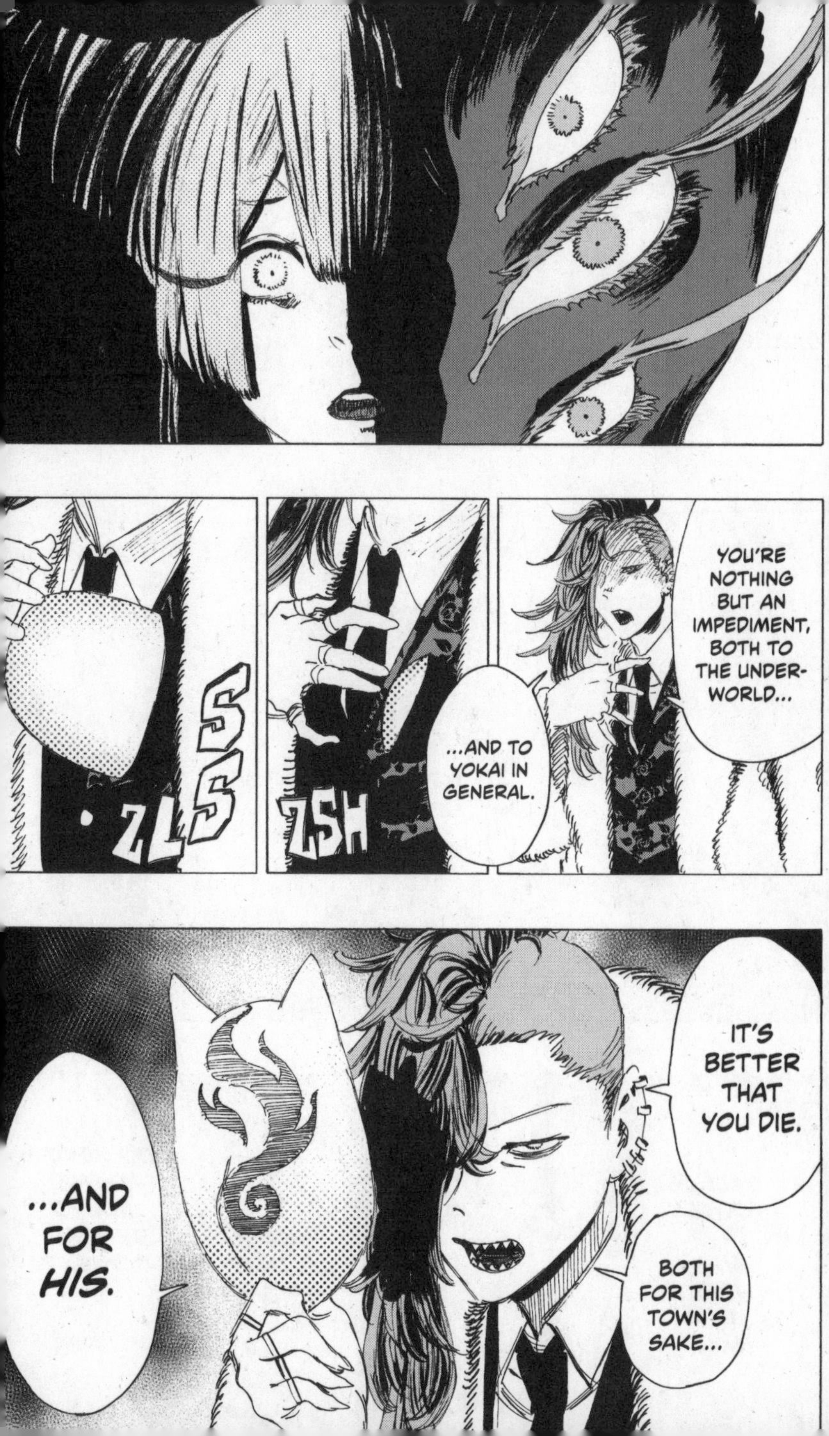
YOU'RE NOTHING BUT AN IMPEDIMENT, BOTH TO THE UNDER-WORLD...
...AND TO YOKAI IN GENERAL.
ZSH
IT'S BETTER THAT YOU DIE.
BOTH FOR THIS TOWN'S SAKE...
...AND FOR *HIS*.

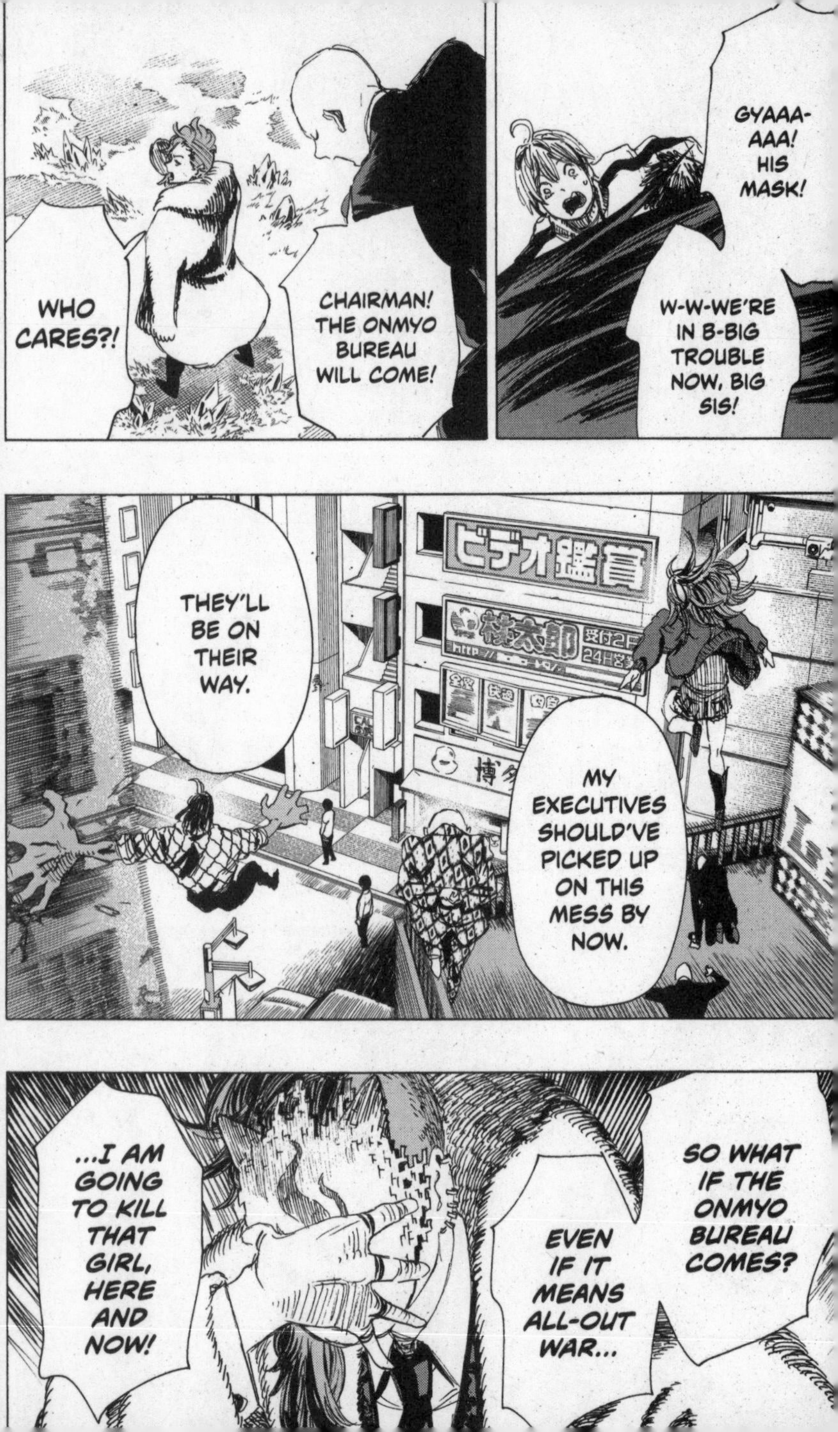

GYAAA-AAA! HIS MASK!
W-W-WE'RE IN B-BIG TROUBLE NOW, BIG SIS!
CHAIRMAN! THE ONMYO BUREAU WILL COME!
WHO CARES?!
ビデオ鑑賞
桃太郎
MY EXECUTIVES SHOULD'VE PICKED UP ON THIS MESS BY NOW.
THEY'LL BE ON THEIR WAY.
SO WHAT IF THE ONMYO BUREAU COMES?
EVEN IF IT MEANS ALL-OUT WAR...
...I AM GOING TO KILL THAT GIRL, HERE AND NOW!

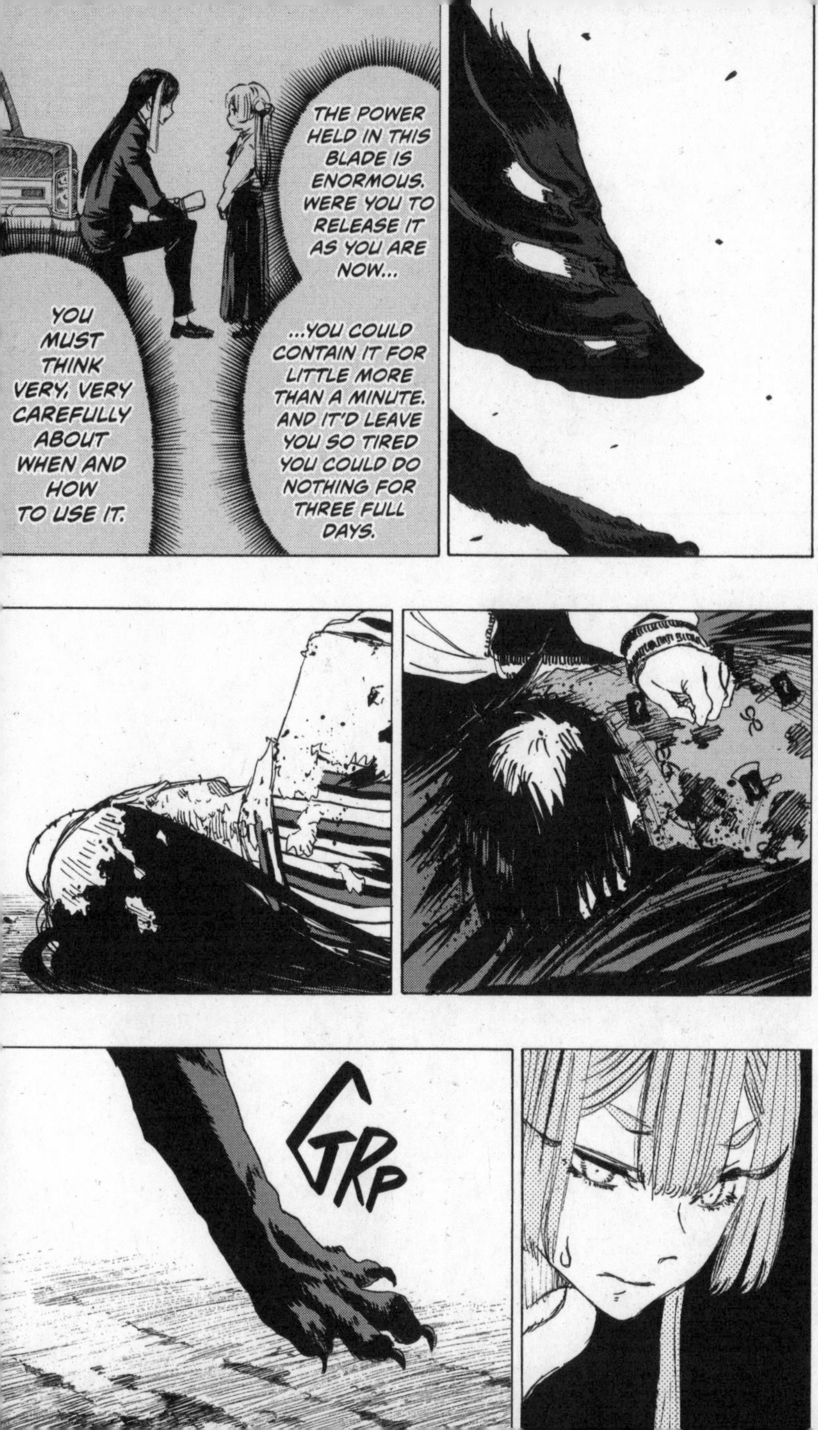
THE POWER HELD IN THIS BLADE IS ENORMOUS. WERE YOU TO RELEASE IT AS YOU ARE NOW...
...YOU COULD CONTAIN IT FOR LITTLE MORE THAN A MINUTE. AND IT'D LEAVE YOU SO TIRED YOU COULD DO NOTHING FOR THREE FULL DAYS.
YOU MUST THINK VERY, VERY CAREFULLY ABOUT WHEN AND HOW TO USE IT.
GRP

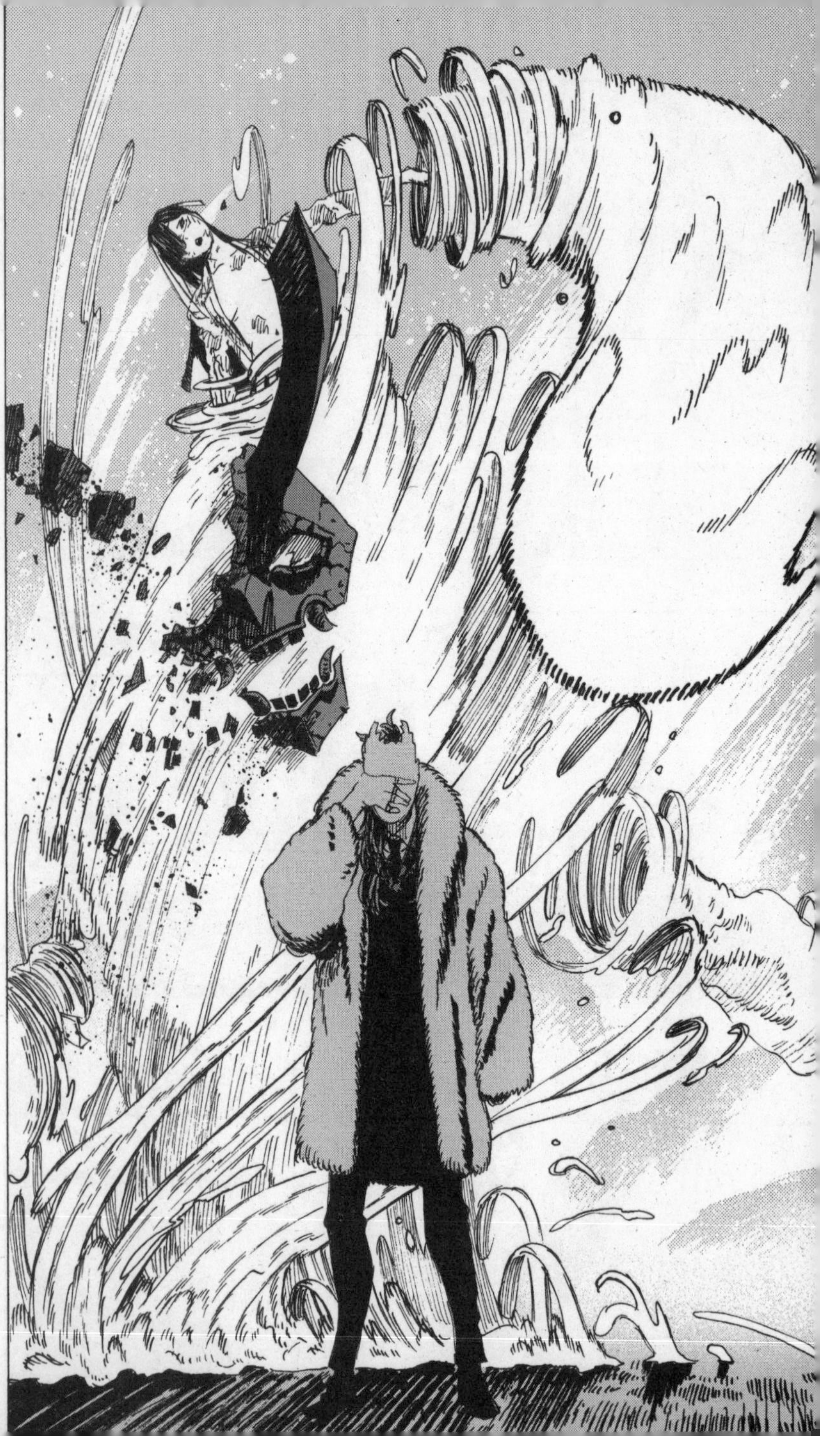

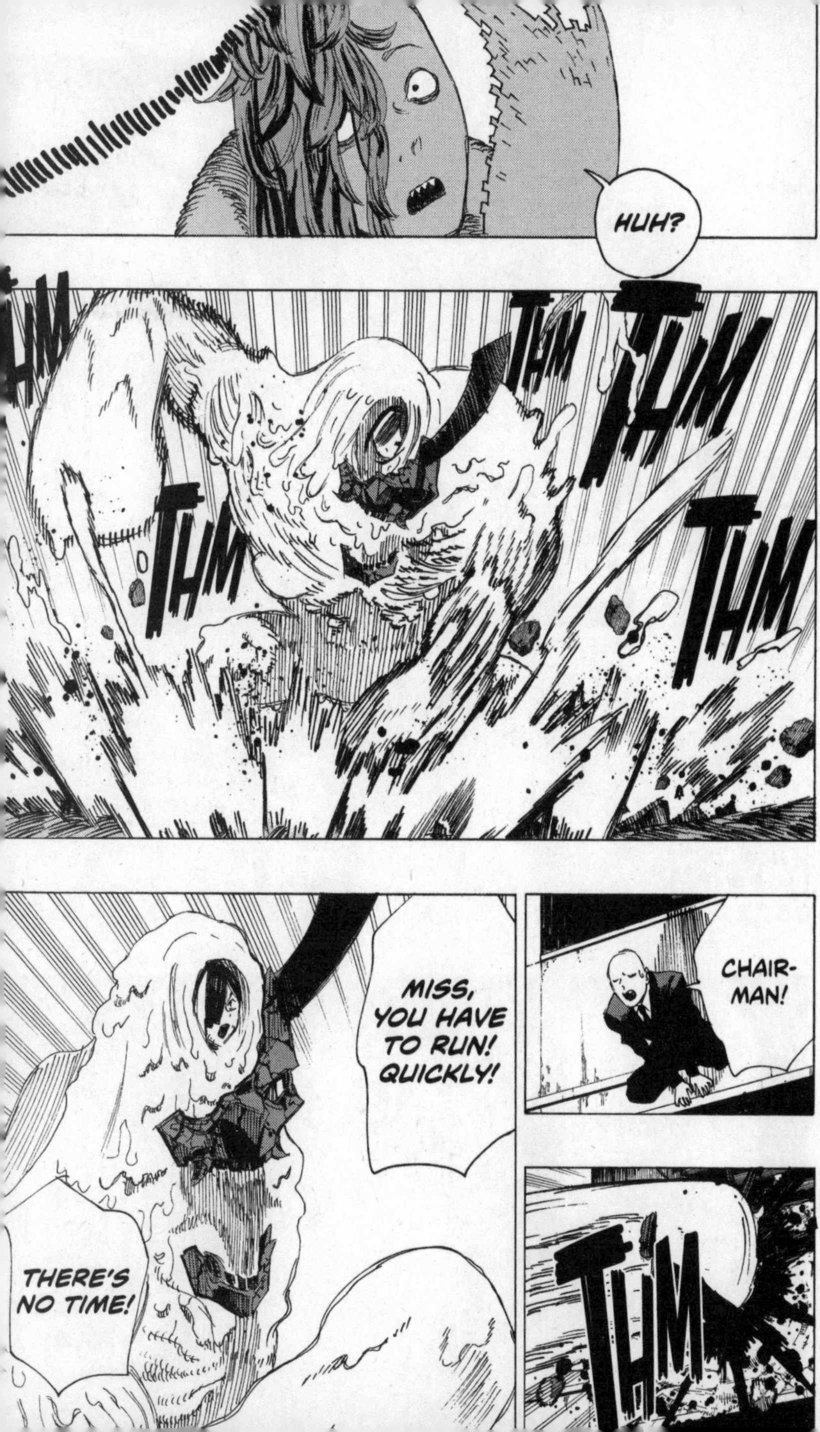
HUH?
THM
THM
THM
THM
THM
CHAIR-MAN!
THM
MISS, YOU HAVE TO RUN! QUICKLY!
THERE'S NO TIME!

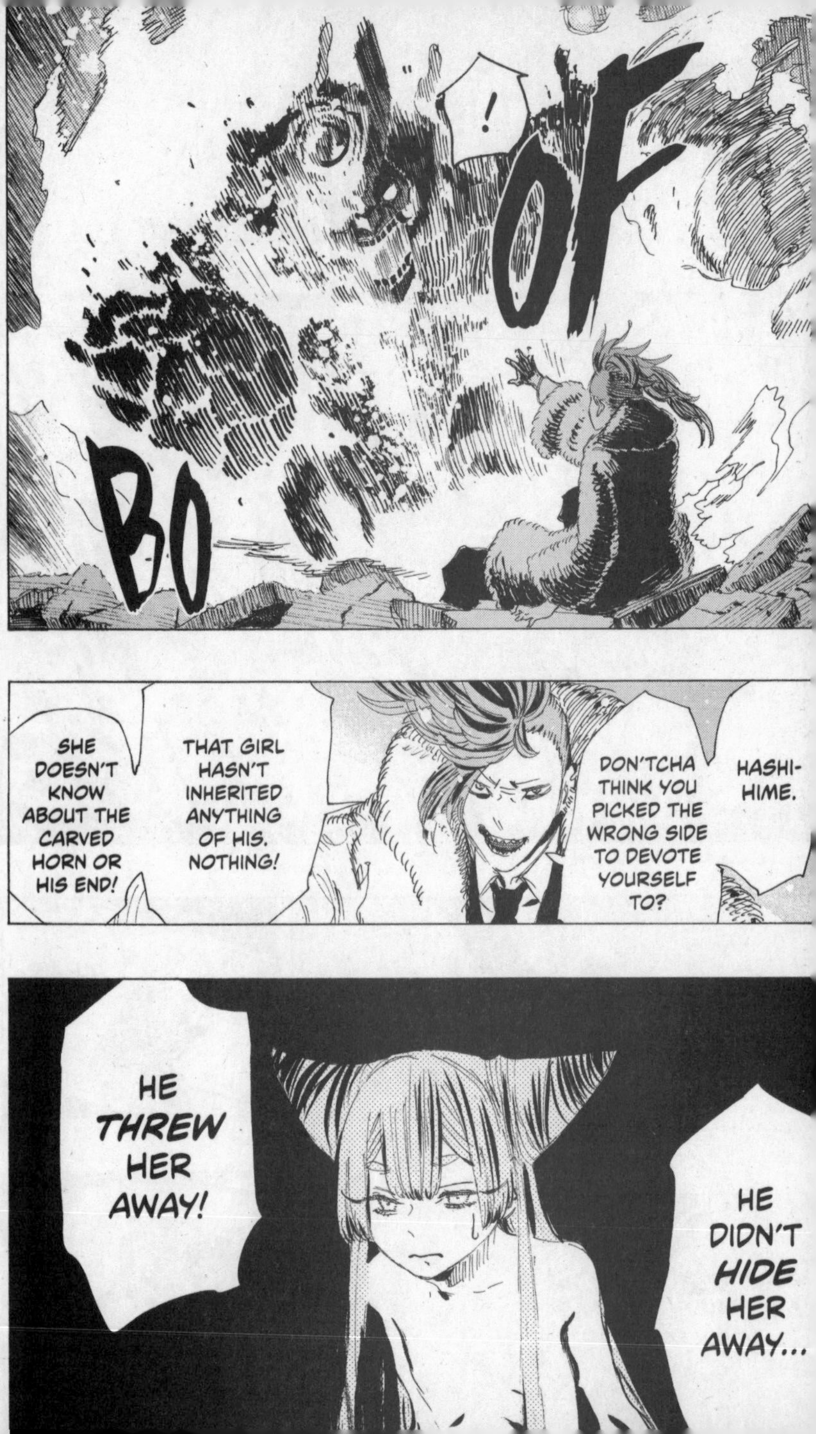
!
BOOF
HASHI-HIME.
DON'TCHA THINK YOU PICKED THE WRONG SIDE TO DEVOTE YOURSELF TO?
THAT GIRL HASN'T INHERITED ANYTHING OF HIS. NOTHING!
SHE DOESN'T KNOW ABOUT THE CARVED HORN OR HIS END!
HE DIDN'T *HIDE* HER AWAY...
HE *THREW* HER AWAY!

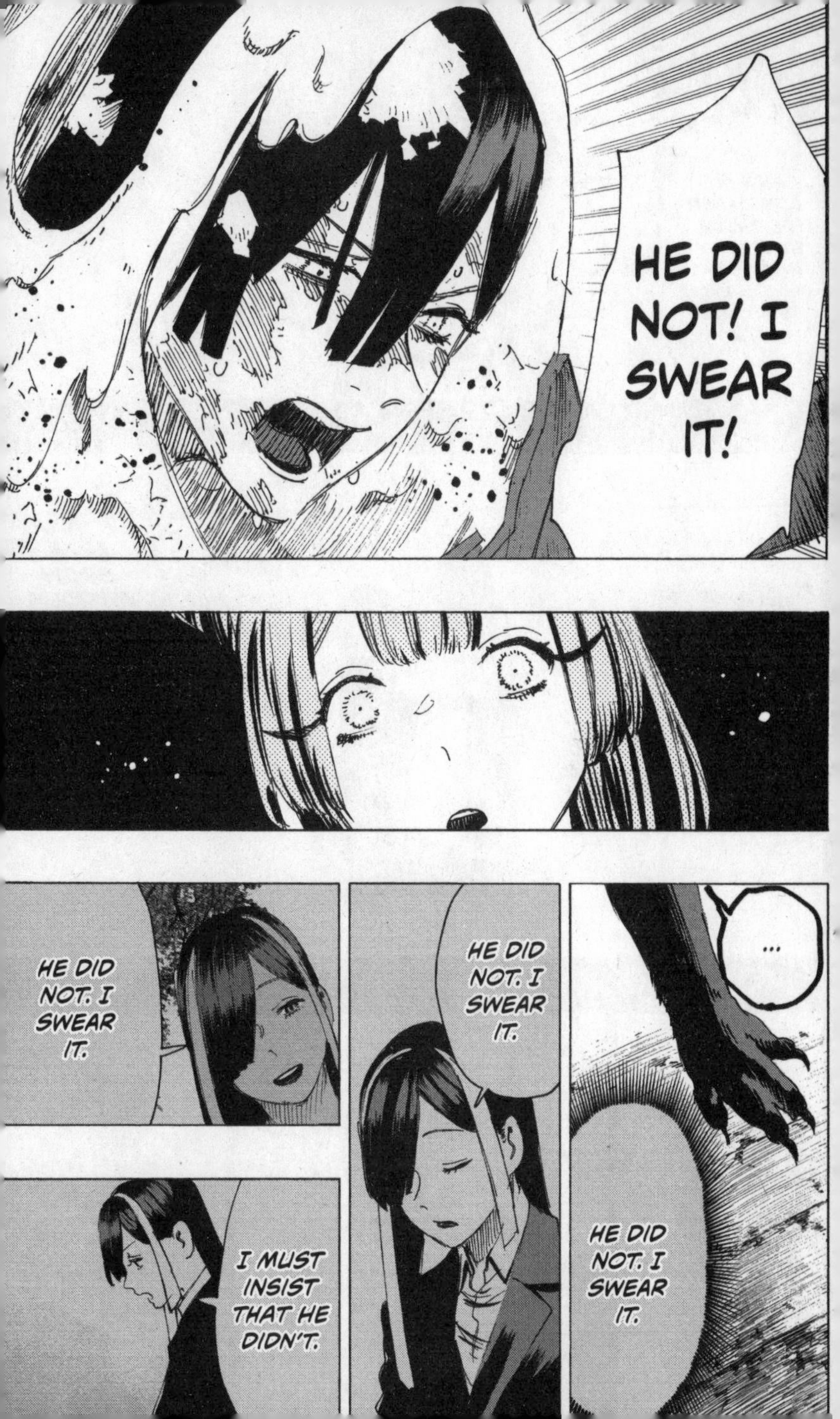
HE DID NOT! I SWEAR IT!
...
HE DID NOT. I SWEAR IT.
HE DID NOT. I SWEAR IT.
HE DID NOT. I SWEAR IT.
I MUST INSIST THAT HE DIDN'T.

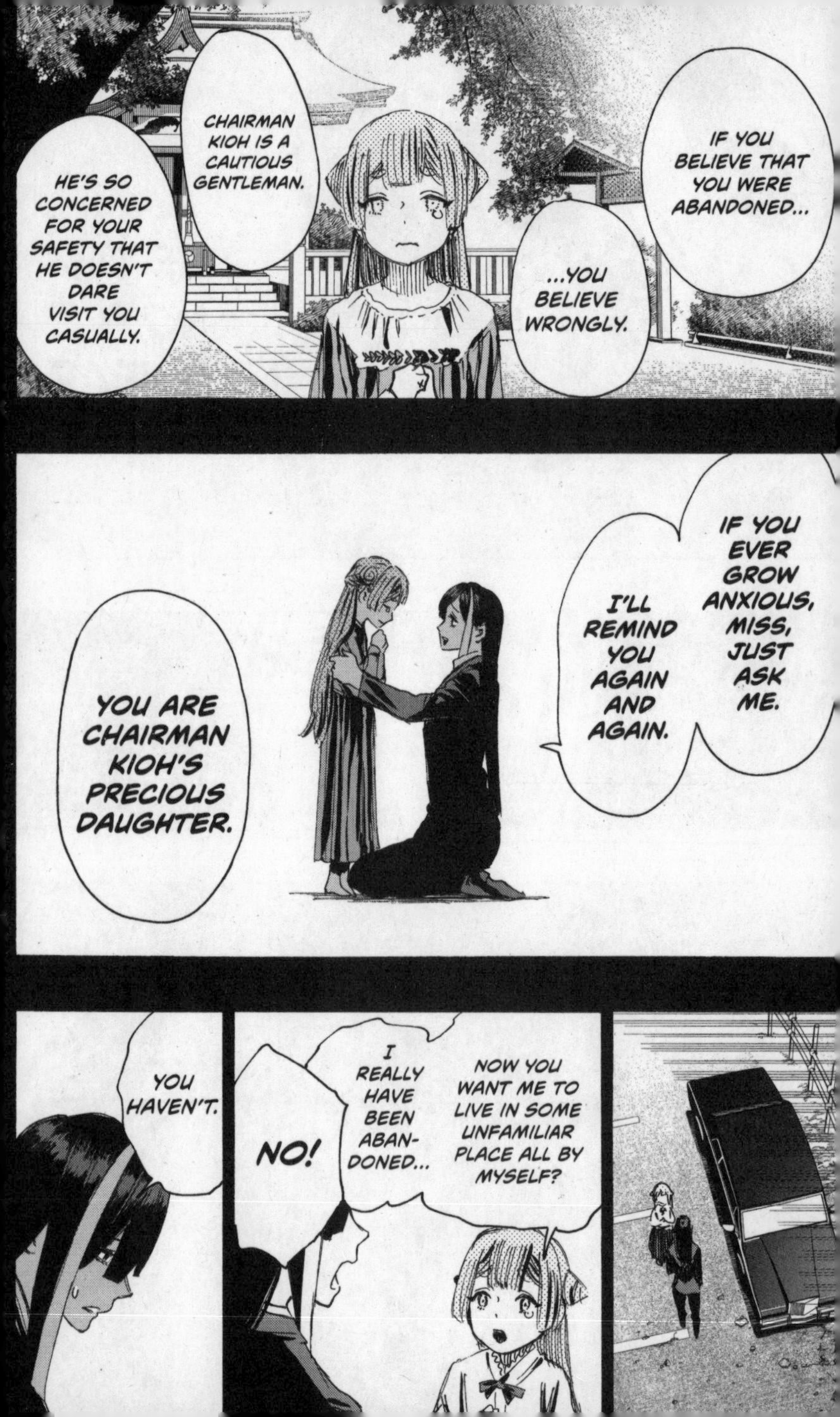
IF YOU BELIEVE THAT YOU WERE ABANDONED...
...YOU BELIEVE WRONGLY.
CHAIRMAN KIOH IS A CAUTIOUS GENTLEMAN.
HE'S SO CONCERNED FOR YOUR SAFETY THAT HE DOESN'T DARE VISIT YOU CASUALLY.
IF YOU EVER GROW ANXIOUS, MISS, JUST ASK ME.
I'LL REMIND YOU AGAIN AND AGAIN.
YOU ARE CHAIRMAN KIOH'S PRECIOUS DAUGHTER.
NOW YOU WANT ME TO LIVE IN SOME UNFAMILIAR PLACE ALL BY MYSELF?
I REALLY HAVE BEEN ABAN-DONED...
NO!
YOU HAVEN'T.

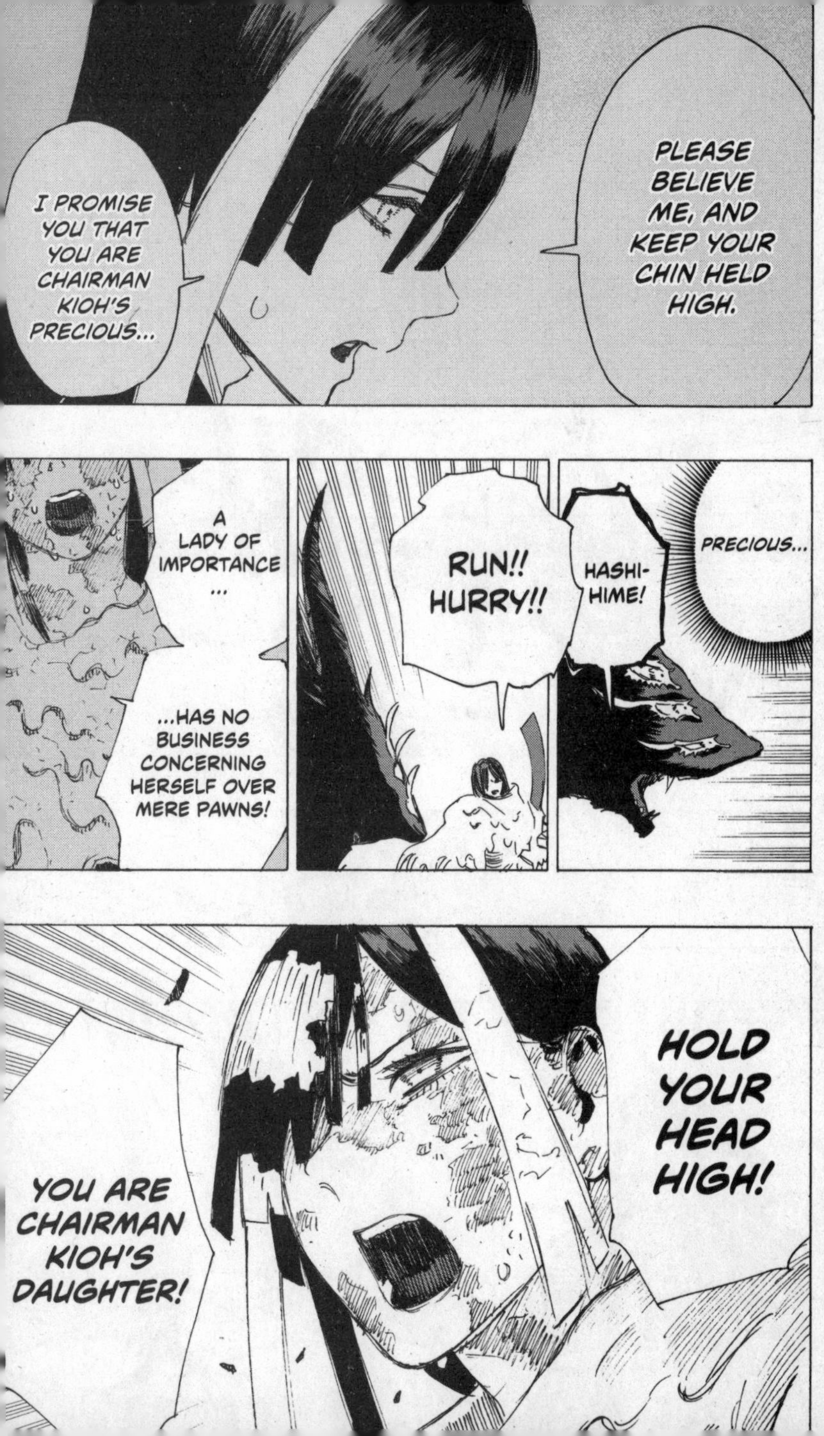
PLEASE BELIEVE ME, AND KEEP YOUR CHIN HELD HIGH.
I PROMISE YOU THAT YOU ARE CHAIRMAN KIOH'S PRECIOUS...
PRECIOUS...
HASHI-HIME!
RUN!! HURRY!!
A LADY OF IMPORTANCE ...
...HAS NO BUSINESS CONCERNING HERSELF OVER MERE PAWNS!
HOLD YOUR HEAD HIGH!
YOU ARE CHAIRMAN KIOH'S DAUGHTER!

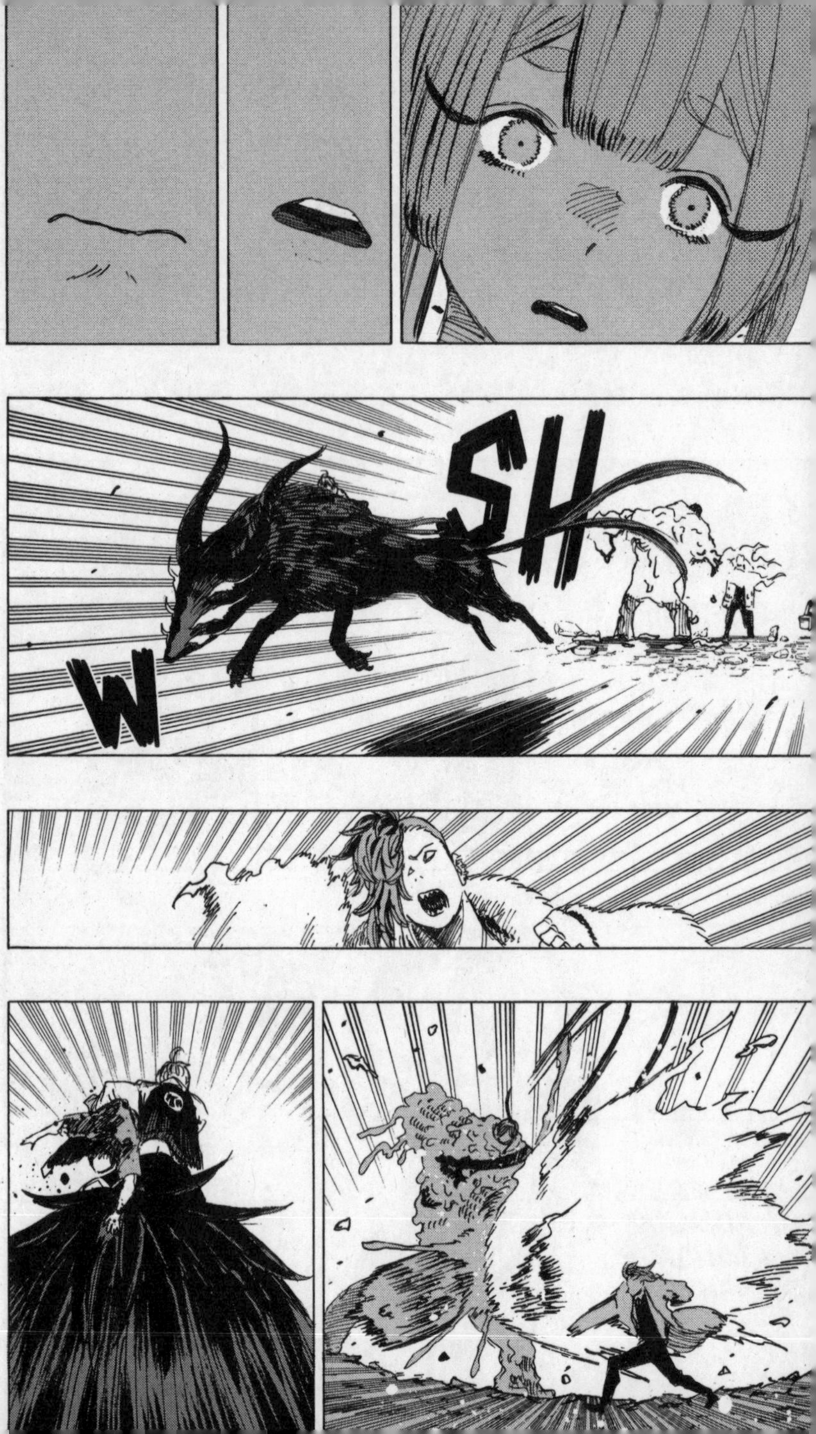
SH
W

MARUO, I LEAVE HER IN YOUR HANDS.

TAKE CARE OF HER. SHE'S CHAIRMAN KIOH'S...! NO.

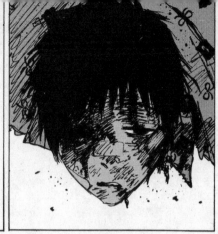

SHE'S MY PRECIOUS CHARGE!

AYASHIMON

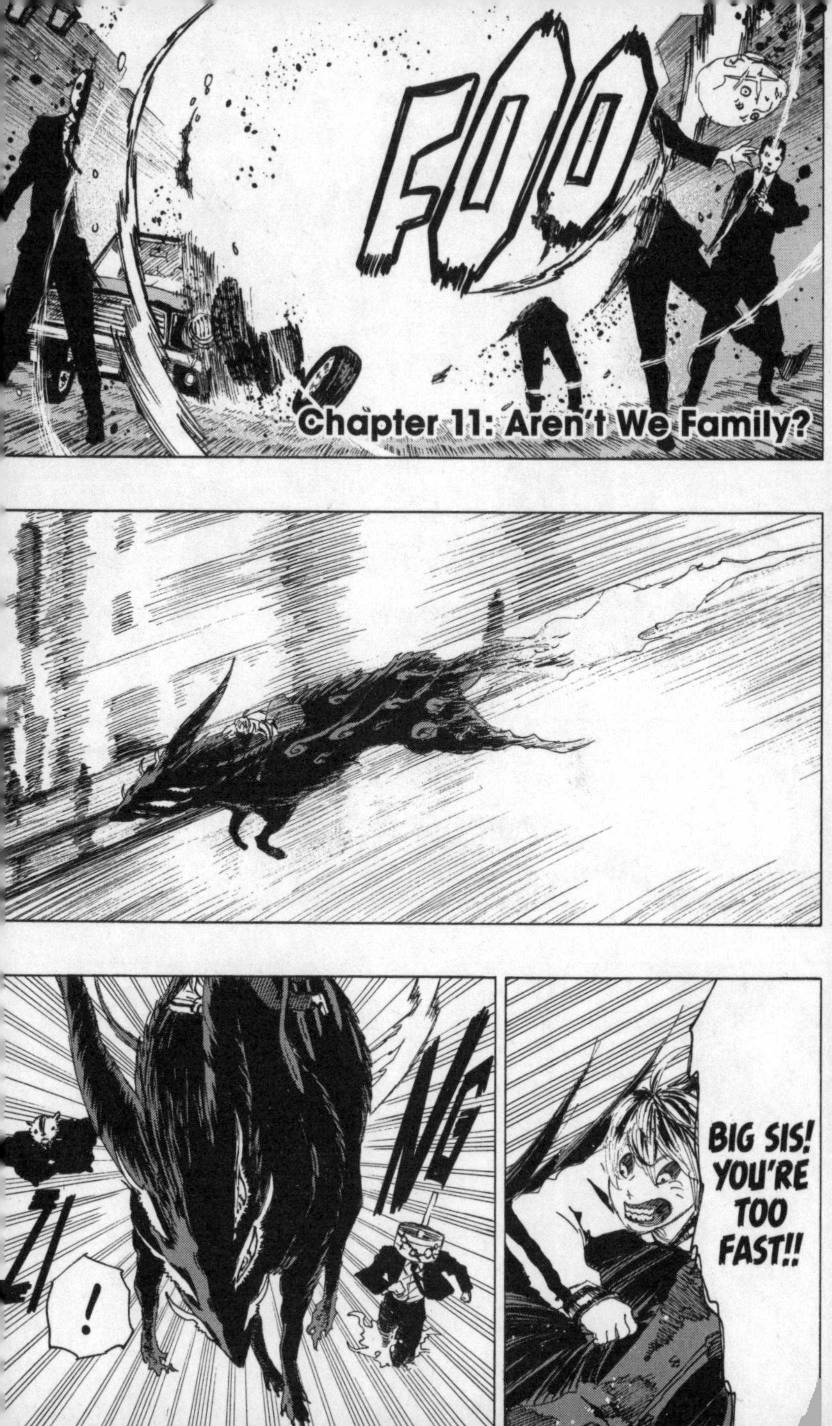
FOOO
Chapter 11: Aren't We Family?
BIG SIS! YOU'RE TOO FAST!!
NG
!

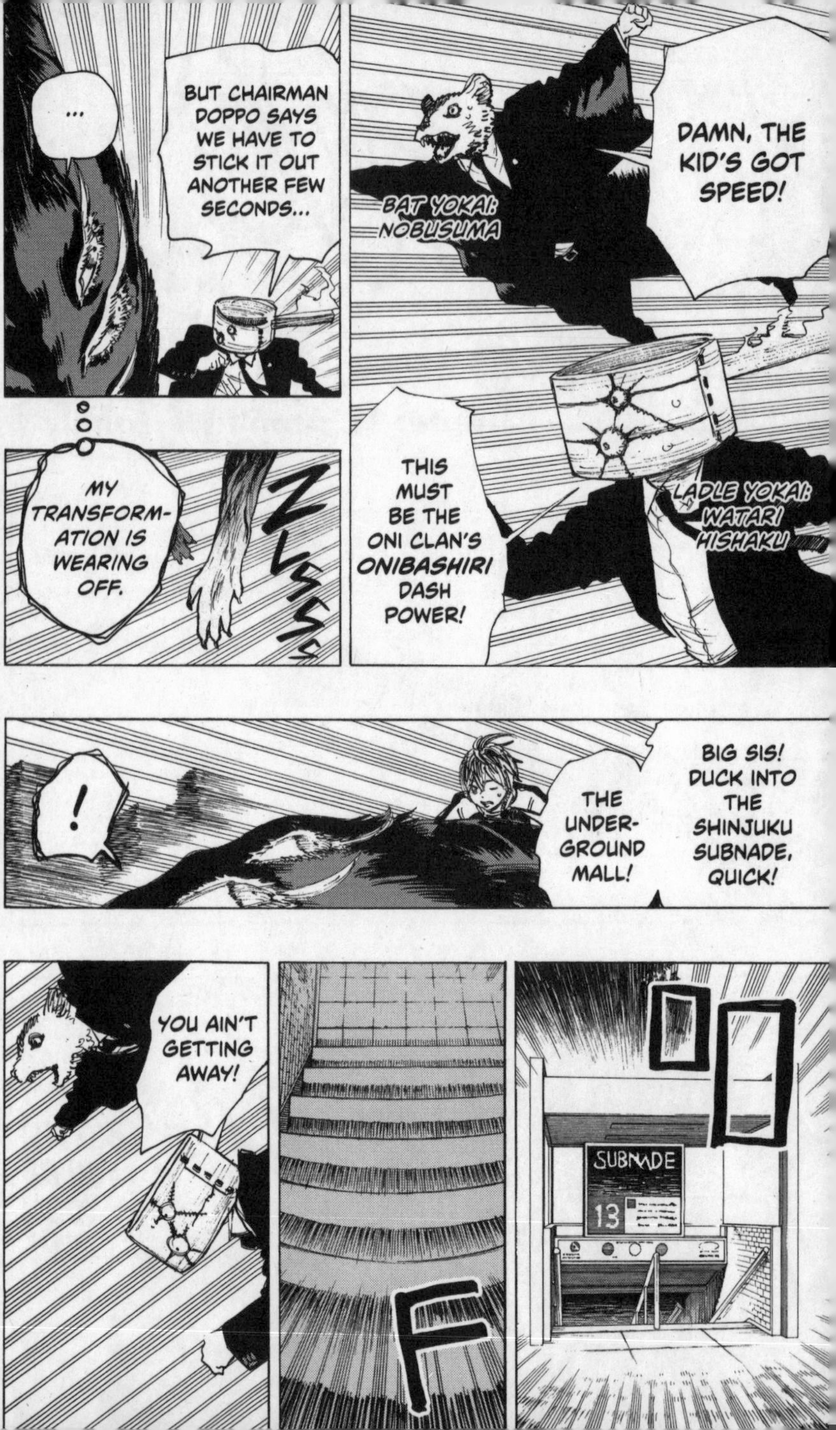
DAMN, THE KID'S GOT SPEED!
BAT YOKAI: NOBUSUMA
THIS MUST BE THE ONI CLAN'S ONIBASHIRI DASH POWER!
LADLE YOKAI: WATARI HISHAKU
...
BUT CHAIRMAN DOPPO SAYS WE HAVE TO STICK IT OUT ANOTHER FEW SECONDS...
MY TRANSFORM-ATION IS WEARING OFF.
BIG SIS! DUCK INTO THE SHINJUKU SUBNADE, QUICK!
THE UNDER-GROUND MALL!
!
SUBNADE
13
YOU AIN'T GETTING AWAY!

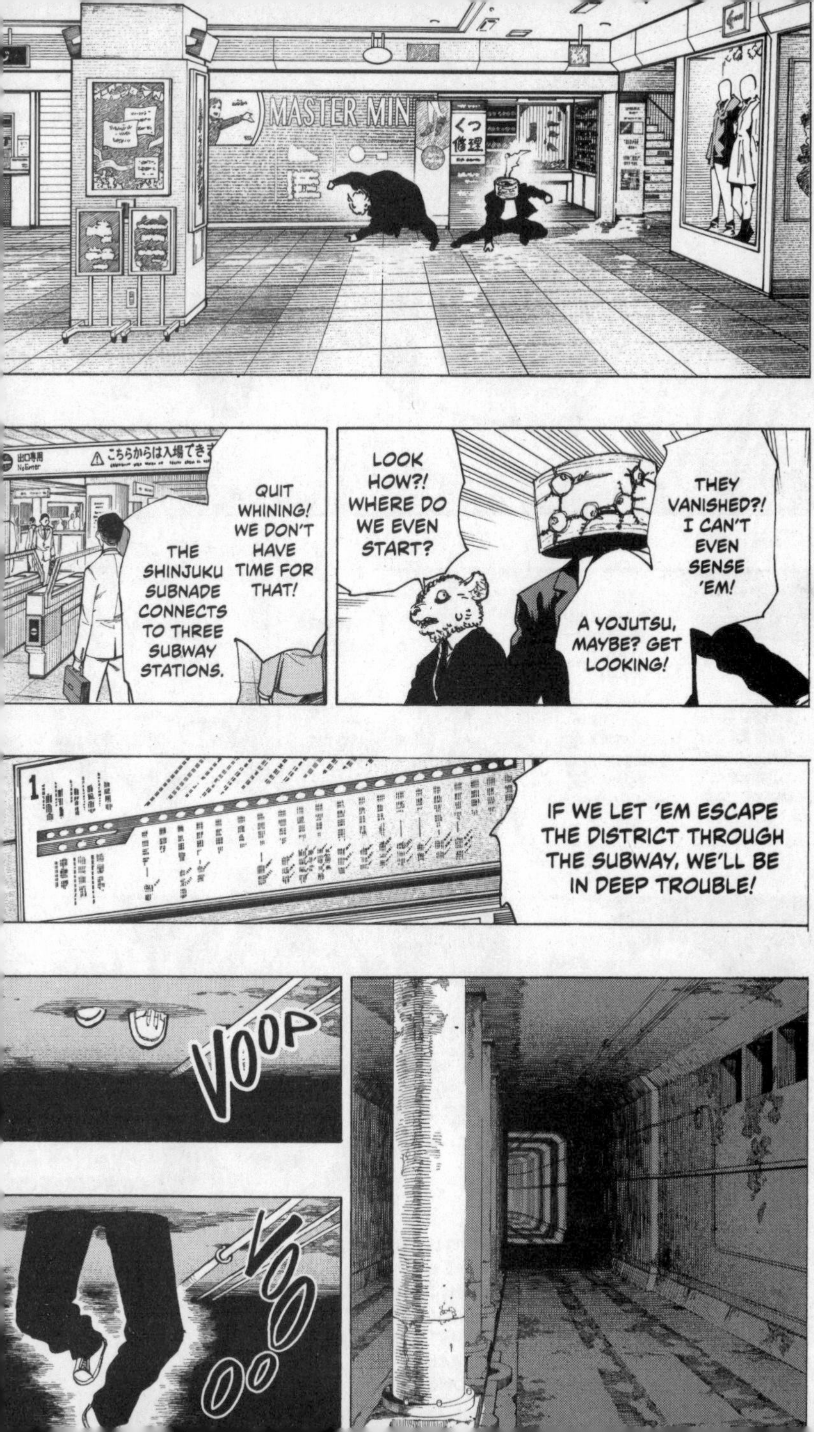
MASTER MIN
くつ修理
THEY VANISHED?! I CAN'T EVEN SENSE 'EM!
LOOK HOW?! WHERE DO WE EVEN START?
A YOJUTSU, MAYBE? GET LOOKING!
QUIT WHINING! WE DON'T HAVE TIME FOR THAT!
出口専用
No Enter
THE SHINJUKU SUBNADE CONNECTS TO THREE SUBWAY STATIONS.
IF WE LET 'EM ESCAPE THE DISTRICT THROUGH THE SUBWAY, WE'LL BE IN DEEP TROUBLE!
VOOP
VOOOO

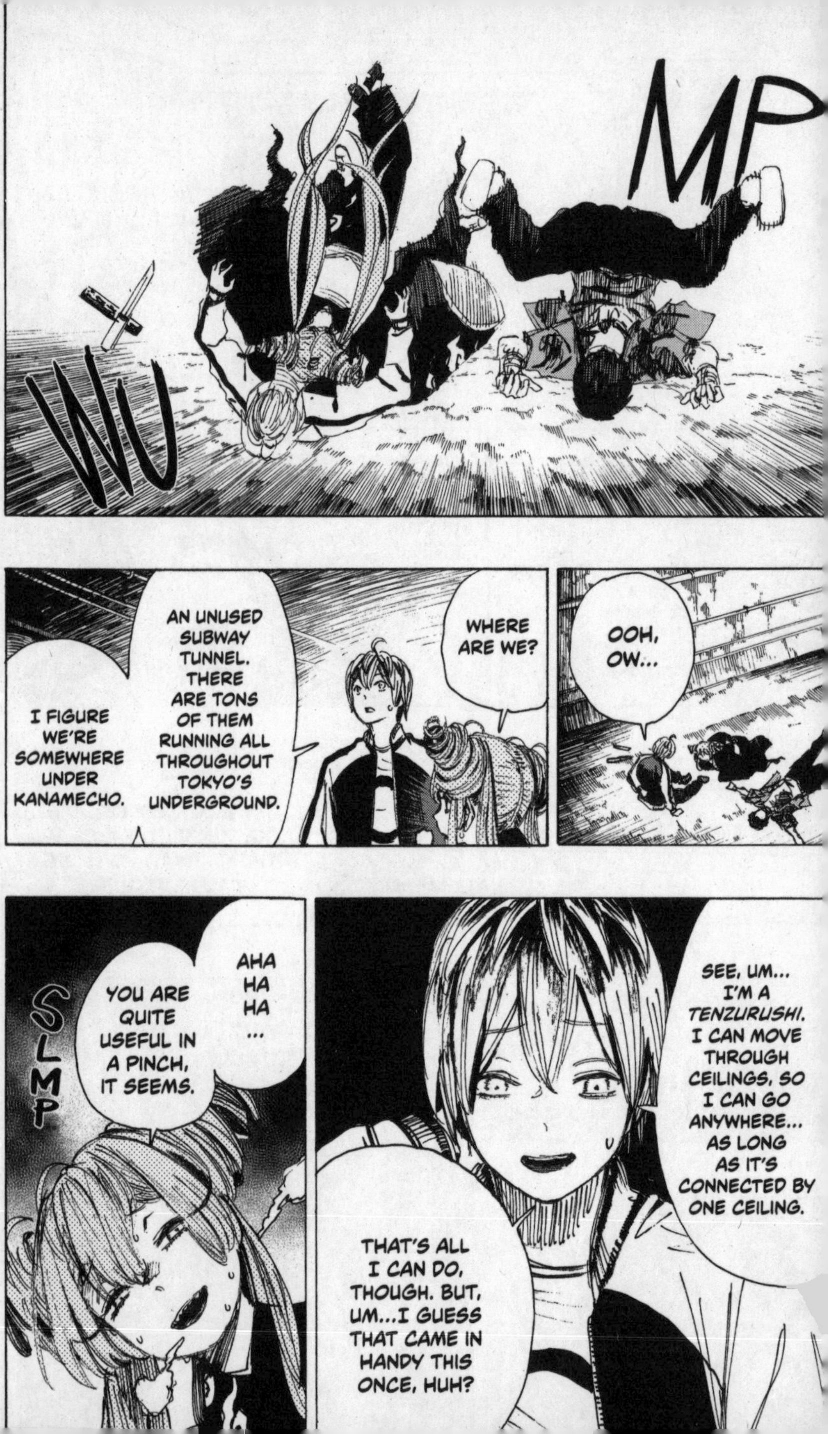
WUMP
OOH, OW...
WHERE ARE WE?
AN UNUSED SUBWAY TUNNEL. THERE ARE TONS OF THEM RUNNING ALL THROUGHOUT TOKYO'S UNDERGROUND.
I FIGURE WE'RE SOMEWHERE UNDER KANAMECHO.
SEE, UM... I'M A TENZURUSHI. I CAN MOVE THROUGH CEILINGS, SO I CAN GO ANYWHERE... AS LONG AS IT'S CONNECTED BY ONE CEILING.
THAT'S ALL I CAN DO, THOUGH. BUT, UM...I GUESS THAT CAME IN HANDY THIS ONCE, HUH?
AHA HA HA ...
YOU ARE QUITE USEFUL IN A PINCH, IT SEEMS.
SLMP

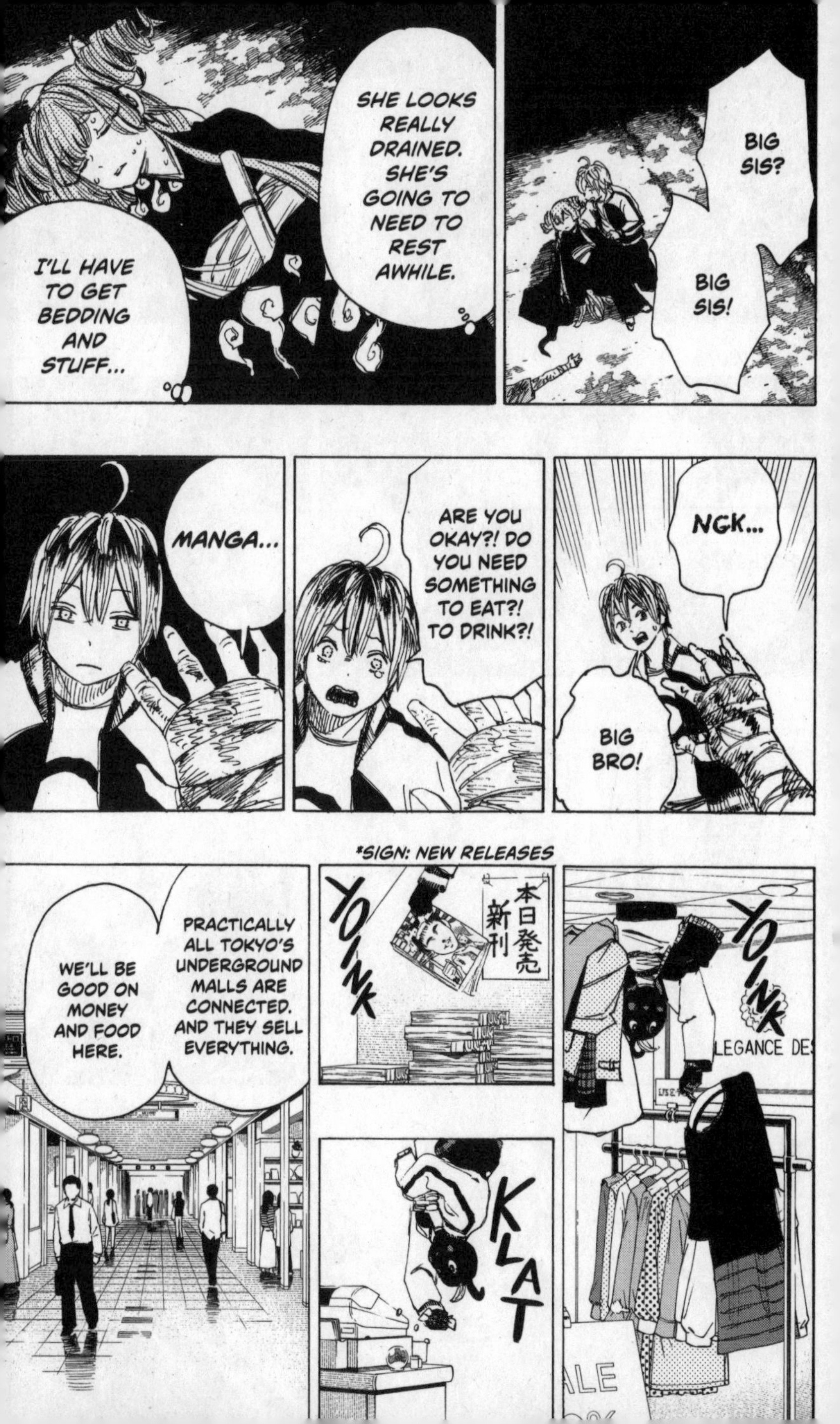
BIG SIS?
BIG SIS!
SHE LOOKS REALLY DRAINED. SHE'S GOING TO NEED TO REST AWHILE.
I'LL HAVE TO GET BEDDING AND STUFF...
NGK...
BIG BRO!
ARE YOU OKAY?! DO YOU NEED SOMETHING TO EAT?! TO DRINK?!
MANGA...
*SIGN: NEW RELEASES
YOINK
YOINK
本日発売
新刊
KLAT
PRACTICALLY ALL TOKYO'S UNDERGROUND MALLS ARE CONNECTED. AND THEY SELL EVERYTHING.
WE'LL BE GOOD ON MONEY AND FOOD HERE.

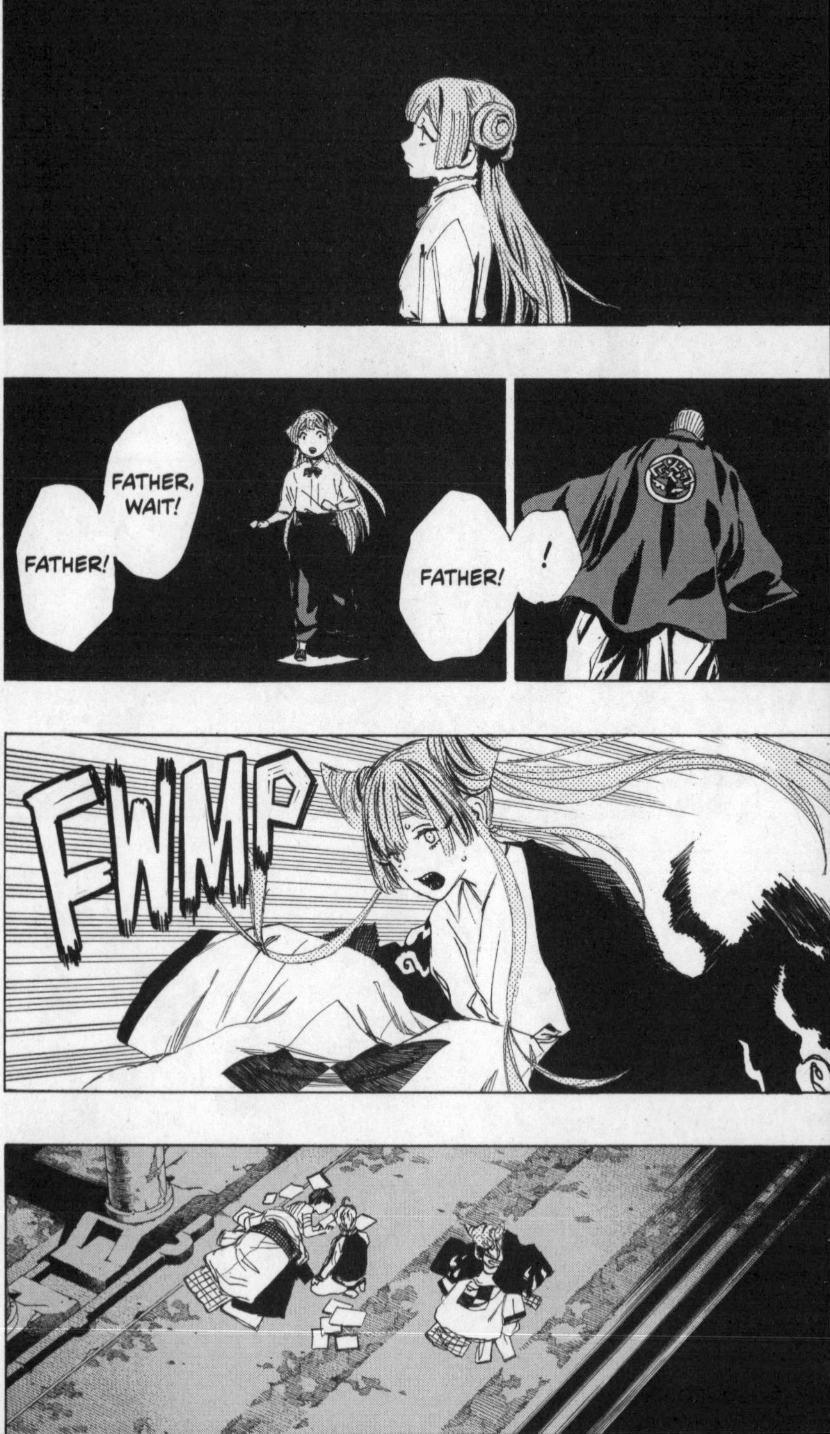
!
FATHER!
FATHER, WAIT!
FATHER!
FWMP

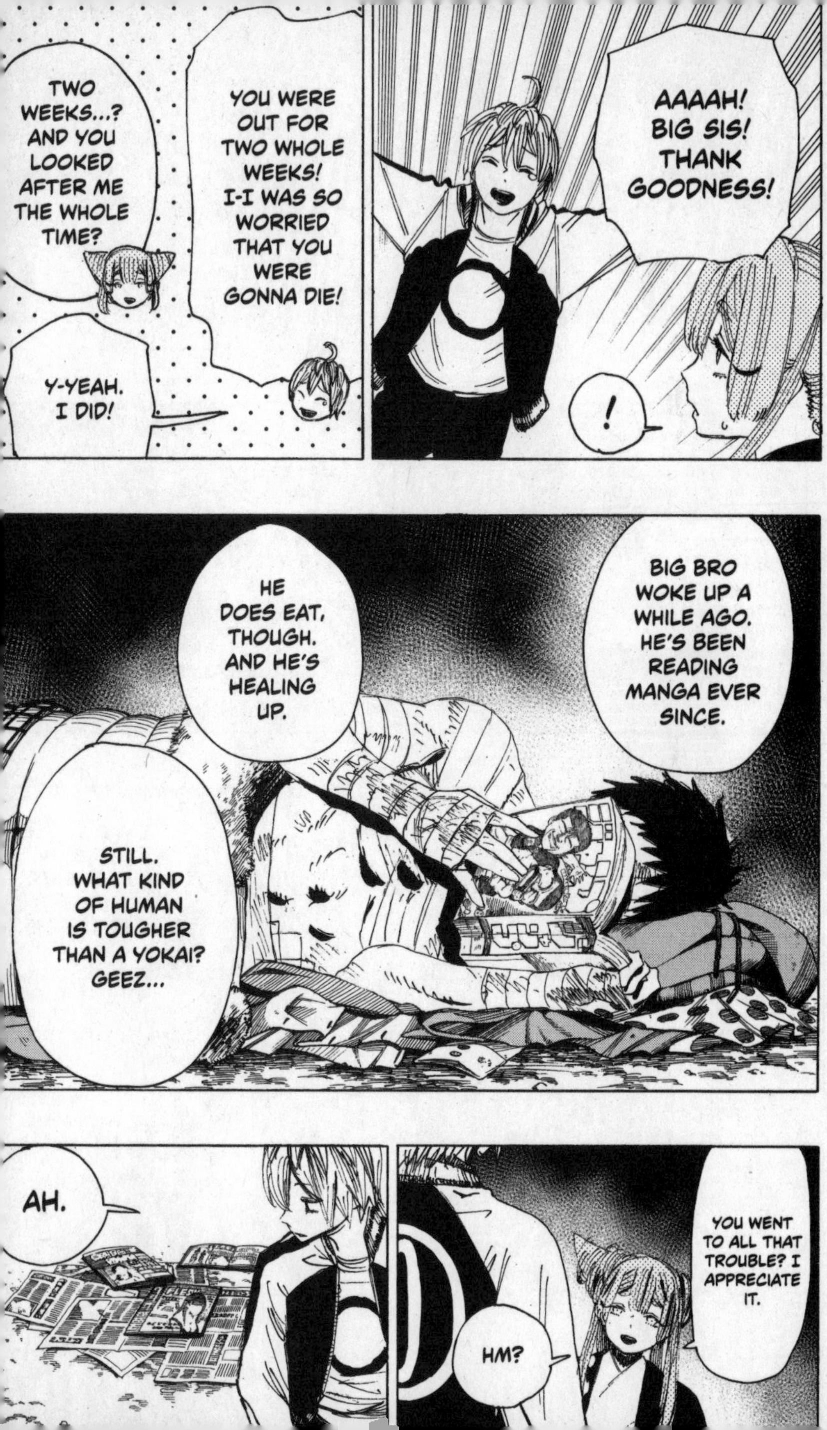
AAAAH! BIG SIS! THANK GOODNESS!
!
YOU WERE OUT FOR TWO WHOLE WEEKS! I-I WAS SO WORRIED THAT YOU WERE GONNA DIE!
TWO WEEKS...? AND YOU LOOKED AFTER ME THE WHOLE TIME?
Y-YEAH. I DID!
BIG BRO WOKE UP A WHILE AGO. HE'S BEEN READING MANGA EVER SINCE.
HE DOES EAT, THOUGH. AND HE'S HEALING UP.
STILL. WHAT KIND OF HUMAN IS TOUGHER THAN A YOKAI? GEEZ...
YOU WENT TO ALL THAT TROUBLE? I APPRECIATE IT.
HM?
AH.

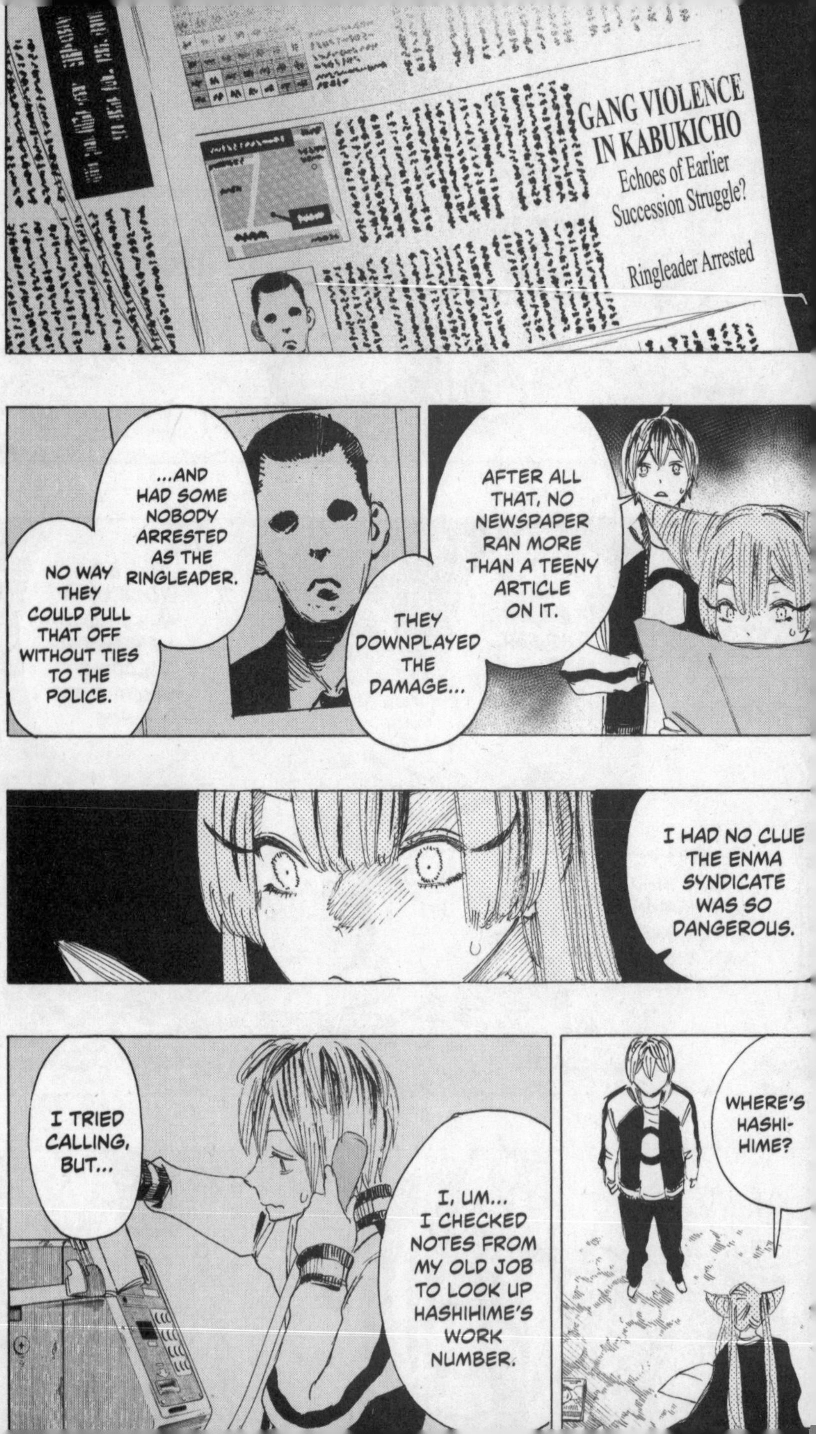
GANG VIOLENCE IN KABUKICHO
Echoes of Earlier Succession Struggle?
Ringleader Arrested
AFTER ALL THAT, NO NEWSPAPER RAN MORE THAN A TEENY ARTICLE ON IT.
THEY DOWNPLAYED THE DAMAGE...
...AND HAD SOME NOBODY ARRESTED AS THE RINGLEADER.
NO WAY THEY COULD PULL THAT OFF WITHOUT TIES TO THE POLICE.
I HAD NO CLUE THE ENMA SYNDICATE WAS SO DANGEROUS.
WHERE'S HASHI-HIME?
I, UM... I CHECKED NOTES FROM MY OLD JOB TO LOOK UP HASHIHIME'S WORK NUMBER.
I TRIED CALLING, BUT...

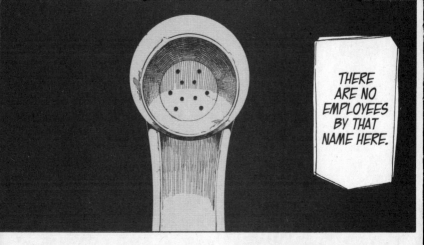

THERE ARE NO EMPLOYEES BY THAT NAME HERE.

I THINK SHE'S PROLLY...

I DON'T KNOW WHAT KIND OF BEEF YOU'VE GOT WITH KIOH, BUT...

UM, BIG SIS?

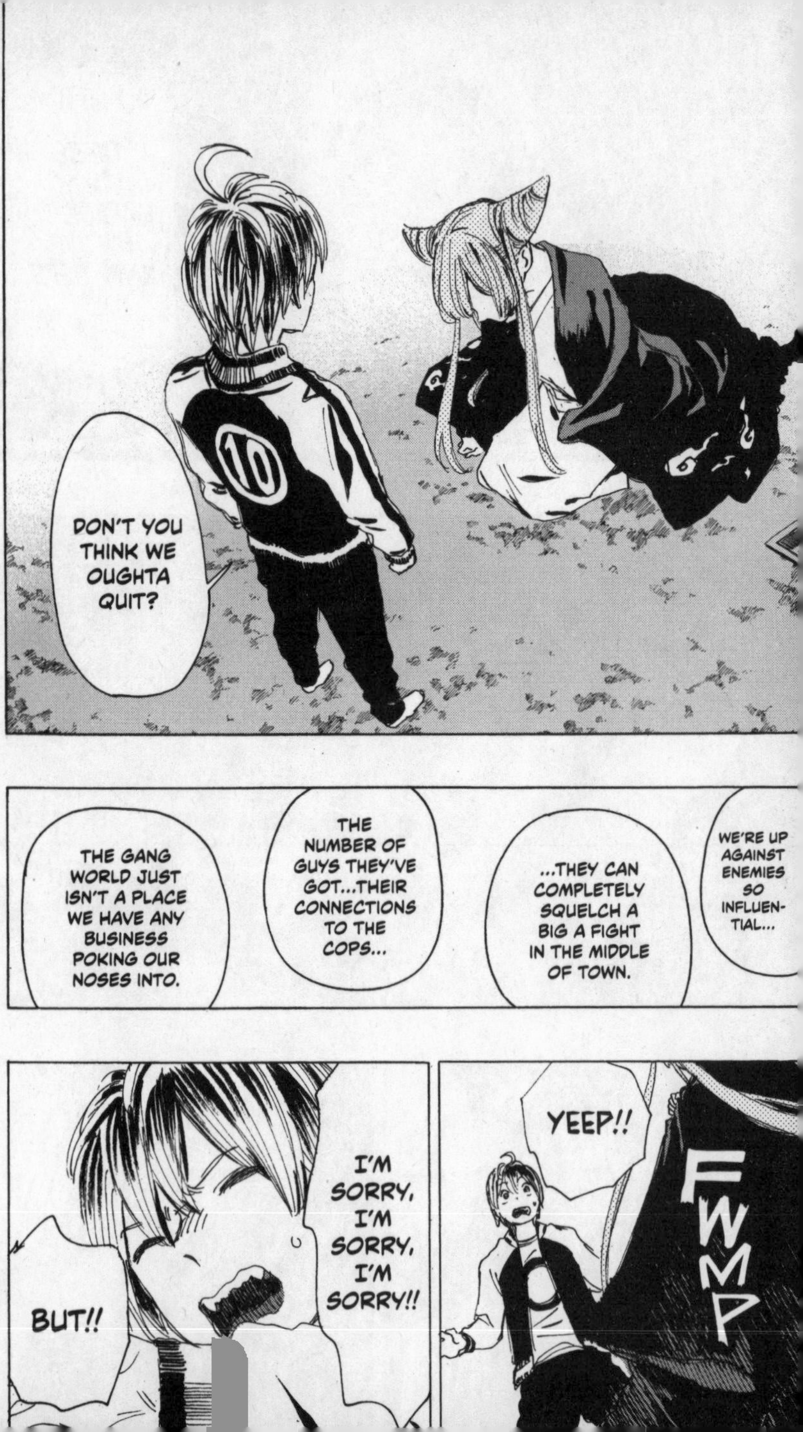
DON'T YOU THINK WE OUGHTA QUIT?
WE'RE UP AGAINST ENEMIES SO INFLUEN-TIAL...
...THEY CAN COMPLETELY SQUELCH A BIG A FIGHT IN THE MIDDLE OF TOWN.
THE NUMBER OF GUYS THEY'VE GOT...THEIR CONNECTIONS TO THE COPS...
THE GANG WORLD JUST ISN'T A PLACE WE HAVE ANY BUSINESS POKING OUR NOSES INTO.
YEEP!!
FWMP
I'M SORRY, I'M SORRY, I'M SORRY!!
BUT!!

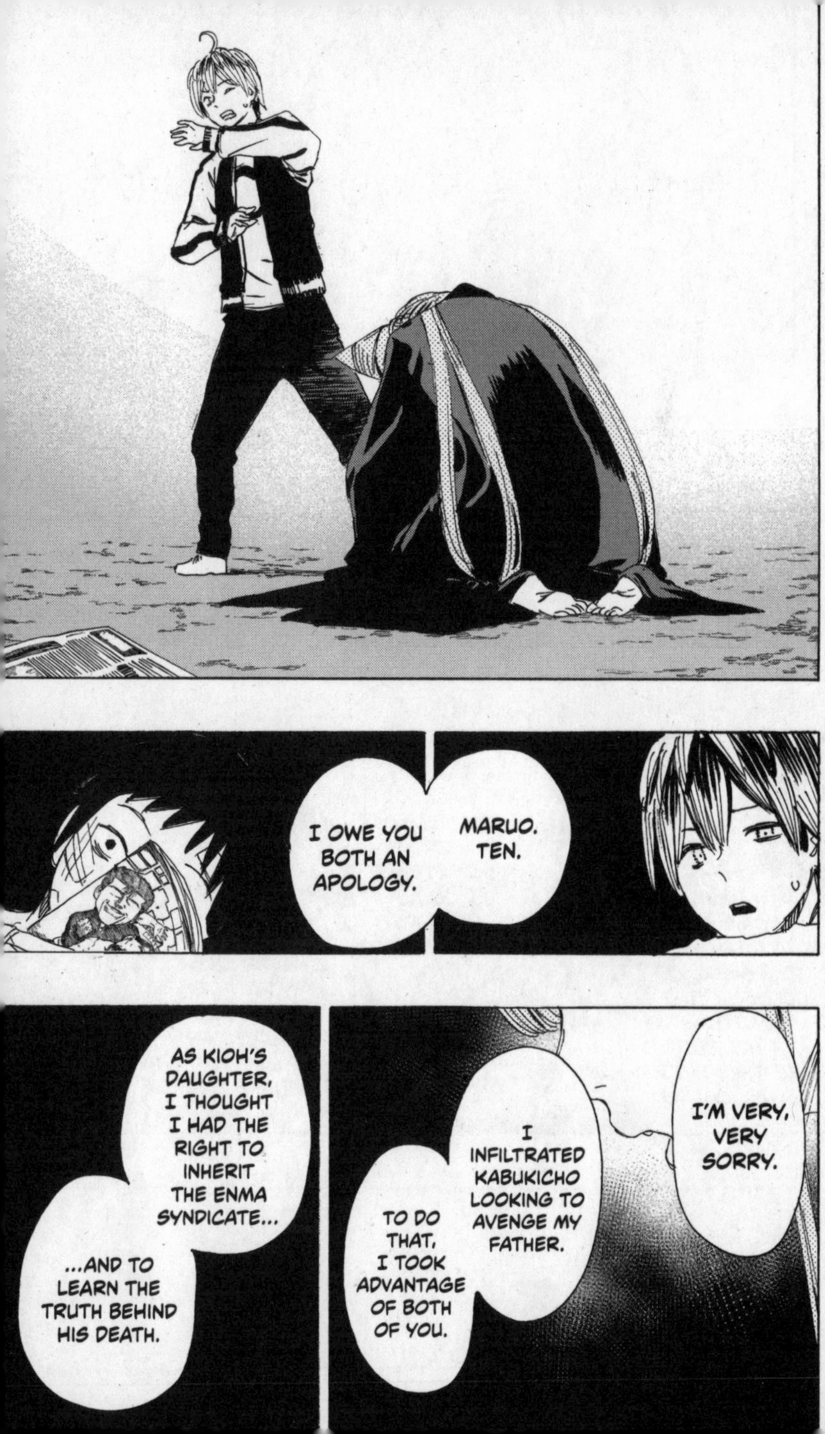
MARUO. TEN.
I OWE YOU BOTH AN APOLOGY.
I'M VERY, VERY SORRY.
I INFILTRATED KABUKICHO LOOKING TO AVENGE MY FATHER.
TO DO THAT, I TOOK ADVANTAGE OF BOTH OF YOU.
AS KIOH'S DAUGHTER, I THOUGHT I HAD THE RIGHT TO INHERIT THE ENMA SYNDICATE...
...AND TO LEARN THE TRUTH BEHIND HIS DEATH.

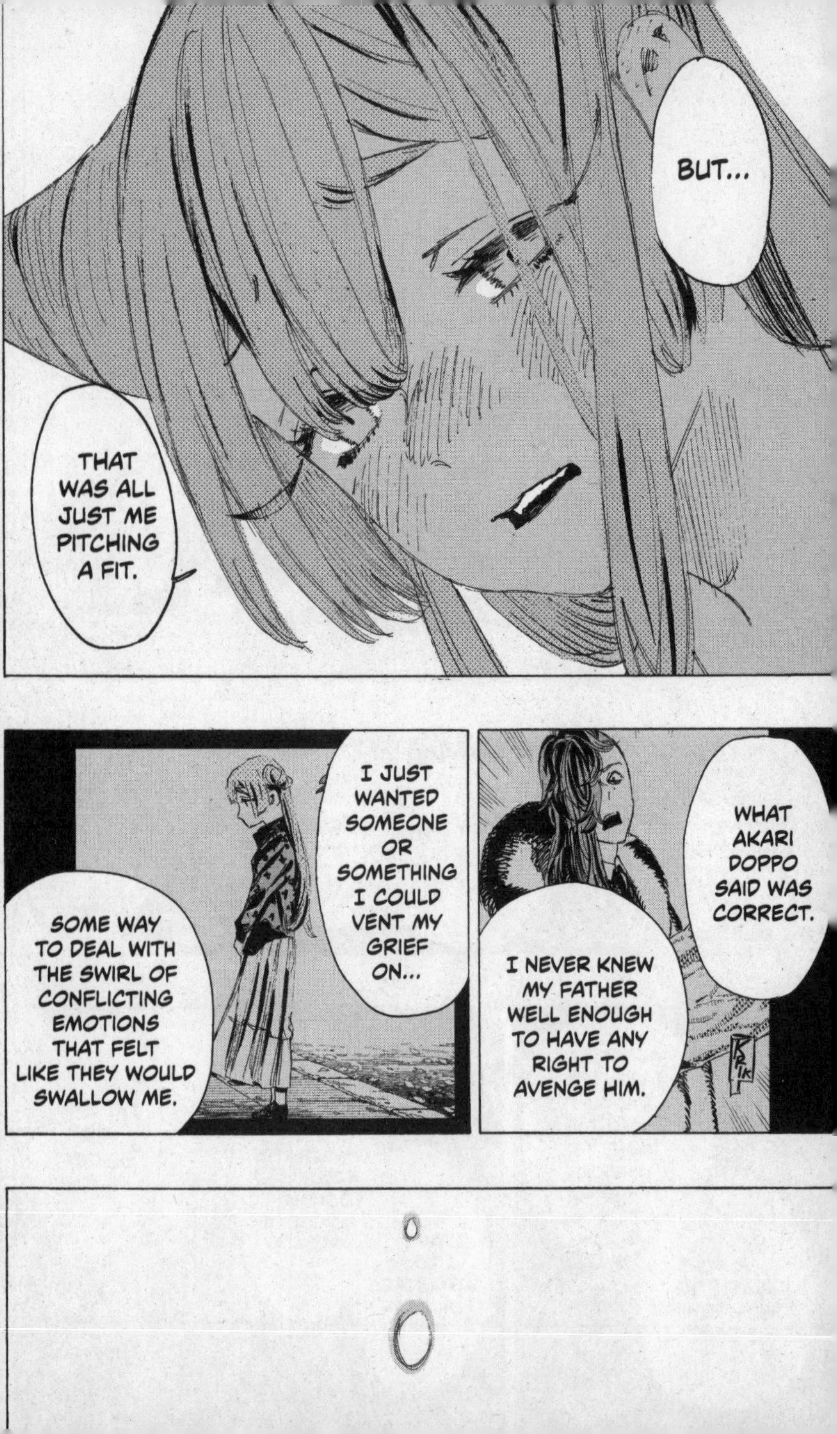
BUT...
THAT WAS ALL JUST ME PITCHING A FIT.
WHAT AKARI DOPPO SAID WAS CORRECT.
I NEVER KNEW MY FATHER WELL ENOUGH TO HAVE ANY RIGHT TO AVENGE HIM.
KRIK
I JUST WANTED SOMEONE OR SOMETHING I COULD VENT MY GRIEF ON...
SOME WAY TO DEAL WITH THE SWIRL OF CONFLICTING EMOTIONS THAT FELT LIKE THEY WOULD SWALLOW ME.

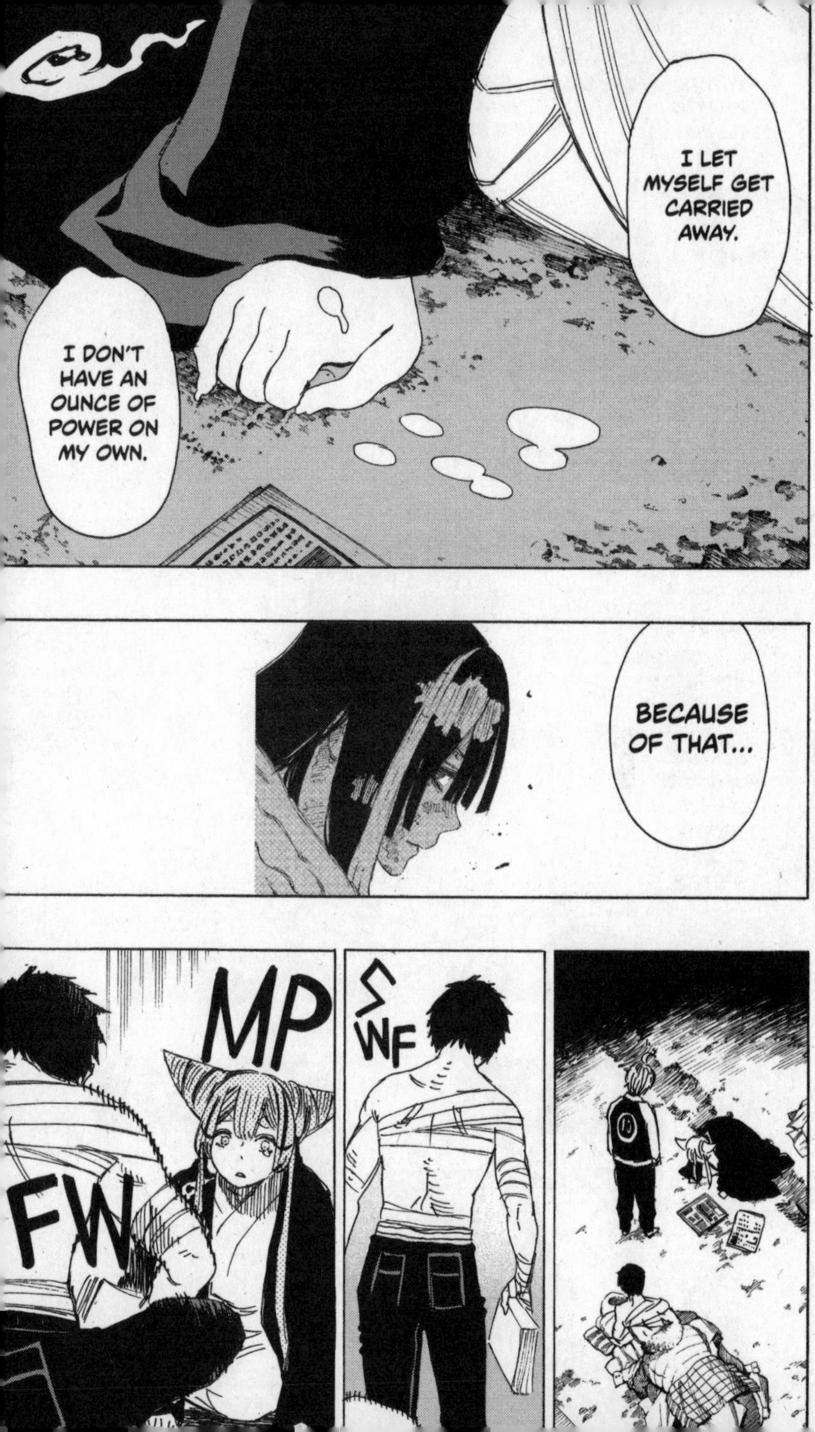
I LET MYSELF GET CARRIED AWAY.
I DON'T HAVE AN OUNCE OF POWER ON MY OWN.
BECAUSE OF THAT...
SWF
MP
FW

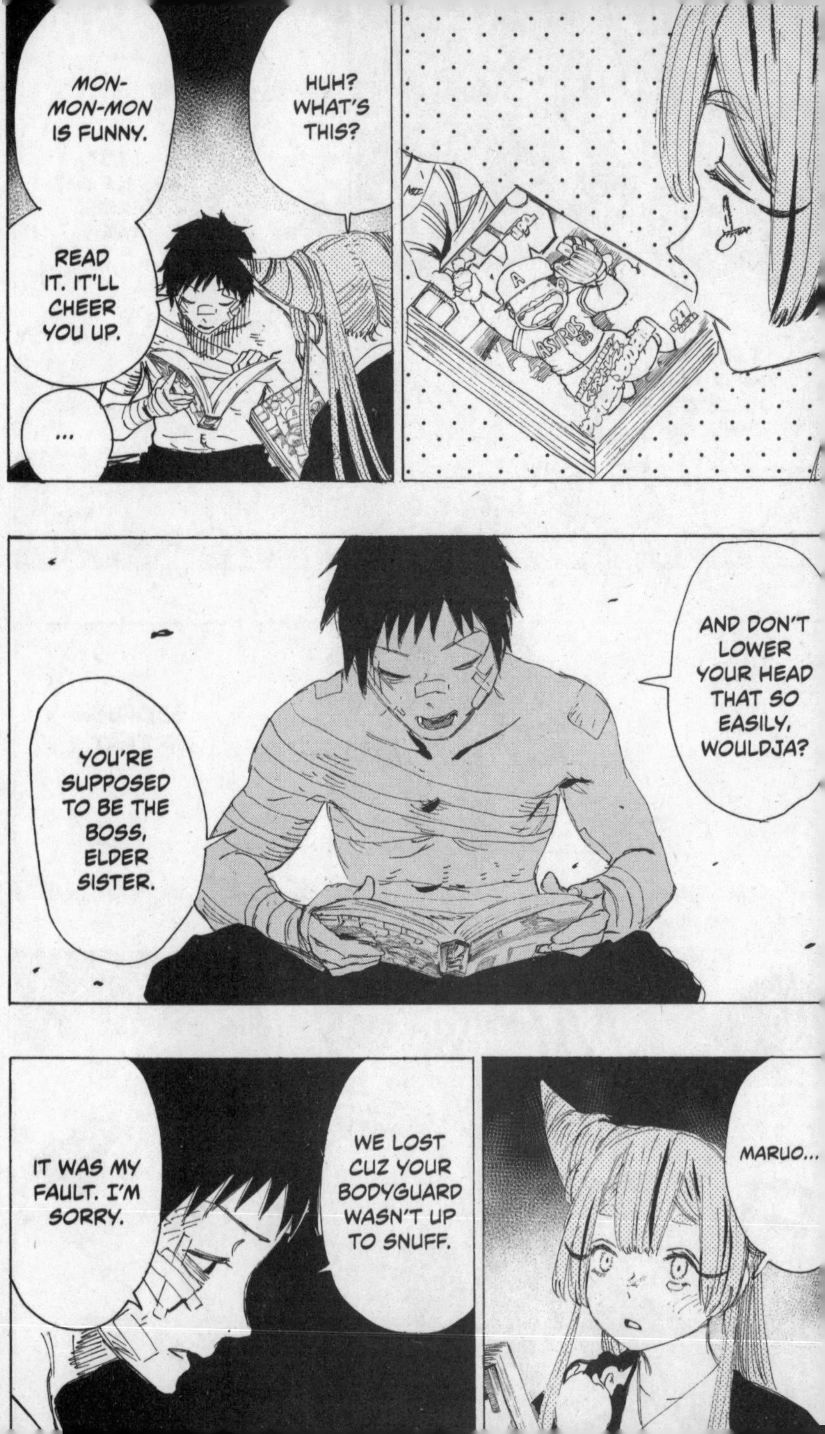
ASTROS
HUH? WHAT'S THIS?
MON-MON-MON IS FUNNY.
READ IT. IT'LL CHEER YOU UP.
...
AND DON'T LOWER YOUR HEAD THAT SO EASILY, WOULDJA?
YOU'RE SUPPOSED TO BE THE BOSS, ELDER SISTER.
MARUO...
WE LOST CUZ YOUR BODYGUARD WASN'T UP TO SNUFF.
IT WAS MY FAULT. I'M SORRY.

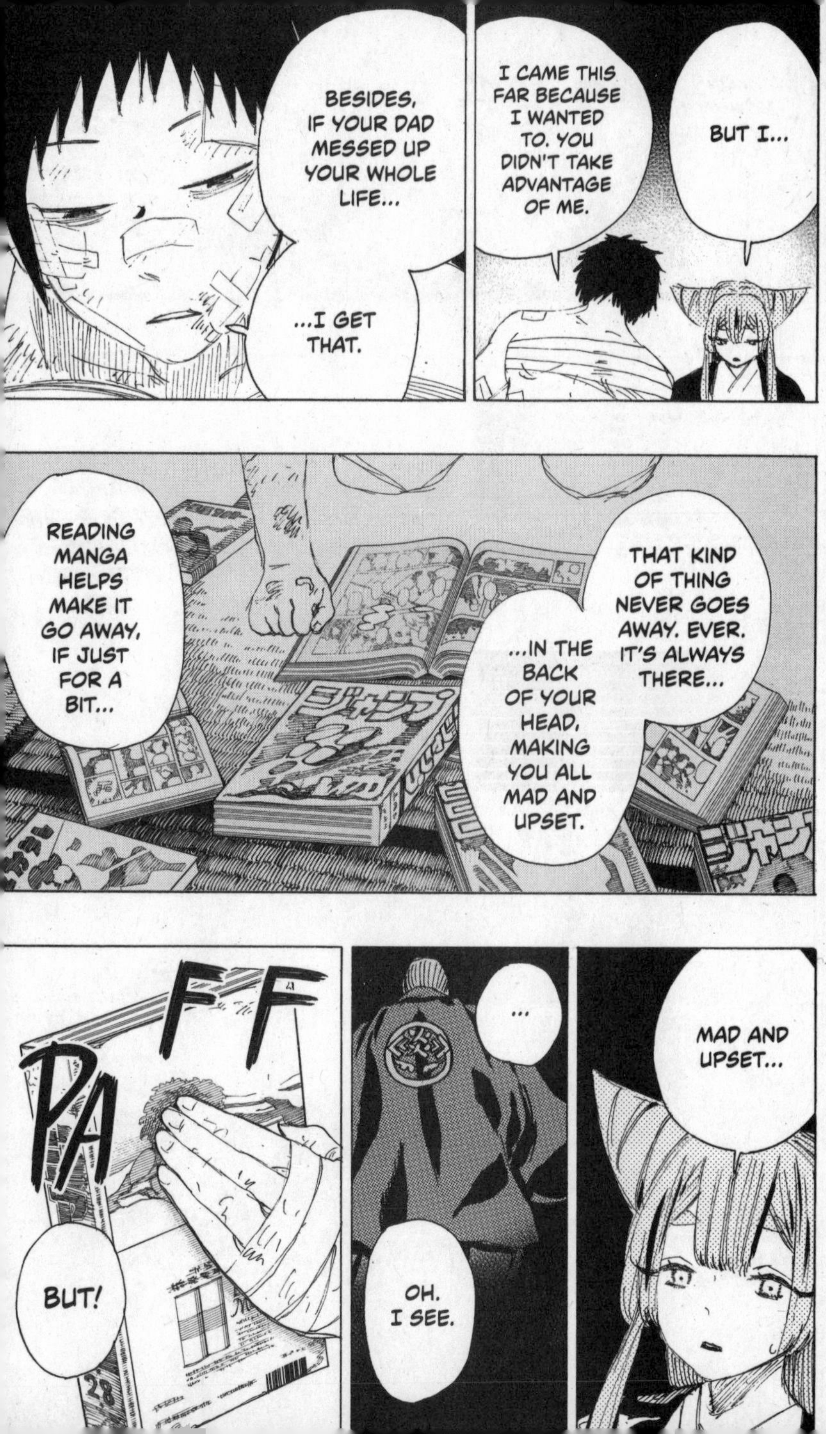
BUT I...
I CAME THIS FAR BECAUSE I WANTED TO. YOU DIDN'T TAKE ADVANTAGE OF ME.
BESIDES, IF YOUR DAD MESSED UP YOUR WHOLE LIFE...
...I GET THAT.
THAT KIND OF THING NEVER GOES AWAY. EVER. IT'S ALWAYS THERE...
...IN THE BACK OF YOUR HEAD, MAKING YOU ALL MAD AND UPSET.
READING MANGA HELPS MAKE IT GO AWAY, IF JUST FOR A BIT...
MAD AND UPSET...
...
OH. I SEE.
PAFF
BUT!

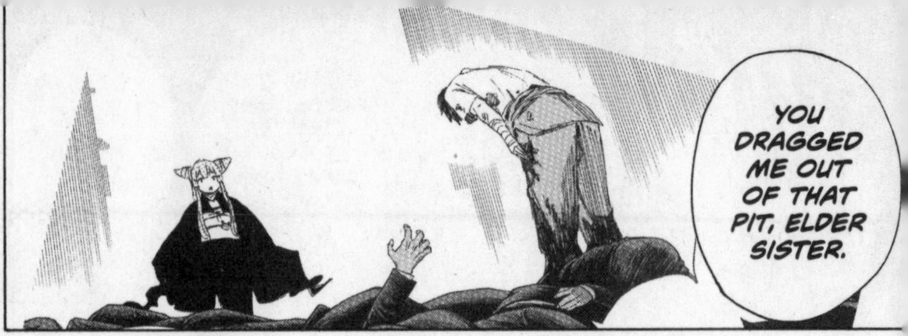
YOU DRAGGED ME OUT OF THAT PIT, ELDER SISTER.

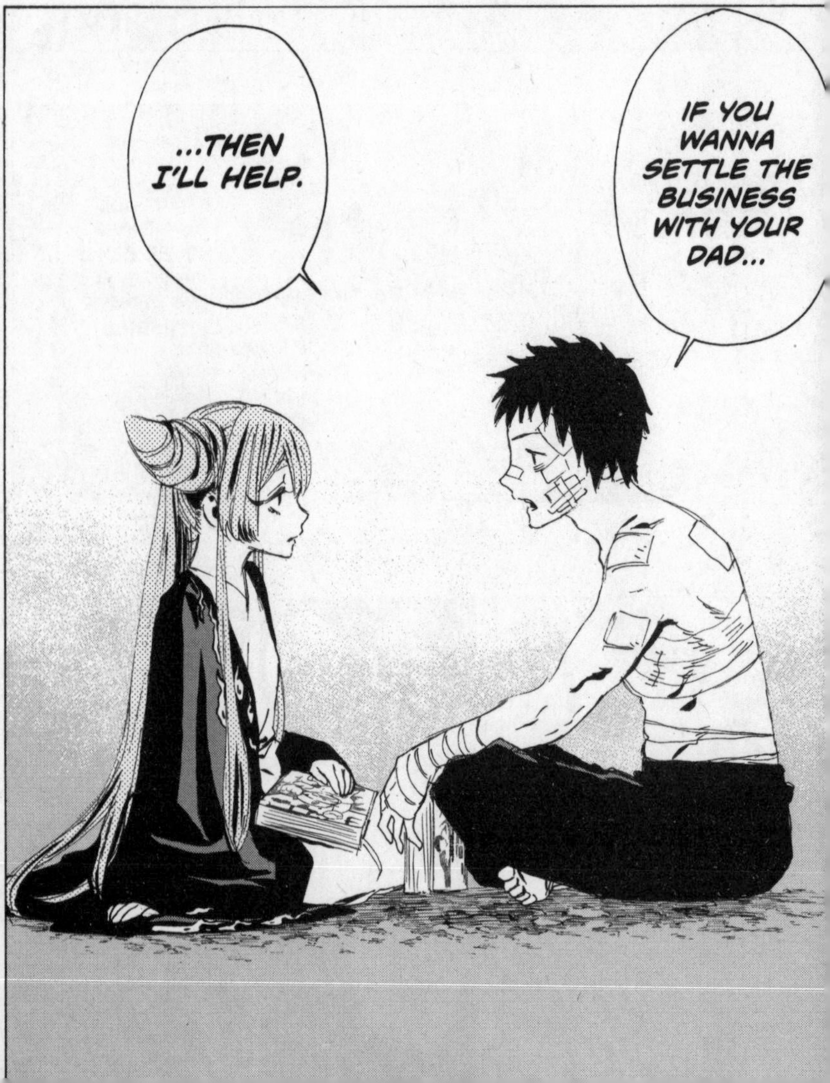
IF YOU WANNA SETTLE THE BUSINESS WITH YOUR DAD...
...THEN I'LL HELP.

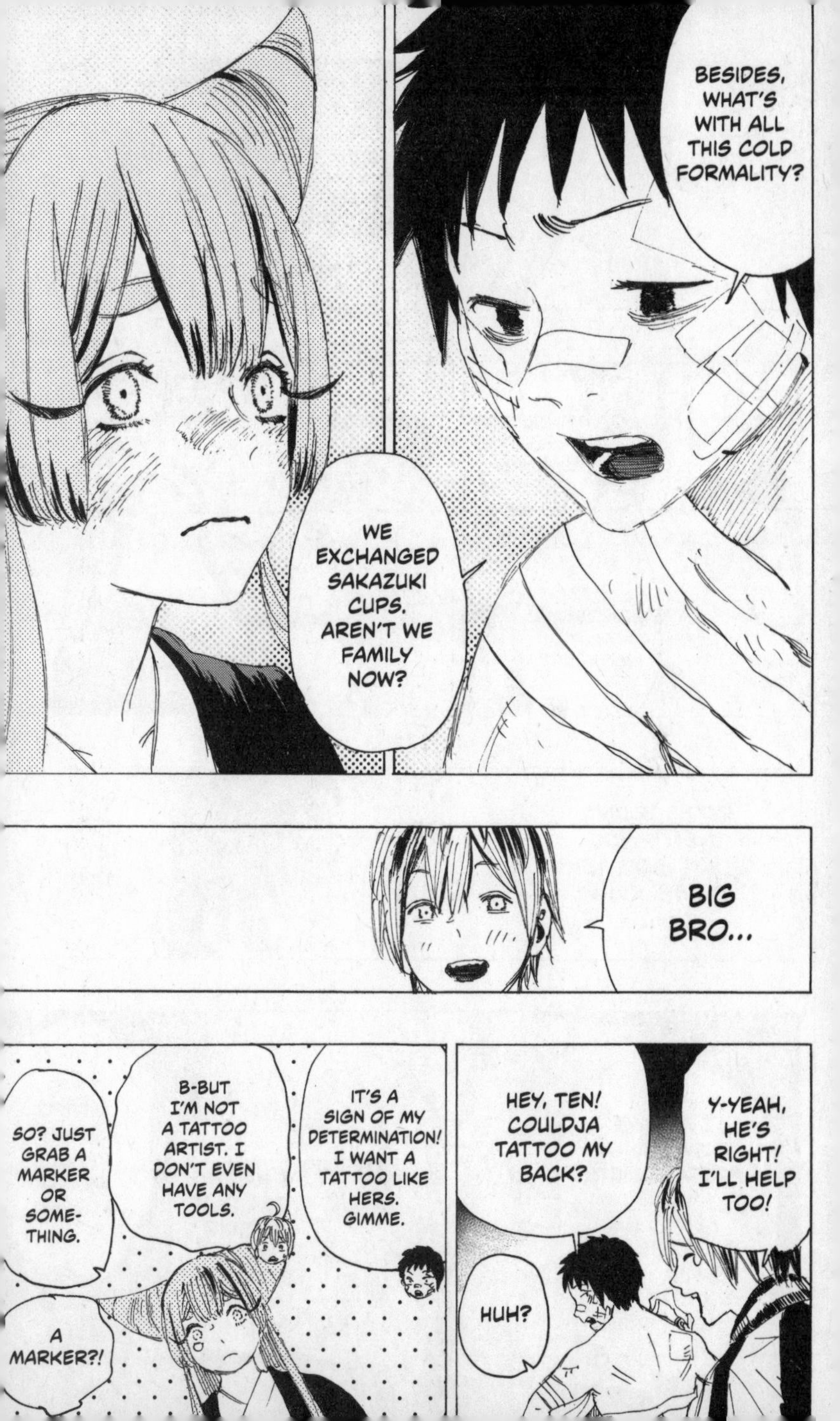
BESIDES, WHAT'S WITH ALL THIS COLD FORMALITY?
WE EXCHANGED SAKAZUKI CUPS. AREN'T WE FAMILY NOW?
BIG BRO...
Y-YEAH, HE'S RIGHT! I'LL HELP TOO!
HEY, TEN! COULDJA TATTOO MY BACK?
HUH?
IT'S A SIGN OF MY DETERMINATION! I WANT A TATTOO LIKE HERS. GIMME.
B-BUT I'M NOT A TATTOO ARTIST. I DON'T EVEN HAVE ANY TOOLS.
SO? JUST GRAB A MARKER OR SOME-THING.
A MARKER?!

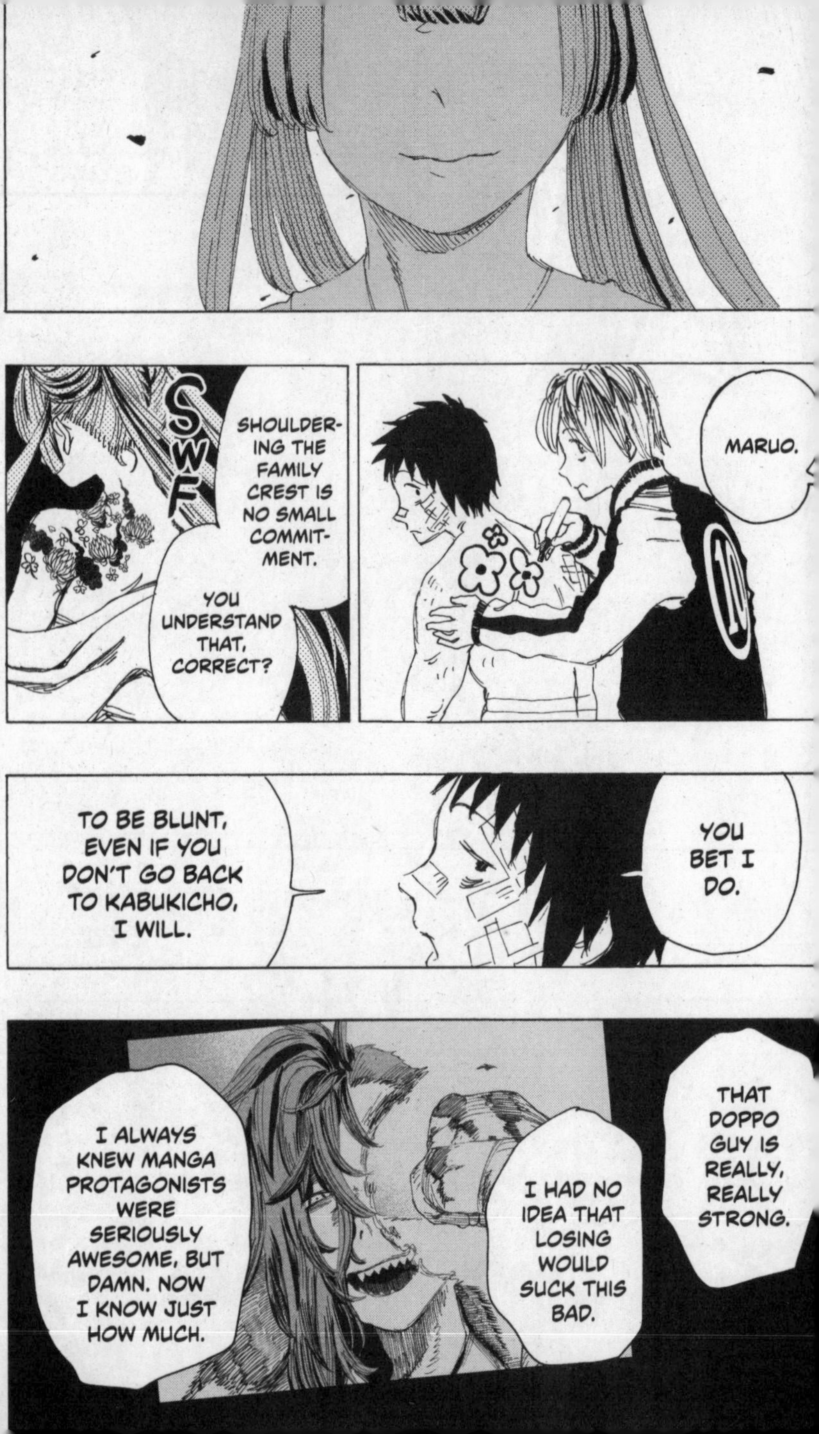
MARUO.
SWF
SHOULDERING THE FAMILY CREST IS NO SMALL COMMITMENT.
YOU UNDERSTAND THAT, CORRECT?
YOU BET I DO.
TO BE BLUNT, EVEN IF YOU DON'T GO BACK TO KABUKICHO, I WILL.
THAT DOPPO GUY IS REALLY, REALLY STRONG.
I HAD NO IDEA THAT LOSING WOULD SUCK THIS BAD.
I ALWAYS KNEW MANGA PROTAGONISTS WERE SERIOUSLY AWESOME, BUT DAMN. NOW I KNOW JUST HOW MUCH.

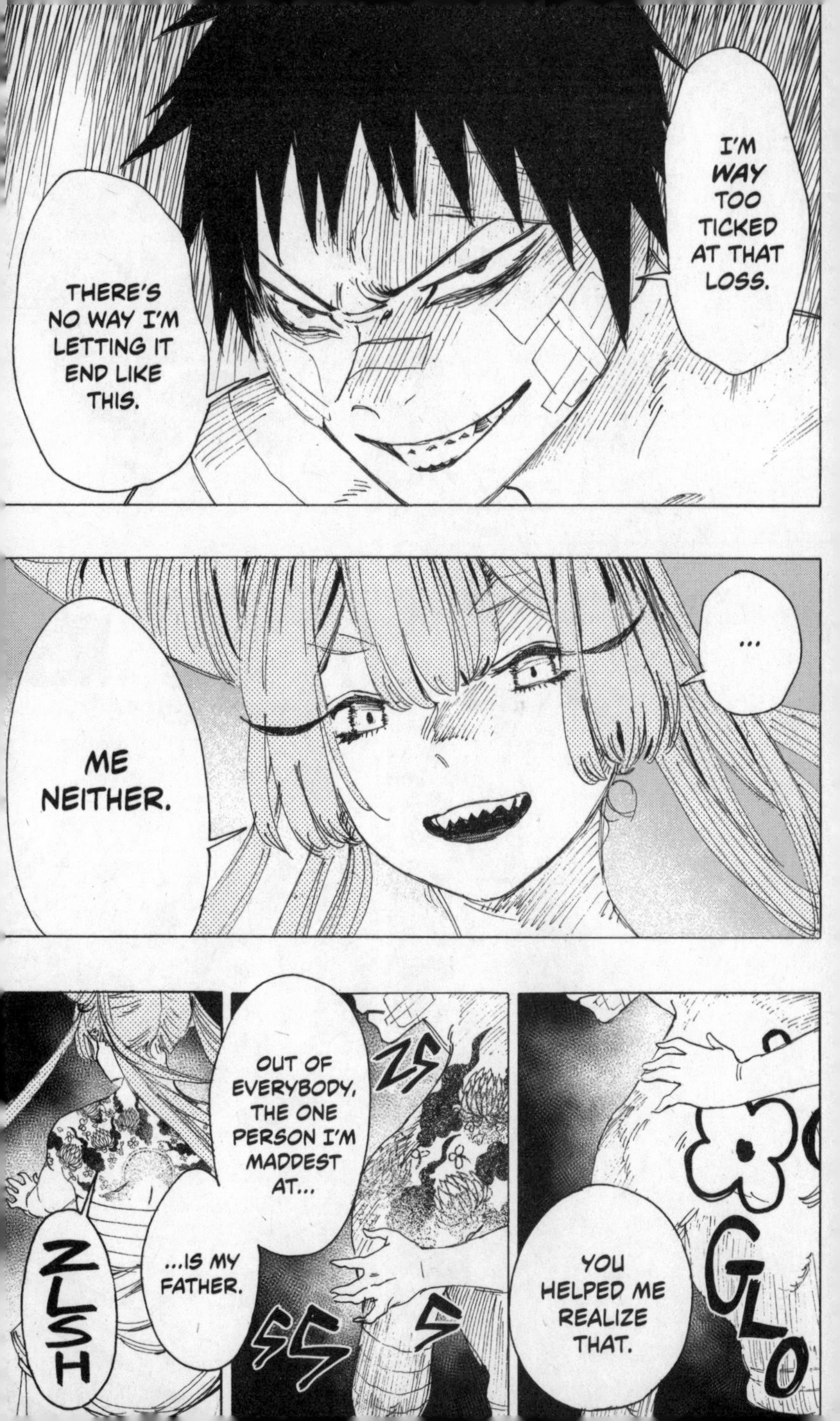
THERE'S NO WAY I'M LETTING IT END LIKE THIS.
I'M WAY TOO TICKED AT THAT LOSS.
ME NEITHER.
...
ZLSH
OUT OF EVERYBODY, THE ONE PERSON I'M MADDEST AT...
...IS MY FATHER.
YOU HELPED ME REALIZE THAT.
GLO

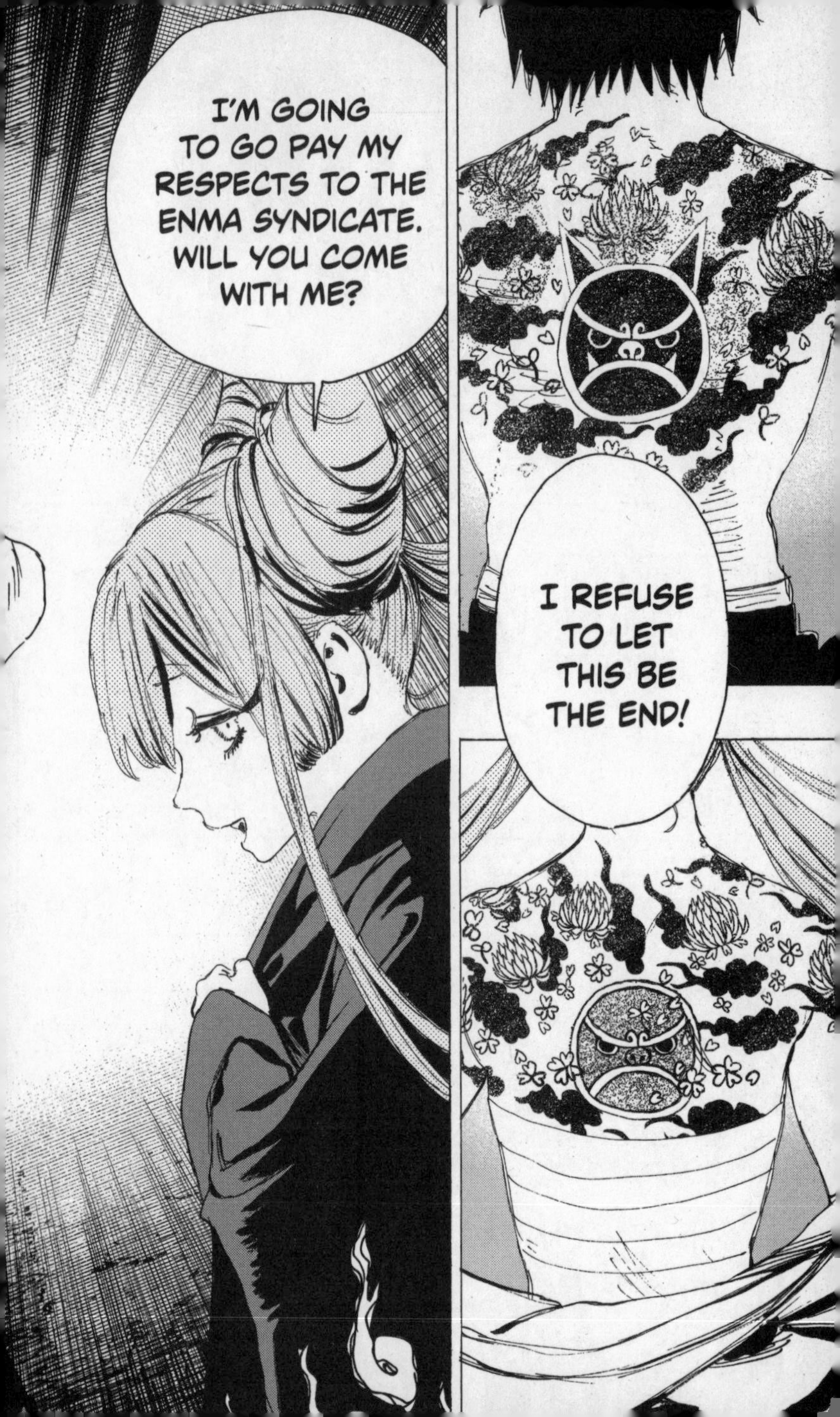
I REFUSE TO LET THIS BE THE END!
I'M GOING TO GO PAY MY RESPECTS TO THE ENMA SYNDICATE. WILL YOU COME WITH ME?

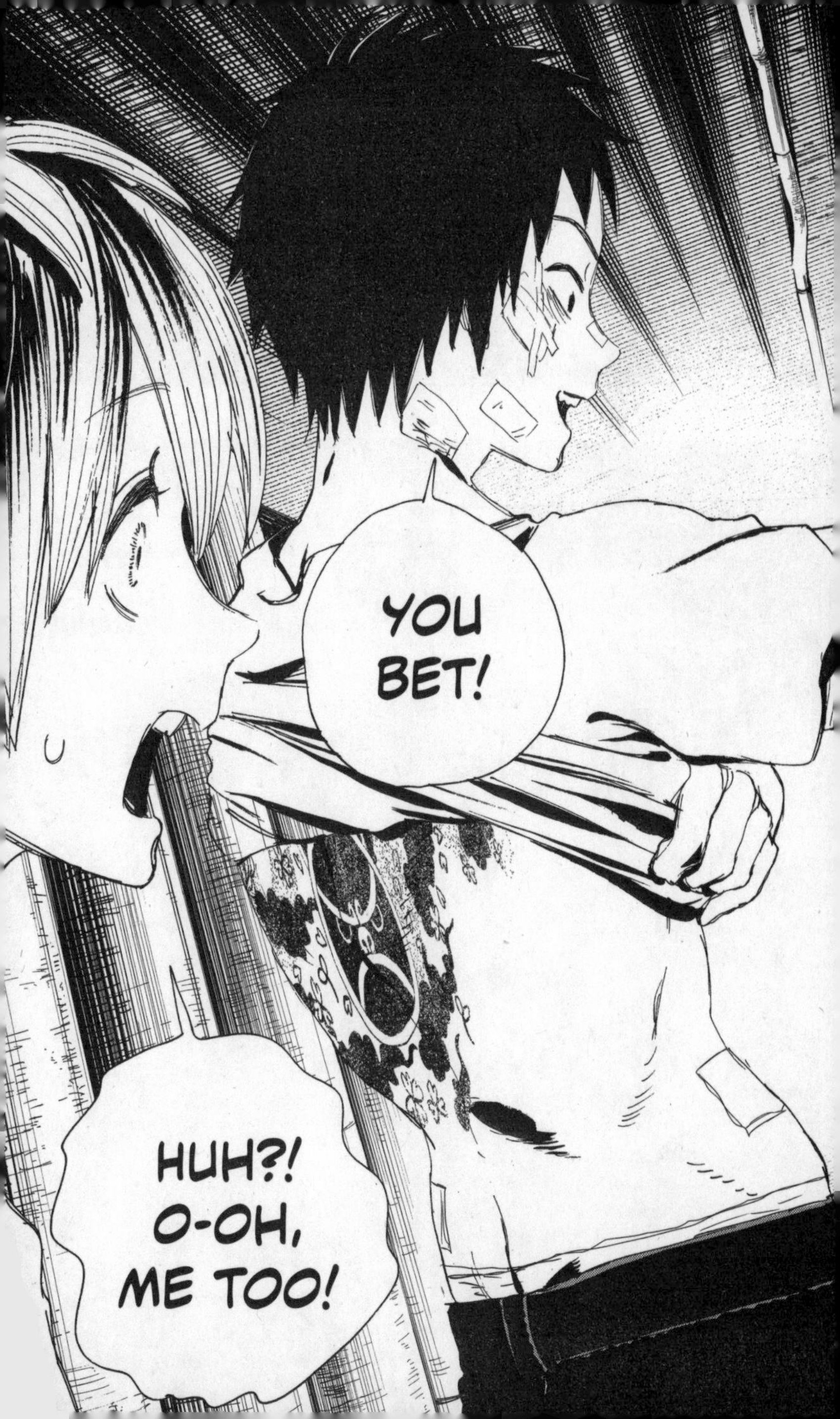
YOU BET!
HUH?! O-OH, ME TOO!

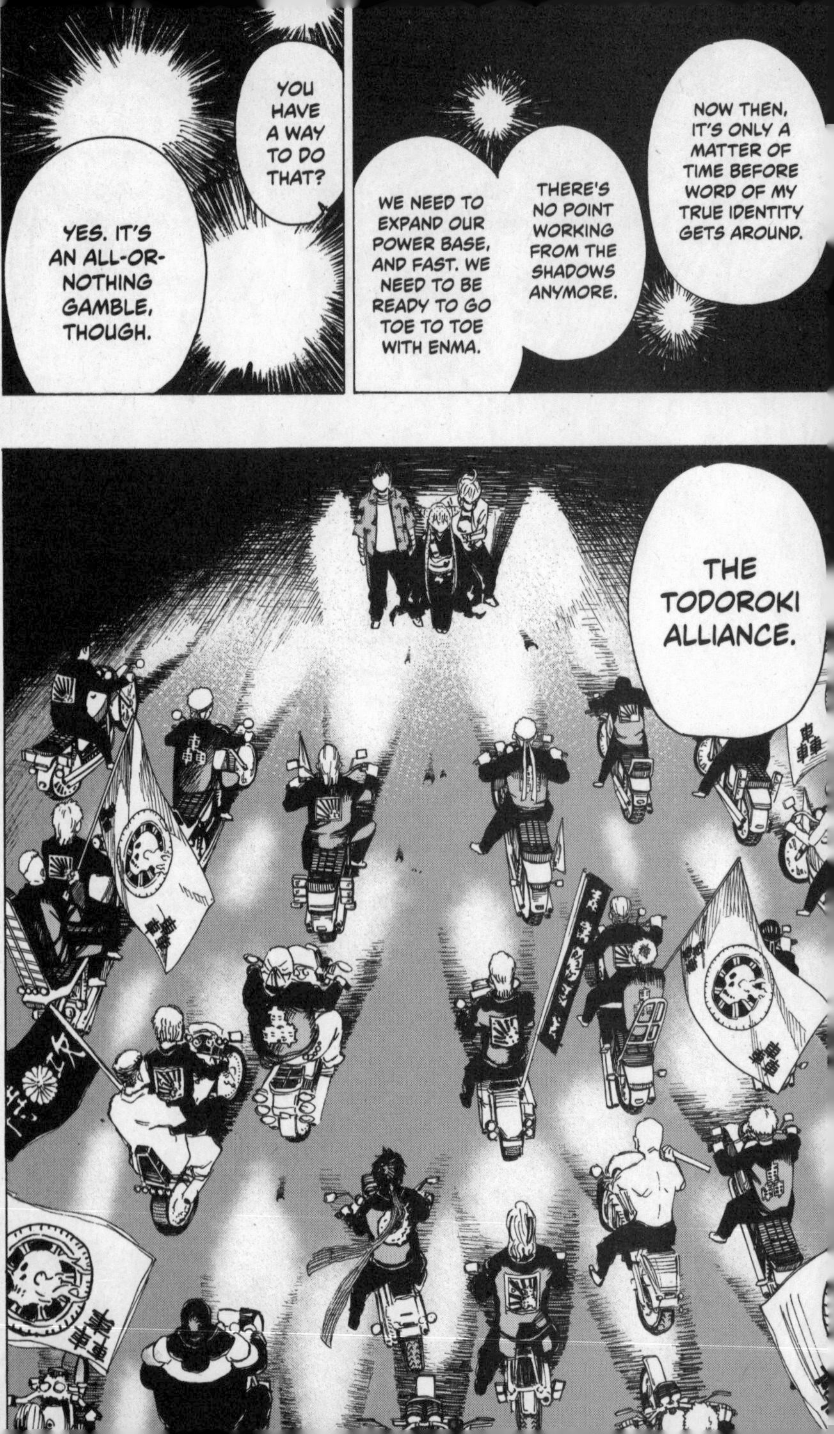
NOW THEN, IT'S ONLY A MATTER OF TIME BEFORE WORD OF MY TRUE IDENTITY GETS AROUND.
THERE'S NO POINT WORKING FROM THE SHADOWS ANYMORE.
WE NEED TO EXPAND OUR POWER BASE, AND FAST. WE NEED TO BE READY TO GO TOE TO TOE WITH ENMA.
YOU HAVE A WAY TO DO THAT?
YES. IT'S AN ALL-OR-NOTHING GAMBLE, THOUGH.
THE TODOROKI ALLIANCE.

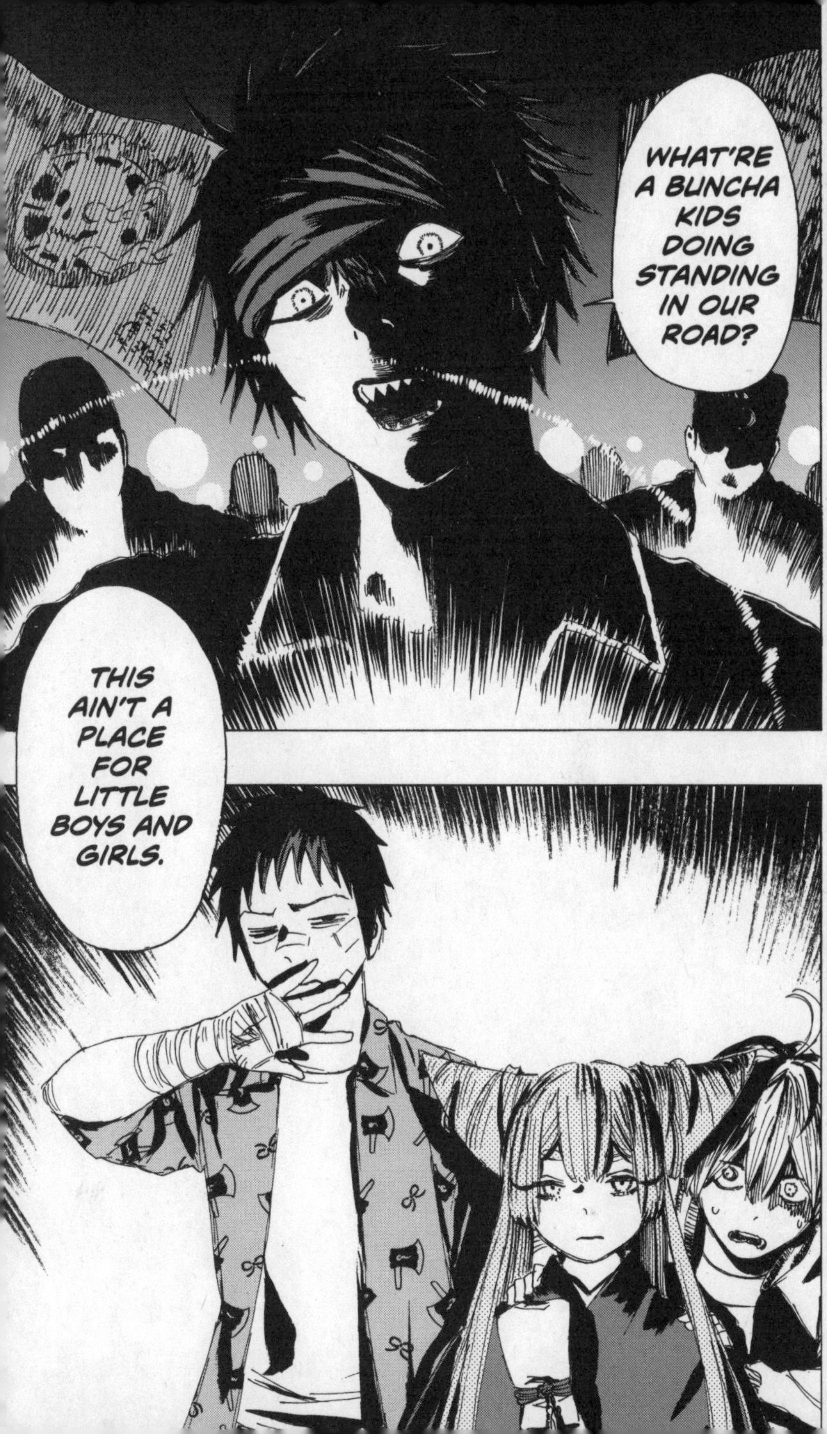
WHAT'RE A BUNCHA KIDS DOING STANDING IN OUR ROAD?
THIS AIN'T A PLACE FOR LITTLE BOYS AND GIRLS.

AYASHIMON

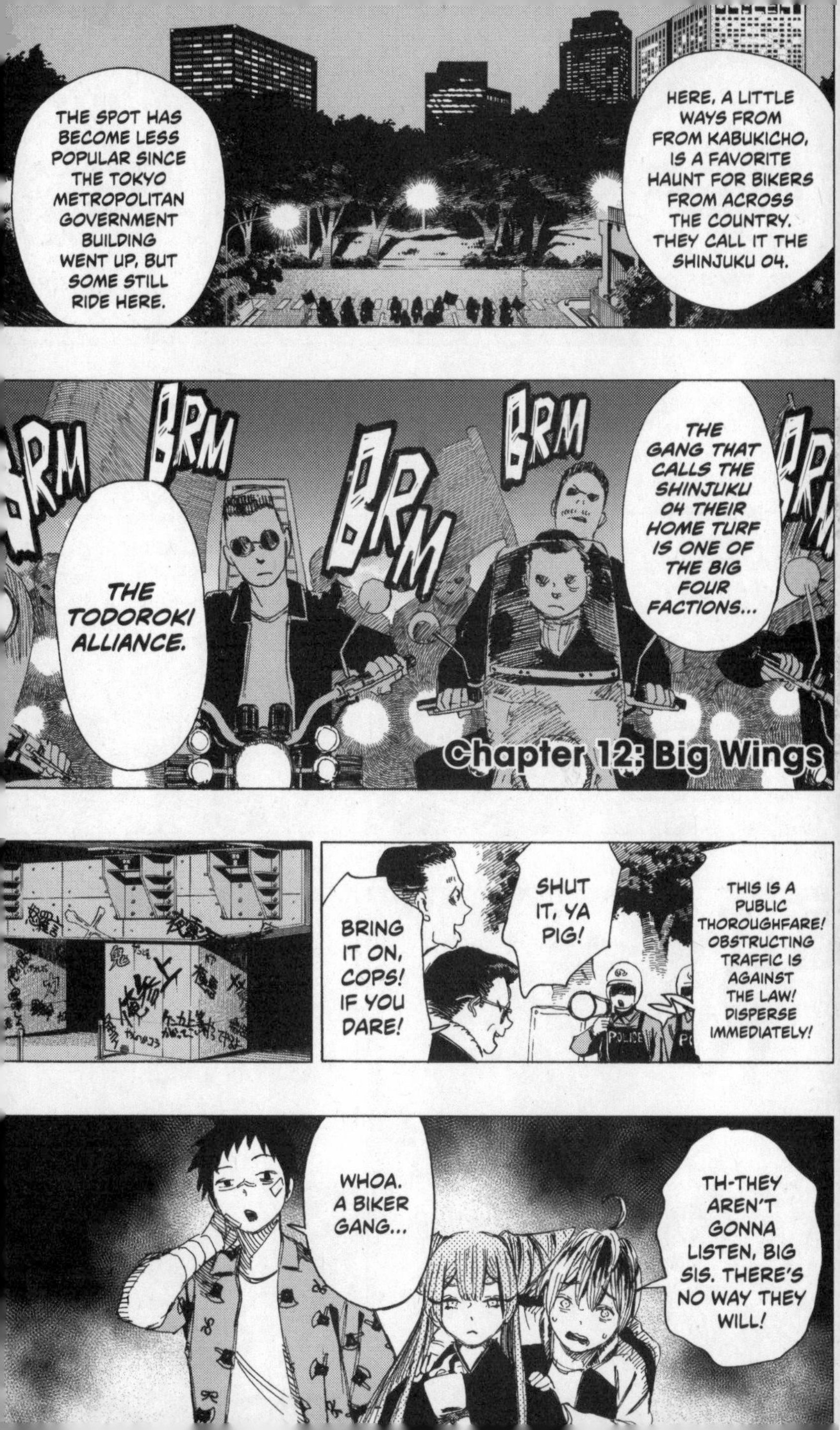
HERE, A LITTLE WAYS FROM FROM KABUKICHO, IS A FAVORITE HAUNT FOR BIKERS FROM ACROSS THE COUNTRY. THEY CALL IT THE SHINJUKU 04.
THE SPOT HAS BECOME LESS POPULAR SINCE THE TOKYO METROPOLITAN GOVERNMENT BUILDING WENT UP, BUT SOME STILL RIDE HERE.
THE GANG THAT CALLS THE SHINJUKU 04 THEIR HOME TURF IS ONE OF THE BIG FOUR FACTIONS...
BRM
BRM
BRM
BRM
BRM
THE TODOROKI ALLIANCE.
Chapter 12: Big Wings
THIS IS A PUBLIC THOROUGHFARE! OBSTRUCTING TRAFFIC IS AGAINST THE LAW! DISPERSE IMMEDIATELY!
POLICE
SHUT IT, YA PIG!
BRING IT ON, COPS! IF YOU DARE!
TH-THEY AREN'T GONNA LISTEN, BIG SIS. THERE'S NO WAY THEY WILL!
WHOA. A BIKER GANG...

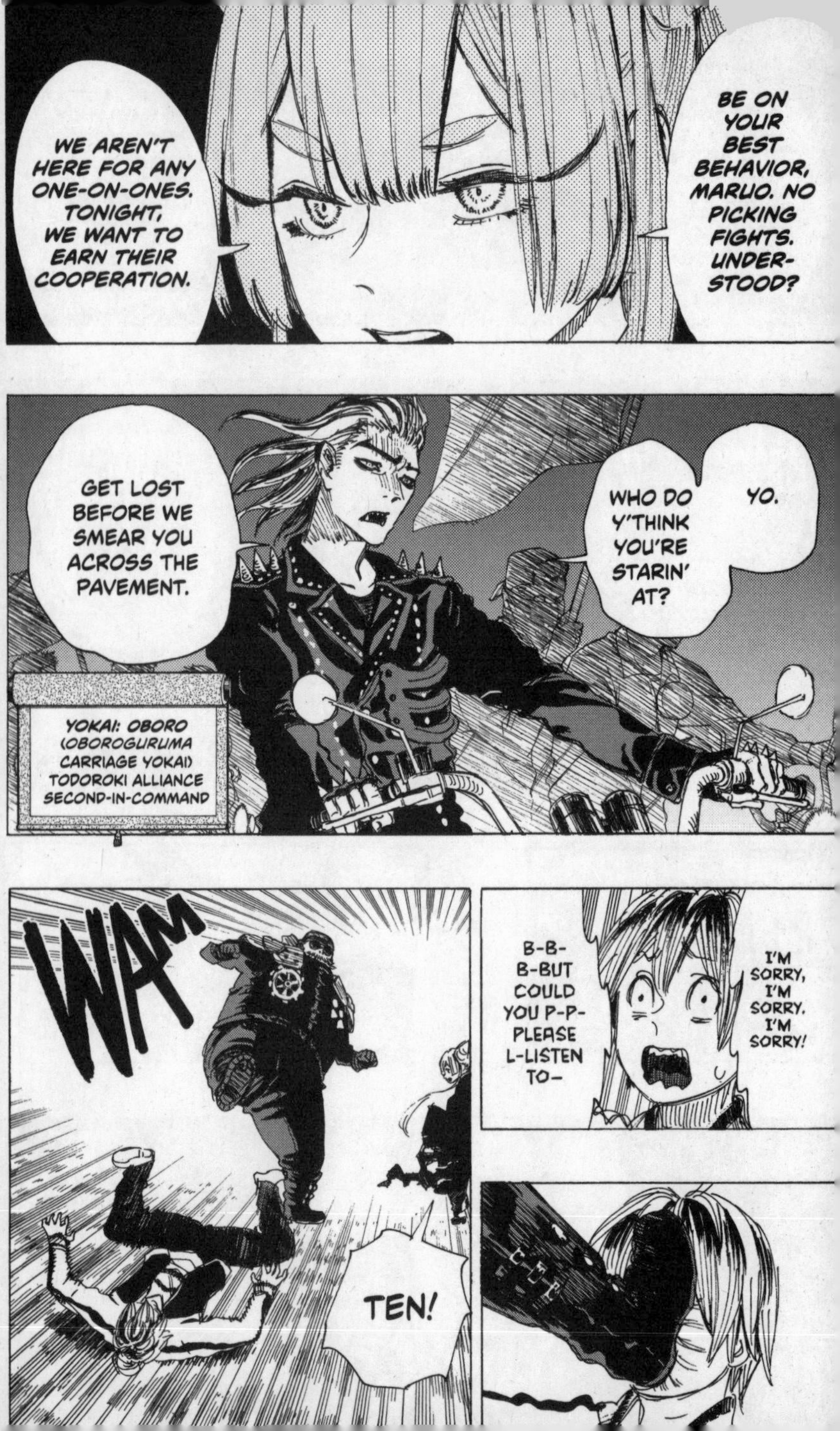
BE ON YOUR BEST BEHAVIOR, MARUO. NO PICKING FIGHTS. UNDERSTOOD?
WE AREN'T HERE FOR ANY ONE-ON-ONES. TONIGHT, WE WANT TO EARN THEIR COOPERATION.
YO.
WHO DO Y'THINK YOU'RE STARIN' AT?
GET LOST BEFORE WE SMEAR YOU ACROSS THE PAVEMENT.
YOKAI: OBORO (OBOROGURUMA CARRIAGE YOKAI) TODOROKI ALLIANCE SECOND-IN-COMMAND
I'M SORRY, I'M SORRY. I'M SORRY!
B-B-B-BUT COULD YOU P-P-PLEASE L-LISTEN TO—
WAM
TEN!

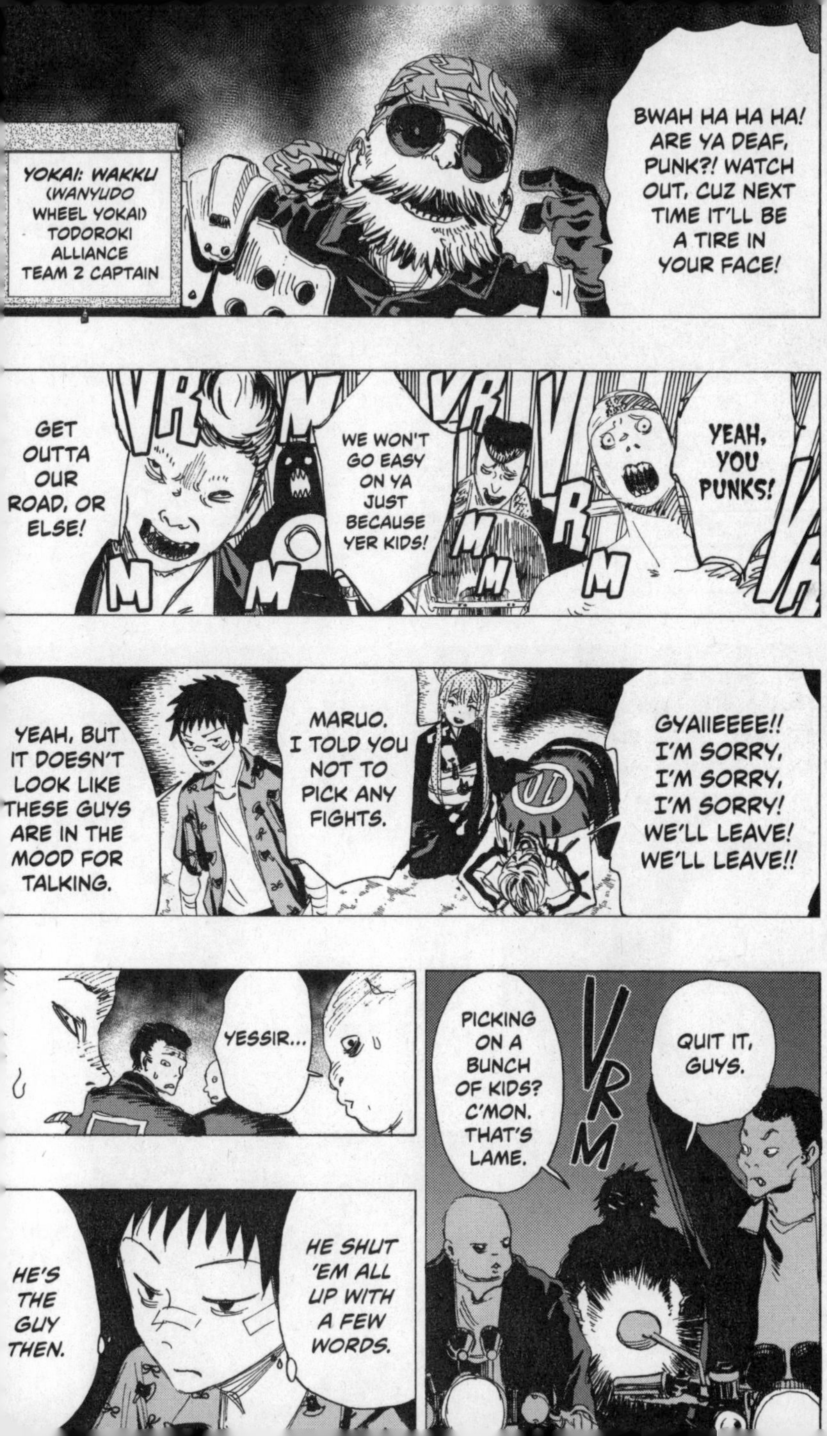
BWAH HA HA HA! ARE YA DEAF, PUNK?! WATCH OUT, CUZ NEXT TIME IT'LL BE A TIRE IN YOUR FACE!
YOKAI: WAKKU (WANYUDO WHEEL YOKAI) TODOROKI ALLIANCE TEAM 2 CAPTAIN
YEAH, YOU PUNKS!
WE WON'T GO EASY ON YA JUST BECAUSE YER KIDS!
GET OUTTA OUR ROAD, OR ELSE!
GYAIIEEEE!! I'M SORRY, I'M SORRY, I'M SORRY! WE'LL LEAVE! WE'LL LEAVE!!
MARUO. I TOLD YOU NOT TO PICK ANY FIGHTS.
YEAH, BUT IT DOESN'T LOOK LIKE THESE GUYS ARE IN THE MOOD FOR TALKING.
QUIT IT, GUYS.
VRM
PICKING ON A BUNCH OF KIDS? C'MON. THAT'S LAME.
YESSIR...
HE SHUT 'EM ALL UP WITH A FEW WORDS.
HE'S THE GUY THEN.

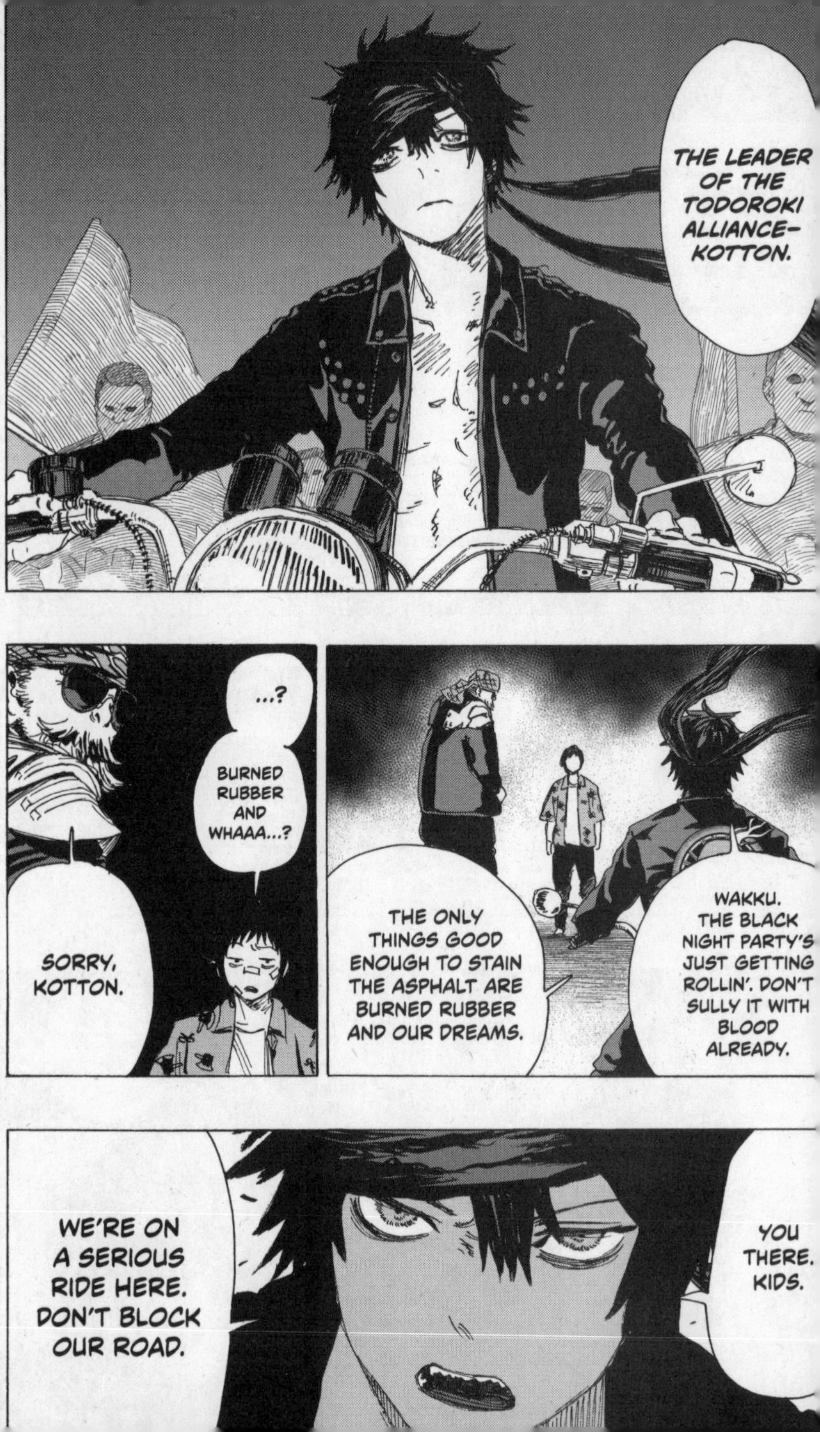
THE LEADER OF THE TODOROKI ALLIANCE- KOTTON.
WAKKU. THE BLACK NIGHT PARTY'S JUST GETTING ROLLIN'. DON'T SULLY IT WITH BLOOD ALREADY.
THE ONLY THINGS GOOD ENOUGH TO STAIN THE ASPHALT ARE BURNED RUBBER AND OUR DREAMS.
...?
BURNED RUBBER AND WHAAA...?
SORRY, KOTTON.
YOU THERE. KIDS.
WE'RE ON A SERIOUS RIDE HERE. DON'T BLOCK OUR ROAD.

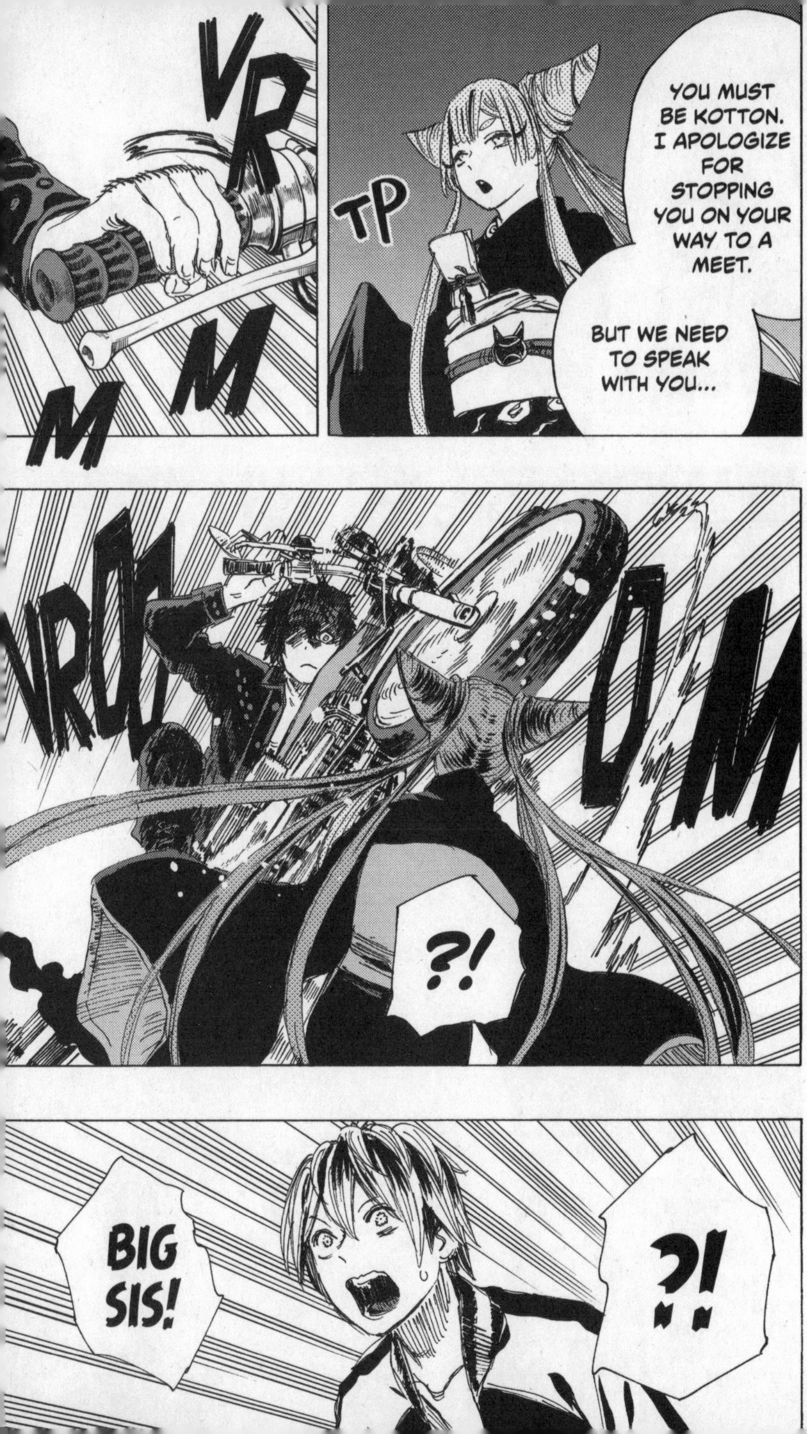
YOU MUST BE KOTTON. I APOLOGIZE FOR STOPPING YOU ON YOUR WAY TO A MEET.
BUT WE NEED TO SPEAK WITH YOU...
TP
VR
MMM
VROO
OM
?!
?!
BIG SIS!

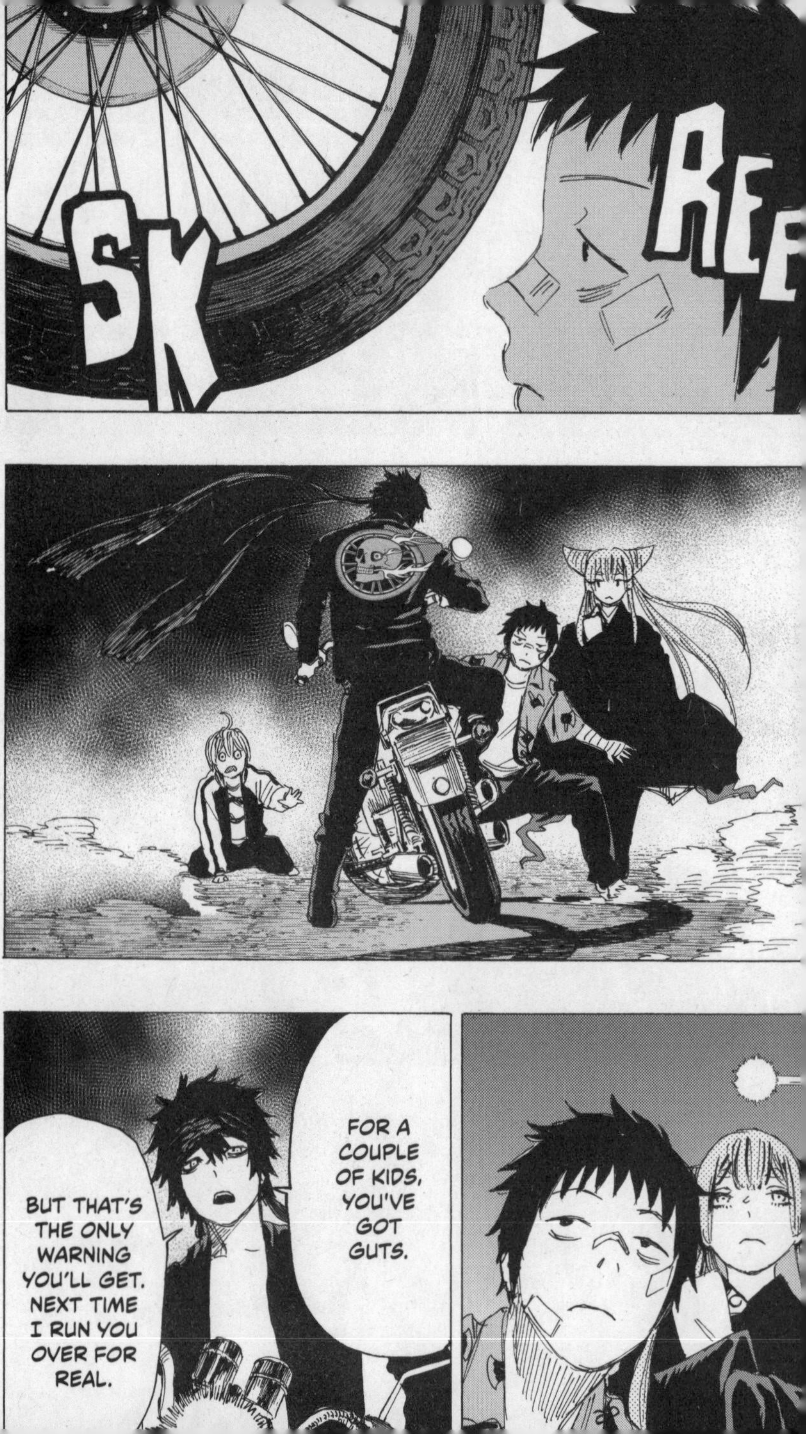
SK REE
FOR A COUPLE OF KIDS, YOU'VE GOT GUTS.
BUT THAT'S THE ONLY WARNING YOU'LL GET. NEXT TIME I RUN YOU OVER FOR REAL.

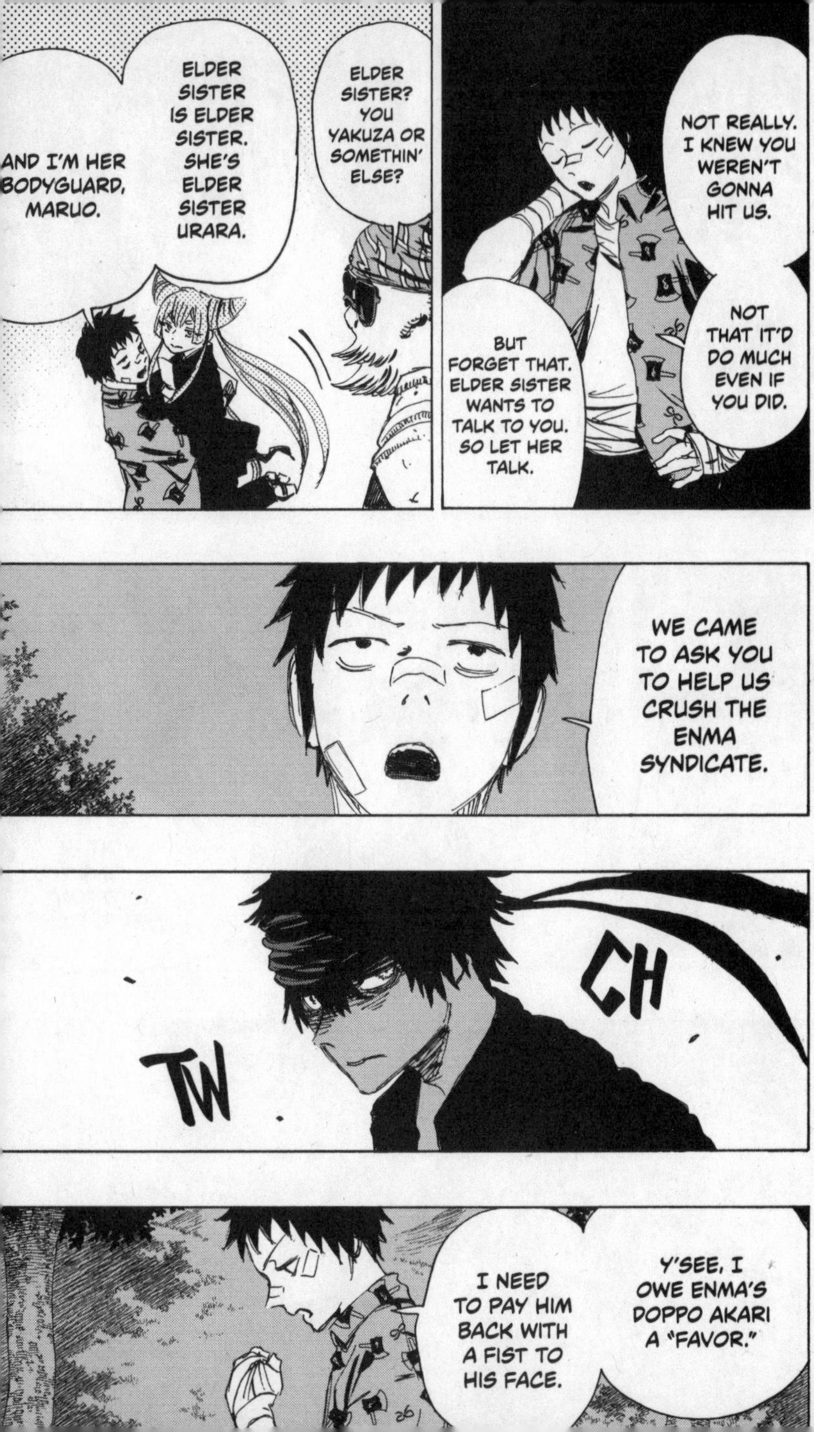
NOT REALLY. I KNEW YOU WEREN'T GONNA HIT US.
NOT THAT IT'D DO MUCH EVEN IF YOU DID.
BUT FORGET THAT. ELDER SISTER WANTS TO TALK TO YOU. SO LET HER TALK.
ELDER SISTER? YOU YAKUZA OR SOMETHIN' ELSE?
ELDER SISTER IS ELDER SISTER. SHE'S ELDER SISTER URARA.
AND I'M HER BODYGUARD, MARUO.
WE CAME TO ASK YOU TO HELP US CRUSH THE ENMA SYNDICATE.
CH
TW
Y'SEE, I OWE ENMA'S DOPPO AKARI A "FAVOR."
I NEED TO PAY HIM BACK WITH A FIST TO HIS FACE.

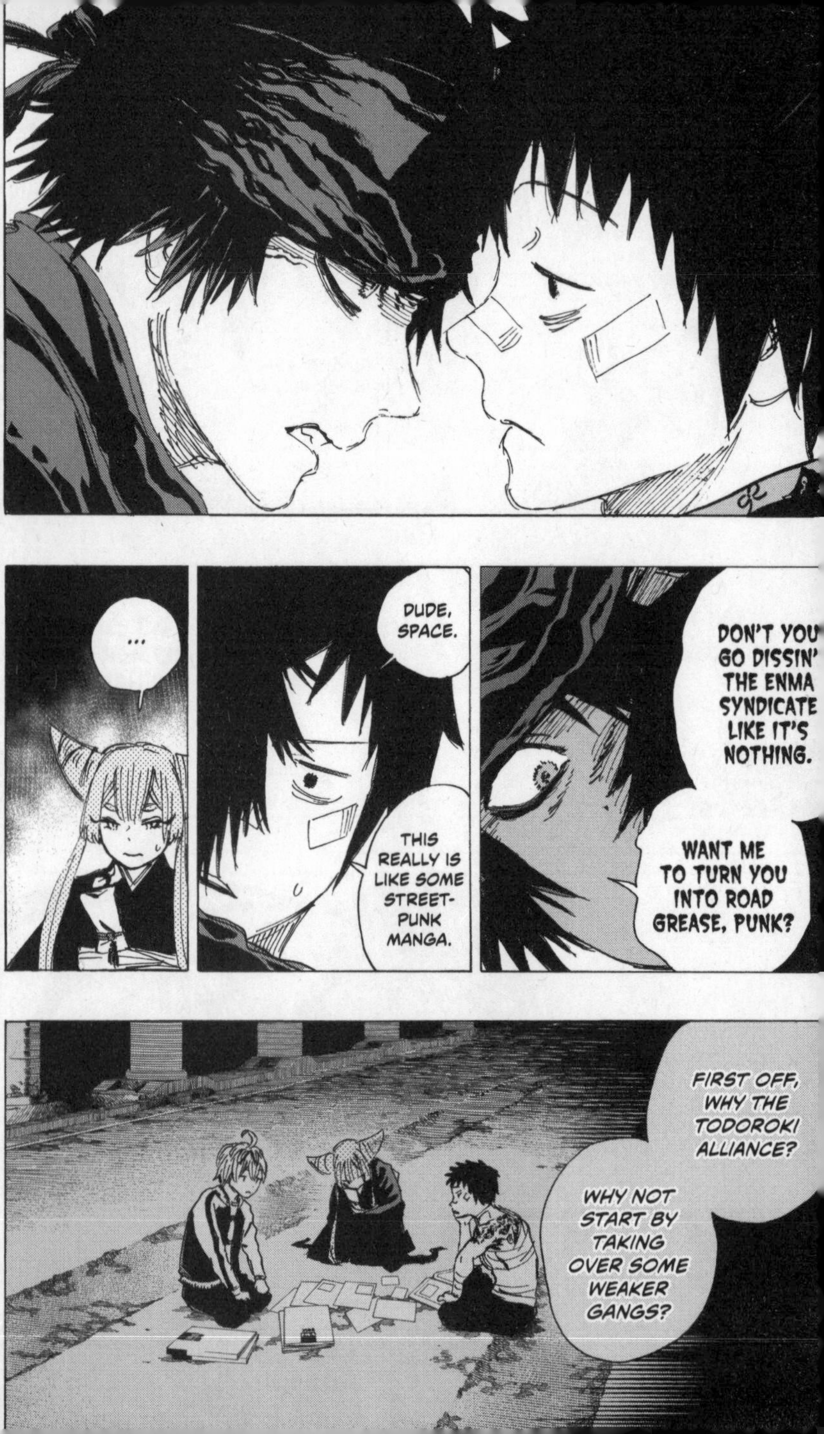
DON'T YOU GO DISSIN' THE ENMA SYNDICATE LIKE IT'S NOTHING.
WANT ME TO TURN YOU INTO ROAD GREASE, PUNK?
DUDE, SPACE.
THIS REALLY IS LIKE SOME STREET-PUNK MANGA.
...
FIRST OFF, WHY THE TODOROKI ALLIANCE?
WHY NOT START BY TAKING OVER SOME WEAKER GANGS?

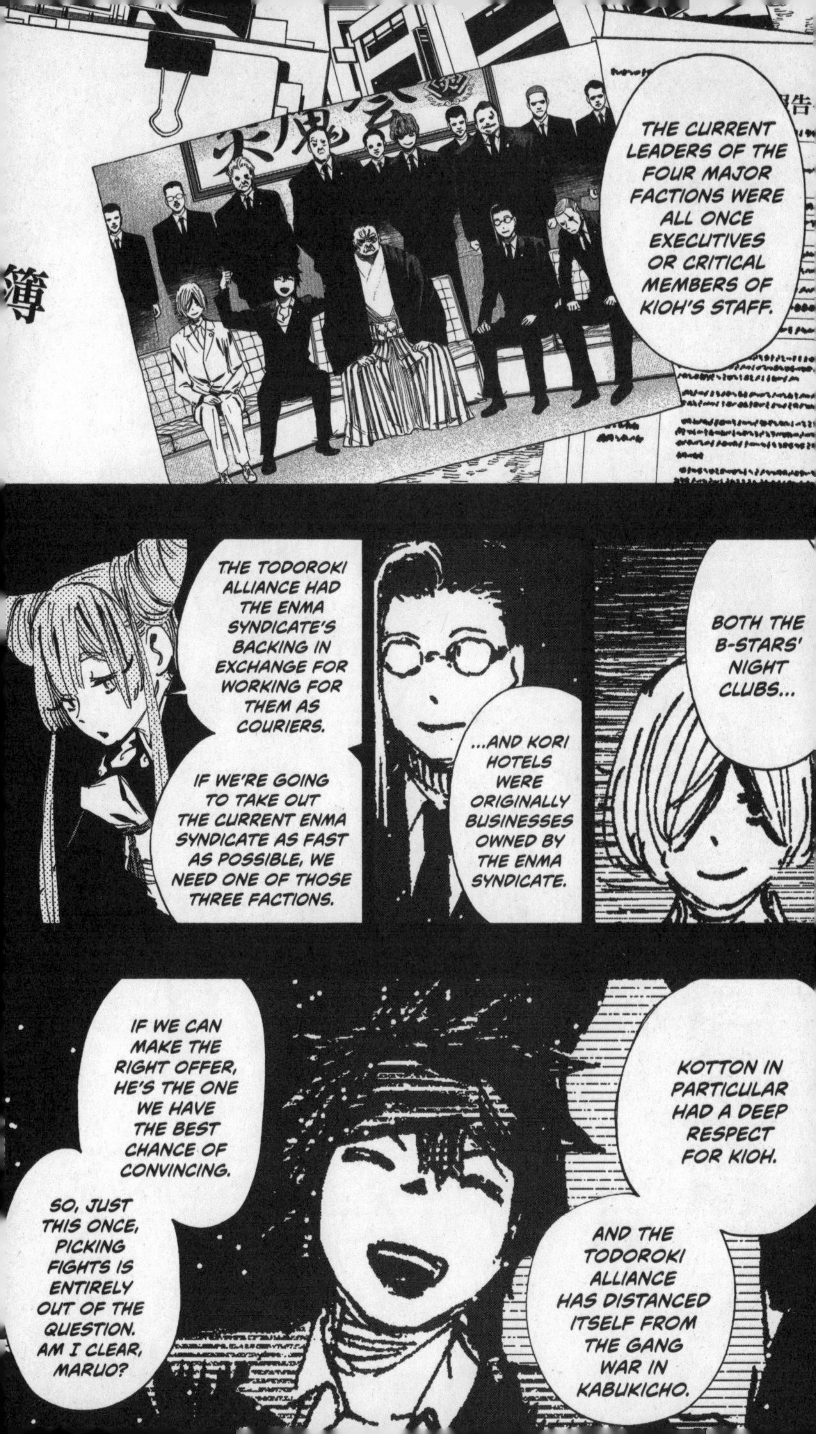
THE CURRENT LEADERS OF THE FOUR MAJOR FACTIONS WERE ALL ONCE EXECUTIVES OR CRITICAL MEMBERS OF KIOH'S STAFF.
簿
BOTH THE B-STARS' NIGHT CLUBS...
...AND KORI HOTELS WERE ORIGINALLY BUSINESSES OWNED BY THE ENMA SYNDICATE.
THE TODOROKI ALLIANCE HAD THE ENMA SYNDICATE'S BACKING IN EXCHANGE FOR WORKING FOR THEM AS COURIERS.
IF WE'RE GOING TO TAKE OUT THE CURRENT ENMA SYNDICATE AS FAST AS POSSIBLE, WE NEED ONE OF THOSE THREE FACTIONS.
KOTTON IN PARTICULAR HAD A DEEP RESPECT FOR KIOH.
AND THE TODOROKI ALLIANCE HAS DISTANCED ITSELF FROM THE GANG WAR IN KABUKICHO.
IF WE CAN MAKE THE RIGHT OFFER, HE'S THE ONE WE HAVE THE BEST CHANCE OF CONVINCING.
SO, JUST THIS ONCE, PICKING FIGHTS IS ENTIRELY OUT OF THE QUESTION. AM I CLEAR, MARUO?

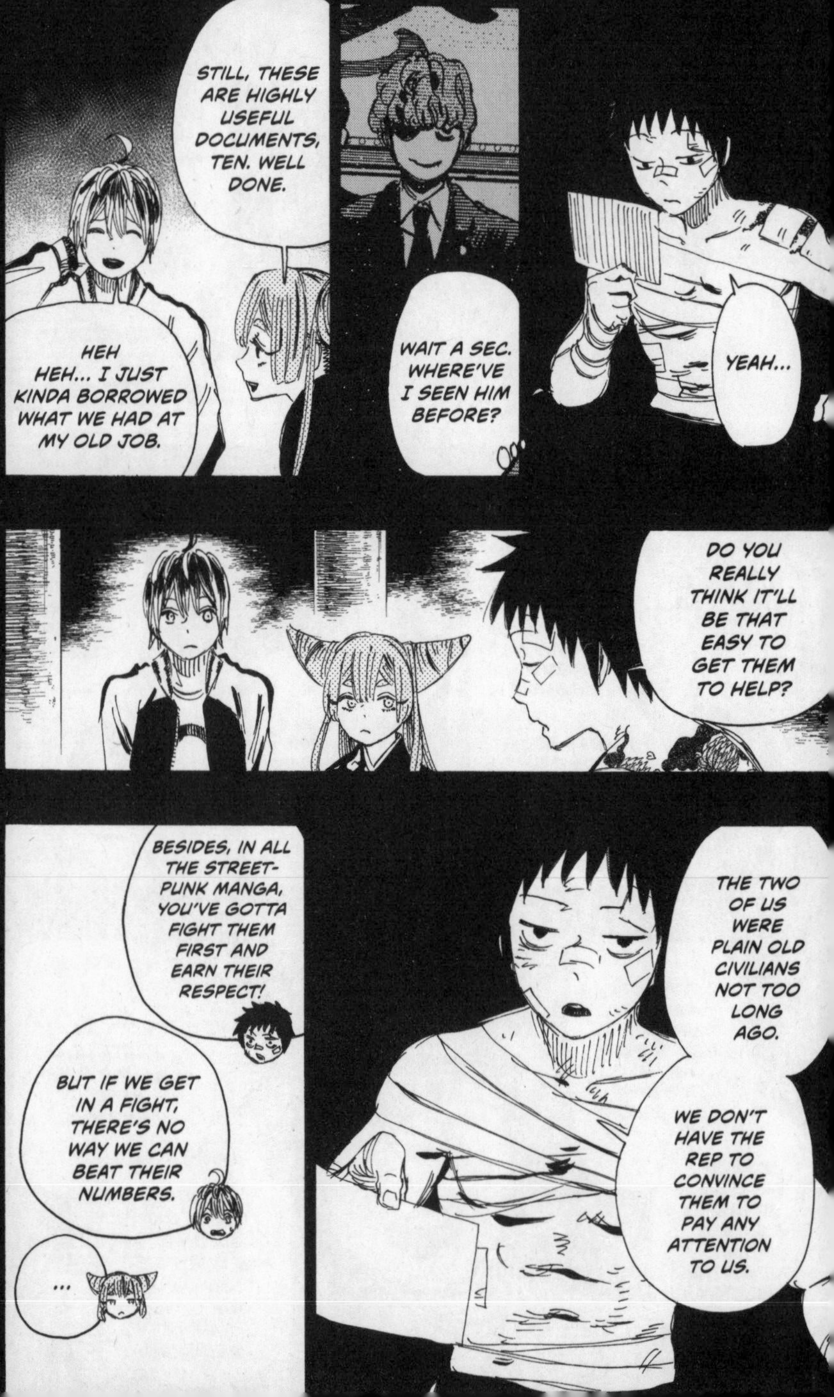
YEAH...
WAIT A SEC. WHERE'VE I SEEN HIM BEFORE?
STILL, THESE ARE HIGHLY USEFUL DOCUMENTS, TEN. WELL DONE.
HEH HEH... I JUST KINDA BORROWED WHAT WE HAD AT MY OLD JOB.
DO YOU REALLY THINK IT'LL BE THAT EASY TO GET THEM TO HELP?
THE TWO OF US WERE PLAIN OLD CIVILIANS NOT TOO LONG AGO.
WE DON'T HAVE THE REP TO CONVINCE THEM TO PAY ANY ATTENTION TO US.
BESIDES, IN ALL THE STREET-PUNK MANGA, YOU'VE GOTTA FIGHT THEM FIRST AND EARN THEIR RESPECT!
BUT IF WE GET IN A FIGHT, THERE'S NO WAY WE CAN BEAT THEIR NUMBERS.
...

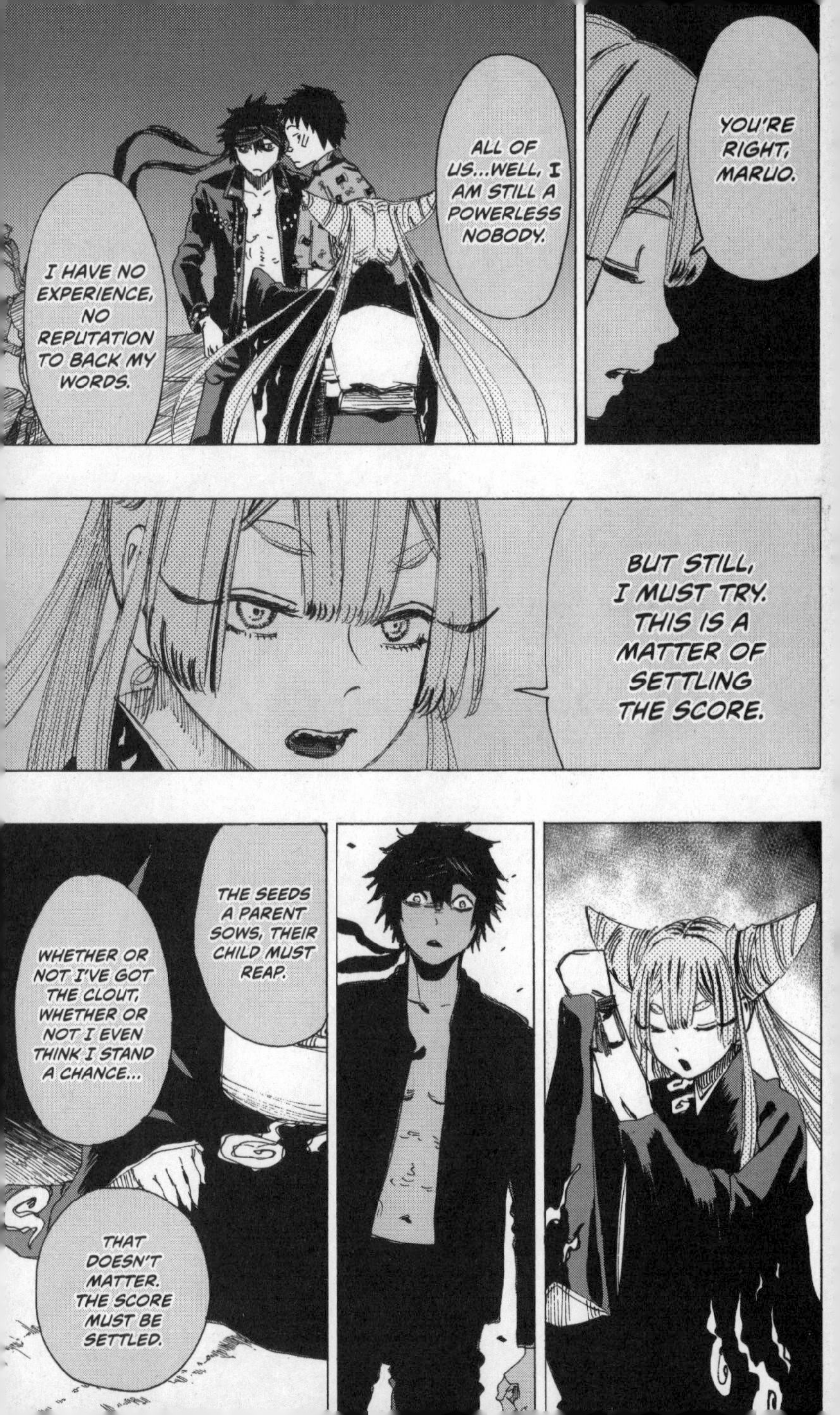
YOU'RE RIGHT, MARUO.
ALL OF US...WELL, I AM STILL A POWERLESS NOBODY.
I HAVE NO EXPERIENCE, NO REPUTATION TO BACK MY WORDS.
BUT STILL, I MUST TRY. THIS IS A MATTER OF SETTLING THE SCORE.
THE SEEDS A PARENT SOWS, THEIR CHILD MUST REAP.
WHETHER OR NOT I'VE GOT THE CLOUT, WHETHER OR NOT I EVEN THINK I STAND A CHANCE...
THAT DOESN'T MATTER. THE SCORE MUST BE SETTLED.

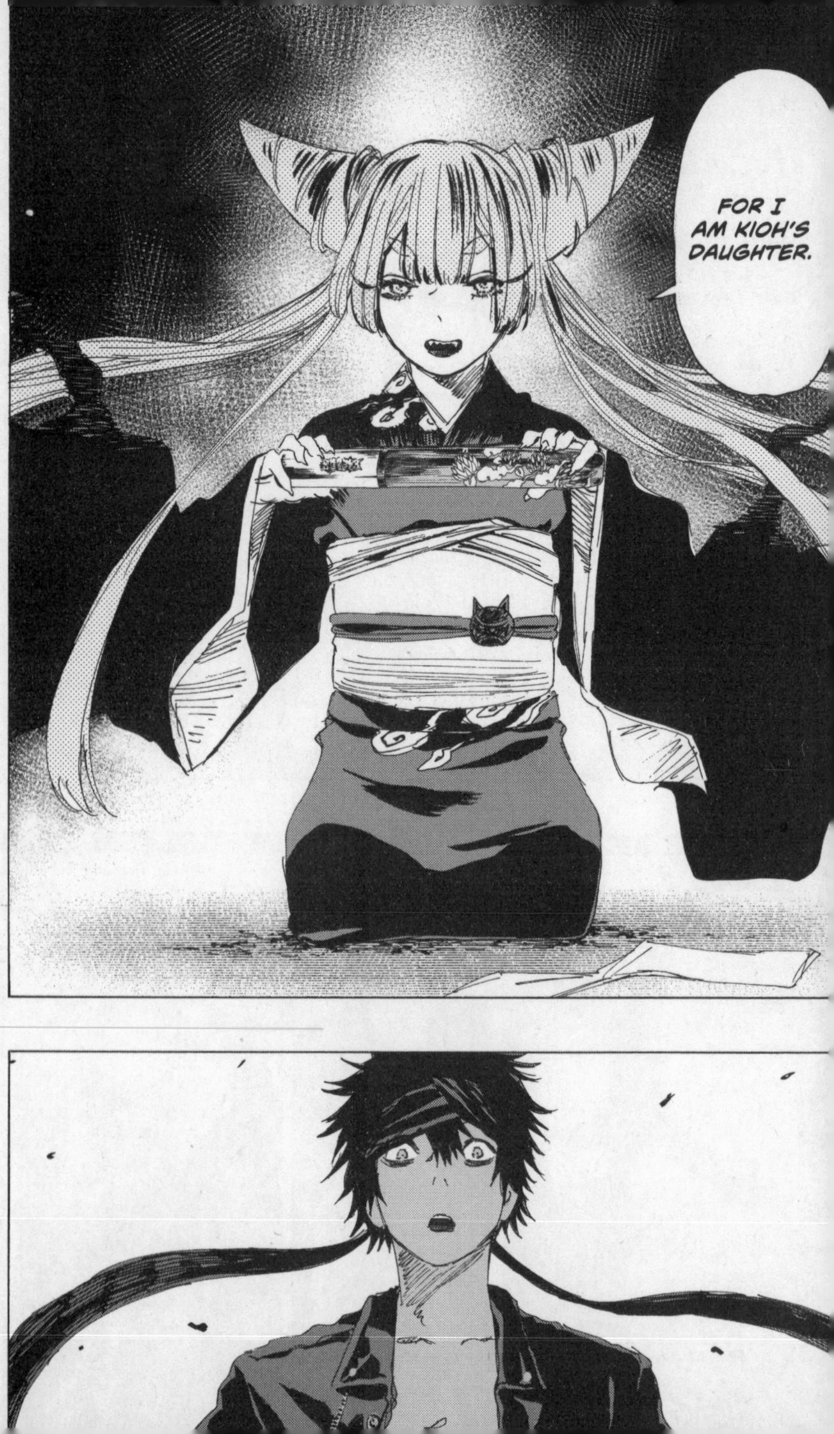
FOR I AM KIOH'S DAUGHTER.

ACCORDINGLY, I ASK FOR THE TODOROKI ALLIANCE'S COOPERATION.

AS PROOF OF MY IDENTITY...THIS HEIRLOOM.

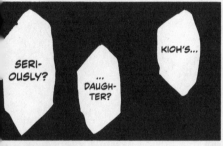

SERI-OUSLY?

...DAUGH-TER?

KIOH'S...

...

WHOA. KOTTON...

STMP

B-BIG SIS...?

STMP

STMP

ST

MP

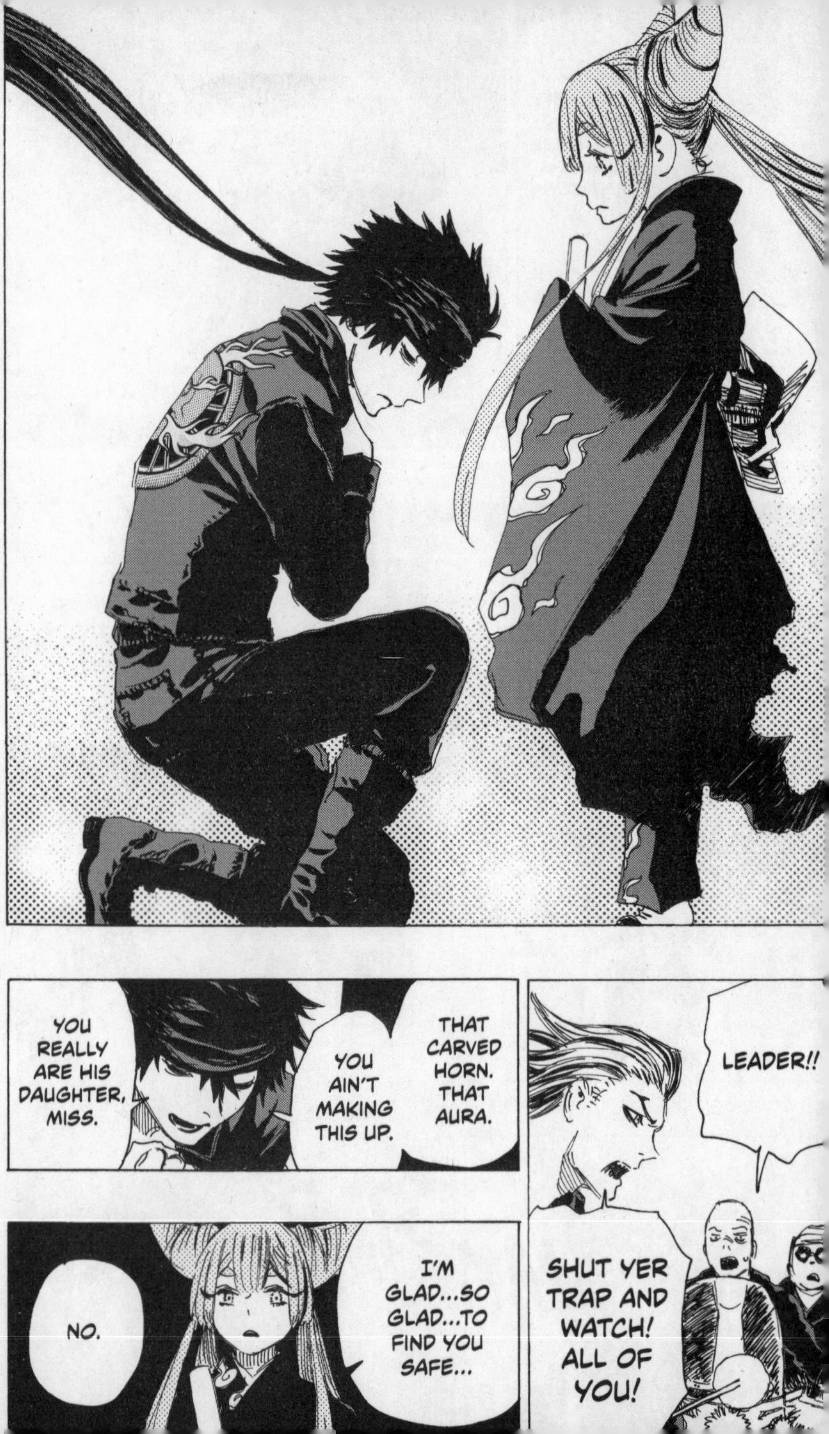
LEADER!!
SHUT YER TRAP AND WATCH! ALL OF YOU!
THAT CARVED HORN. THAT AURA.
YOU AIN'T MAKING THIS UP.
YOU REALLY ARE HIS DAUGHTER, MISS.
I'M GLAD...SO GLAD...TO FIND YOU SAFE...
NO.

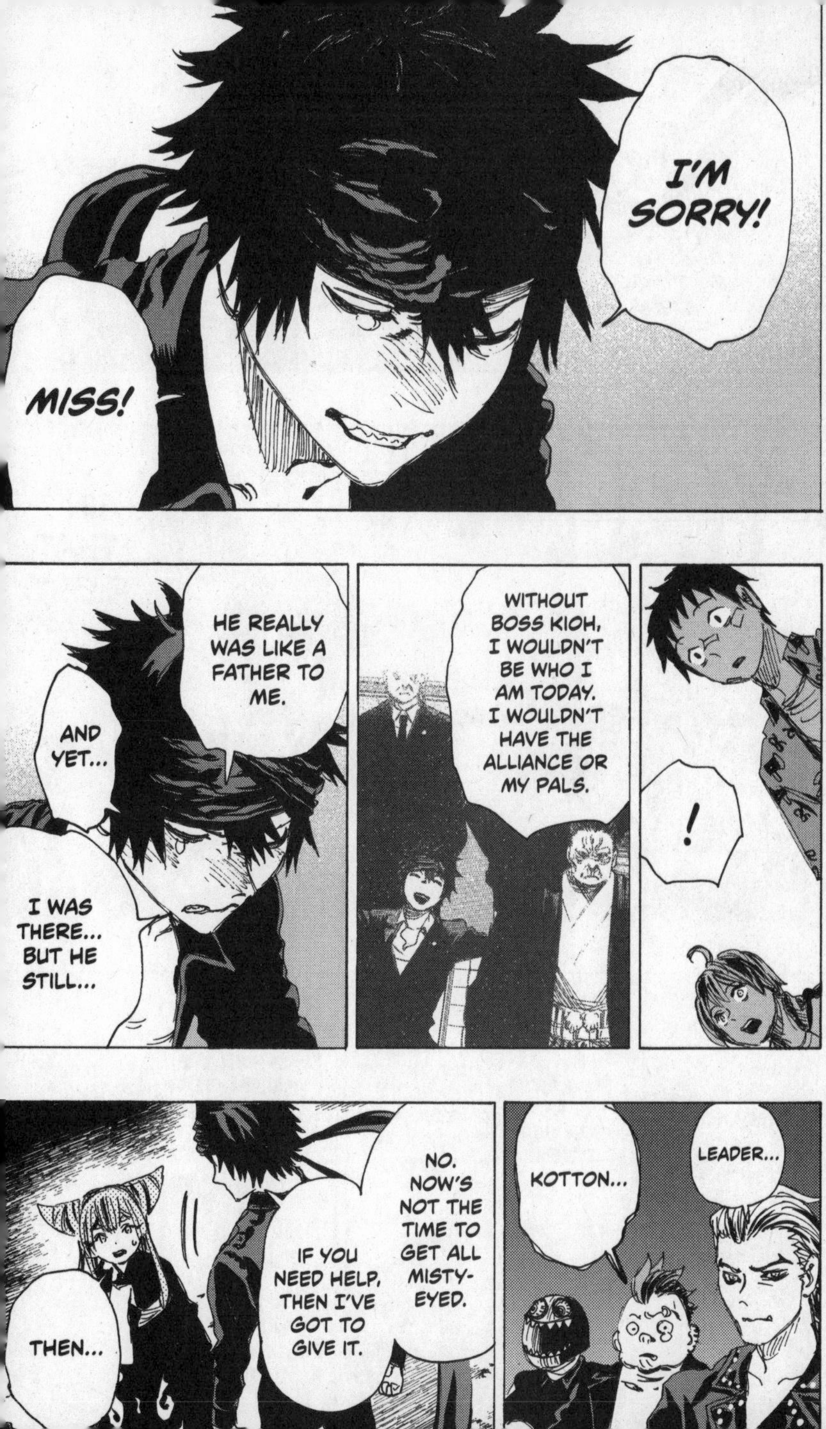
I'M SORRY!
MISS!
!
WITHOUT BOSS KIOH, I WOULDN'T BE WHO I AM TODAY. I WOULDN'T HAVE THE ALLIANCE OR MY PALS.
HE REALLY WAS LIKE A FATHER TO ME.
AND YET...
I WAS THERE... BUT HE STILL...
LEADER...
KOTTON...
NO. NOW'S NOT THE TIME TO GET ALL MISTY-EYED.
IF YOU NEED HELP, THEN I'VE GOT TO GIVE IT.
THEN...

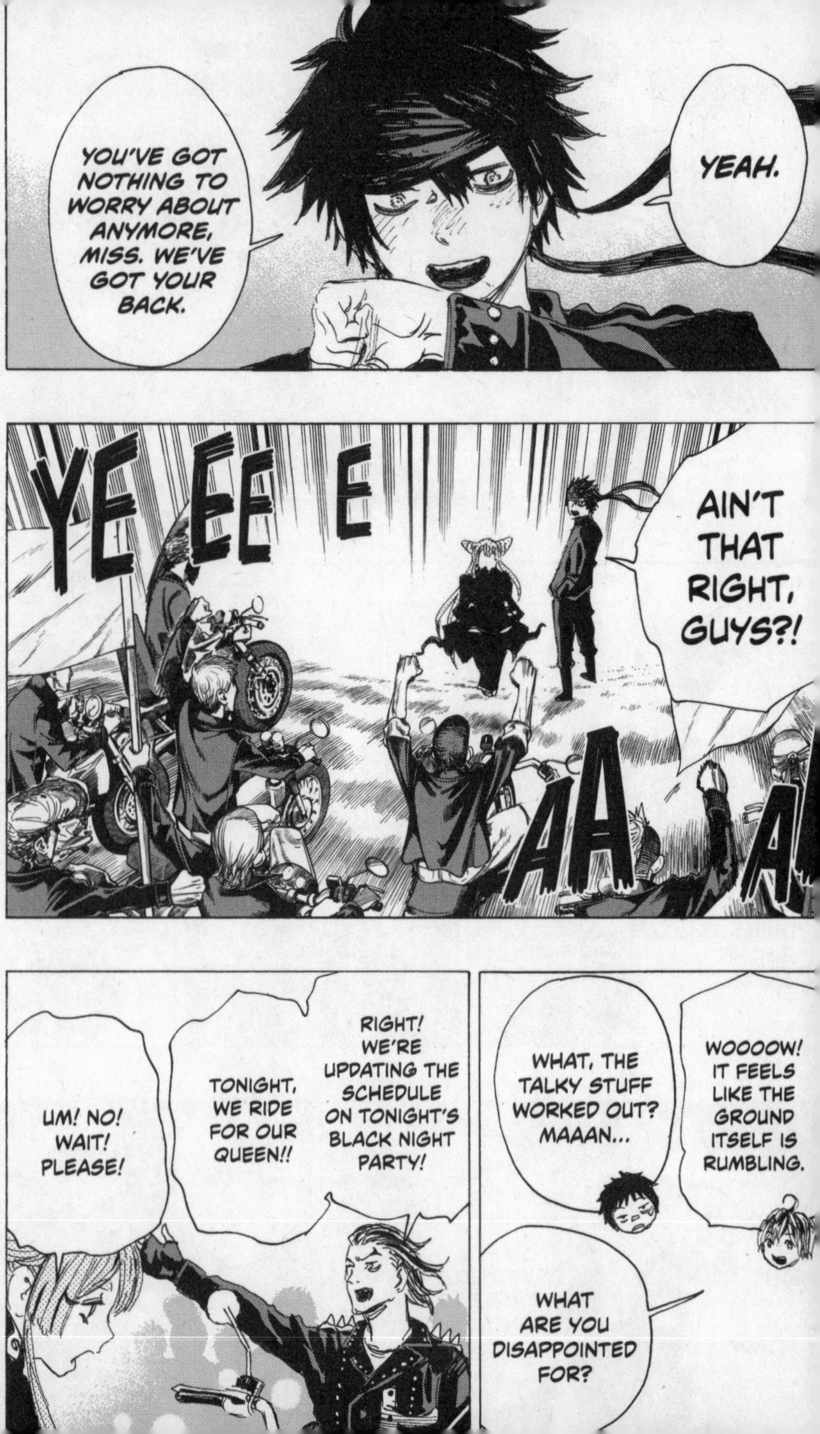
YEAH.
YOU'VE GOT NOTHING TO WORRY ABOUT ANYMORE, MISS. WE'VE GOT YOUR BACK.
AIN'T THAT RIGHT, GUYS?!
YE EE E
AA A
WOOOOW! IT FEELS LIKE THE GROUND ITSELF IS RUMBLING.
WHAT, THE TALKY STUFF WORKED OUT? MAAAN...
WHAT ARE YOU DISAPPOINTED FOR?
RIGHT! WE'RE UPDATING THE SCHEDULE ON TONIGHT'S BLACK NIGHT PARTY!
TONIGHT, WE RIDE FOR OUR QUEEN!!
UM! NO! WAIT! PLEASE!

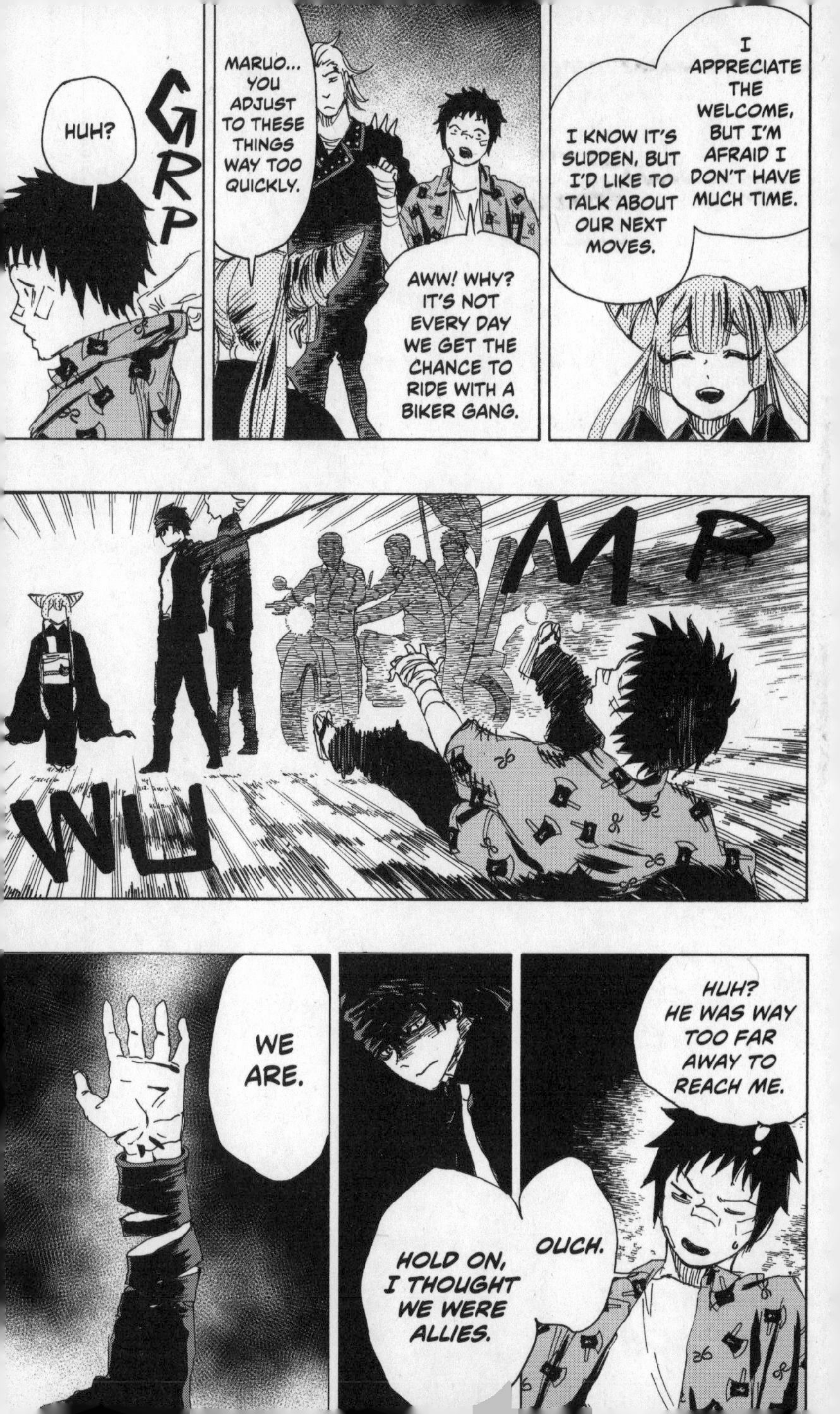
I APPRECIATE THE WELCOME, BUT I'M AFRAID I DON'T HAVE MUCH TIME.
I KNOW IT'S SUDDEN, BUT I'D LIKE TO TALK ABOUT OUR NEXT MOVES.
AWW! WHY? IT'S NOT EVERY DAY WE GET THE CHANCE TO RIDE WITH A BIKER GANG.
MARUO... YOU ADJUST TO THESE THINGS WAY TOO QUICKLY.
GRP
HUH?
WUMP
HUH? HE WAS WAY TOO FAR AWAY TO REACH ME.
OUCH.
HOLD ON, I THOUGHT WE WERE ALLIES.
WE ARE.

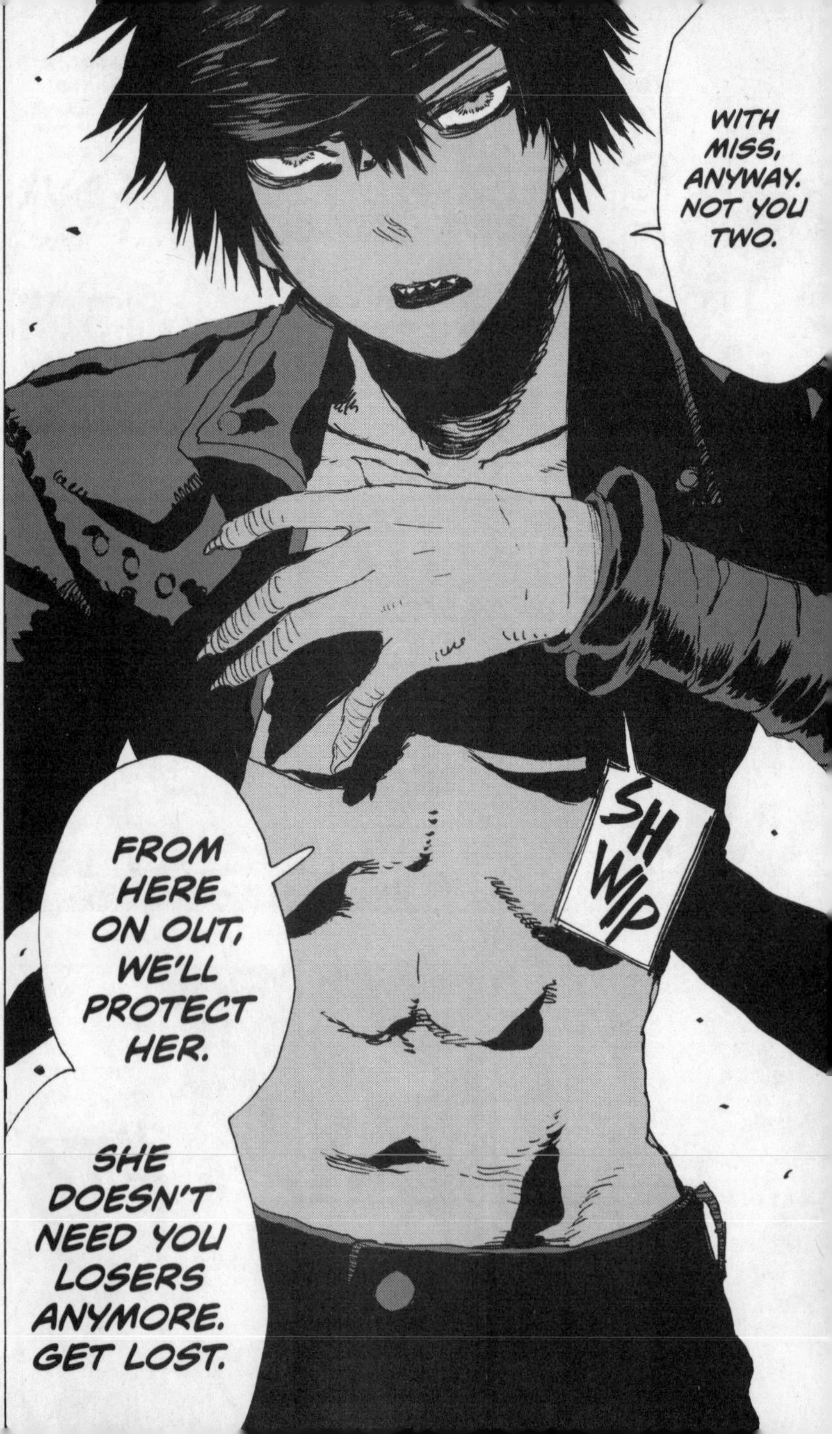
WITH MISS, ANYWAY. NOT YOU TWO.
SHWIP
FROM HERE ON OUT, WE'LL PROTECT HER.
SHE DOESN'T NEED YOU LOSERS ANYMORE. GET LOST.

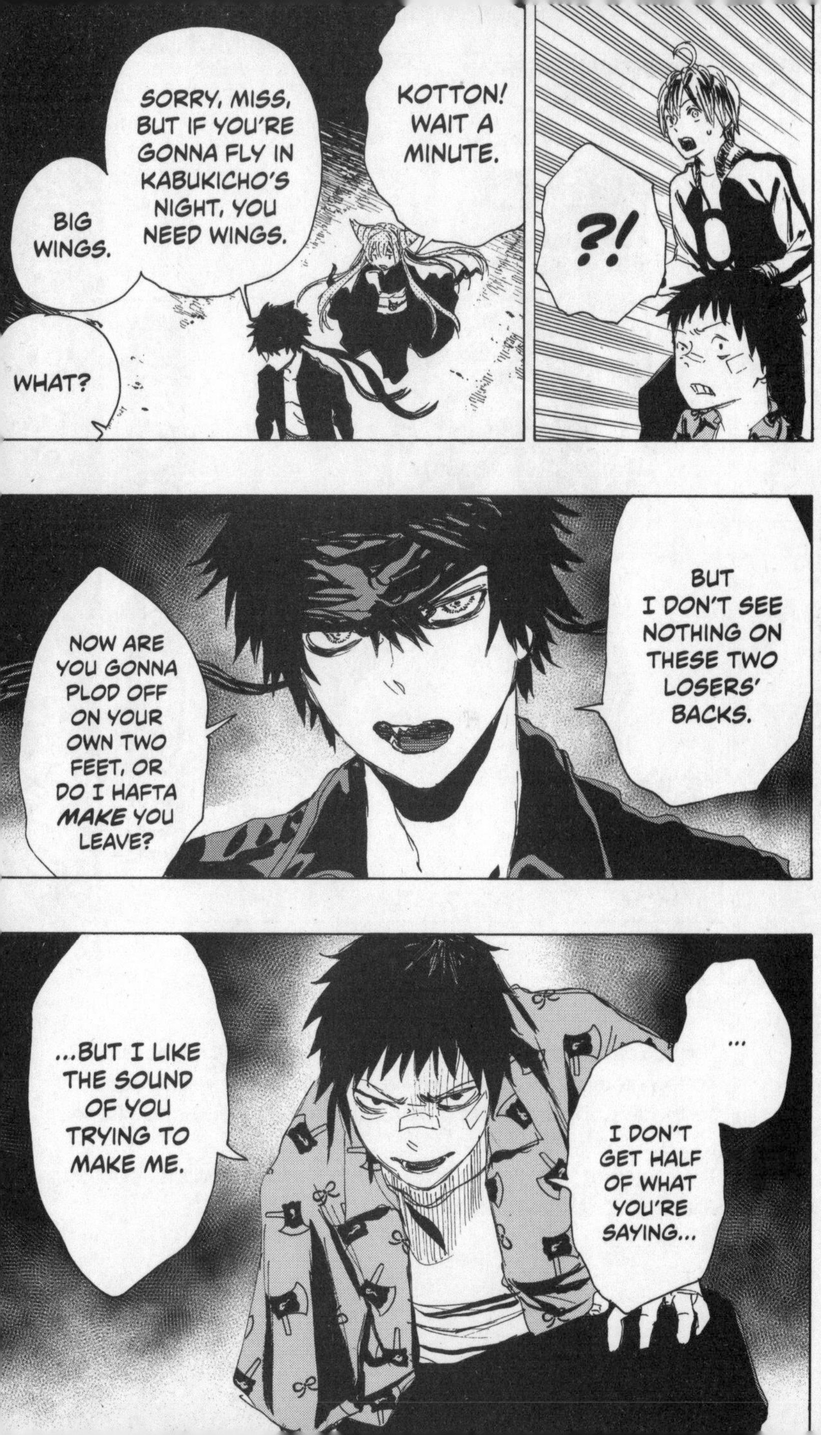
?!
KOTTON! WAIT A MINUTE.
SORRY, MISS, BUT IF YOU'RE GONNA FLY IN KABUKICHO'S NIGHT, YOU NEED WINGS.
BIG WINGS.
WHAT?
BUT I DON'T SEE NOTHING ON THESE TWO LOSERS' BACKS.
NOW ARE YOU GONNA PLOD OFF ON YOUR OWN TWO FEET, OR DO I HAFTA *MAKE* YOU LEAVE?
...
I DON'T GET HALF OF WHAT YOU'RE SAYING...
...BUT I LIKE THE SOUND OF YOU TRYING TO MAKE ME.

KABUKICHO MONSTER MANUAL

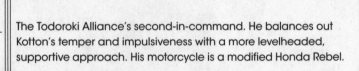

Oboro (Oboro Guruma)

The Todoroki Alliance's second-in-command. He balances out Kotton's temper and impulsiveness with a more levelheaded, supportive approach. His motorcycle is a modified Honda Rebel.

They say that he's the one who actually established the Todoroki Alliance's code of conduct.

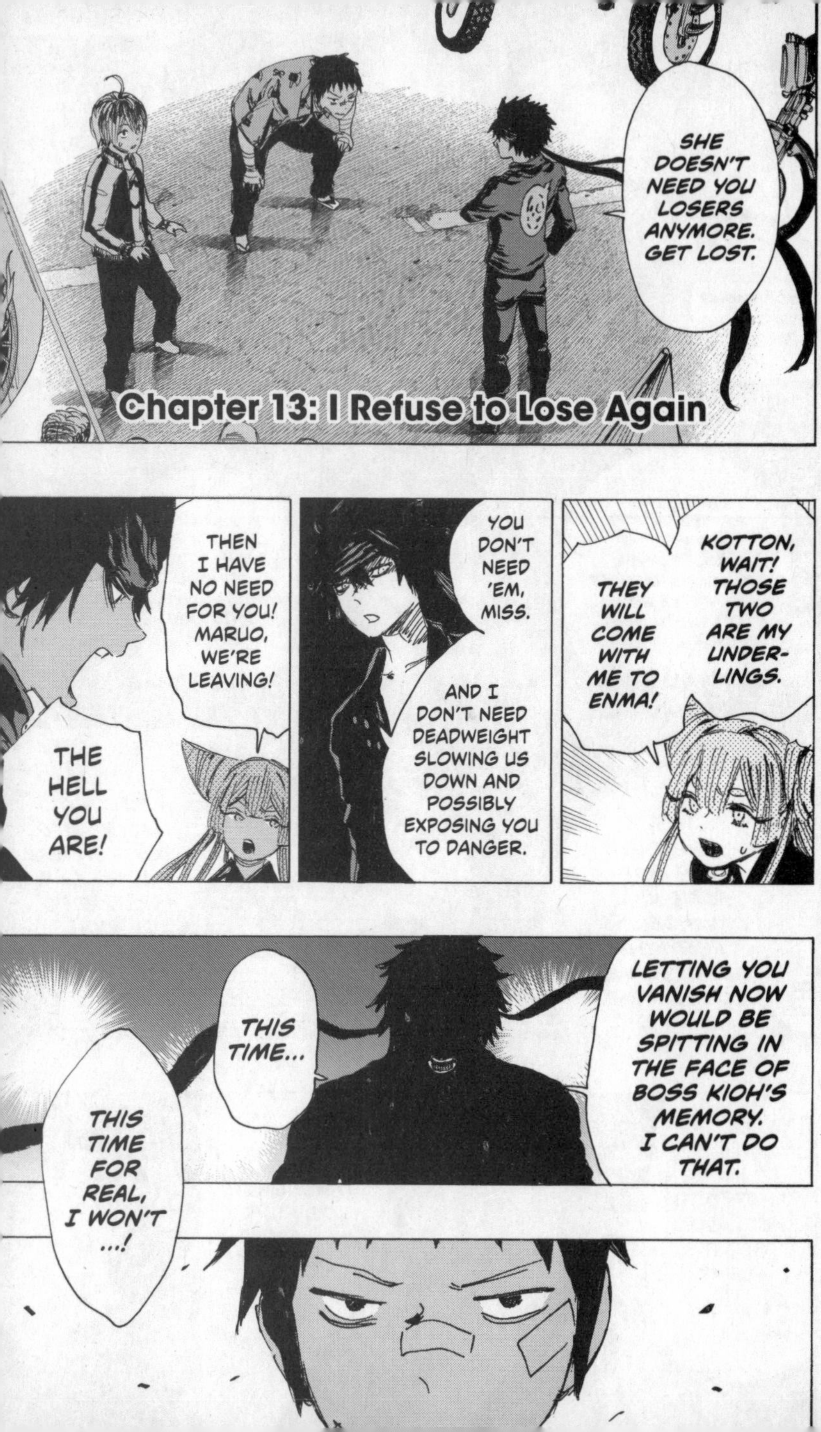
SHE DOESN'T NEED YOU LOSERS ANYMORE. GET LOST.
Chapter 13: I Refuse to Lose Again
KOTTON, WAIT! THOSE TWO ARE MY UNDER-LINGS.
THEY WILL COME WITH ME TO ENMA!
YOU DON'T NEED 'EM, MISS.
AND I DON'T NEED DEADWEIGHT SLOWING US DOWN AND POSSIBLY EXPOSING YOU TO DANGER.
THEN I HAVE NO NEED FOR YOU! MARUO, WE'RE LEAVING!
THE HELL YOU ARE!
LETTING YOU VANISH NOW WOULD BE SPITTING IN THE FACE OF BOSS KIOH'S MEMORY. I CAN'T DO THAT.
THIS TIME...
THIS TIME FOR REAL, I WON'T ...!

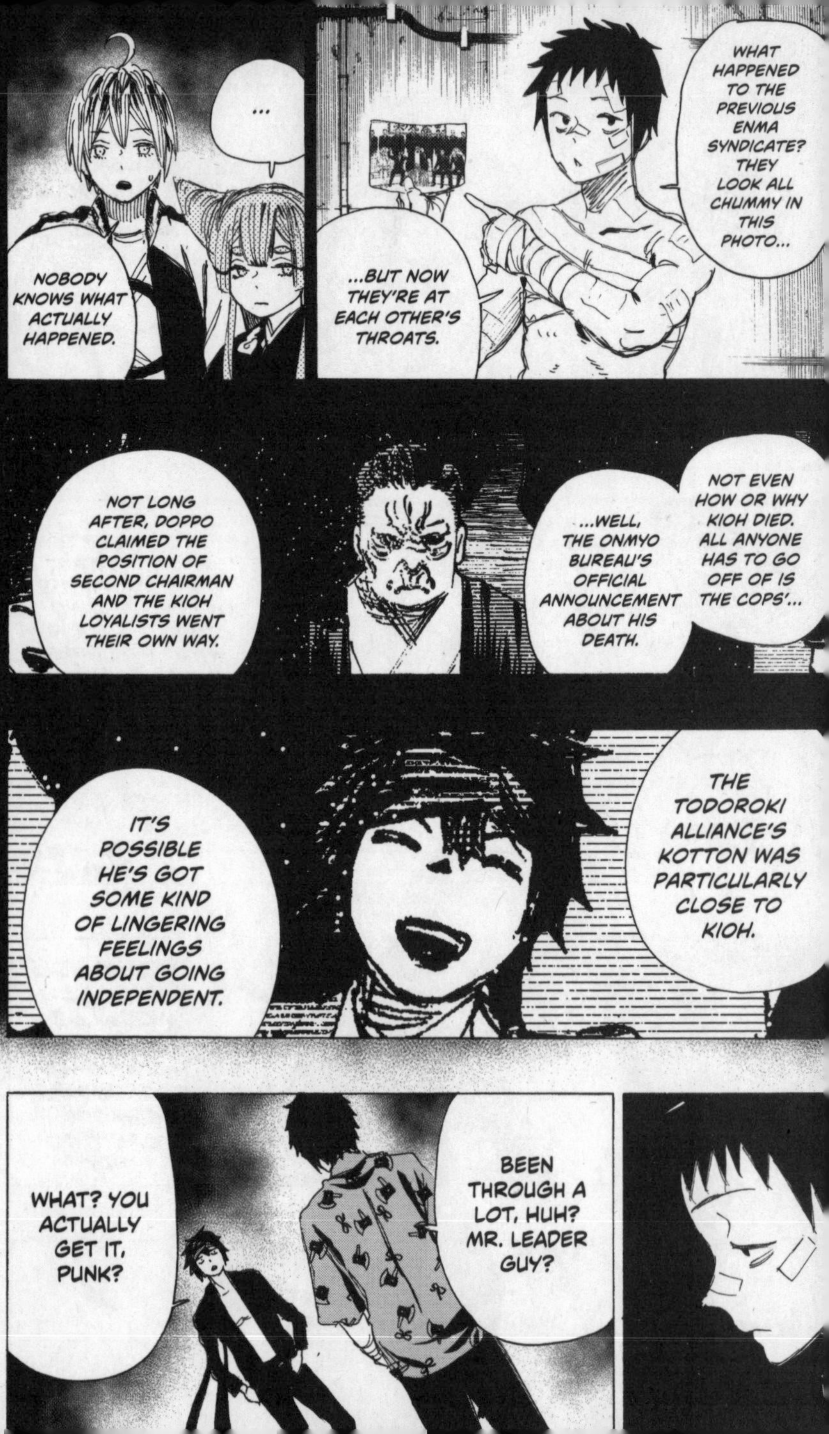
WHAT HAPPENED TO THE PREVIOUS ENMA SYNDICATE? THEY LOOK ALL CHUMMY IN THIS PHOTO...
...BUT NOW THEY'RE AT EACH OTHER'S THROATS.
...
NOBODY KNOWS WHAT ACTUALLY HAPPENED.
NOT EVEN HOW OR WHY KIOH DIED. ALL ANYONE HAS TO GO OFF OF IS THE COPS'...
...WELL, THE ONMYO BUREAU'S OFFICIAL ANNOUNCEMENT ABOUT HIS DEATH.
NOT LONG AFTER, DOPPO CLAIMED THE POSITION OF SECOND CHAIRMAN AND THE KIOH LOYALISTS WENT THEIR OWN WAY.
THE TODOROKI ALLIANCE'S KOTTON WAS PARTICULARLY CLOSE TO KIOH.
IT'S POSSIBLE HE'S GOT SOME KIND OF LINGERING FEELINGS ABOUT GOING INDEPENDENT.
BEEN THROUGH A LOT, HUH? MR. LEADER GUY?
WHAT? YOU ACTUALLY GET IT, PUNK?

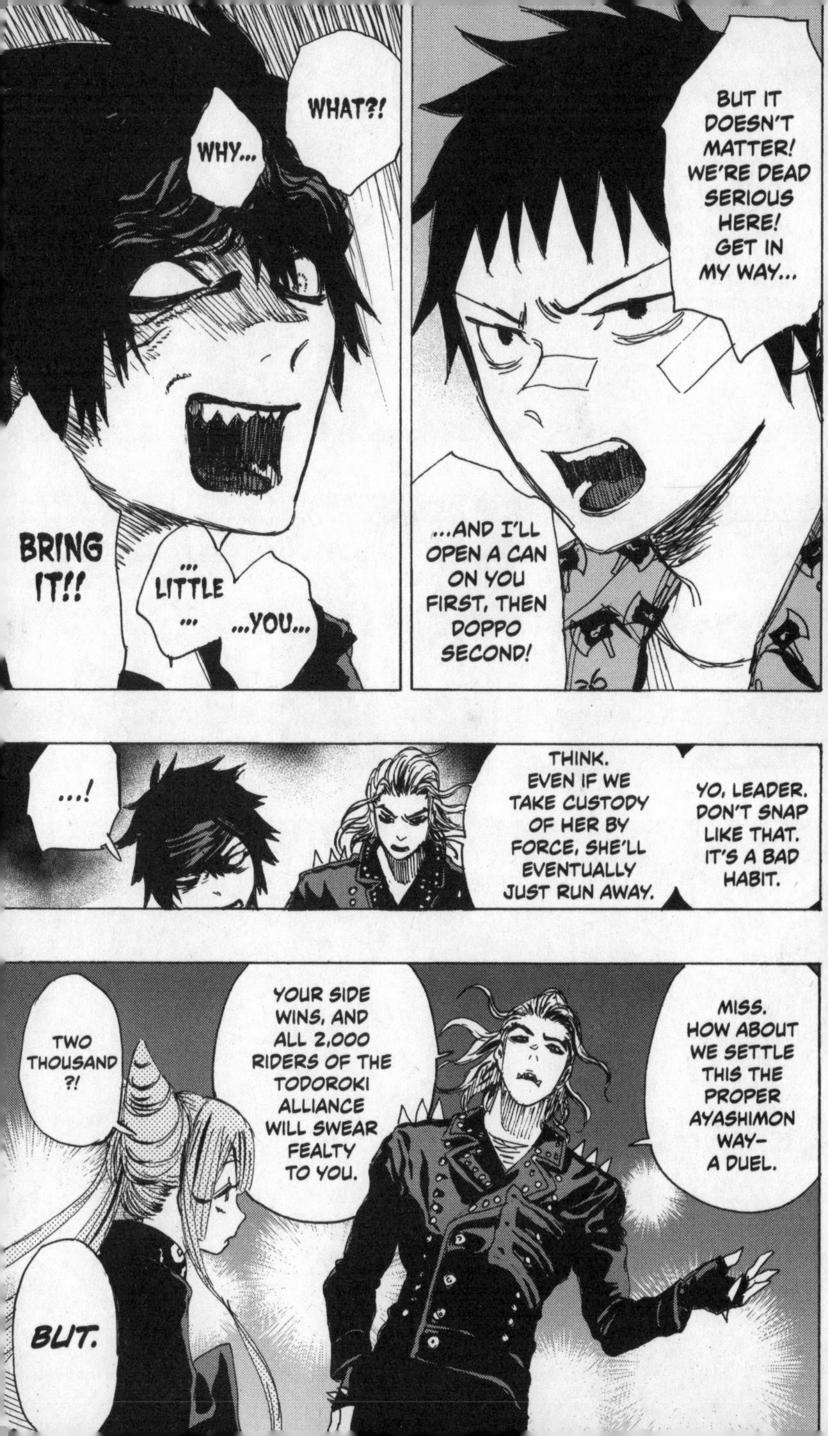
BUT IT DOESN'T MATTER! WE'RE DEAD SERIOUS HERE! GET IN MY WAY...
...AND I'LL OPEN A CAN ON YOU FIRST, THEN DOPPO SECOND!
WHAT?!
WHY...
...YOU...
... LITTLE ...
BRING IT!!
YO, LEADER. DON'T SNAP LIKE THAT. IT'S A BAD HABIT.
THINK. EVEN IF WE TAKE CUSTODY OF HER BY FORCE, SHE'LL EVENTUALLY JUST RUN AWAY.
...!
MISS. HOW ABOUT WE SETTLE THIS THE PROPER AYASHIMON WAY— A DUEL.
YOUR SIDE WINS, AND ALL 2,000 RIDERS OF THE TODOROKI ALLIANCE WILL SWEAR FEALTY TO YOU.
TWO THOUSAND?!
BUT.

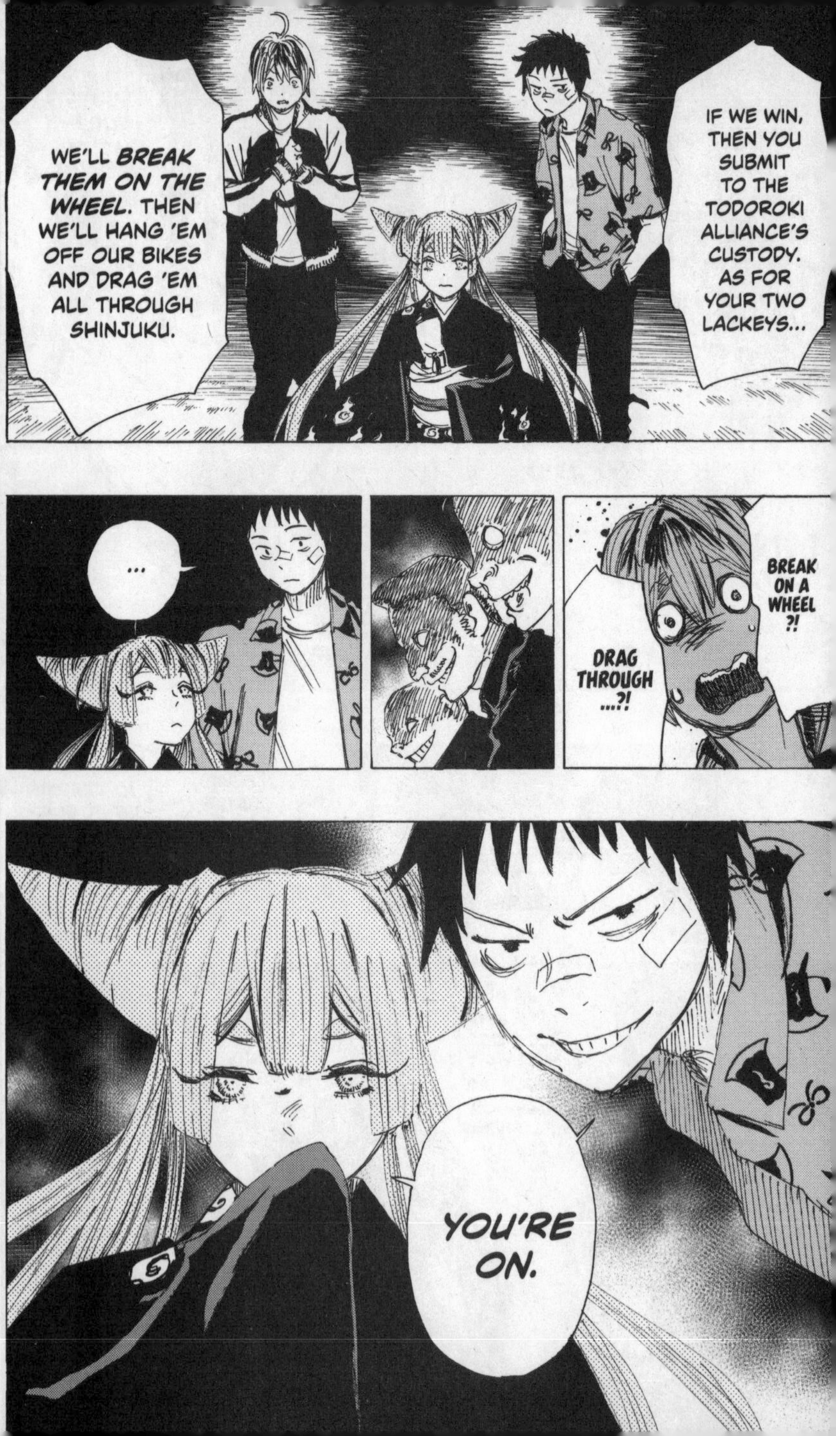
IF WE WIN, THEN YOU SUBMIT TO THE TODOROKI ALLIANCE'S CUSTODY. AS FOR YOUR TWO LACKEYS...
WE'LL *BREAK THEM ON THE WHEEL*. THEN WE'LL HANG 'EM OFF OUR BIKES AND DRAG 'EM ALL THROUGH SHINJUKU.
BREAK ON A WHEEL ?!
DRAG THROUGH ....?!
...
YOU'RE ON.

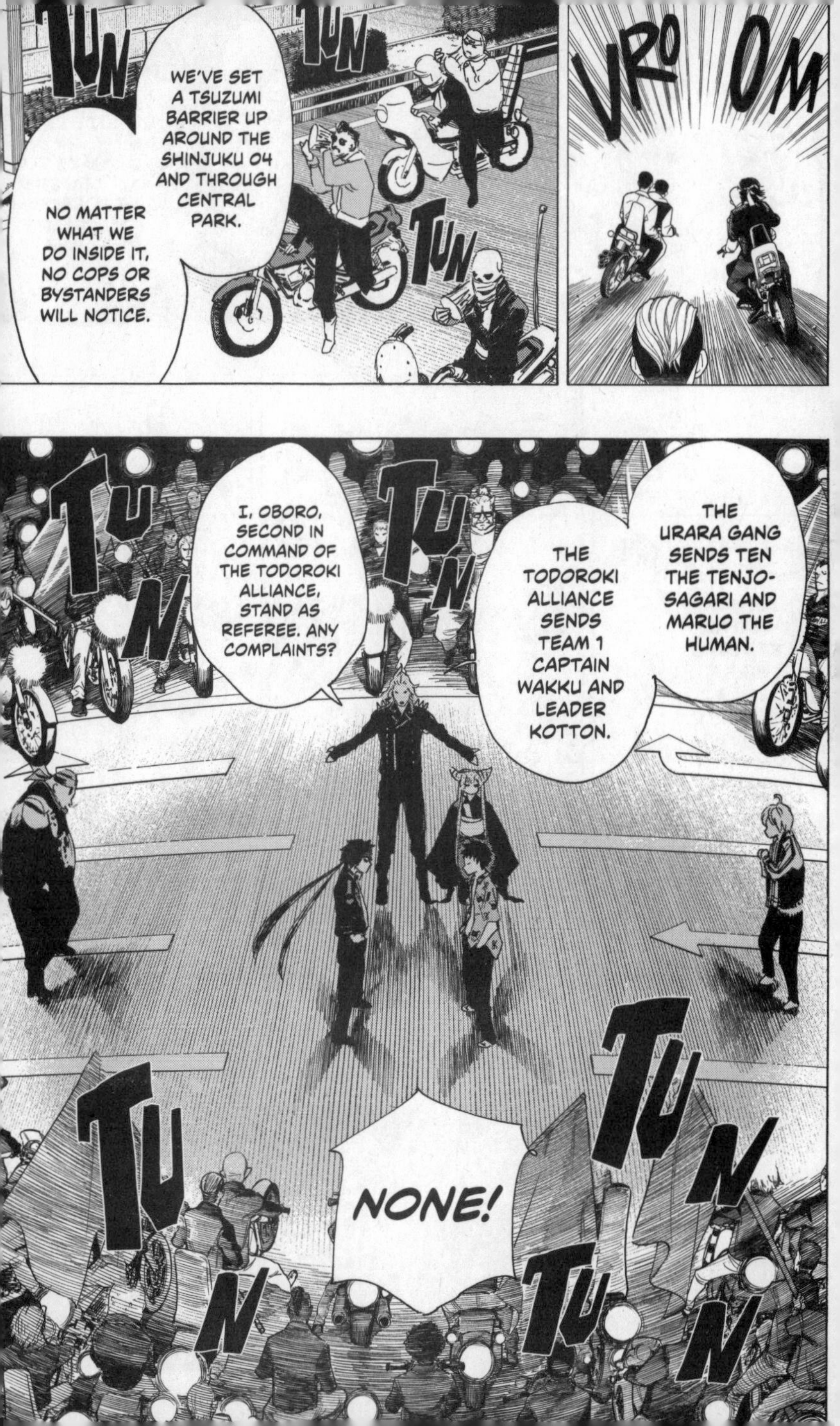
VROOM
TUN
TUN
WE'VE SET A TSUZUMI BARRIER UP AROUND THE SHINJUKU 04 AND THROUGH CENTRAL PARK.
NO MATTER WHAT WE DO INSIDE IT, NO COPS OR BYSTANDERS WILL NOTICE.
TUN
THE URARA GANG SENDS TEN THE TENJO-SAGARI AND MARUO THE HUMAN.
THE TODOROKI ALLIANCE SENDS TEAM 1 CAPTAIN WAKKU AND LEADER KOTTON.
TUN
I, OBORO, SECOND IN COMMAND OF THE TODOROKI ALLIANCE, STAND AS REFEREE. ANY COMPLAINTS?
TUN
TUN
TUN
NONE!
TUN

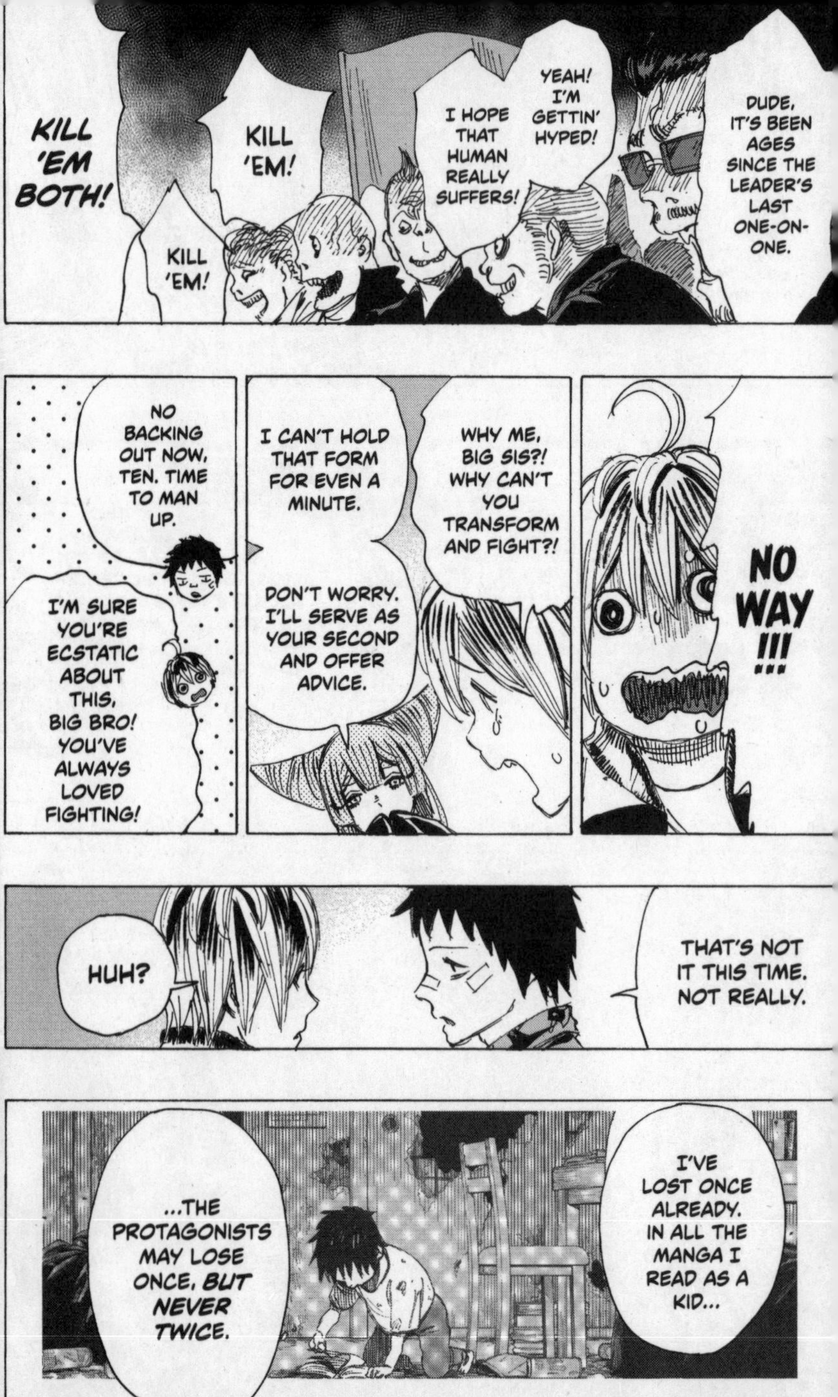
DUDE, IT'S BEEN AGES SINCE THE LEADER'S LAST ONE-ON-ONE.
YEAH! I'M GETTIN' HYPED!
I HOPE THAT HUMAN REALLY SUFFERS!
KILL 'EM!
KILL 'EM!
KILL 'EM BOTH!
NO WAY!!!
WHY ME, BIG SIS?! WHY CAN'T YOU TRANSFORM AND FIGHT?!
I CAN'T HOLD THAT FORM FOR EVEN A MINUTE.
DON'T WORRY. I'LL SERVE AS YOUR SECOND AND OFFER ADVICE.
NO BACKING OUT NOW, TEN. TIME TO MAN UP.
I'M SURE YOU'RE ECSTATIC ABOUT THIS, BIG BRO! YOU'VE ALWAYS LOVED FIGHTING!
THAT'S NOT IT THIS TIME. NOT REALLY.
HUH?
I'VE LOST ONCE ALREADY. IN ALL THE MANGA I READ AS A KID...
...THE PROTAGONISTS MAY LOSE ONCE, BUT NEVER TWICE.

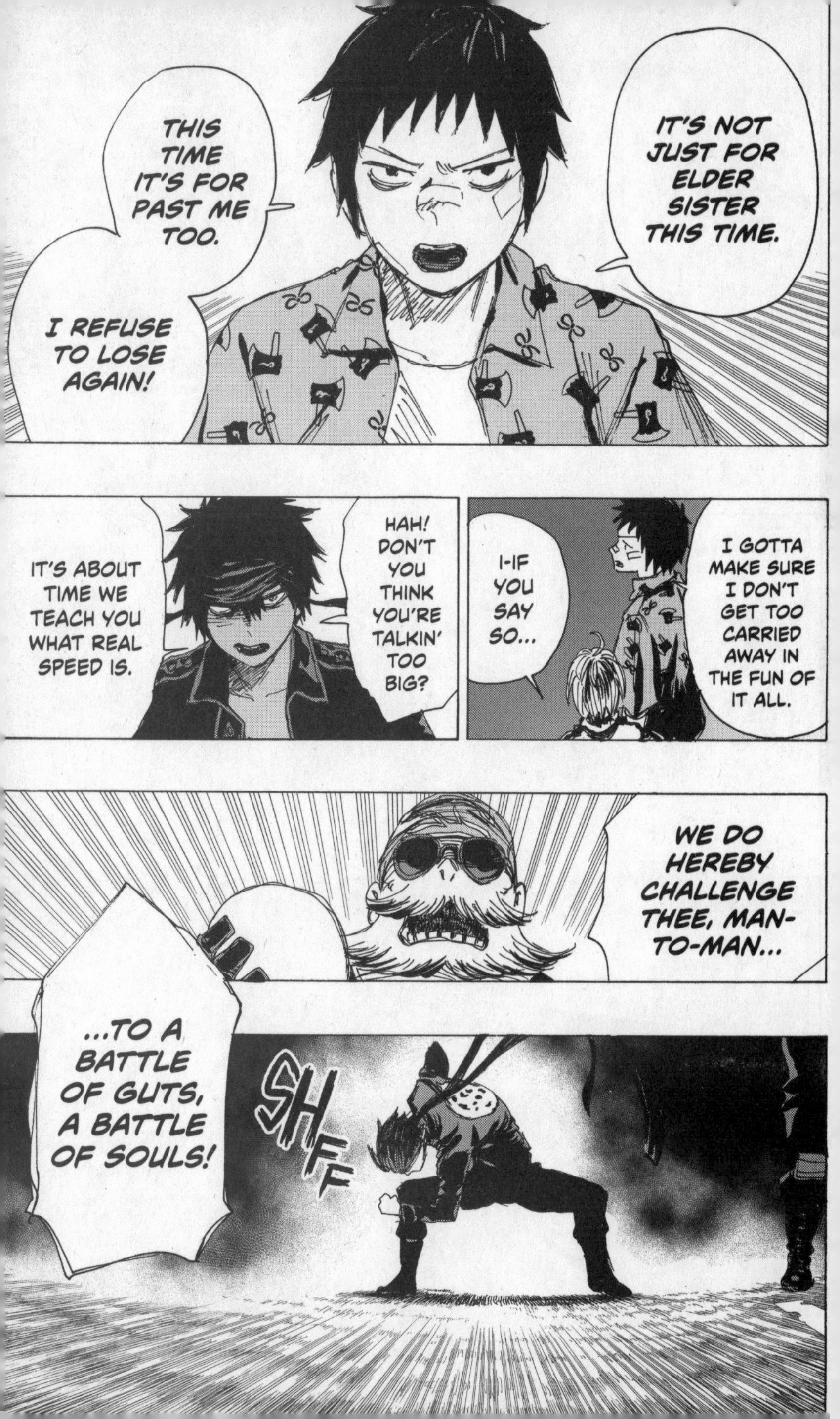
IT'S NOT JUST FOR ELDER SISTER THIS TIME.
THIS TIME IT'S FOR PAST ME TOO.
I REFUSE TO LOSE AGAIN!
I GOTTA MAKE SURE I DON'T GET TOO CARRIED AWAY IN THE FUN OF IT ALL.
I-IF YOU SAY SO...
HAH! DON'T YOU THINK YOU'RE TALKIN' TOO BIG?
IT'S ABOUT TIME WE TEACH YOU WHAT REAL SPEED IS.
WE DO HEREBY CHALLENGE THEE, MAN-TO-MAN...
...TO A BATTLE OF GUTS, A BATTLE OF SOULS!
SHFF

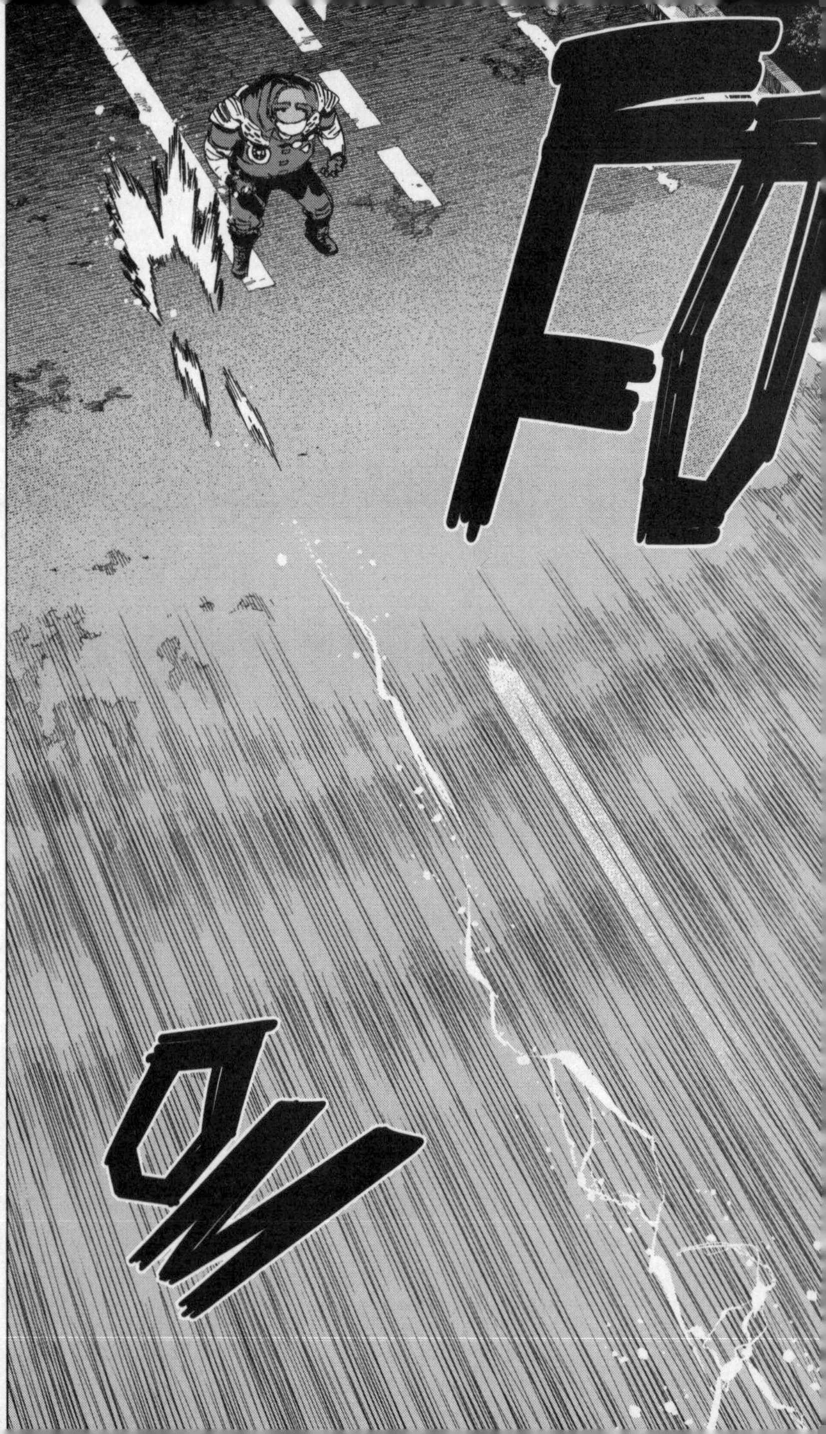

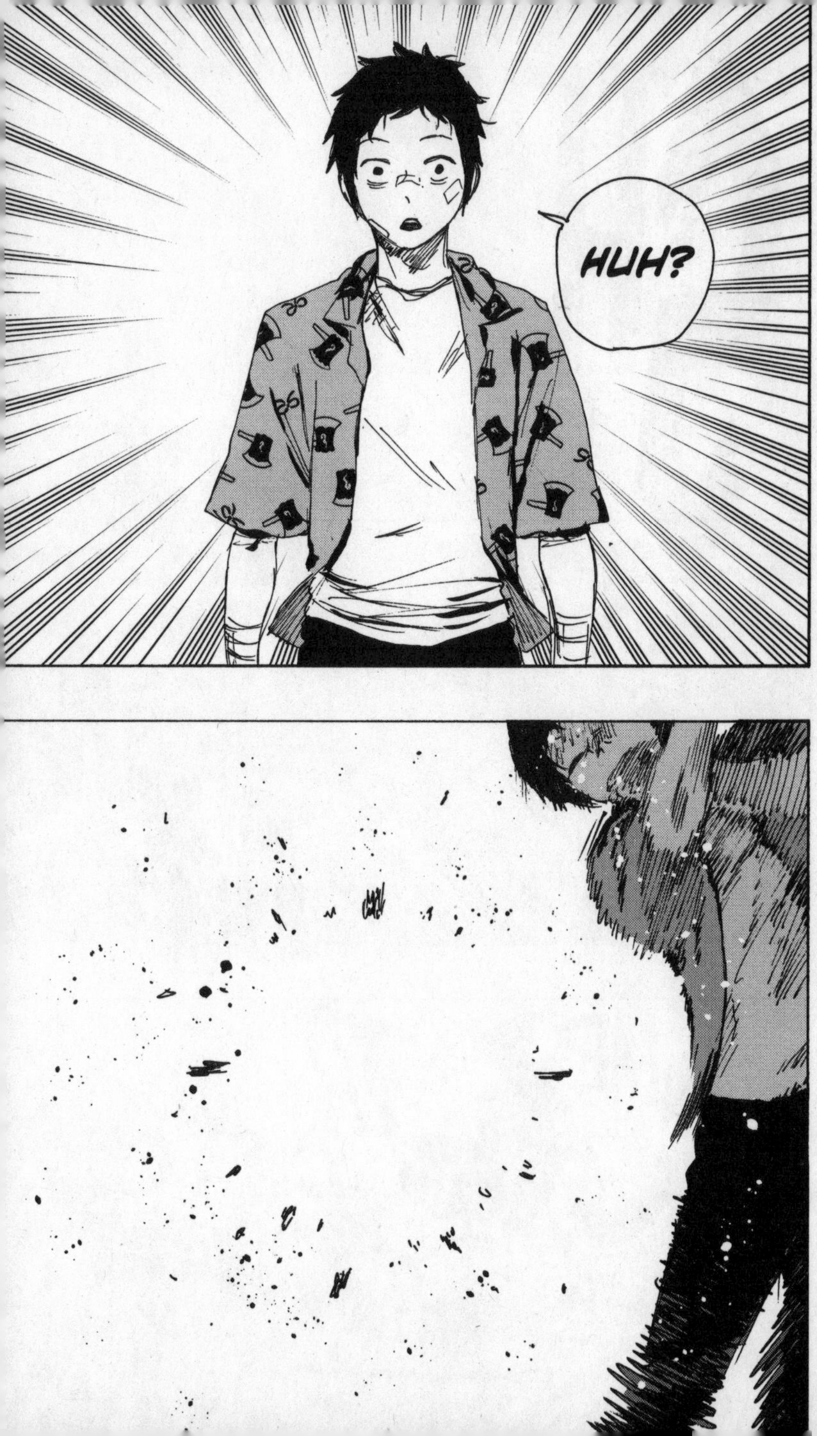
HUH?

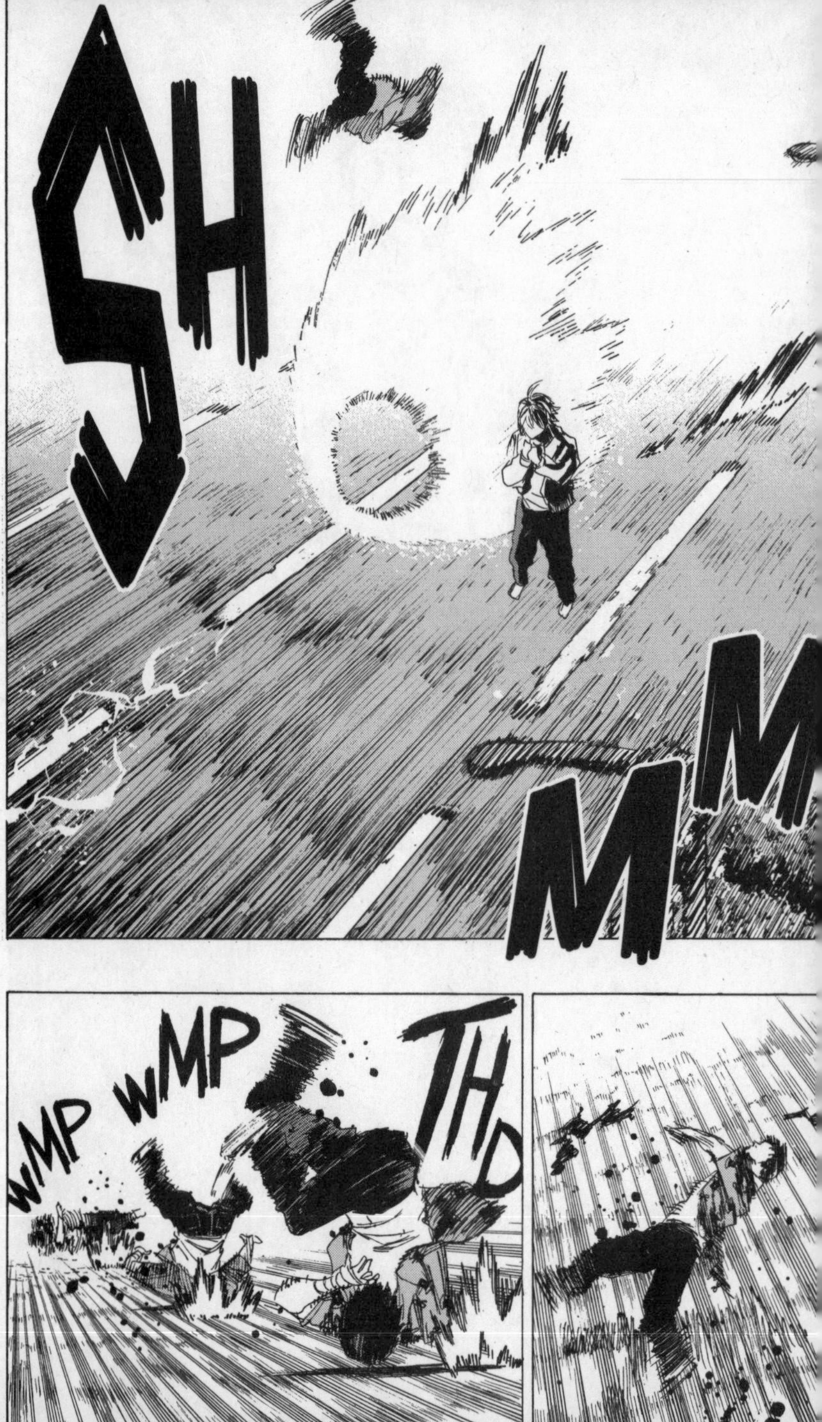
SH
MM
WMP WMP
THD

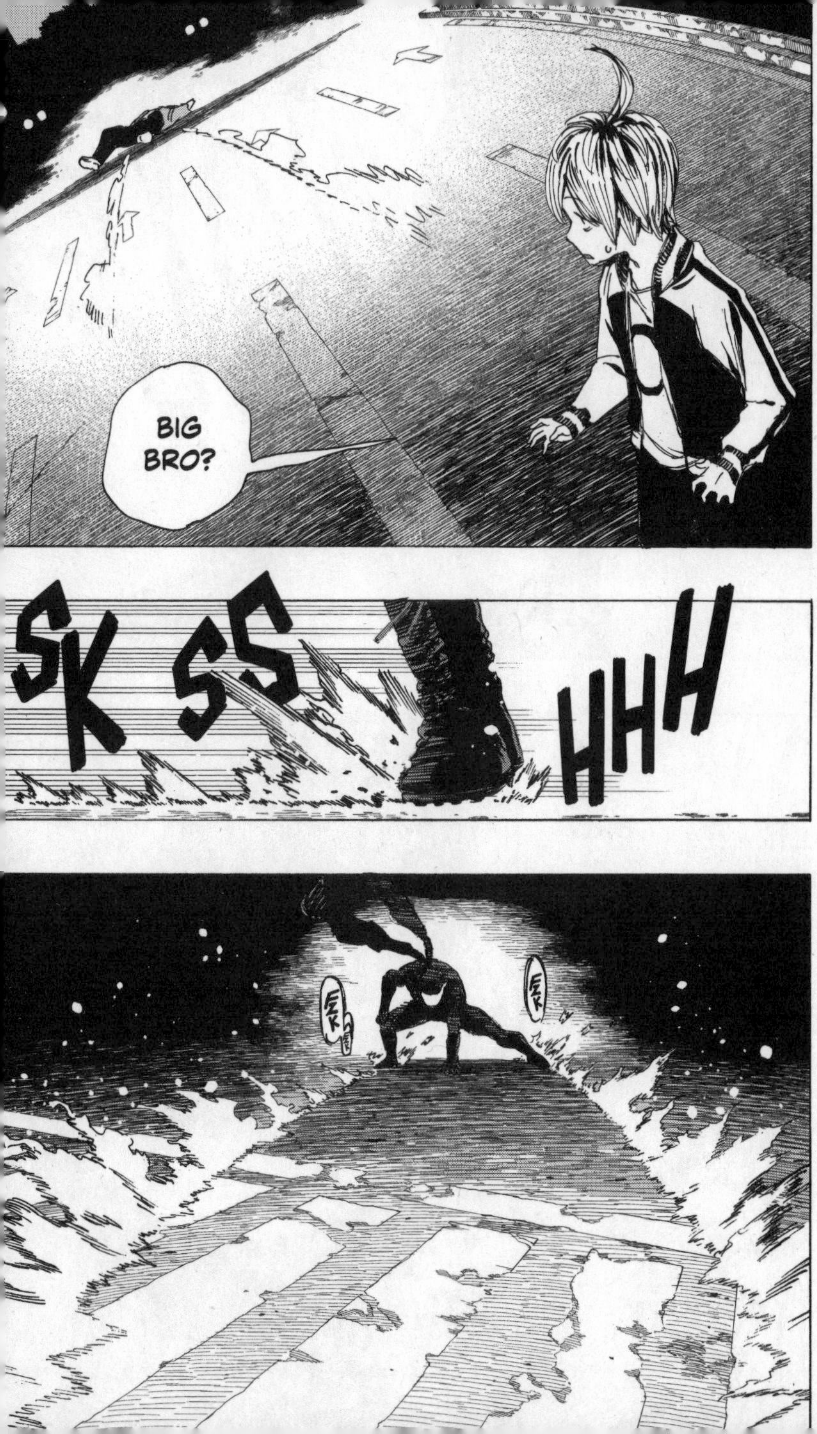
BIG BRO?
SKSSHHH
EEK
EEK
EEK

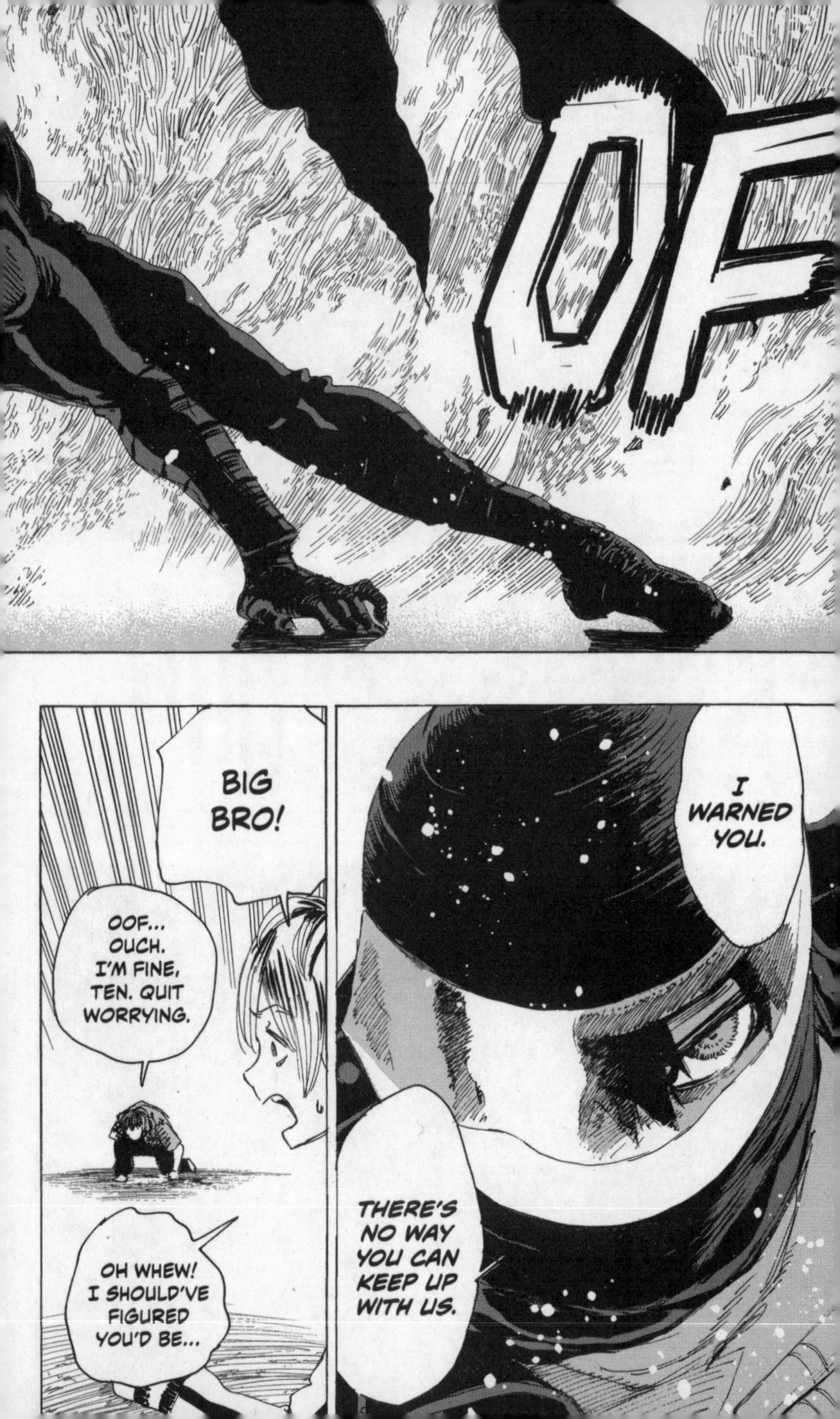
I WARNED YOU.
THERE'S NO WAY YOU CAN KEEP UP WITH US.
BIG BRO!
OOF... OUCH. I'M FINE, TEN. QUIT WORRYING.
OH WHEW! I SHOULD'VE FIGURED YOU'D BE...

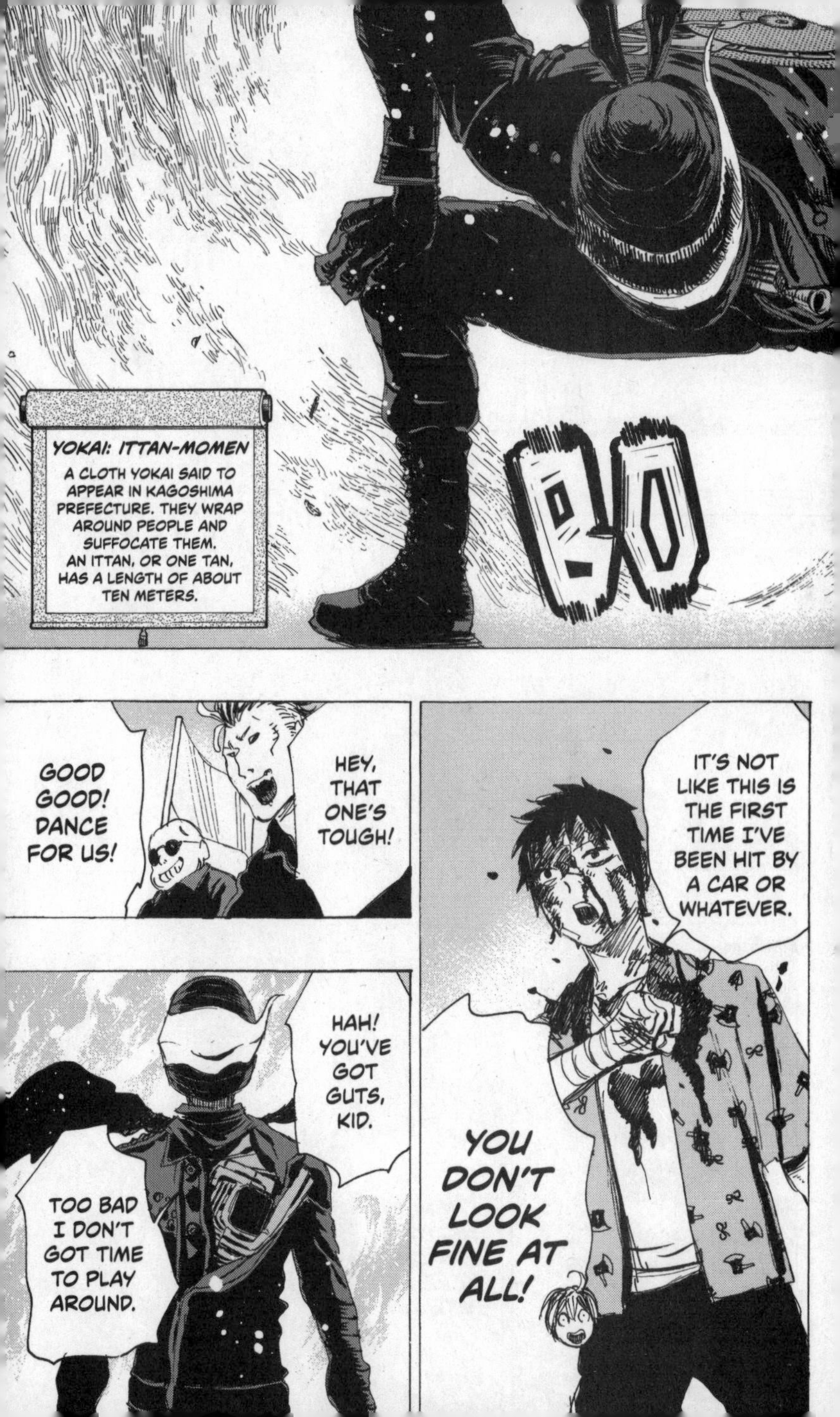
YOKAI: ITTAN-MOMEN
A CLOTH YOKAI SAID TO APPEAR IN KAGOSHIMA PREFECTURE. THEY WRAP AROUND PEOPLE AND SUFFOCATE THEM. AN ITTAN, OR ONE TAN, HAS A LENGTH OF ABOUT TEN METERS.
IT'S NOT LIKE THIS IS THE FIRST TIME I'VE BEEN HIT BY A CAR OR WHATEVER.
YOU DON'T LOOK FINE AT ALL!
HEY, THAT ONE'S TOUGH!
GOOD GOOD! DANCE FOR US!
HAH! YOU'VE GOT GUTS, KID.
TOO BAD I DON'T GOT TIME TO PLAY AROUND.

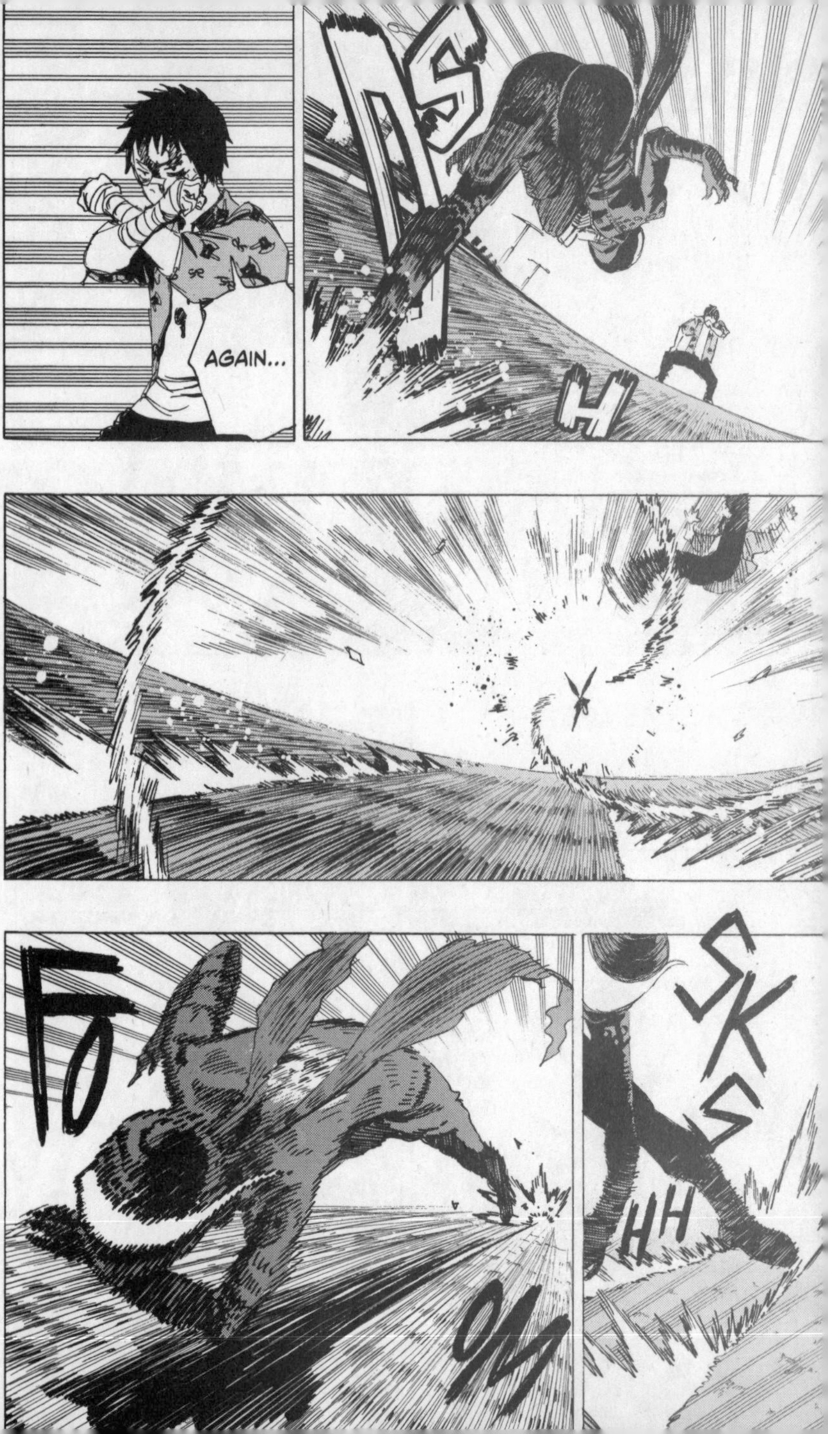

DASH
AGAIN...
SKSHH
FOOM

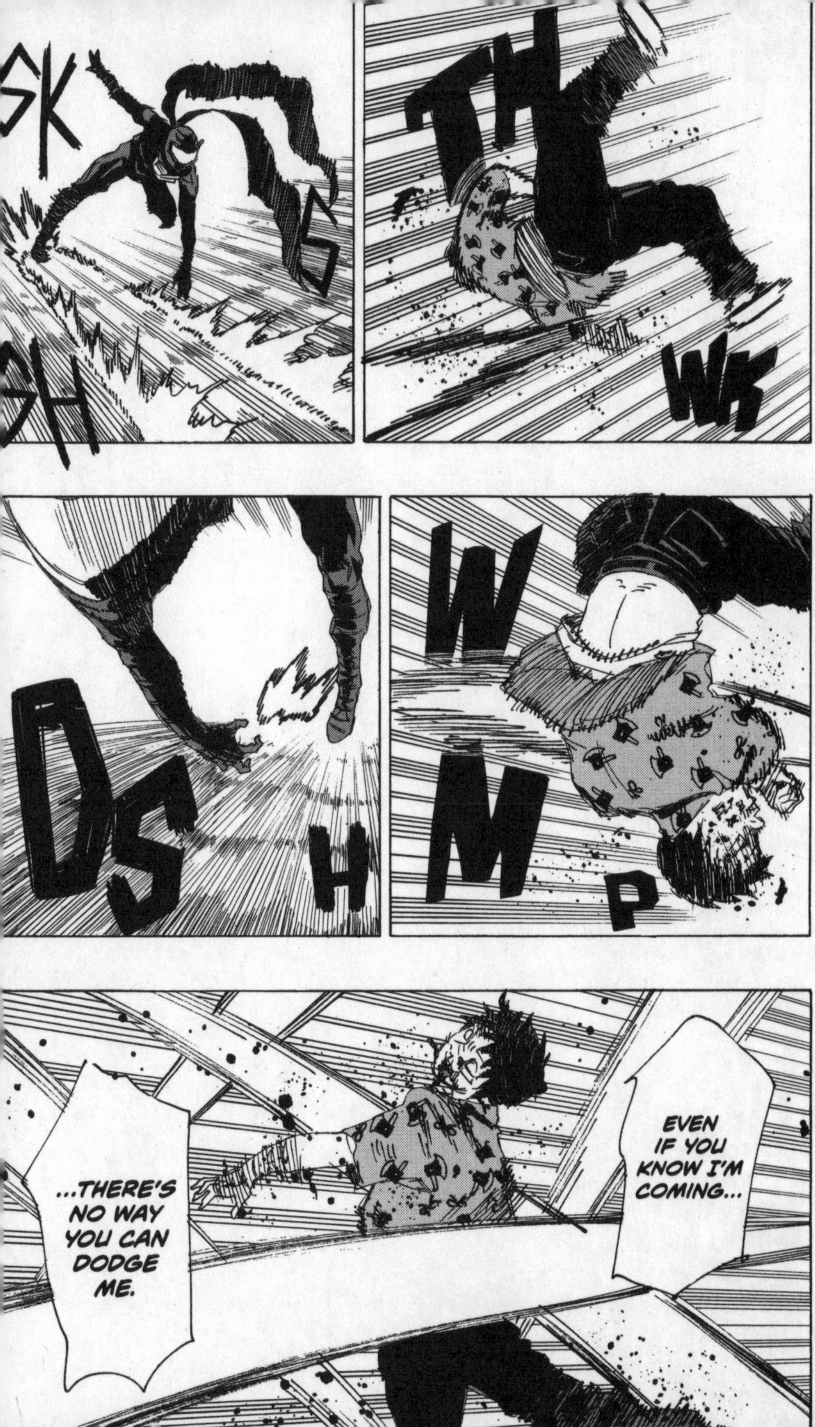
TH
WK
SK
S
SH
W
M
P
D
S
H
EVEN IF YOU KNOW I'M COMING...
...THERE'S NO WAY YOU CAN DODGE ME.

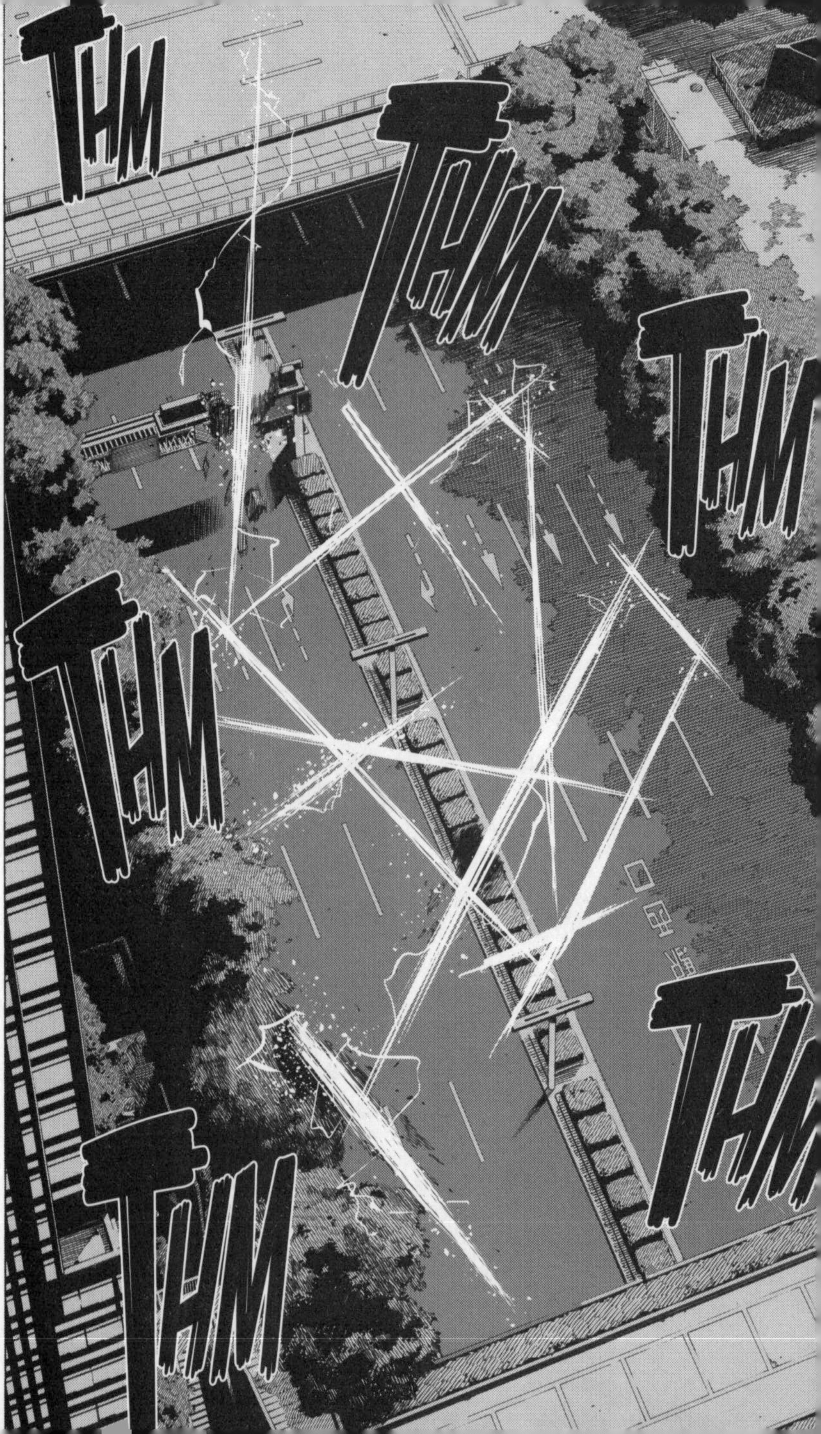
THM
THM
THM
THM
THM
THM

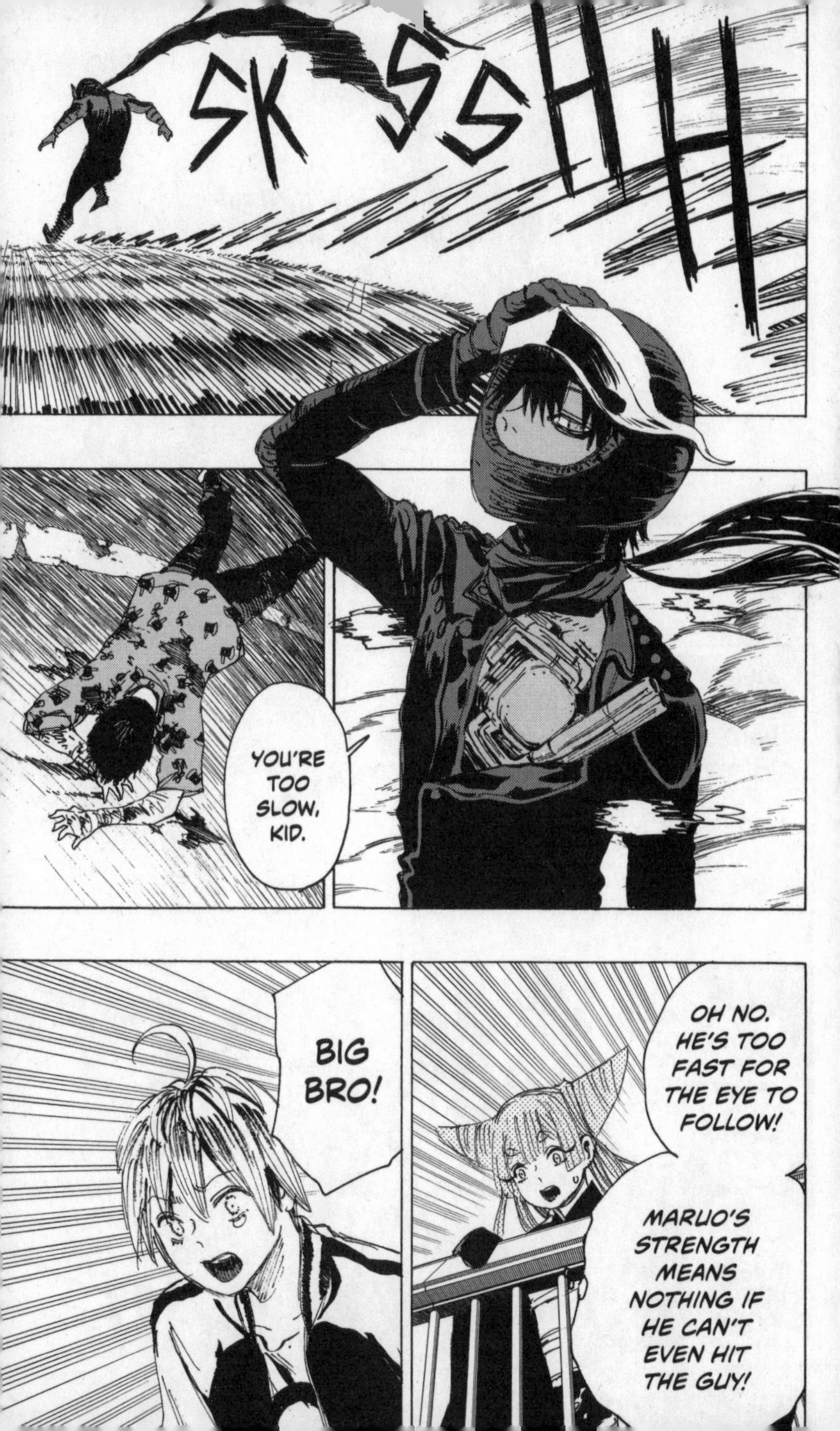
SK SSHH
YOU'RE TOO SLOW, KID.
OH NO. HE'S TOO FAST FOR THE EYE TO FOLLOW!
MARUO'S STRENGTH MEANS NOTHING IF HE CAN'T EVEN HIT THE GUY!
BIG BRO!

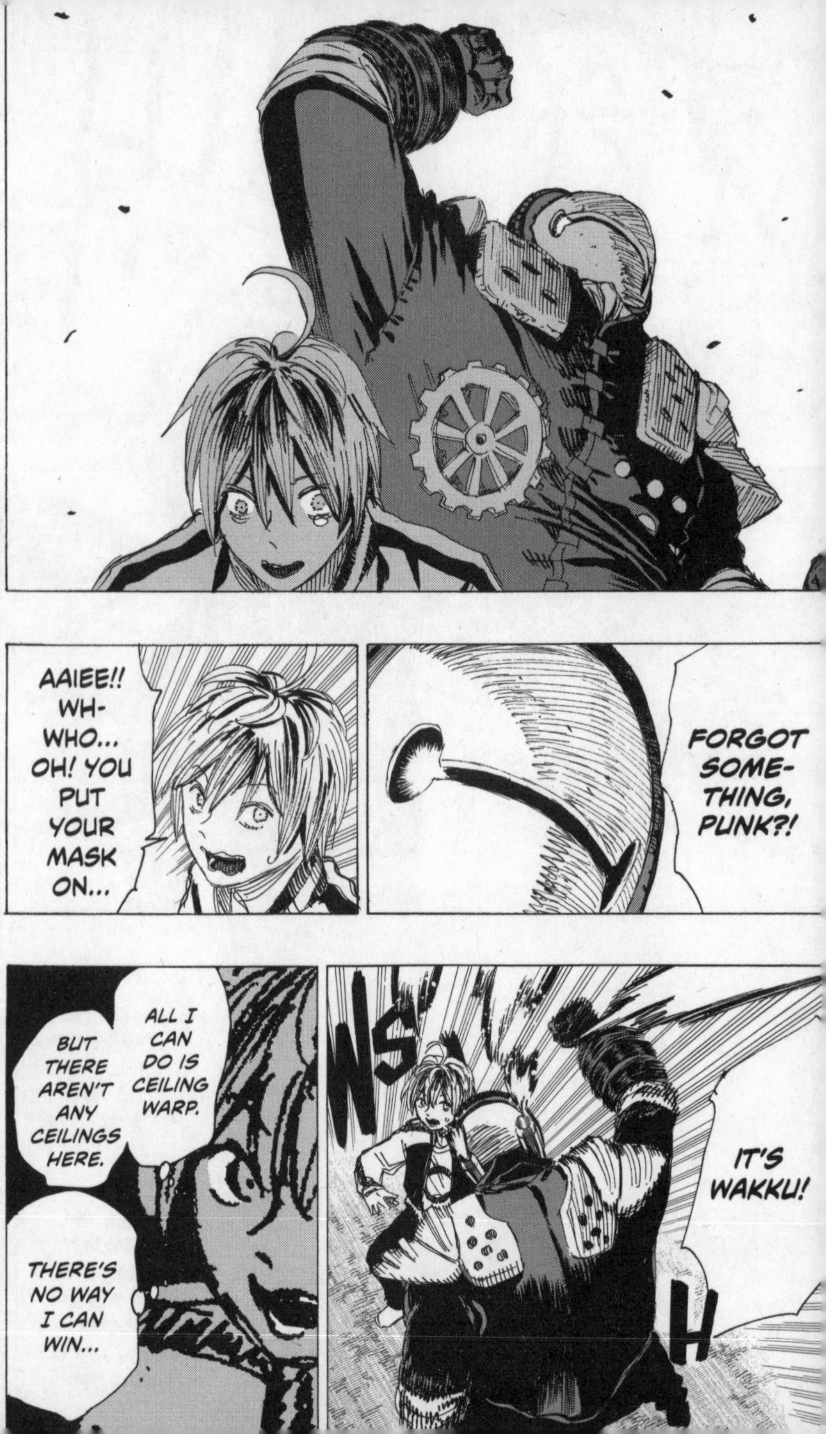
FORGOT SOME-THING, PUNK?!
AAIEE!! WH-WHO... OH! YOU PUT YOUR MASK ON...
IT'S WAKKU!
ALL I CAN DO IS CEILING WARP.
BUT THERE AREN'T ANY CEILINGS HERE.
THERE'S NO WAY I CAN WIN...

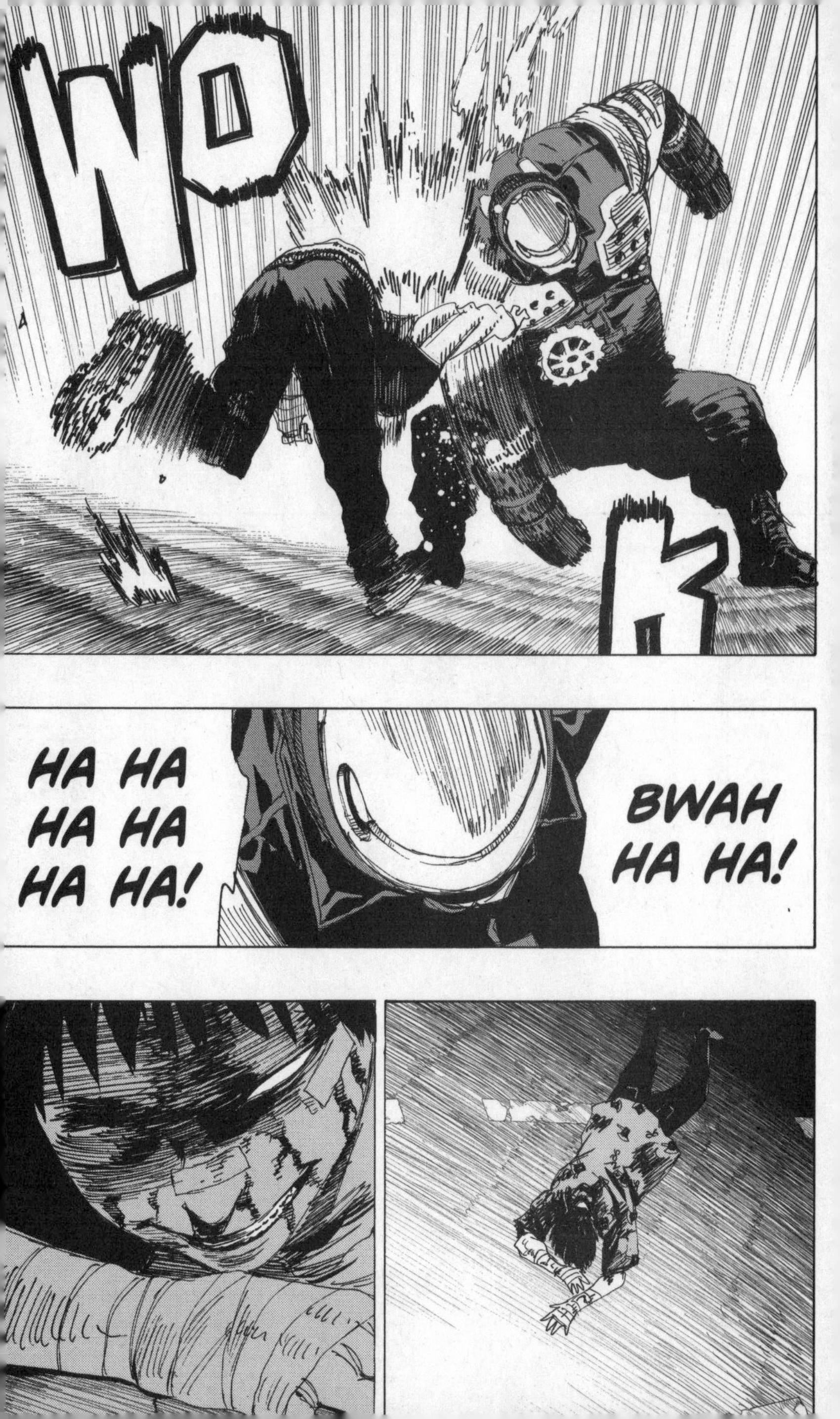
WO
K
BWAH HA HA!
HA HA HA HA HA HA!

KABUKICHO MONSTER MANUAL

Kotton (Ittan-momen)

The Todoroki Alliance's leader. He collects English leather jackets and likes how they feel when worn without a shirt. His motorcycle is a Kawasaki Mach 750SS. He is very, very impatient.

His scarf is not an accessory but part of his body. It never gets caught in his motorcycle's wheels.

Chapter 14: What About You?

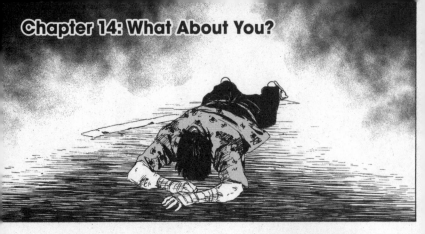

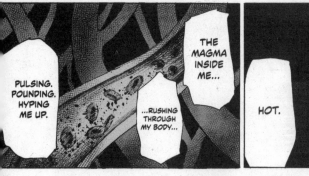

BLOOD.
HOT.
PULS-ING.
THE MAGMA INSIDE ME...
...RUSHING THROUGH MY BODY...
PULSING. POUNDING. HYPING ME UP.
GEH HEH...
GEH HEH HEH...
HEH HEH HEH!

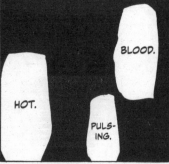

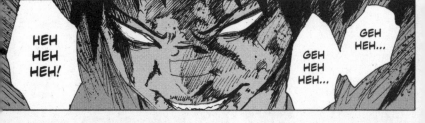

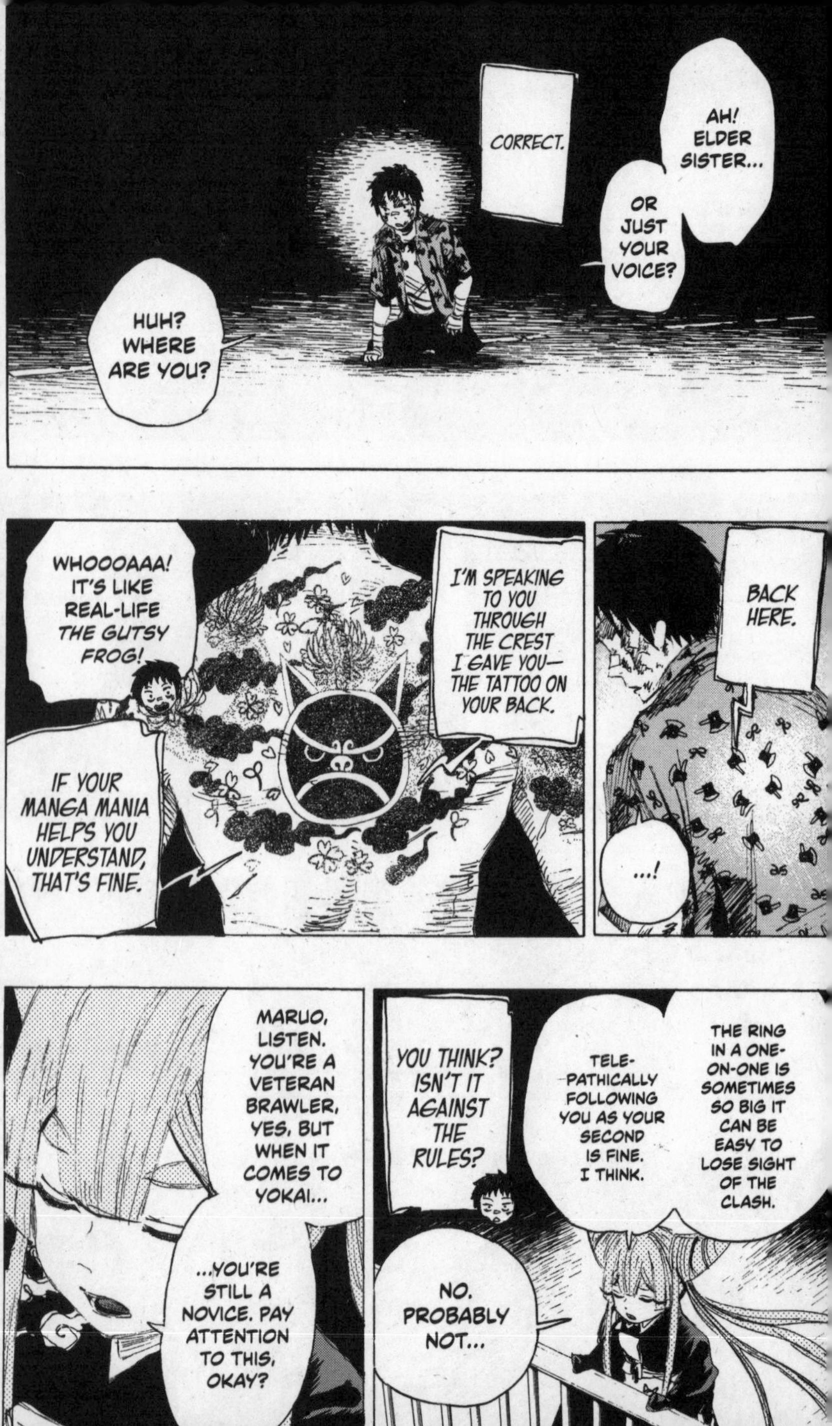

AH! ELDER SISTER...
OR JUST YOUR VOICE?
CORRECT.
HUH? WHERE ARE YOU?
BACK HERE.
...!
I'M SPEAKING TO YOU THROUGH THE CREST I GAVE YOU—THE TATTOO ON YOUR BACK.
WHOOOAAA! IT'S LIKE REAL-LIFE THE GUTSY FROG!
IF YOUR MANGA MANIA HELPS YOU UNDERSTAND, THAT'S FINE.
THE RING IN A ONE-ON-ONE IS SOMETIMES SO BIG IT CAN BE EASY TO LOSE SIGHT OF THE CLASH.
TELE-PATHICALLY FOLLOWING YOU AS YOUR SECOND IS FINE. I THINK.
YOU THINK? ISN'T IT AGAINST THE RULES?
NO. PROBABLY NOT...
MARUO, LISTEN. YOU'RE A VETERAN BRAWLER, YES, BUT WHEN IT COMES TO YOKAI...
...YOU'RE STILL A NOVICE. PAY ATTENTION TO THIS, OKAY?

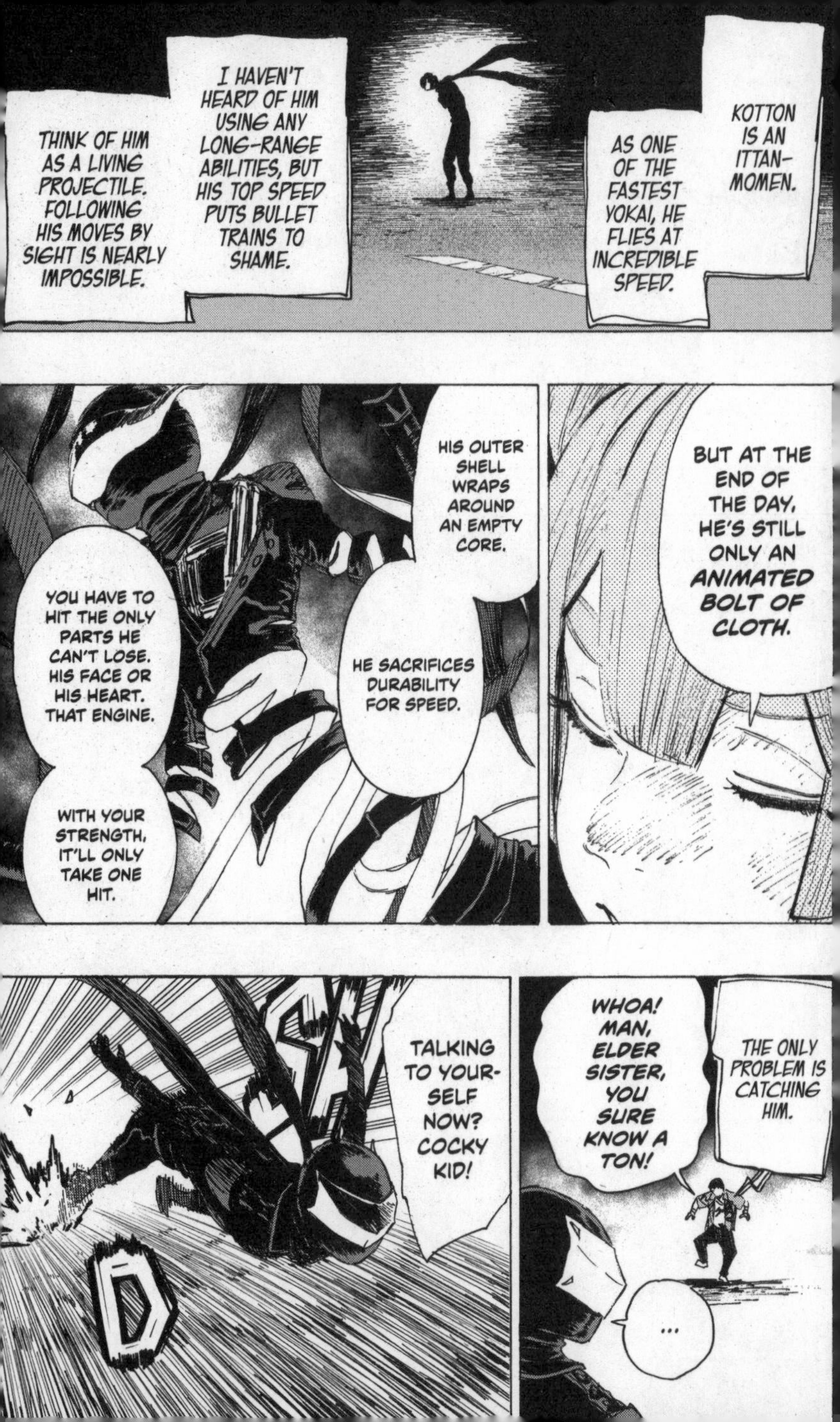
KOTTON IS AN ITTAN-MOMEN.
AS ONE OF THE FASTEST YOKAI, HE FLIES AT INCREDIBLE SPEED.
I HAVEN'T HEARD OF HIM USING ANY LONG-RANGE ABILITIES, BUT HIS TOP SPEED PUTS BULLET TRAINS TO SHAME.
THINK OF HIM AS A LIVING PROJECTILE. FOLLOWING HIS MOVES BY SIGHT IS NEARLY IMPOSSIBLE.
BUT AT THE END OF THE DAY, HE'S STILL ONLY AN ***ANIMATED BOLT OF CLOTH.***
HIS OUTER SHELL WRAPS AROUND AN EMPTY CORE.
HE SACRIFICES DURABILITY FOR SPEED.
YOU HAVE TO HIT THE ONLY PARTS HE CAN'T LOSE. HIS FACE OR HIS HEART. THAT ENGINE.
WITH YOUR STRENGTH, IT'LL ONLY TAKE ONE HIT.
THE ONLY PROBLEM IS CATCHING HIM.
WHOA! MAN, ELDER SISTER, YOU SURE KNOW A TON!
...
TALKING TO YOUR-SELF NOW? COCKY KID!

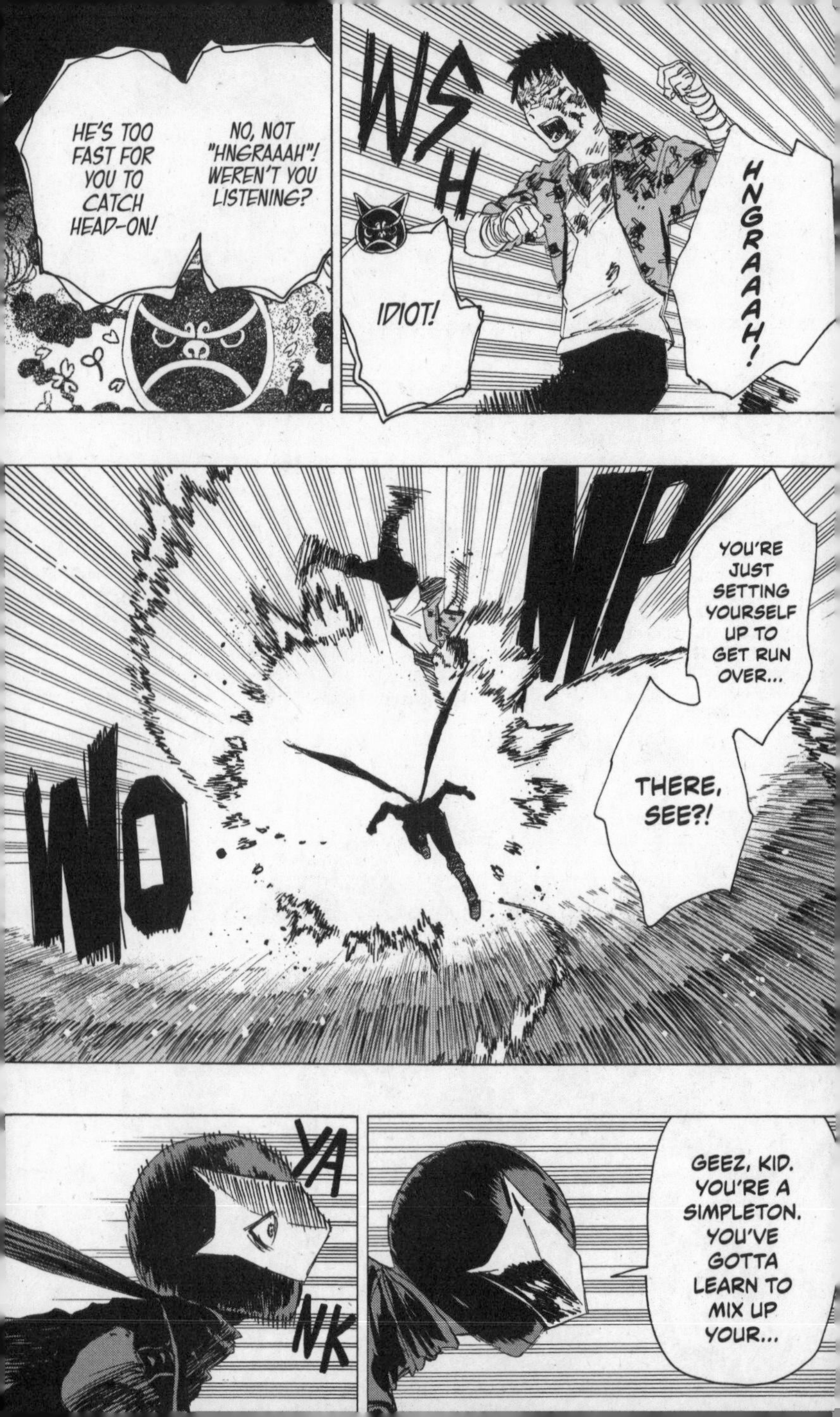
WSH
HNGRAAAH!
IDIOT!
NO, NOT "HNGRAAAH"! WEREN'T YOU LISTENING?
HE'S TOO FAST FOR YOU TO CATCH HEAD-ON!
YOU'RE JUST SETTING YOURSELF UP TO GET RUN OVER...
THERE, SEE?!
WO
GEEZ, KID. YOU'RE A SIMPLETON. YOU'VE GOTTA LEARN TO MIX UP YOUR...
YA
NK

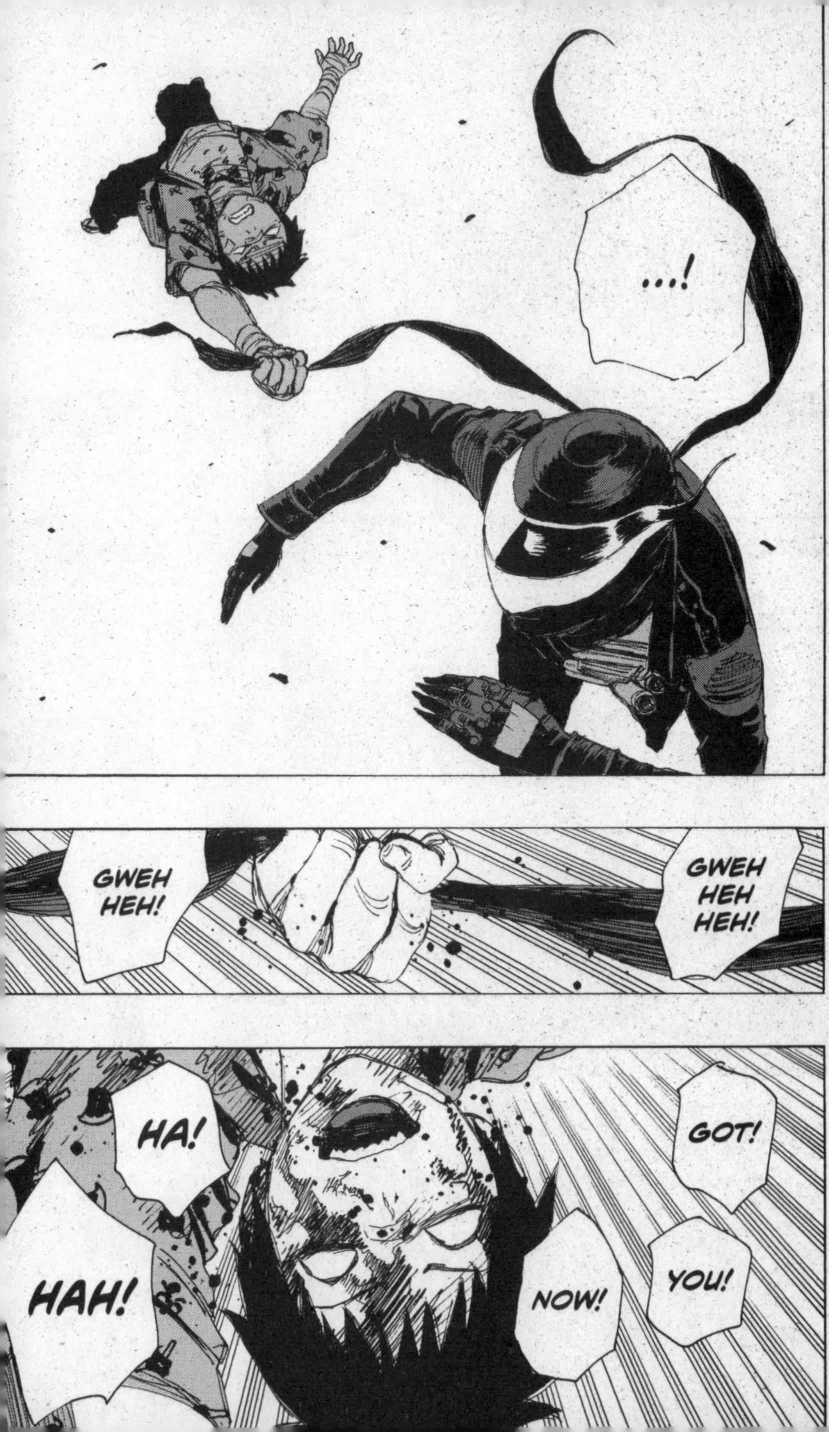
...!
GWEH HEH HEH!
GWEH HEH!
GOT!
YOU!
NOW!
HA!
HAH!

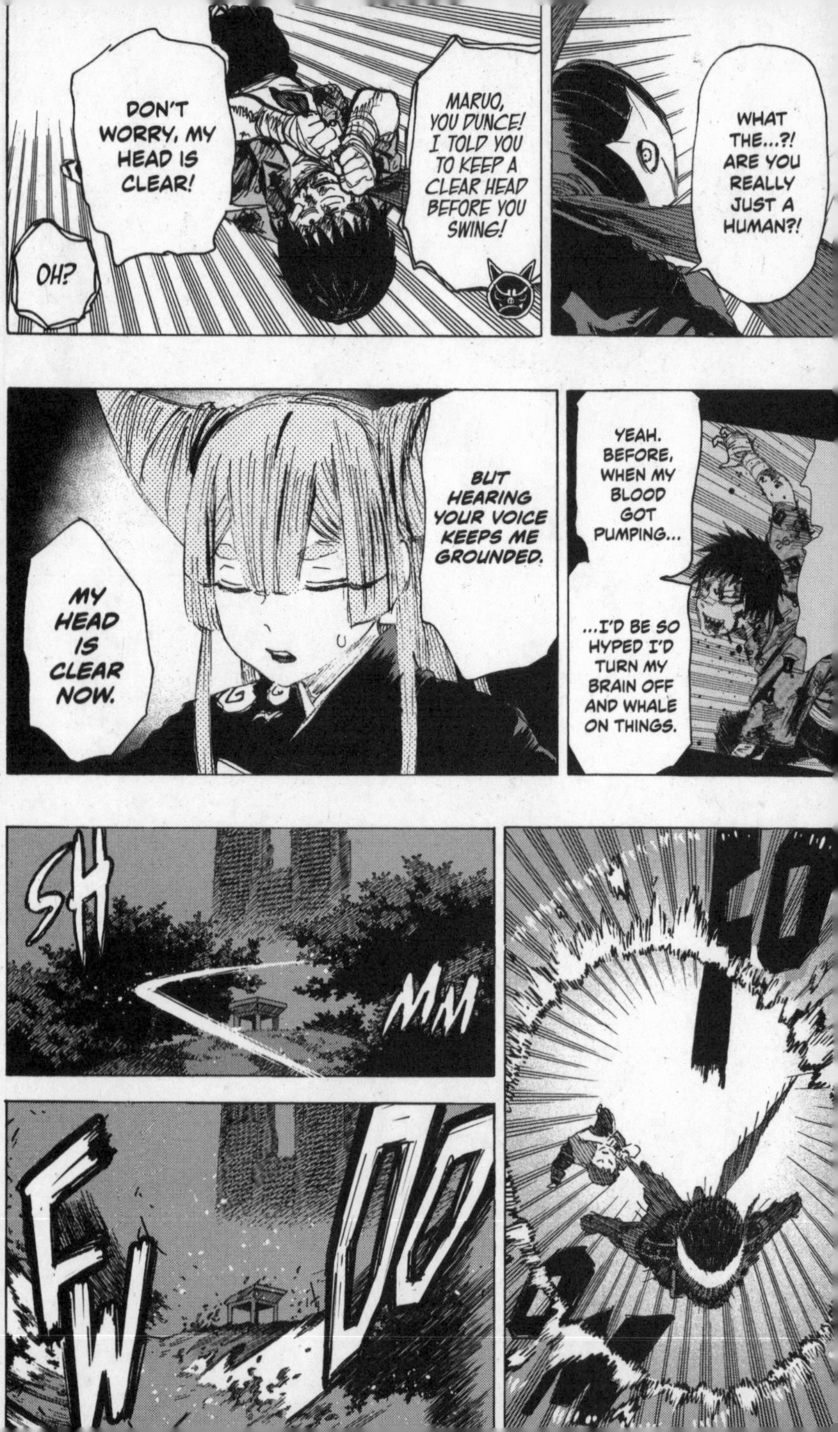
WHAT THE...?! ARE YOU REALLY JUST A HUMAN?!
MARUO, YOU DUNCE! I TOLD YOU TO KEEP A CLEAR HEAD BEFORE YOU SWING!
DON'T WORRY, MY HEAD IS CLEAR!
OH?
YEAH. BEFORE, WHEN MY BLOOD GOT PUMPING...
...I'D BE SO HYPED I'D TURN MY BRAIN OFF AND WHALE ON THINGS.
BUT HEARING YOUR VOICE KEEPS ME GROUNDED.
MY HEAD IS CLEAR NOW.
CO
SH
MM
FW
OO

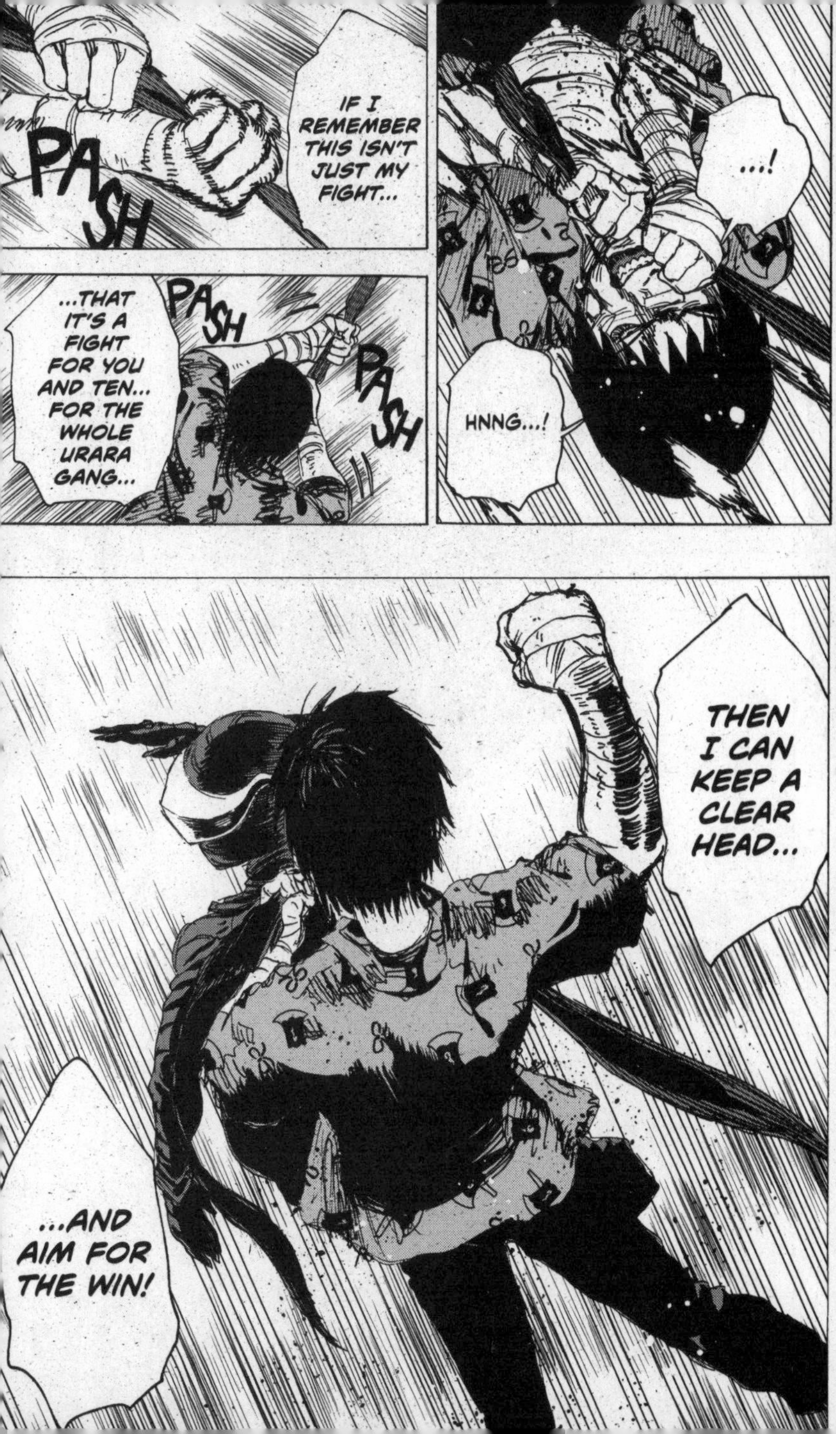
...!
HNNG...!
IF I REMEMBER THIS ISN'T JUST MY FIGHT...
PASH
...THAT IT'S A FIGHT FOR YOU AND TEN... FOR THE WHOLE URARA GANG...
PASH
PASH
THEN I CAN KEEP A CLEAR HEAD...
...AND AIM FOR THE WIN!

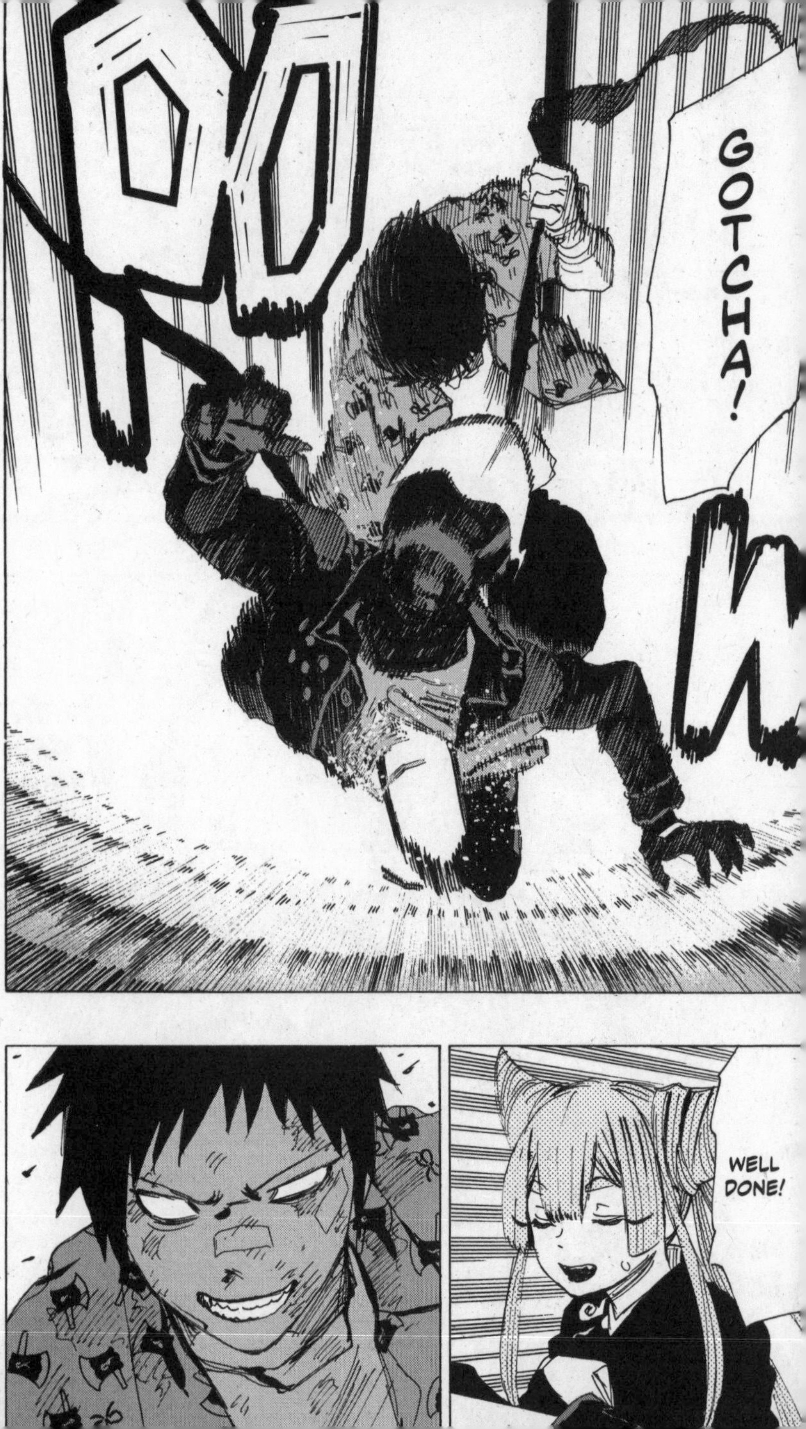
GOTCHA!
WELL DONE!

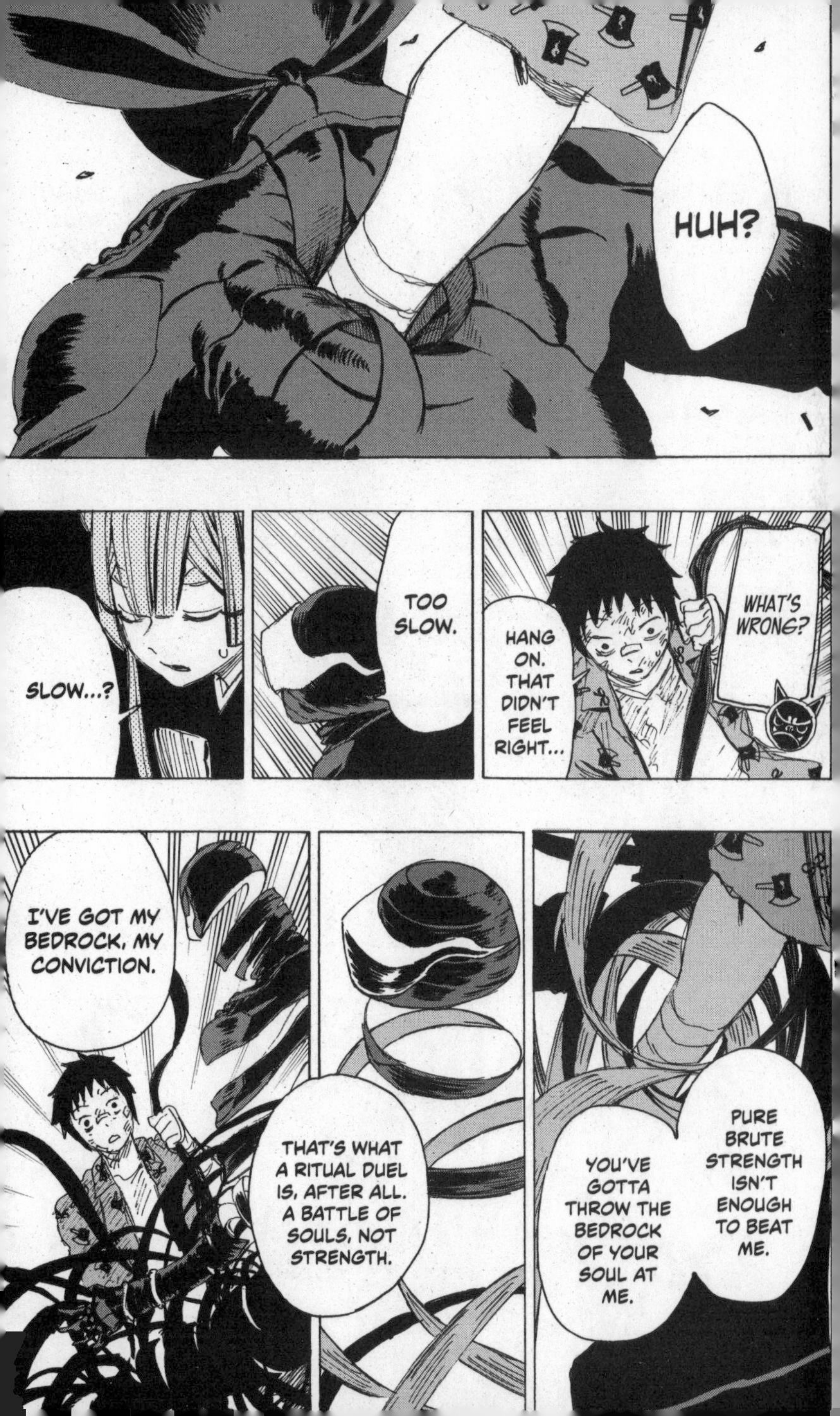
HUH?
WHAT'S WRONG?
HANG ON. THAT DIDN'T FEEL RIGHT...
TOO SLOW.
SLOW...?
PURE BRUTE STRENGTH ISN'T ENOUGH TO BEAT ME.
YOU'VE GOTTA THROW THE BEDROCK OF YOUR SOUL AT ME.
THAT'S WHAT A RITUAL DUEL IS, AFTER ALL. A BATTLE OF SOULS, NOT STRENGTH.
I'VE GOT MY BEDROCK, MY CONVICTION.

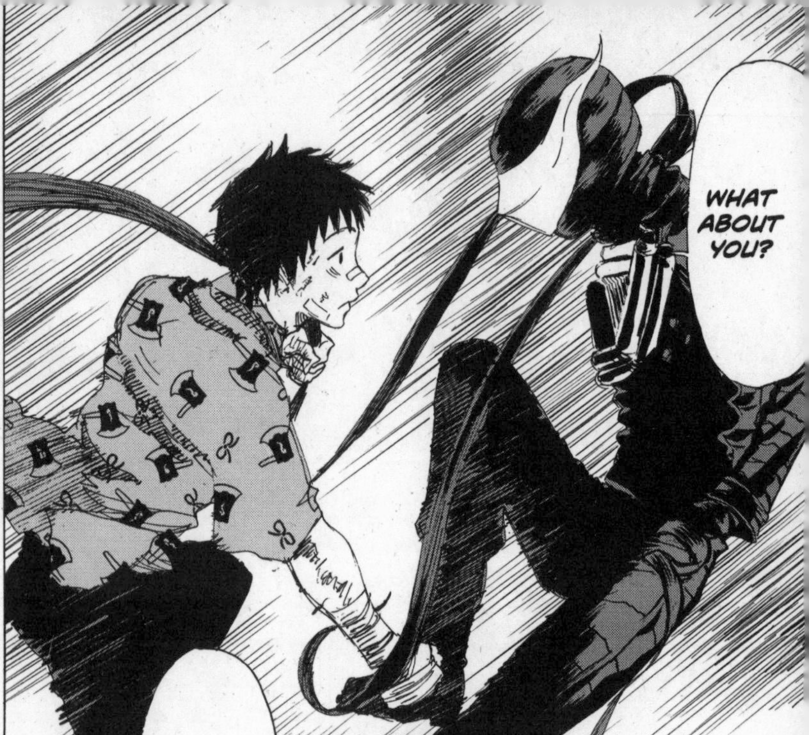
WHAT ABOUT YOU?
KID.

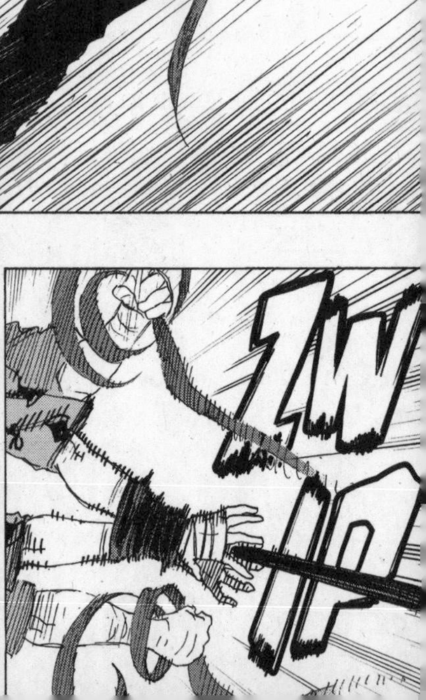

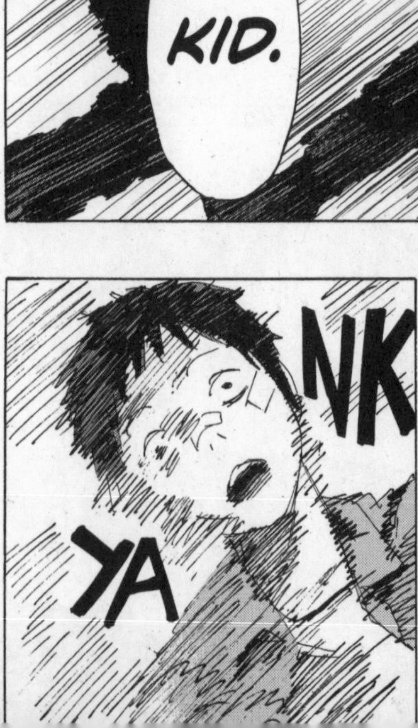
YA
NK

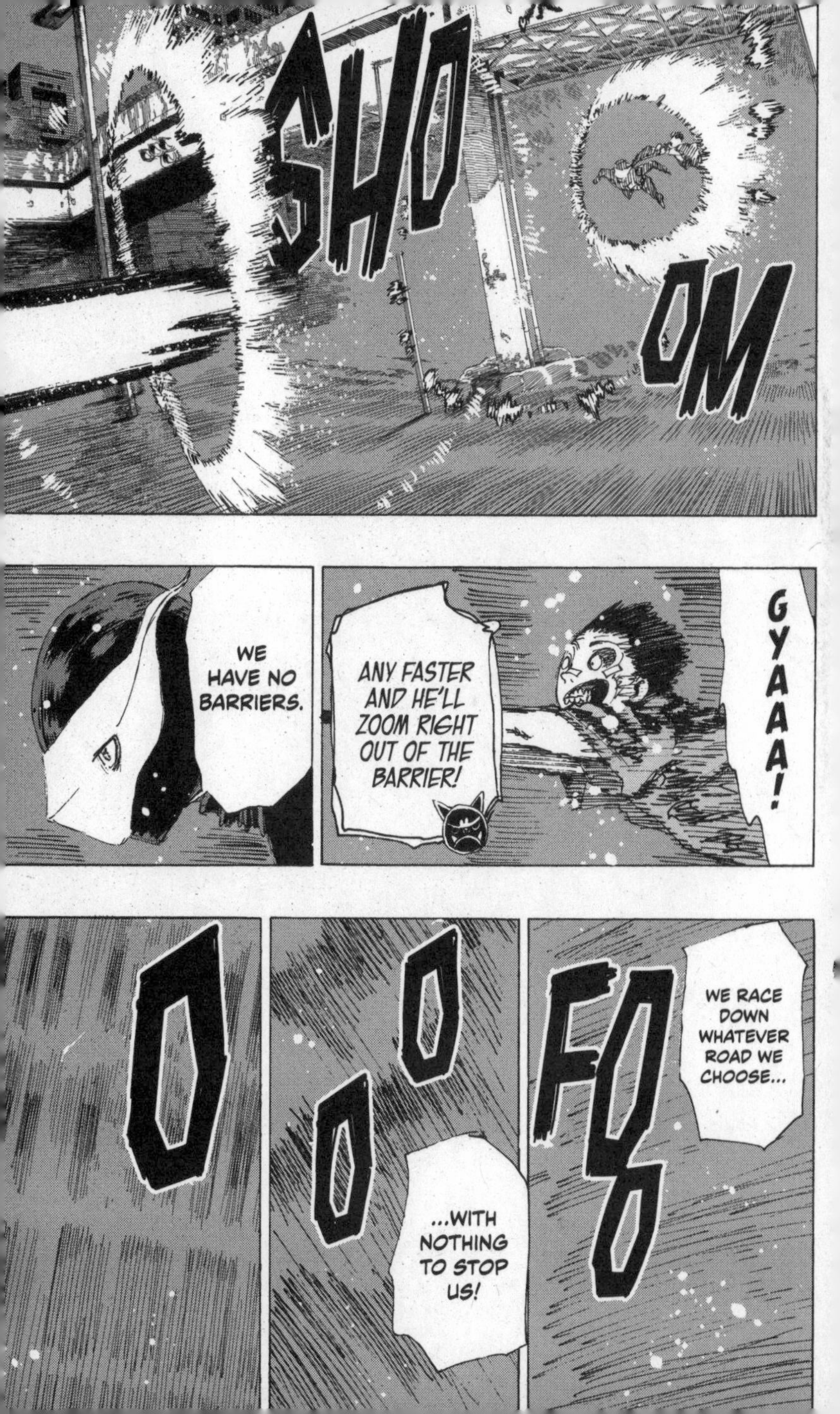
SHO
OM
GYAAA!
ANY FASTER AND HE'LL ZOOM RIGHT OUT OF THE BARRIER!
WE HAVE NO BARRIERS.
WE RACE DOWN WHATEVER ROAD WE CHOOSE...
...WITH NOTHING TO STOP US!

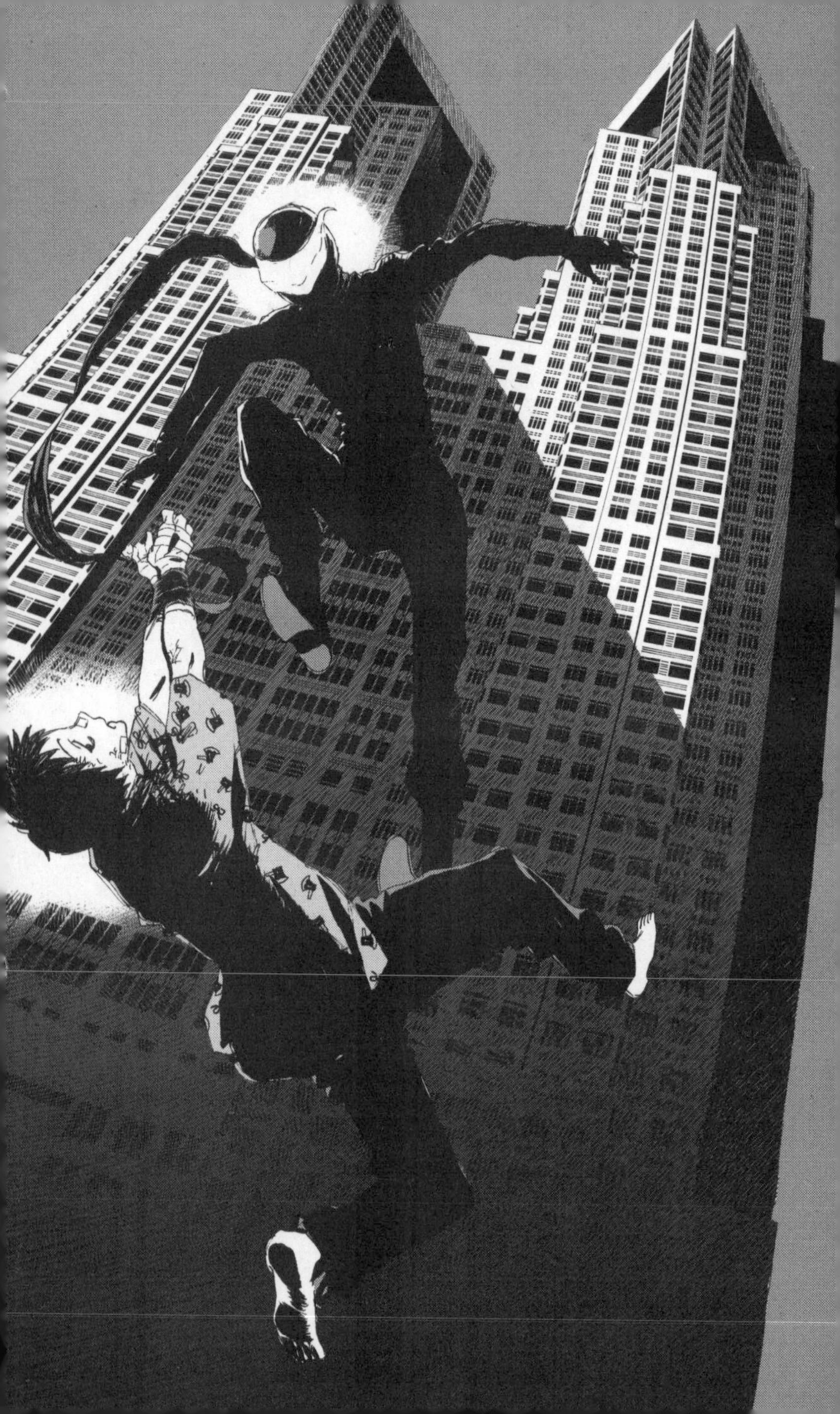

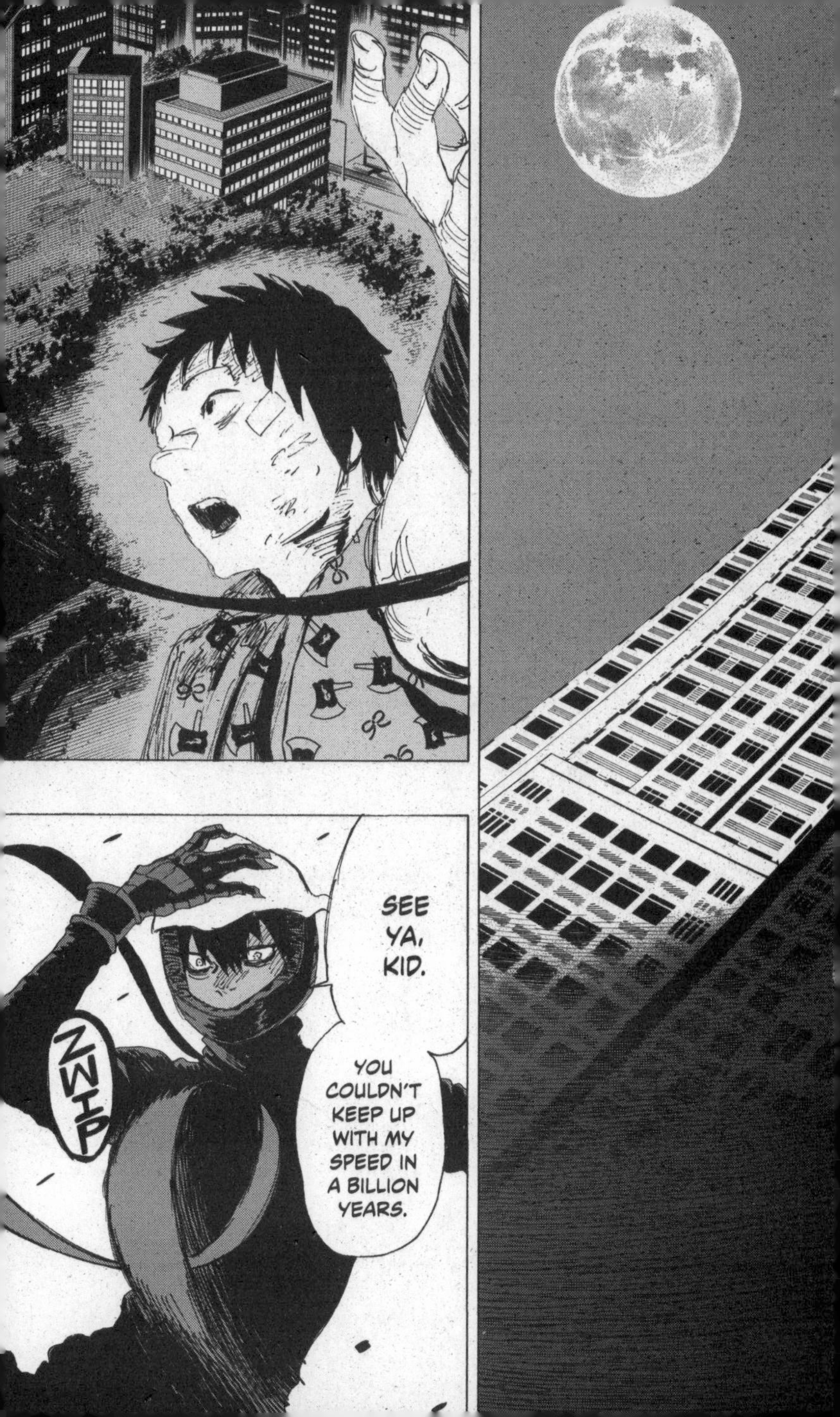
SEE YA, KID.
YOU COULDN'T KEEP UP WITH MY SPEED IN A BILLION YEARS.
ZWIP

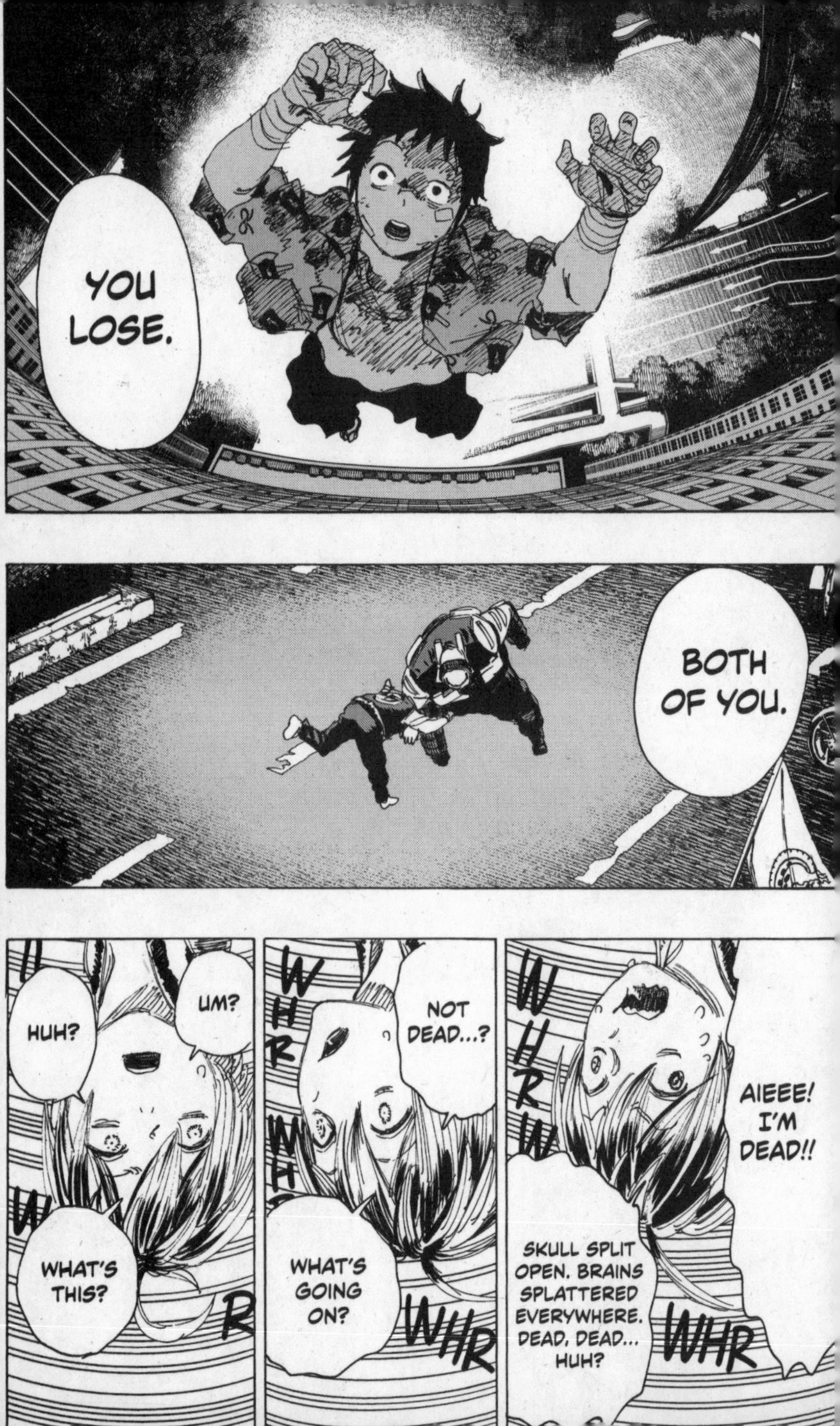
YOU LOSE.
BOTH OF YOU.
WHRW
AIEEE! I'M DEAD!!
SKULL SPLIT OPEN. BRAINS SPLATTERED EVERYWHERE. DEAD, DEAD... HUH?
WHR
WHR
NOT DEAD...?
WHAT'S GOING ON?
WHR
UM?
HUH?
WHAT'S THIS?
R

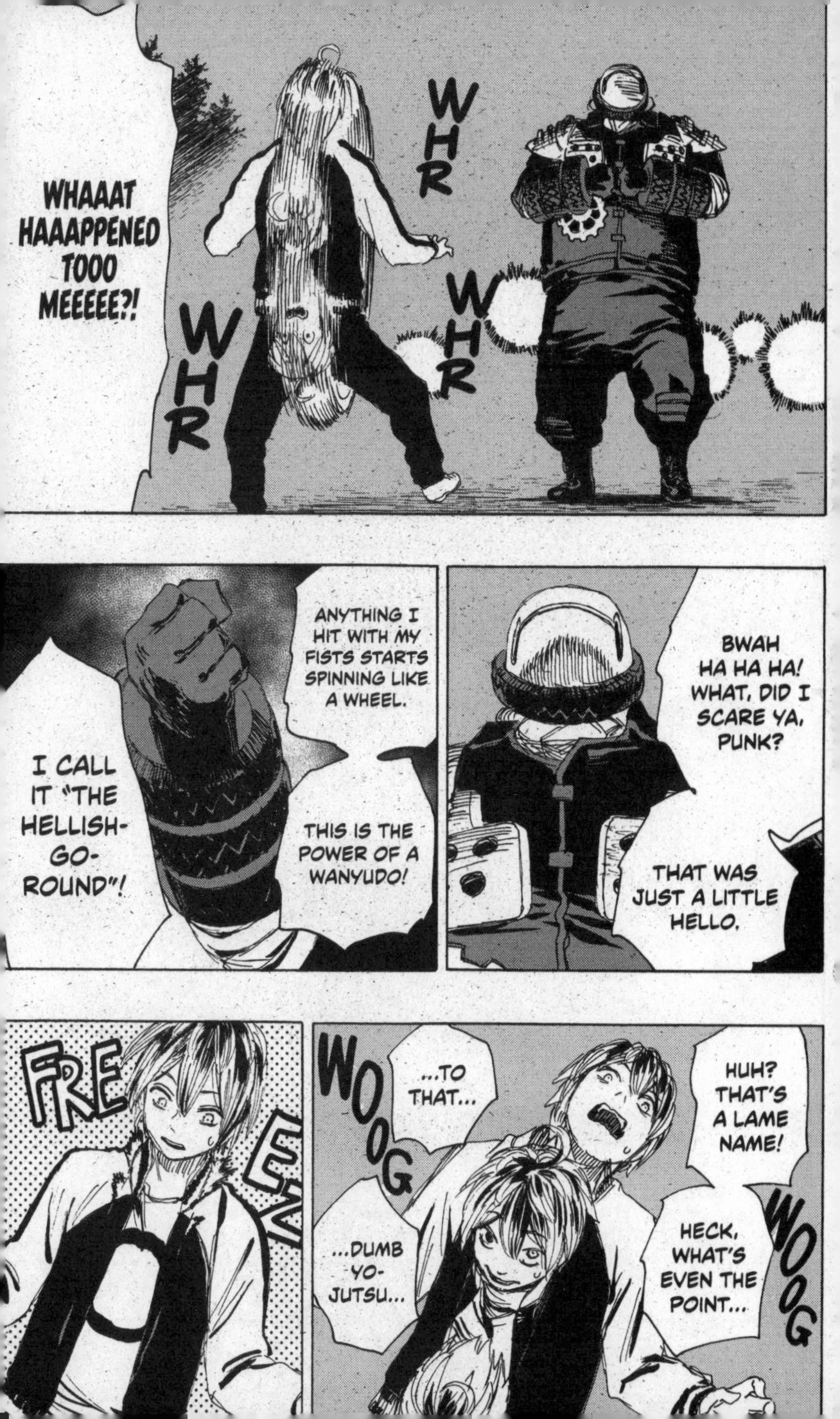
WHR
WHR
WHAAAT HAAAPPENED TOOO MEEEEE?!
WHR
BWAH HA HA HA! WHAT, DID I SCARE YA, PUNK?
THAT WAS JUST A LITTLE HELLO.
ANYTHING I HIT WITH MY FISTS STARTS SPINNING LIKE A WHEEL.
THIS IS THE POWER OF A WANYUDO!
I CALL IT "THE HELLISH-GO-ROUND"!
HUH? THAT'S A LAME NAME!
...TO THAT...
WOOG
WOOG
HECK, WHAT'S EVEN THE POINT...
...DUMB YO-JUTSU...
FREEZ

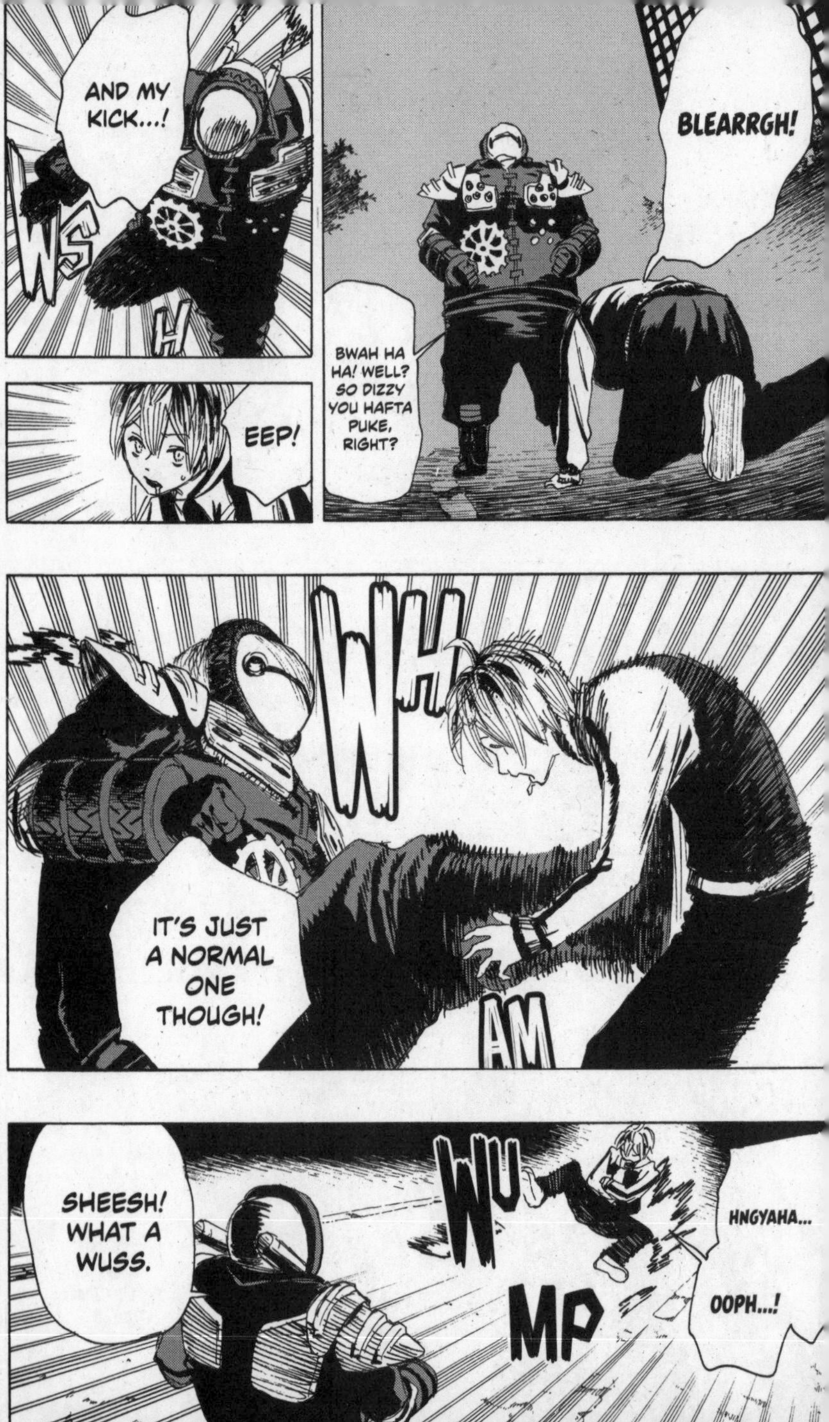
BLEARRGH!
BWAH HA HA! WELL? SO DIZZY YOU HAFTA PUKE, RIGHT?
AND MY KICK...!
WSH
EEP!
WH
IT'S JUST A NORMAL ONE THOUGH!
AM
HNGYAHA...
OOPH...!
WU
MP
SHEESH! WHAT A WUSS.

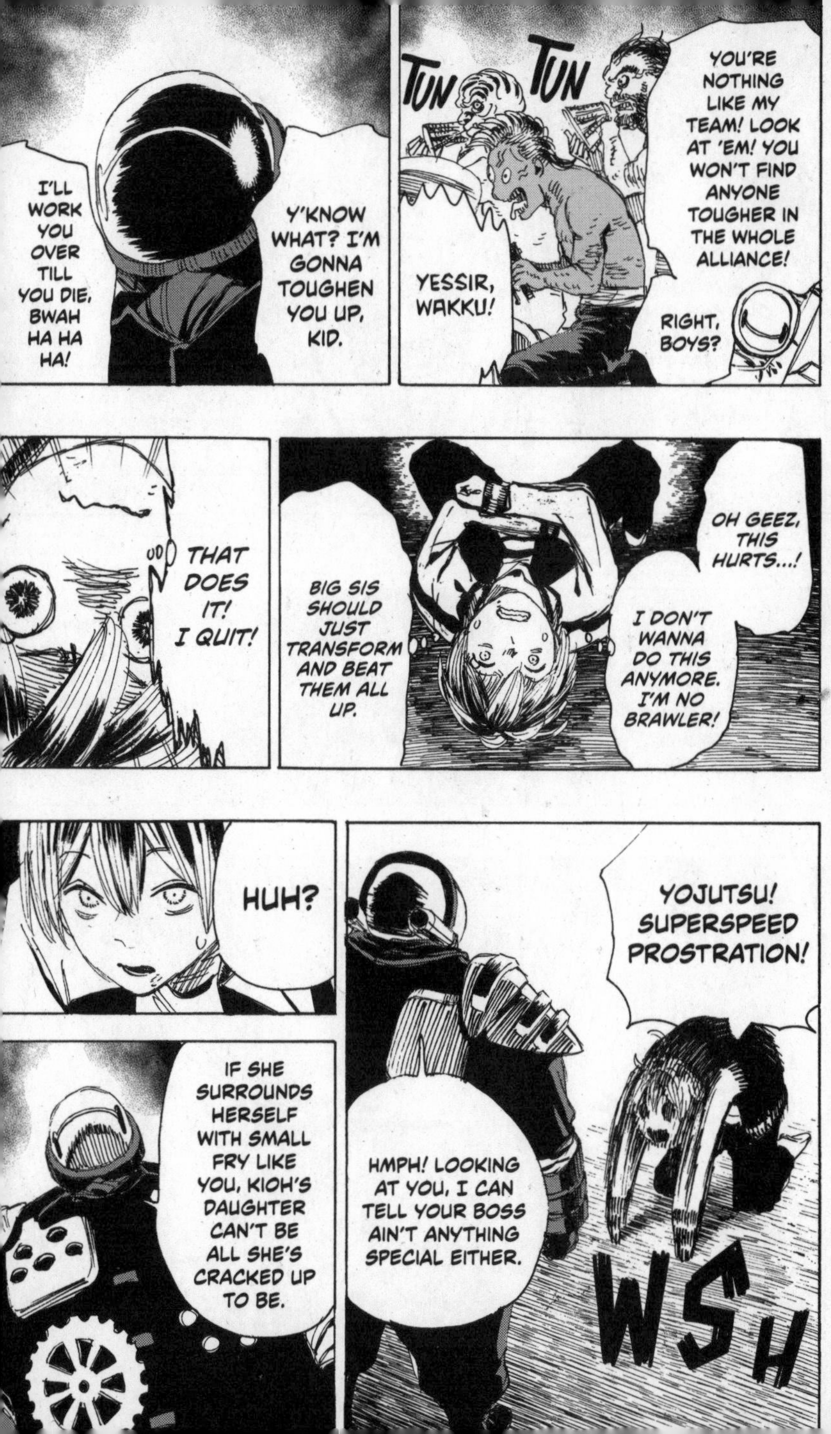
YOU'RE NOTHING LIKE MY TEAM! LOOK AT 'EM! YOU WON'T FIND ANYONE TOUGHER IN THE WHOLE ALLIANCE!
TUN
TUN
RIGHT, BOYS?
YESSIR, WAKKU!
Y'KNOW WHAT? I'M GONNA TOUGHEN YOU UP, KID.
I'LL WORK YOU OVER TILL YOU DIE, BWAH HA HA HA!
OH GEEZ, THIS HURTS...!
I DON'T WANNA DO THIS ANYMORE. I'M NO BRAWLER!
BIG SIS SHOULD JUST TRANSFORM AND BEAT THEM ALL UP.
THAT DOES IT! I QUIT!
YOJUTSU! SUPERSPEED PROSTRATION!
WSH
HMPH! LOOKING AT YOU, I CAN TELL YOUR BOSS AIN'T ANYTHING SPECIAL EITHER.
HUH?
IF SHE SURROUNDS HERSELF WITH SMALL FRY LIKE YOU, KIOH'S DAUGHTER CAN'T BE ALL SHE'S CRACKED UP TO BE.

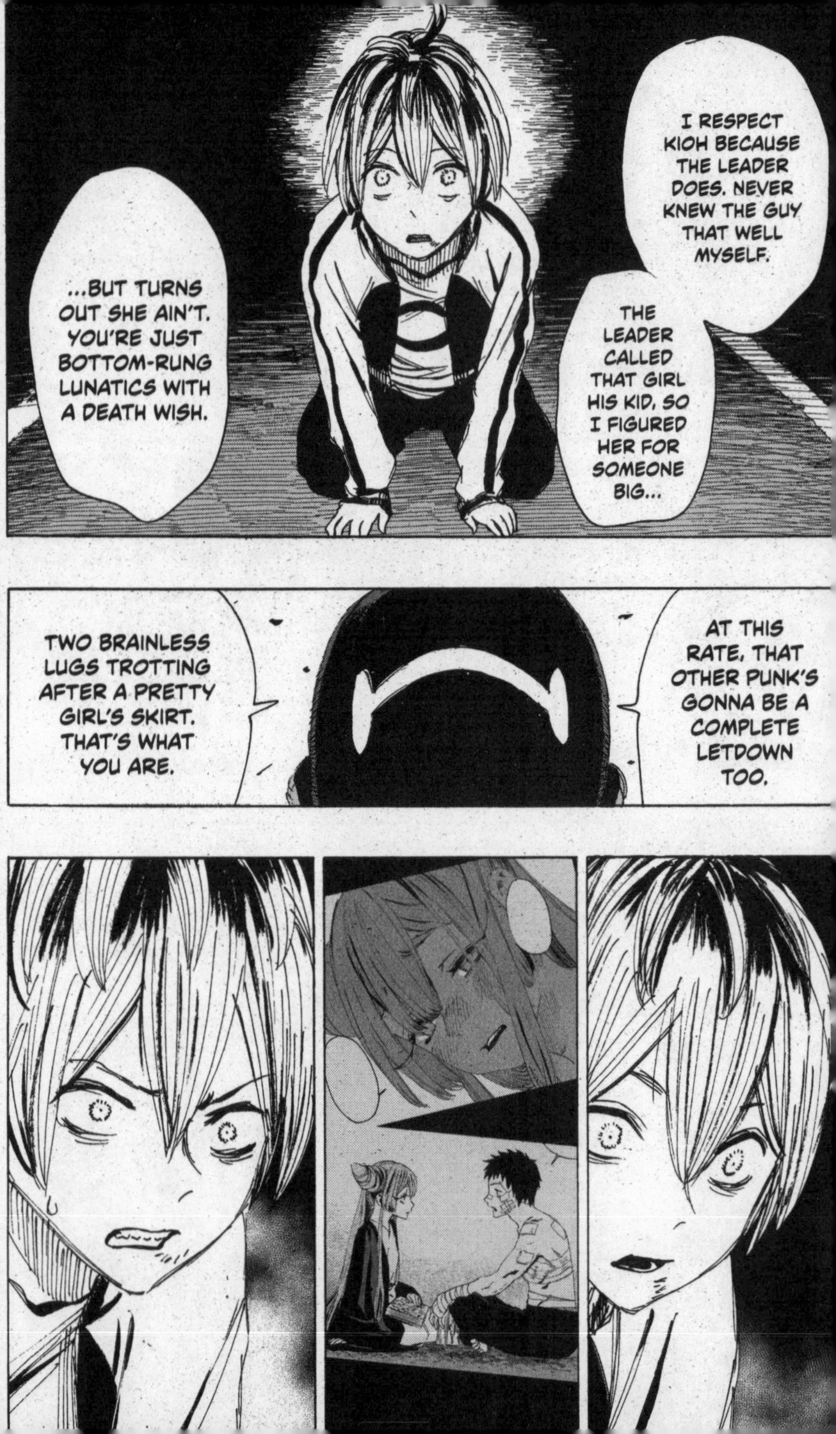
I RESPECT KIOH BECAUSE THE LEADER DOES. NEVER KNEW THE GUY THAT WELL MYSELF.
THE LEADER CALLED THAT GIRL HIS KID, SO I FIGURED HER FOR SOMEONE BIG...
...BUT TURNS OUT SHE AIN'T. YOU'RE JUST BOTTOM-RUNG LUNATICS WITH A DEATH WISH.
AT THIS RATE, THAT OTHER PUNK'S GONNA BE A COMPLETE LETDOWN TOO.
TWO BRAINLESS LUGS TROTTING AFTER A PRETTY GIRL'S SKIRT. THAT'S WHAT YOU ARE.

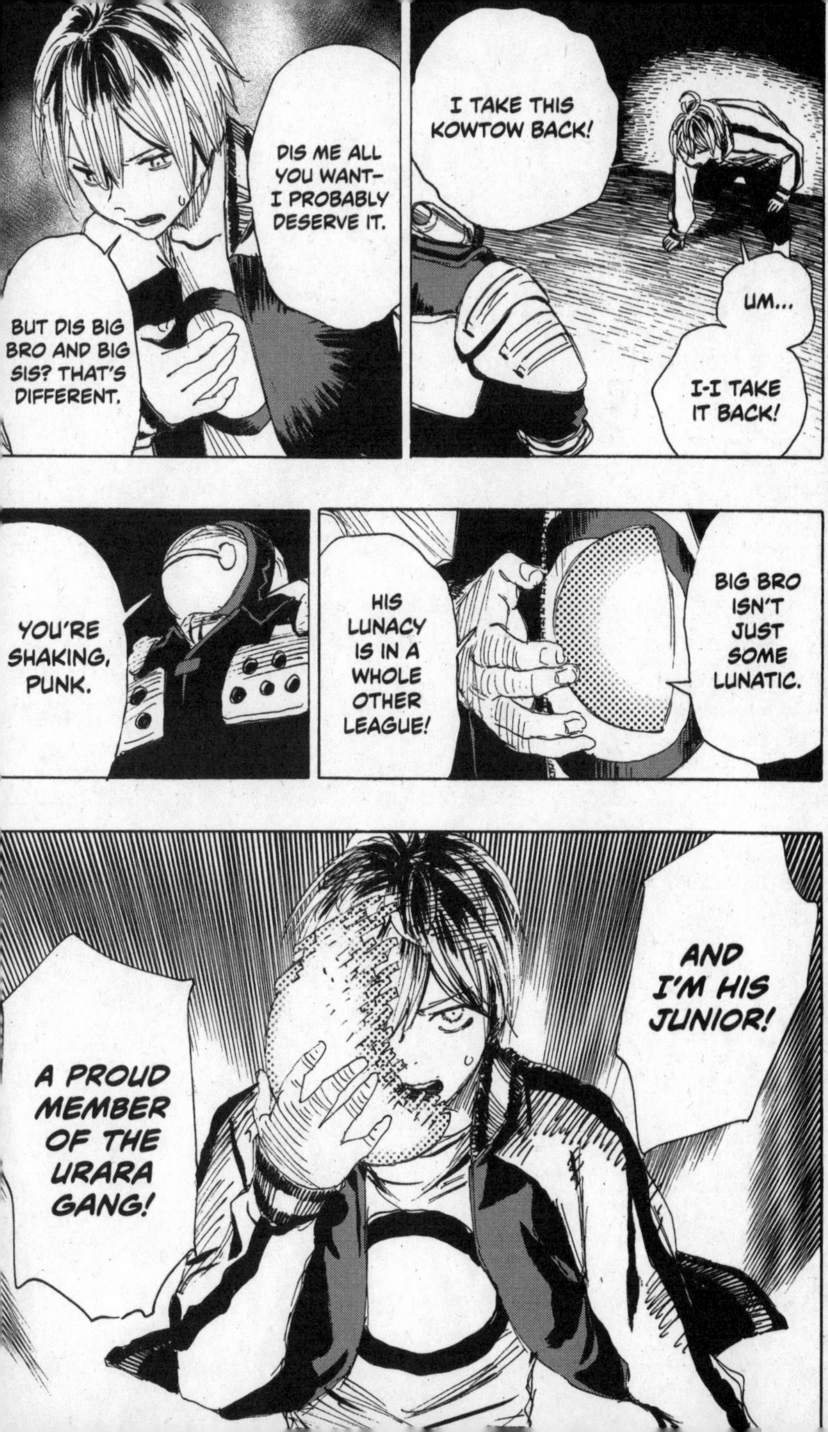
I TAKE THIS KOWTOW BACK!
UM...
I-I TAKE IT BACK!
DIS ME ALL YOU WANT- I PROBABLY DESERVE IT.
BUT DIS BIG BRO AND BIG SIS? THAT'S DIFFERENT.
BIG BRO ISN'T JUST SOME LUNATIC.
HIS LUNACY IS IN A WHOLE OTHER LEAGUE!
YOU'RE SHAKING, PUNK.
AND I'M HIS JUNIOR!
A PROUD MEMBER OF THE URARA GANG!

AYASHIMON

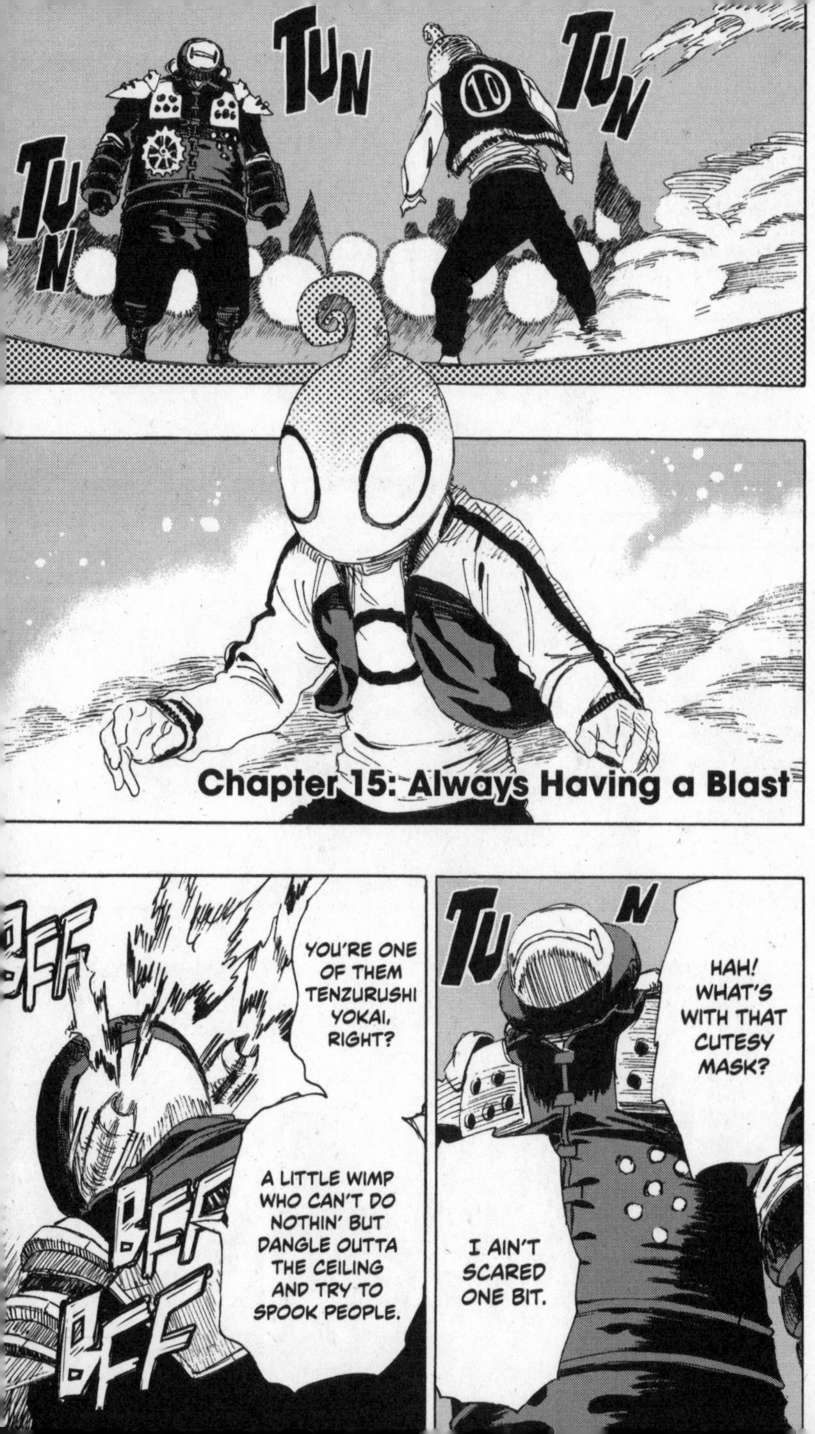
TUN
TUN
TUN
Chapter 15: Always Having a Blast
TUN
HAH! WHAT'S WITH THAT CUTESY MASK?
I AIN'T SCARED ONE BIT.
BFF
YOU'RE ONE OF THEM TENZURUSHI YOKAI, RIGHT?
A LITTLE WIMP WHO CAN'T DO NOTHIN' BUT DANGLE OUTTA THE CEILING AND TRY TO SPOOK PEOPLE.
BFF
BFF

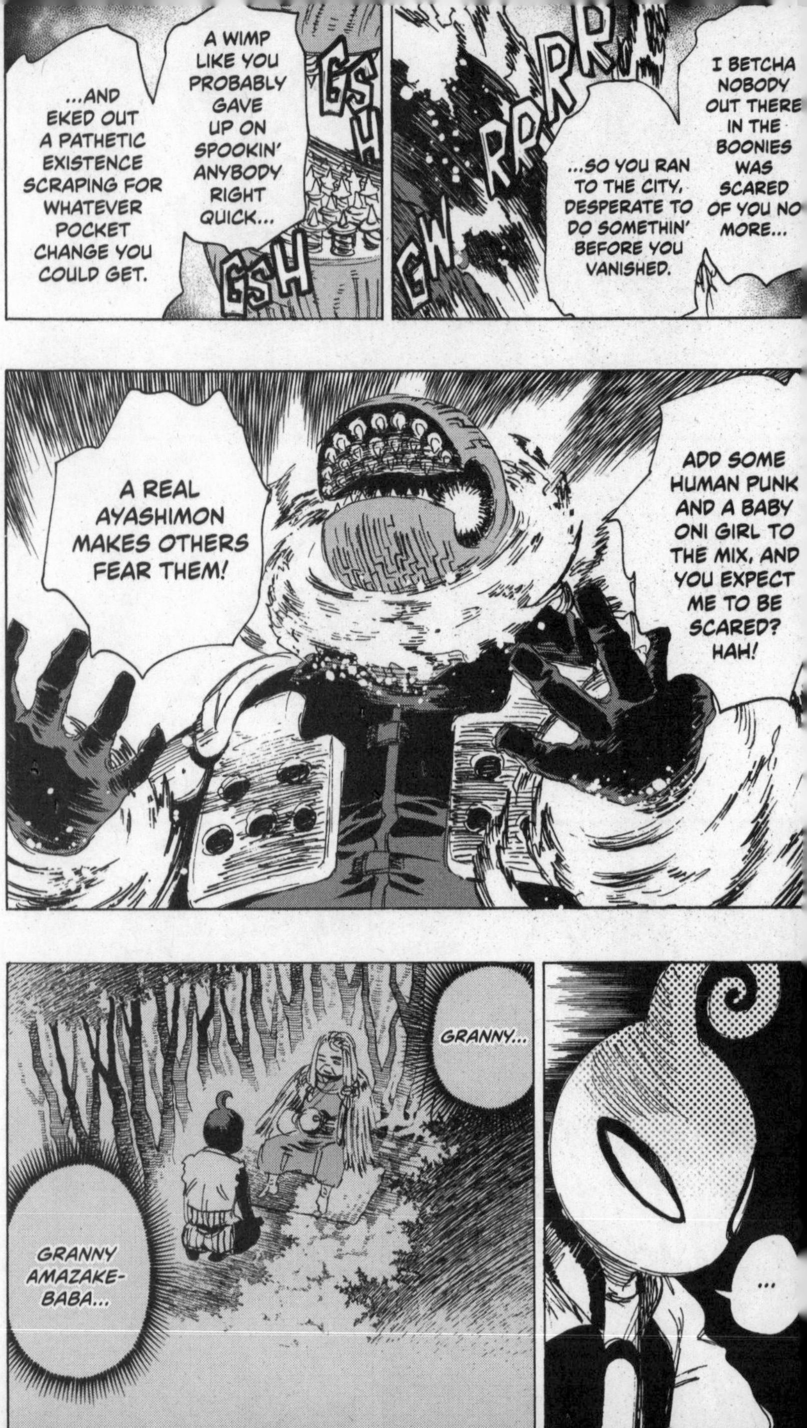
I BETCHA NOBODY OUT THERE IN THE BOONIES WAS SCARED OF YOU NO MORE...
...SO YOU RAN TO THE CITY, DESPERATE TO DO SOMETHIN' BEFORE YOU VANISHED.
GWRRRR
A WIMP LIKE YOU PROBABLY GAVE UP ON SPOOKIN' ANYBODY RIGHT QUICK...
GSH
GSH
...AND EKED OUT A PATHETIC EXISTENCE SCRAPING FOR WHATEVER POCKET CHANGE YOU COULD GET.
ADD SOME HUMAN PUNK AND A BABY ONI GIRL TO THE MIX, AND YOU EXPECT ME TO BE SCARED? HAH!
A REAL AYASHIMON MAKES OTHERS FEAR THEM!
...
GRANNY...
GRANNY AMAZAKE-BABA...

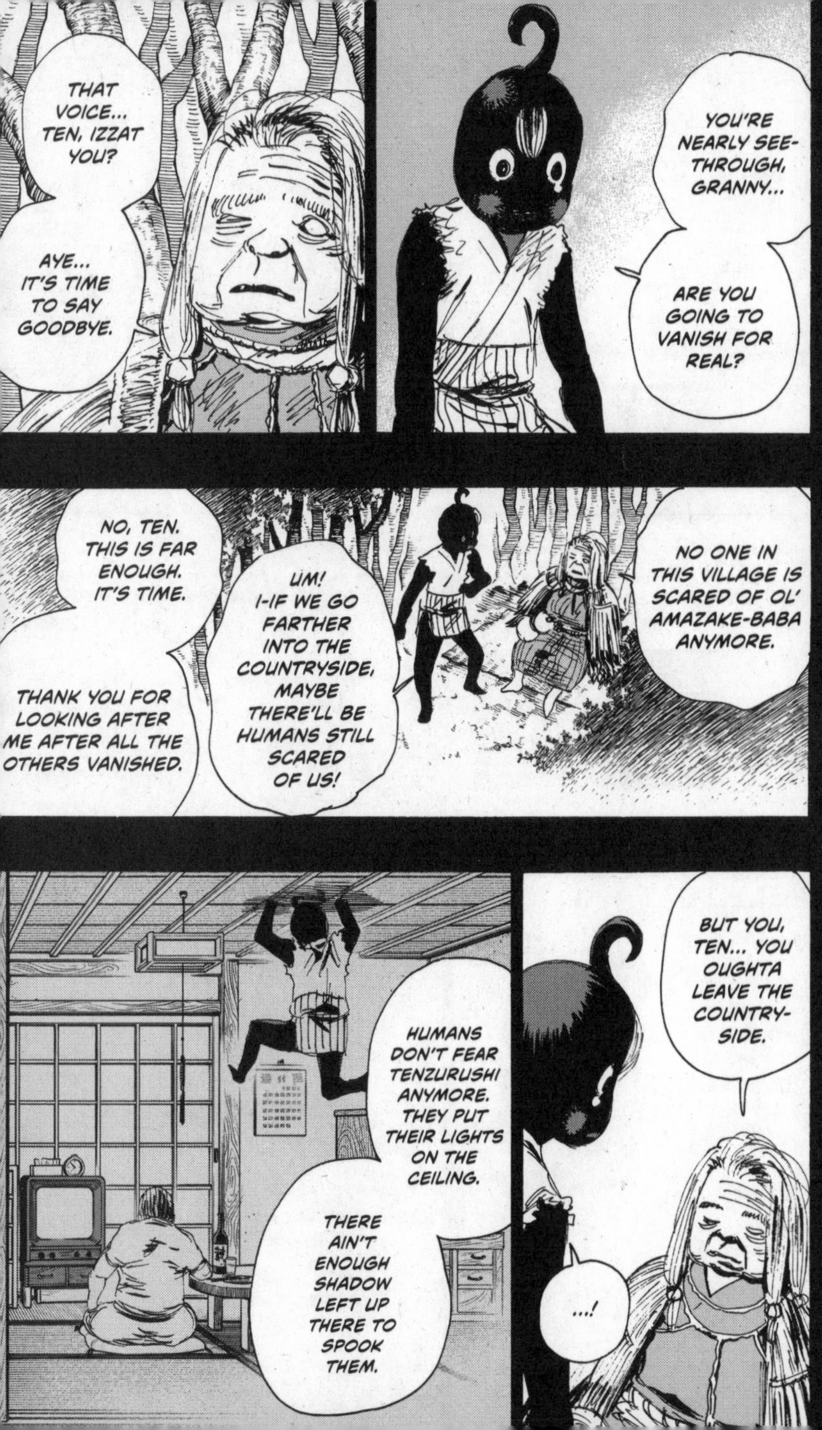
YOU'RE NEARLY SEE-THROUGH, GRANNY...
ARE YOU GOING TO VANISH FOR REAL?
THAT VOICE... TEN, IZZAT YOU?
AYE... IT'S TIME TO SAY GOODBYE.
NO ONE IN THIS VILLAGE IS SCARED OF OL' AMAZAKE-BABA ANYMORE.
UM! I-IF WE GO FARTHER INTO THE COUNTRYSIDE, MAYBE THERE'LL BE HUMANS STILL SCARED OF US!
NO, TEN. THIS IS FAR ENOUGH. IT'S TIME.
THANK YOU FOR LOOKING AFTER ME AFTER ALL THE OTHERS VANISHED.
BUT YOU, TEN... YOU OUGHTA LEAVE THE COUNTRY-SIDE.
...!
HUMANS DON'T FEAR TENZURUSHI ANYMORE. THEY PUT THEIR LIGHTS ON THE CEILING.
THERE AIN'T ENOUGH SHADOW LEFT UP THERE TO SPOOK THEM.

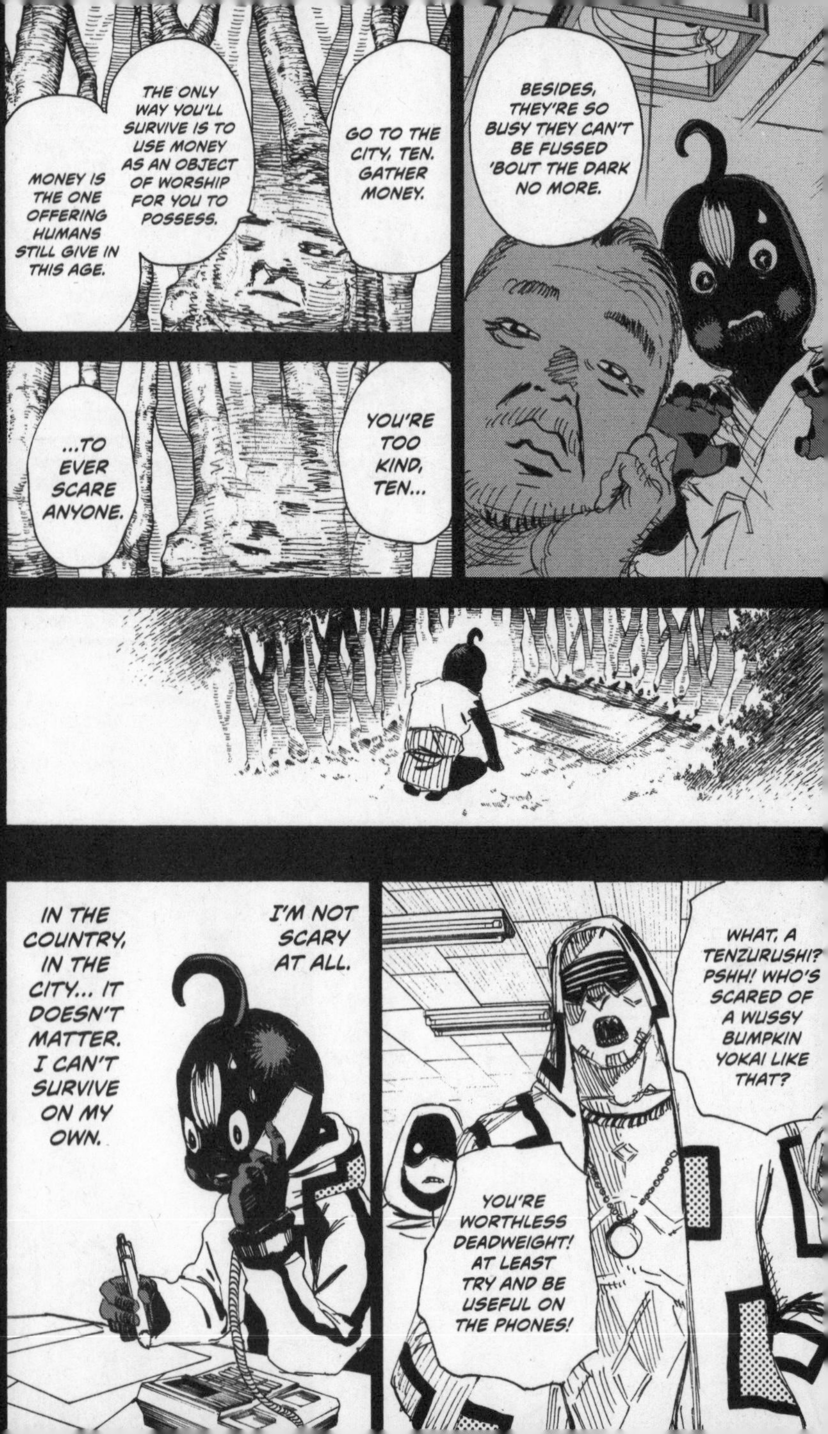
BESIDES, THEY'RE SO BUSY THEY CAN'T BE FUSSED 'BOUT THE DARK NO MORE.
GO TO THE CITY, TEN. GATHER MONEY.
THE ONLY WAY YOU'LL SURVIVE IS TO USE MONEY AS AN OBJECT OF WORSHIP FOR YOU TO POSSESS.
MONEY IS THE ONE OFFERING HUMANS STILL GIVE IN THIS AGE.
YOU'RE TOO KIND, TEN...
...TO EVER SCARE ANYONE.
WHAT, A TENZURUSHI? PSHH! WHO'S SCARED OF A WUSSY BUMPKIN YOKAI LIKE THAT?
YOU'RE WORTHLESS DEADWEIGHT! AT LEAST TRY AND BE USEFUL ON THE PHONES!
I'M NOT SCARY AT ALL.
IN THE COUNTRY, IN THE CITY... IT DOESN'T MATTER. I CAN'T SURVIVE ON MY OWN.

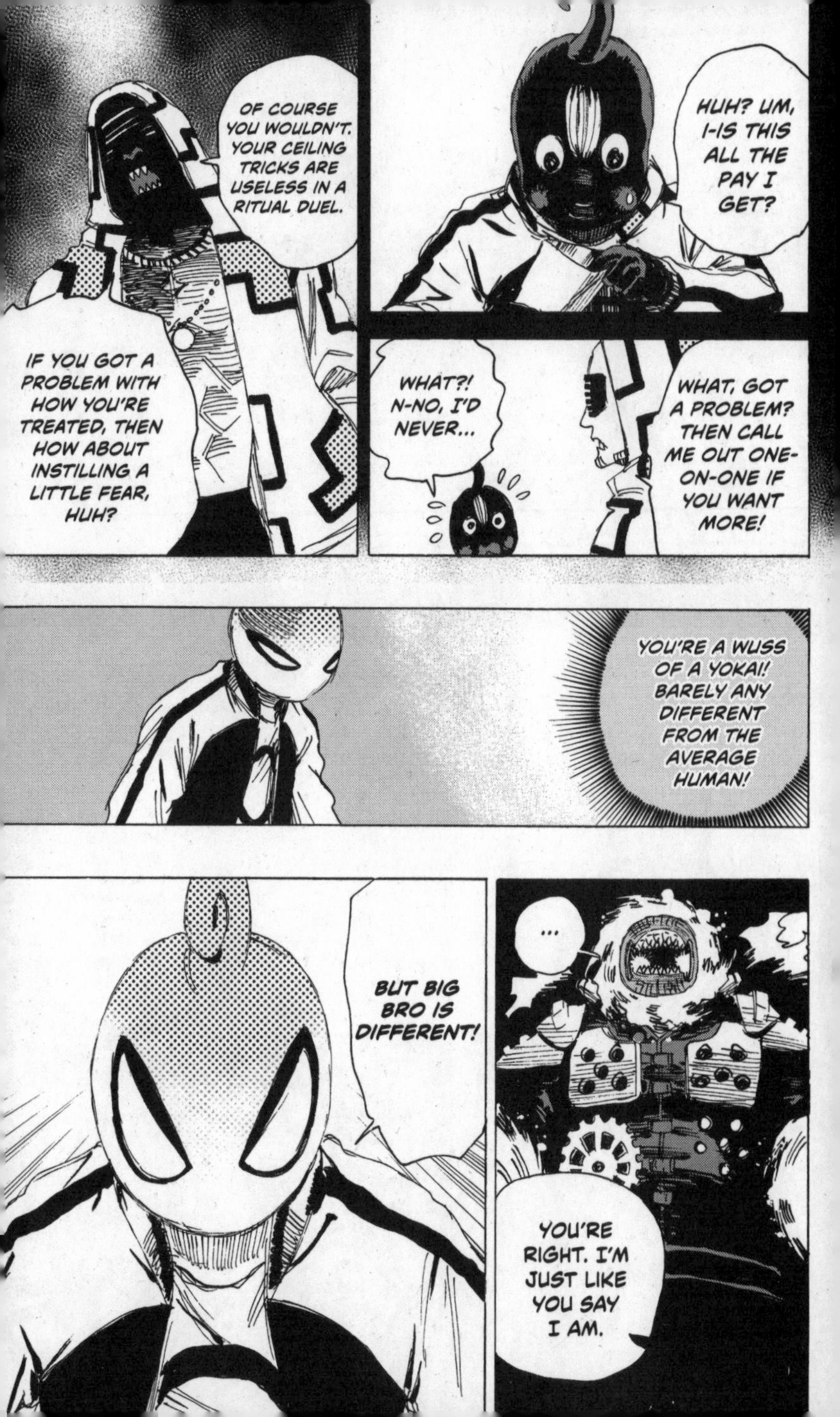

HUH? UM, I-IS THIS ALL THE PAY I GET?
WHAT, GOT A PROBLEM? THEN CALL ME OUT ONE-ON-ONE IF YOU WANT MORE!
WHAT?! N-NO, I'D NEVER...
OF COURSE YOU WOULDN'T. YOUR CEILING TRICKS ARE USELESS IN A RITUAL DUEL.
IF YOU GOT A PROBLEM WITH HOW YOU'RE TREATED, THEN HOW ABOUT INSTILLING A LITTLE FEAR, HUH?
YOU'RE A WUSS OF A YOKAI! BARELY ANY DIFFERENT FROM THE AVERAGE HUMAN!
...
YOU'RE RIGHT. I'M JUST LIKE YOU SAY I AM.
BUT BIG BRO IS DIFFERENT!

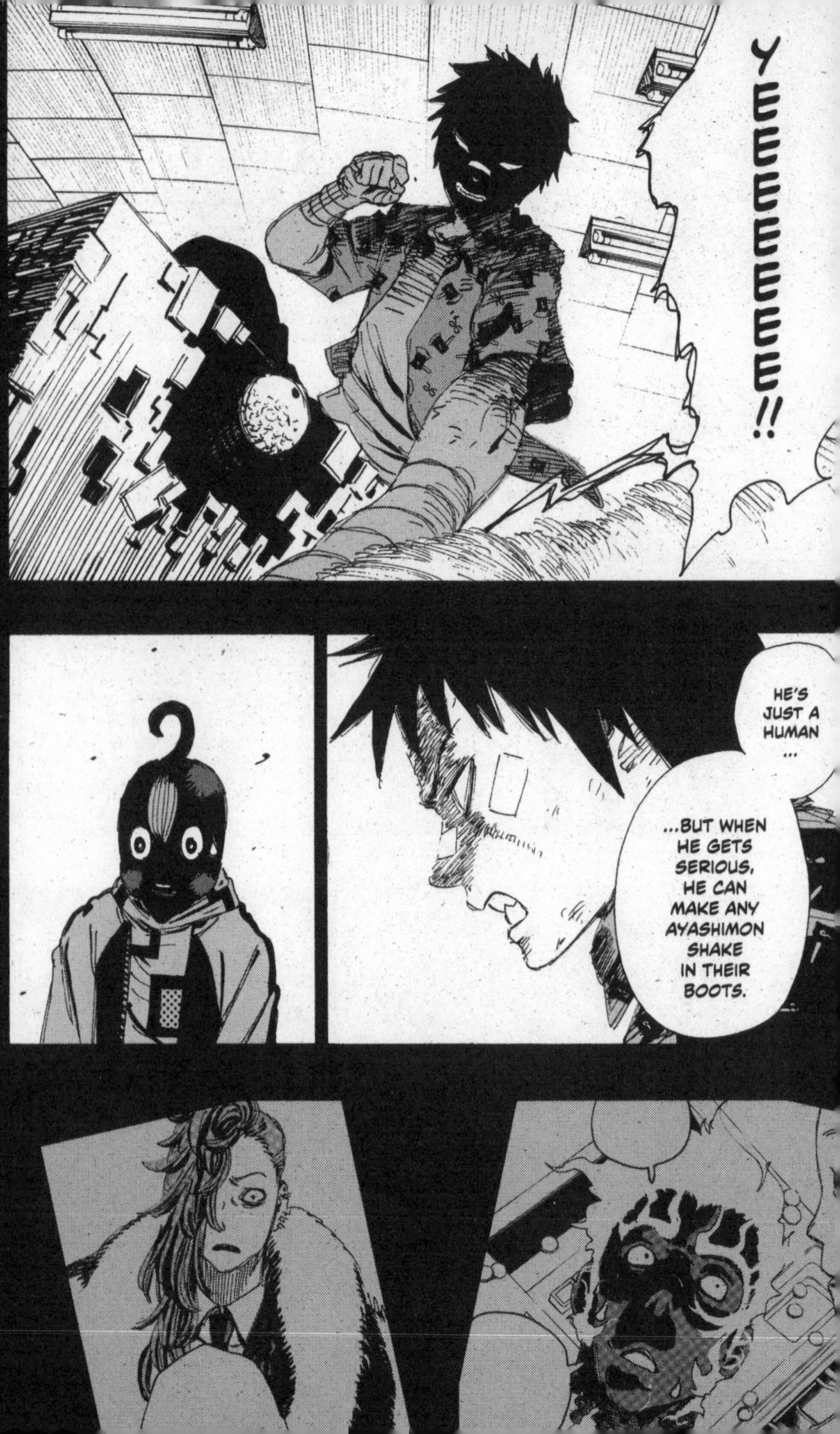
YEEEEEEEEE!!
HE'S JUST A HUMAN...
...BUT WHEN HE GETS SERIOUS, HE CAN MAKE ANY AYASHIMON SHAKE IN THEIR BOOTS.

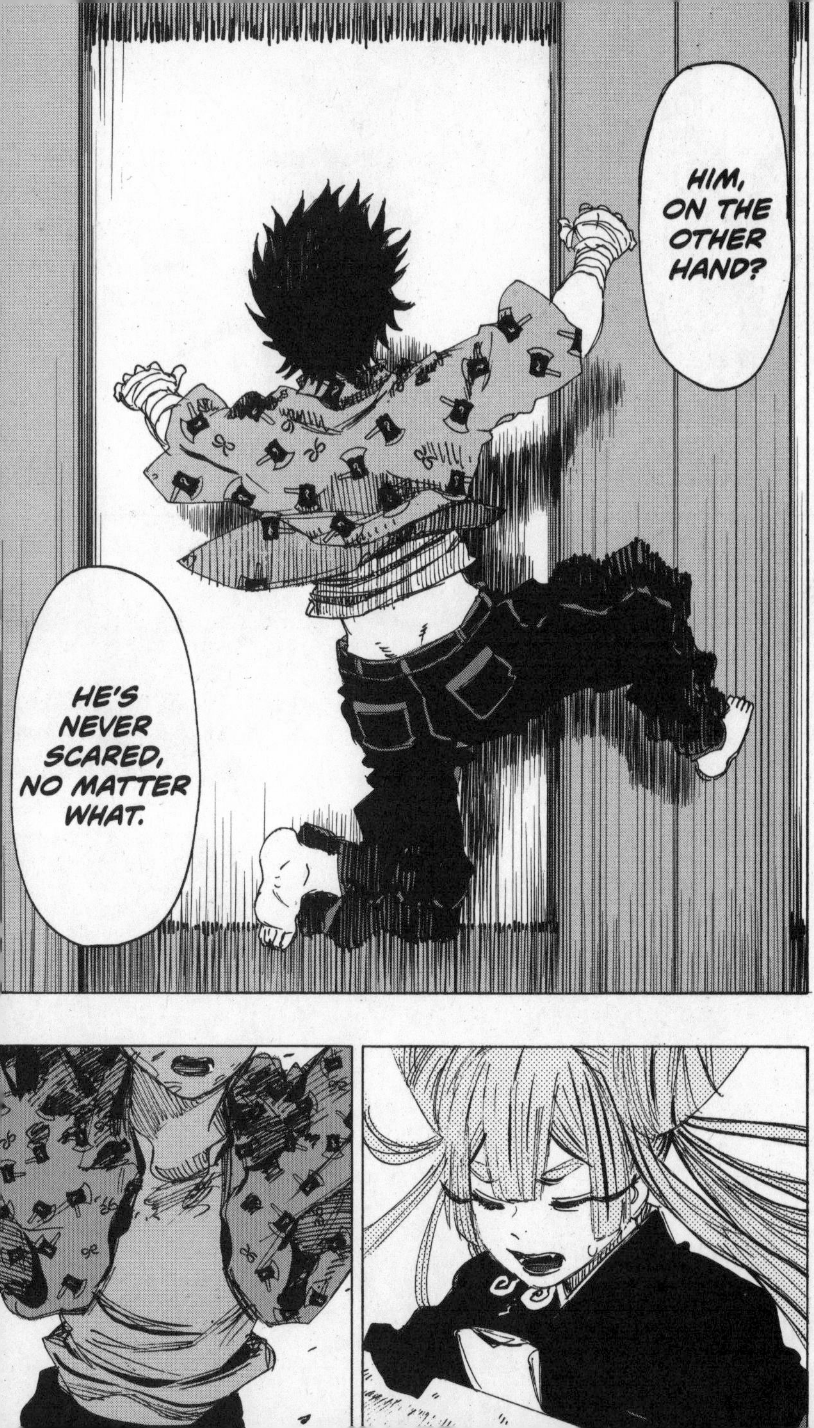
HIM, ON THE OTHER HAND?
HE'S NEVER SCARED, NO MATTER WHAT.

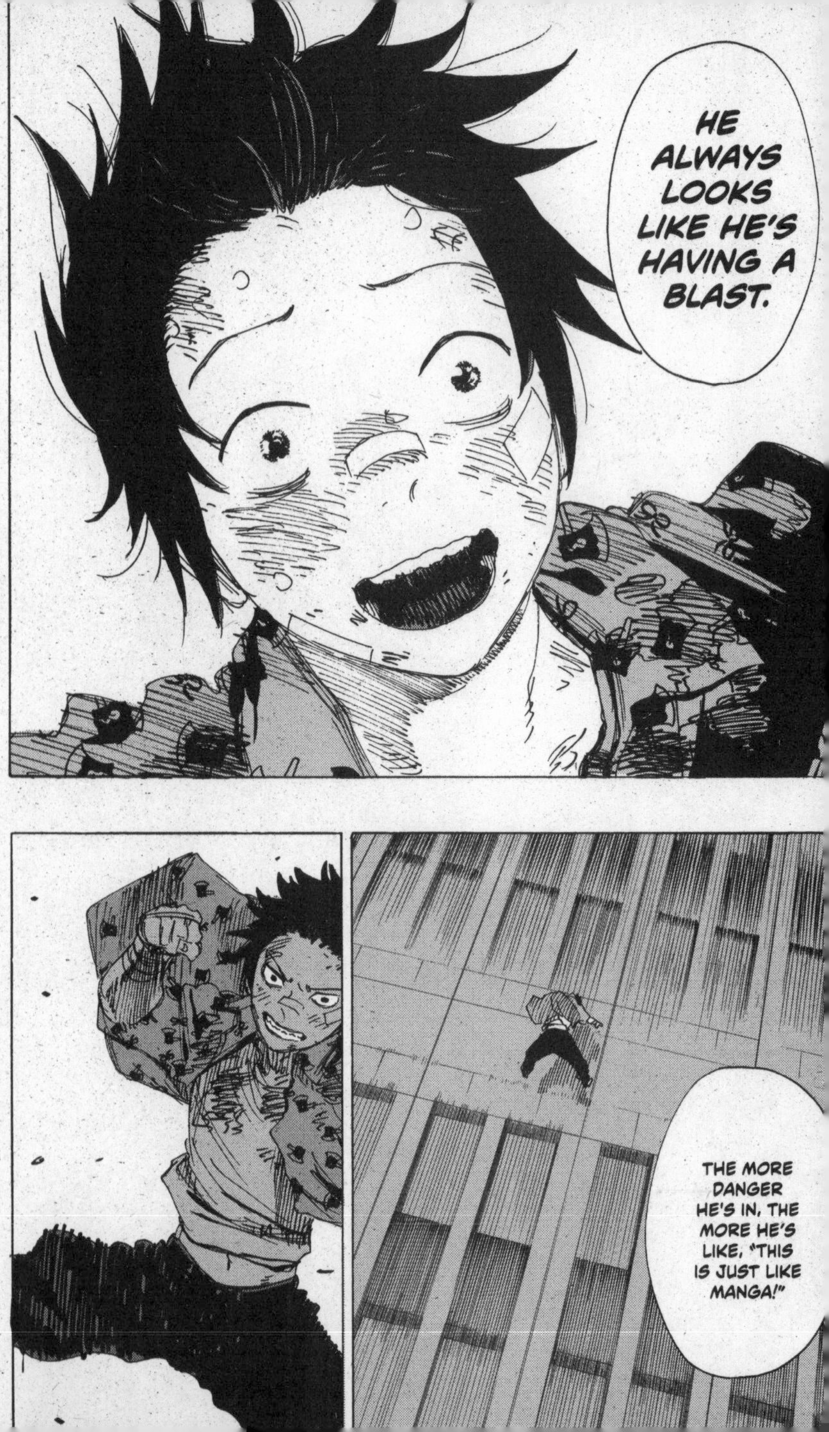
HE ALWAYS LOOKS LIKE HE'S HAVING A BLAST.
THE MORE DANGER HE'S IN, THE MORE HE'S LIKE, "THIS IS JUST LIKE MANGA!"

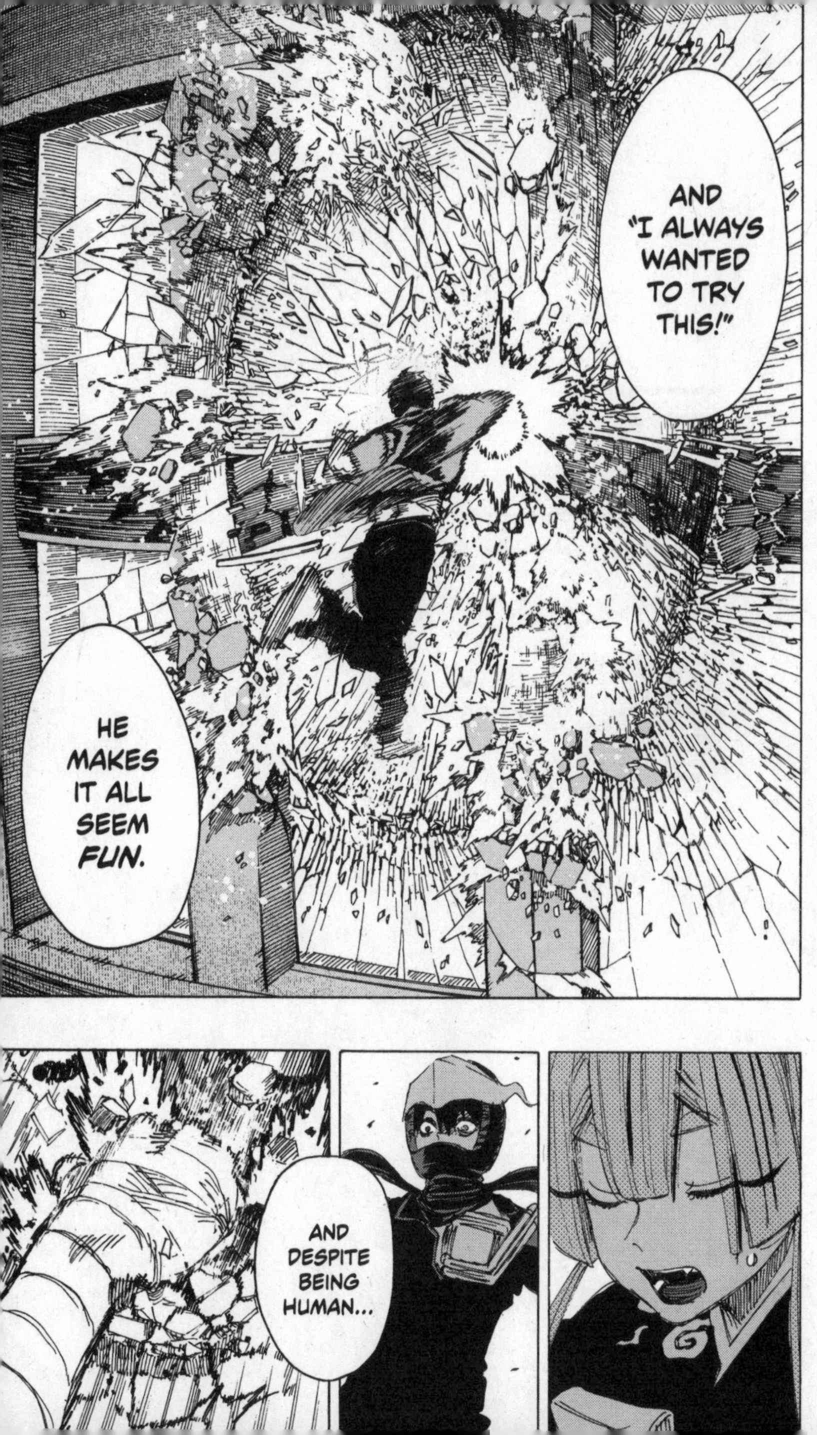
AND "I ALWAYS WANTED TO TRY THIS!"
HE MAKES IT ALL SEEM *FUN.*
AND DESPITE BEING HUMAN...

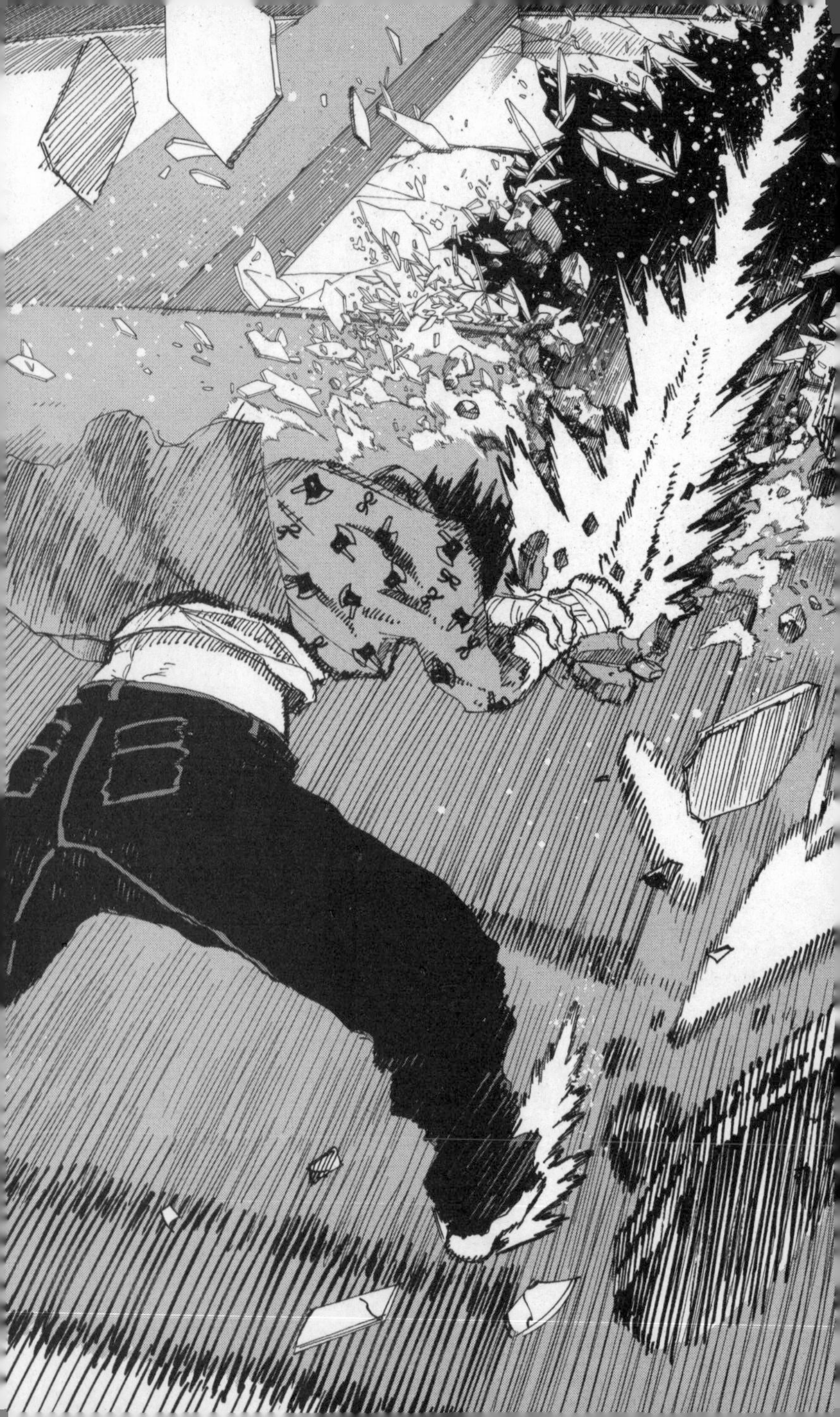

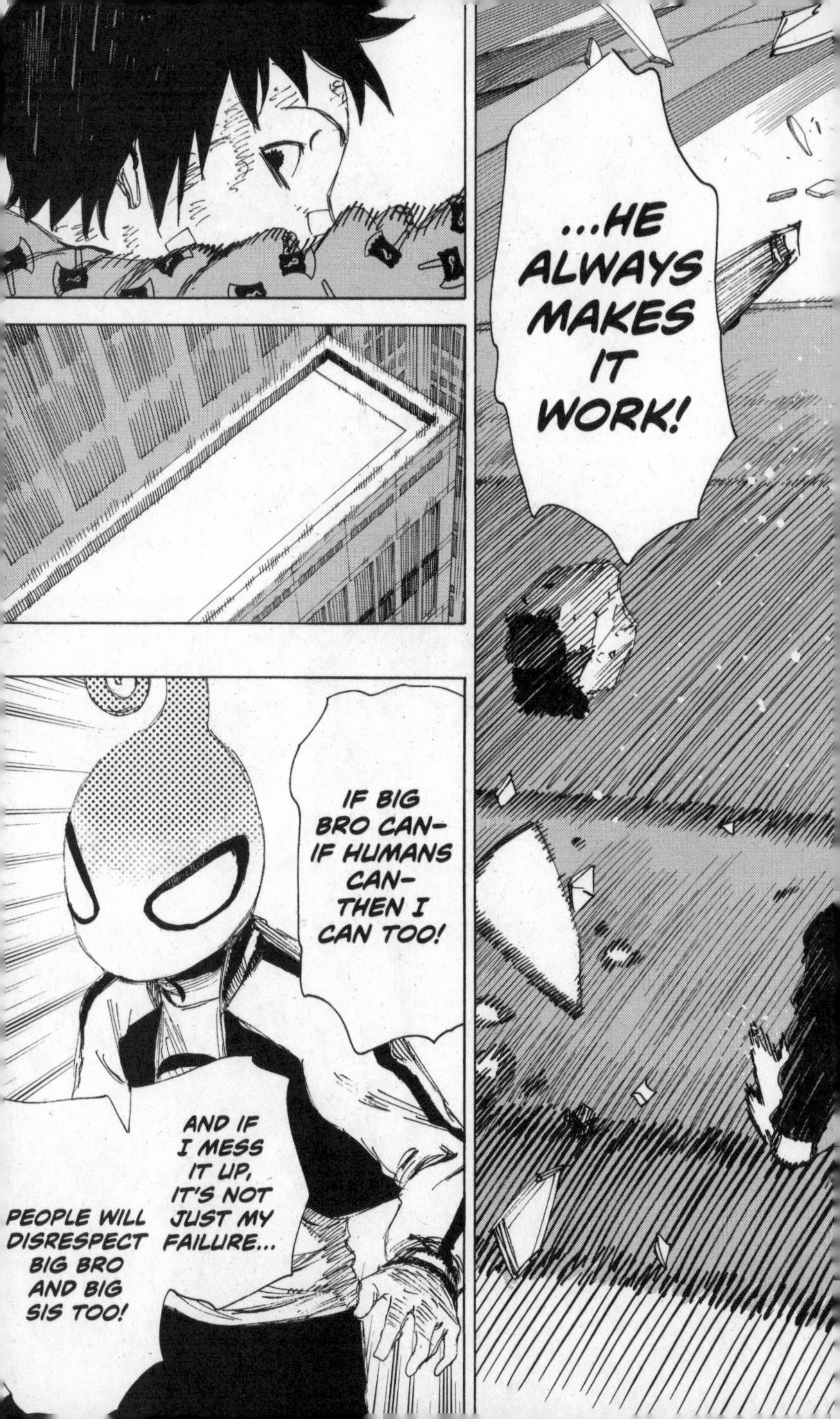
...HE ALWAYS MAKES IT WORK!
IF BIG BRO CAN- IF HUMANS CAN- THEN I CAN TOO!
AND IF I MESS IT UP, IT'S NOT JUST MY FAILURE...
PEOPLE WILL DISRESPECT BIG BRO AND BIG SIS TOO!

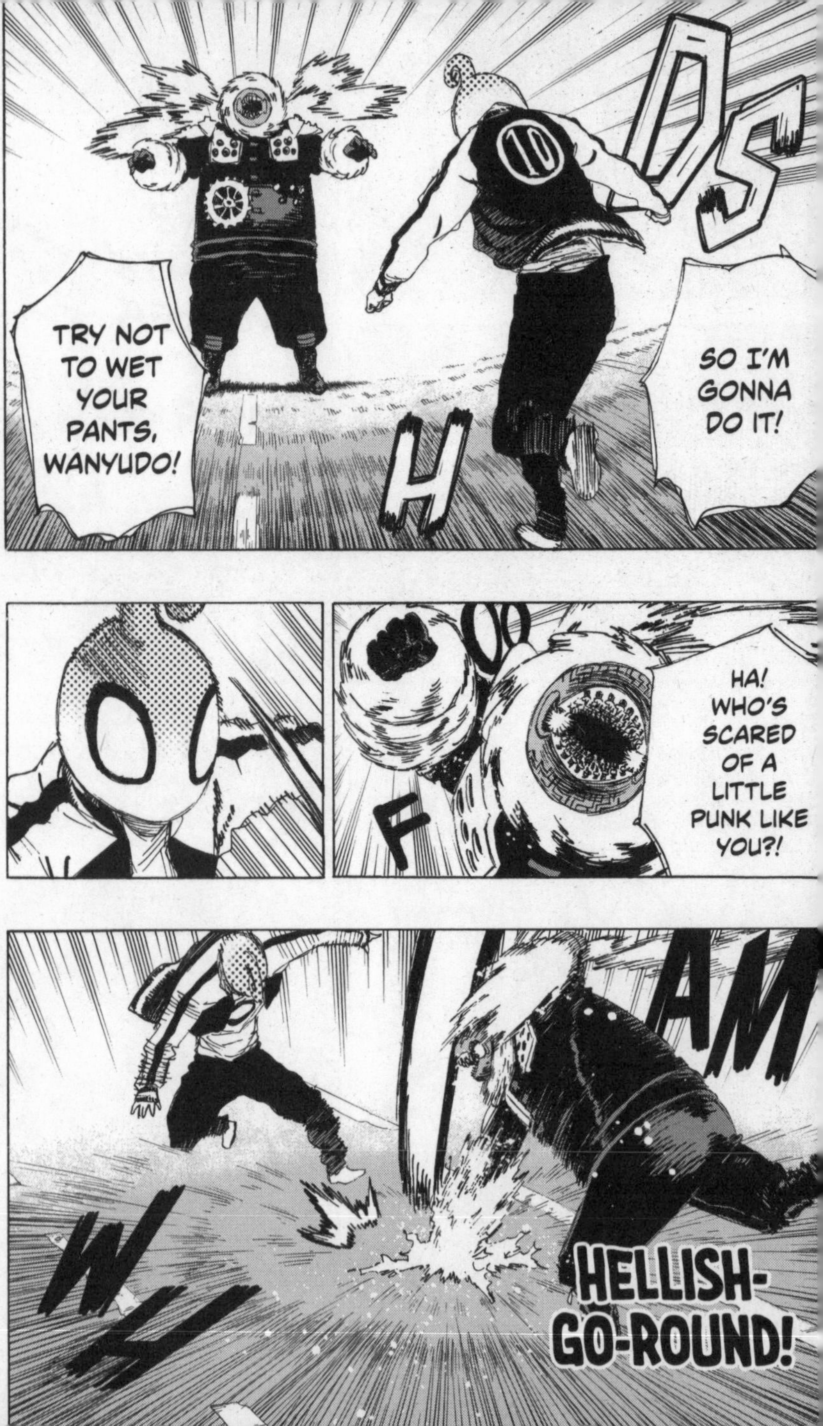
DS
SO I'M GONNA DO IT!
TRY NOT TO WET YOUR PANTS, WANYUDO!
H
HA! WHO'S SCARED OF A LITTLE PUNK LIKE YOU?!
F
AM
HELLISH-GO-ROUND!

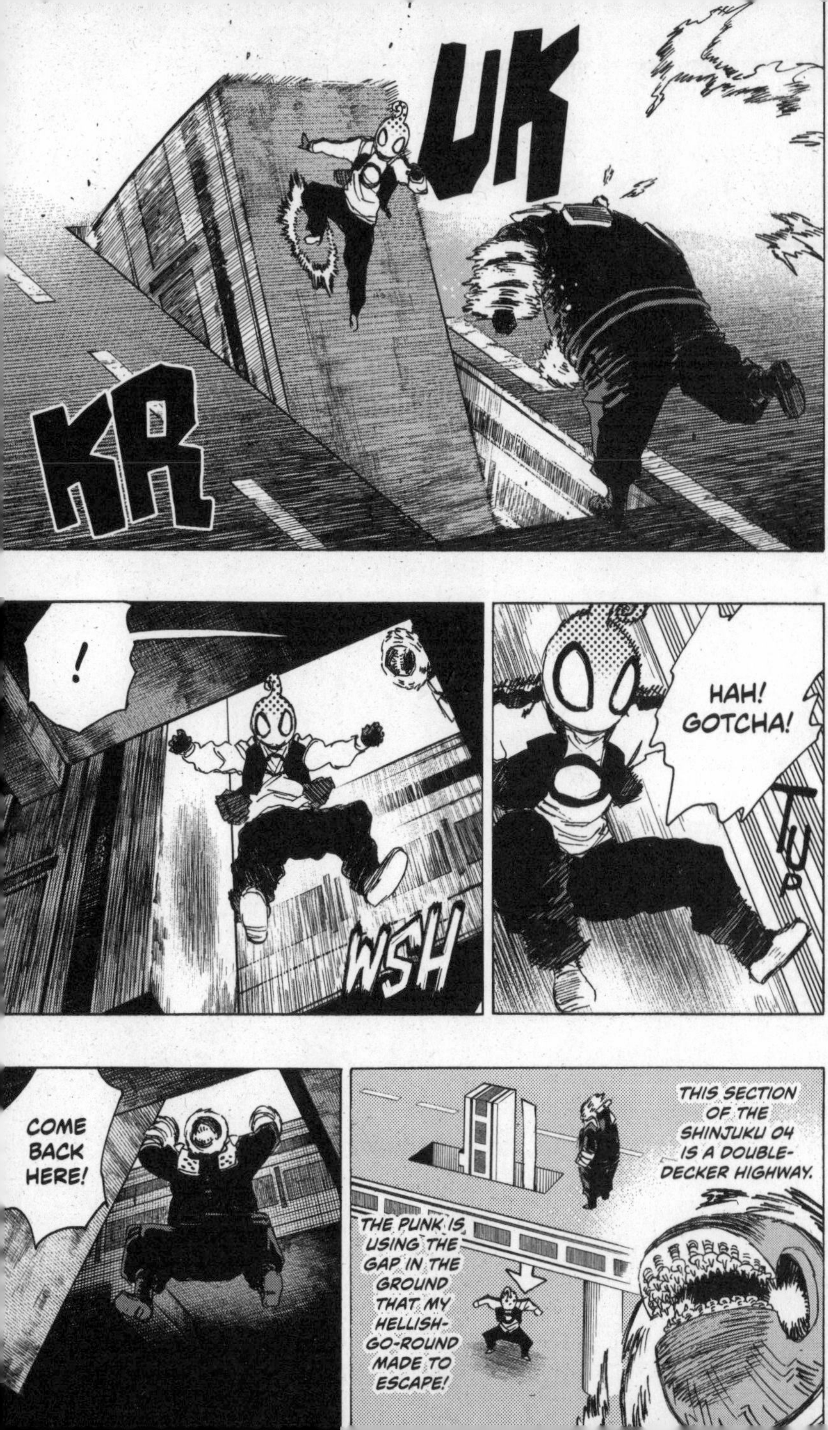
UK
KR
HAH! GOTCHA!
TUP
!
WSH
THIS SECTION OF THE SHINJUKU 04 IS A DOUBLE-DECKER HIGHWAY.
THE PUNK IS USING THE GAP IN THE GROUND THAT MY HELLISH-GO-ROUND MADE TO ESCAPE!
COME BACK HERE!

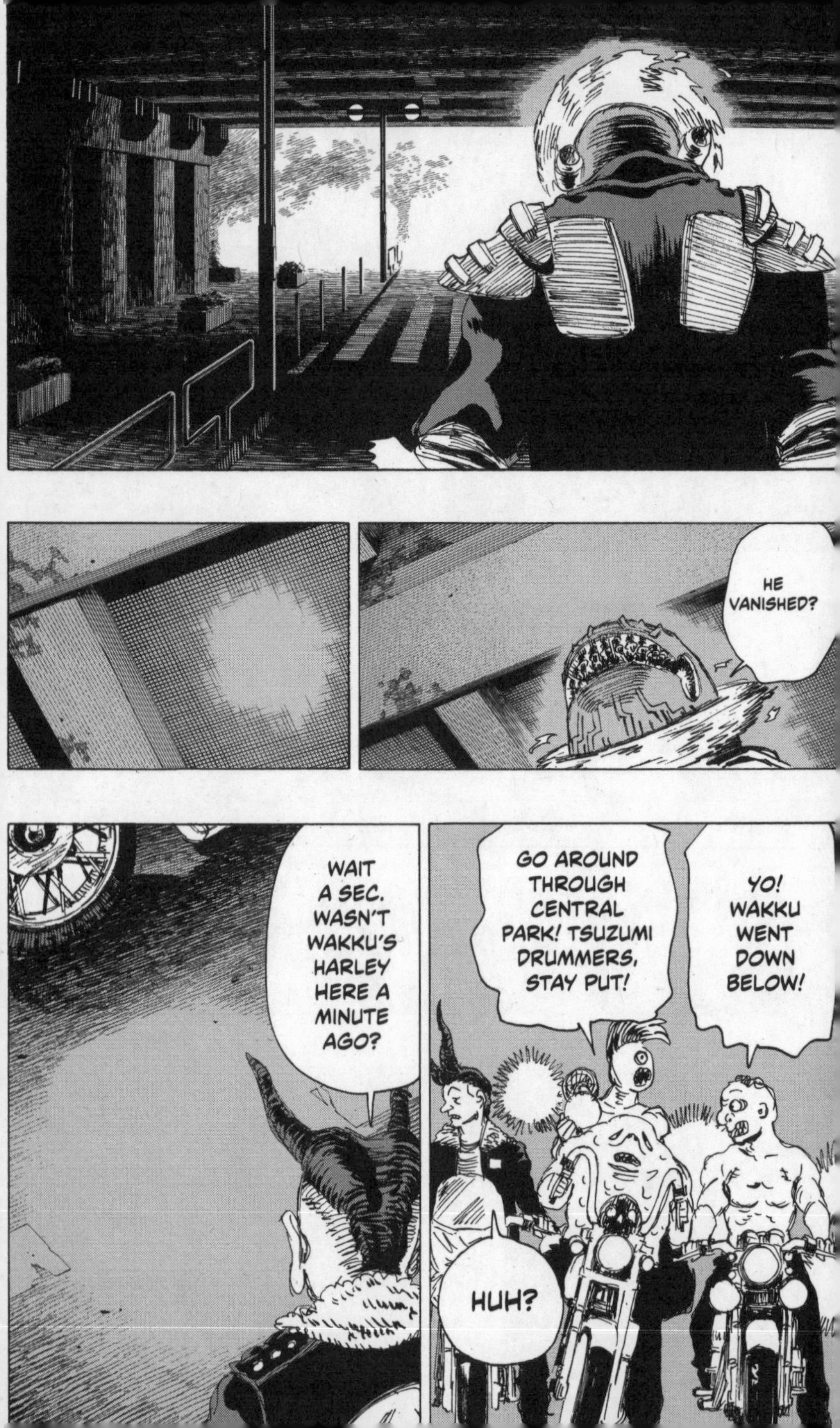
HE VANISHED?
YO! WAKKU WENT DOWN BELOW!
GO AROUND THROUGH CENTRAL PARK! TSUZUMI DRUMMERS, STAY PUT!
HUH?
WAIT A SEC. WASN'T WAKKU'S HARLEY HERE A MINUTE AGO?

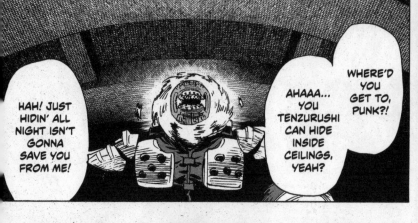

WHERE'D YOU GET TO, PUNK?!
AHAAA... YOU TENZURUSHI CAN HIDE INSIDE CEILINGS, YEAH?
HAH! JUST HIDIN' ALL NIGHT ISN'T GONNA SAVE YOU FROM ME!
ZLSS
HUH?
HOLD ON...
WAAA-AAAA-AAAHH!!!
VOOP

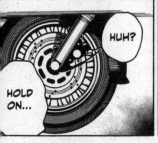

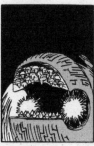

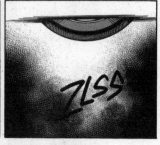

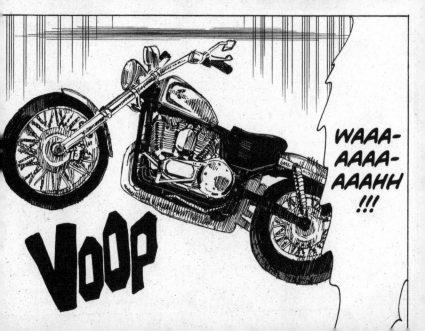

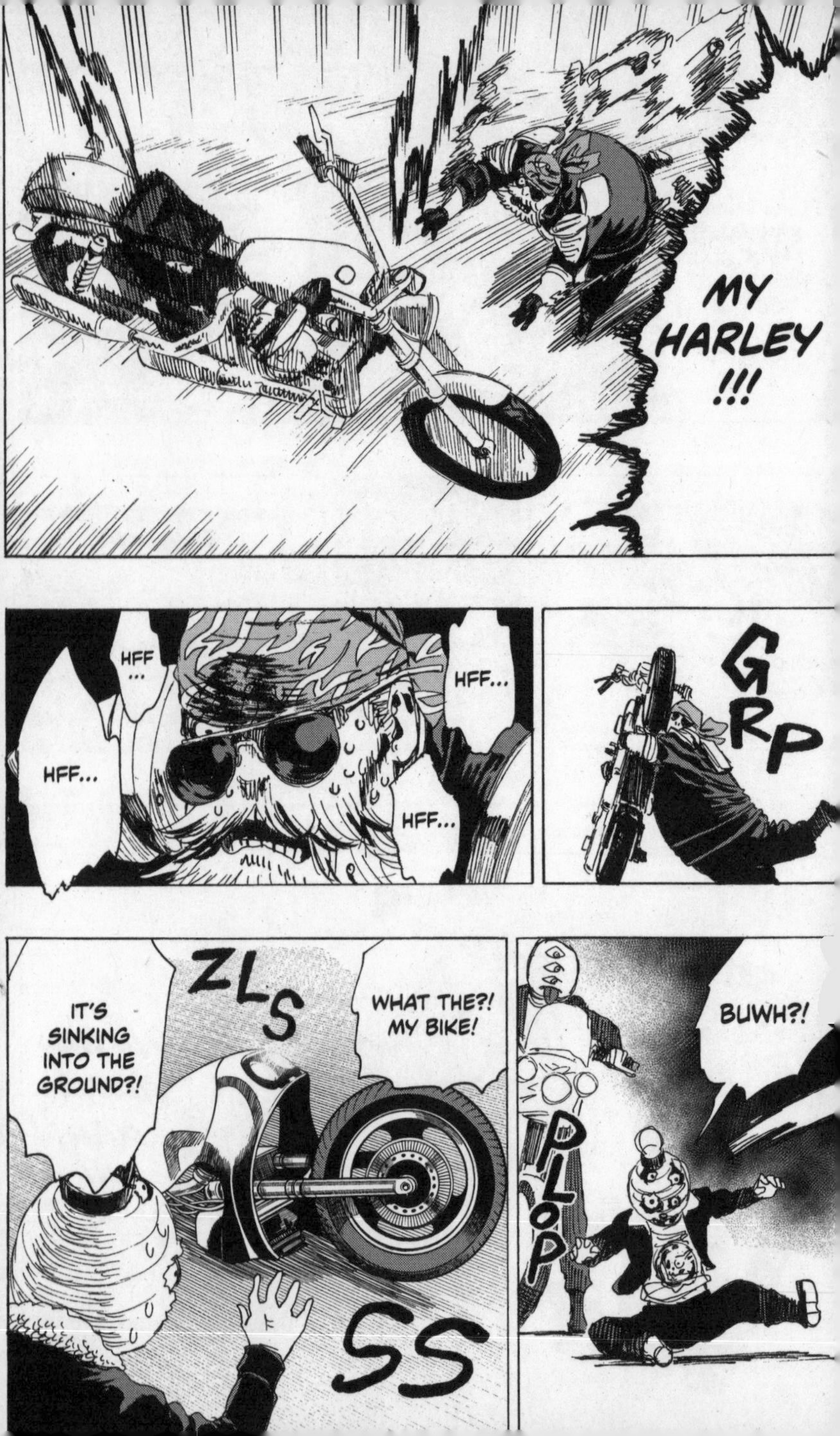
MY HARLEY !!!
GRP
HFF...
HFF ...
HFF...
HFF...
BUWH?!
PLOP
WHAT THE?! MY BIKE!
ZLS
IT'S SINKING INTO THE GROUND?!
SS

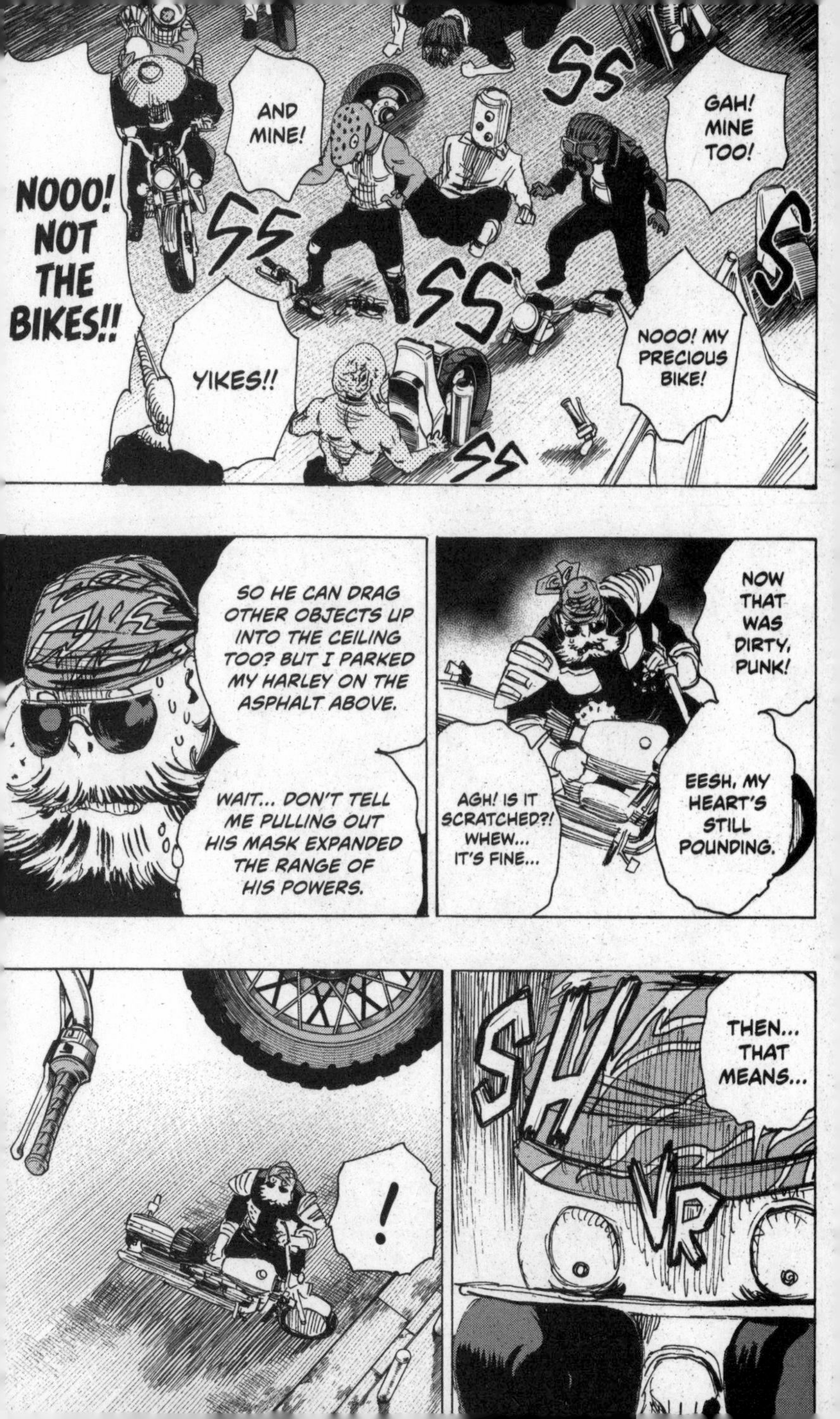
SS
GAH! MINE TOO!
S
AND MINE!
SS
NOOO! MY PRECIOUS BIKE!
SS
YIKES!!
NOOO! NOT THE BIKES!!
SS
NOW THAT WAS DIRTY, PUNK!
EESH, MY HEART'S STILL POUNDING.
AGH! IS IT SCRATCHED?! WHEW... IT'S FINE...
SO HE CAN DRAG OTHER OBJECTS UP INTO THE CEILING TOO? BUT I PARKED MY HARLEY ON THE ASPHALT ABOVE.
WAIT... DON'T TELL ME PULLING OUT HIS MASK EXPANDED THE RANGE OF HIS POWERS.
THEN... THAT MEANS...
SH
VR
!

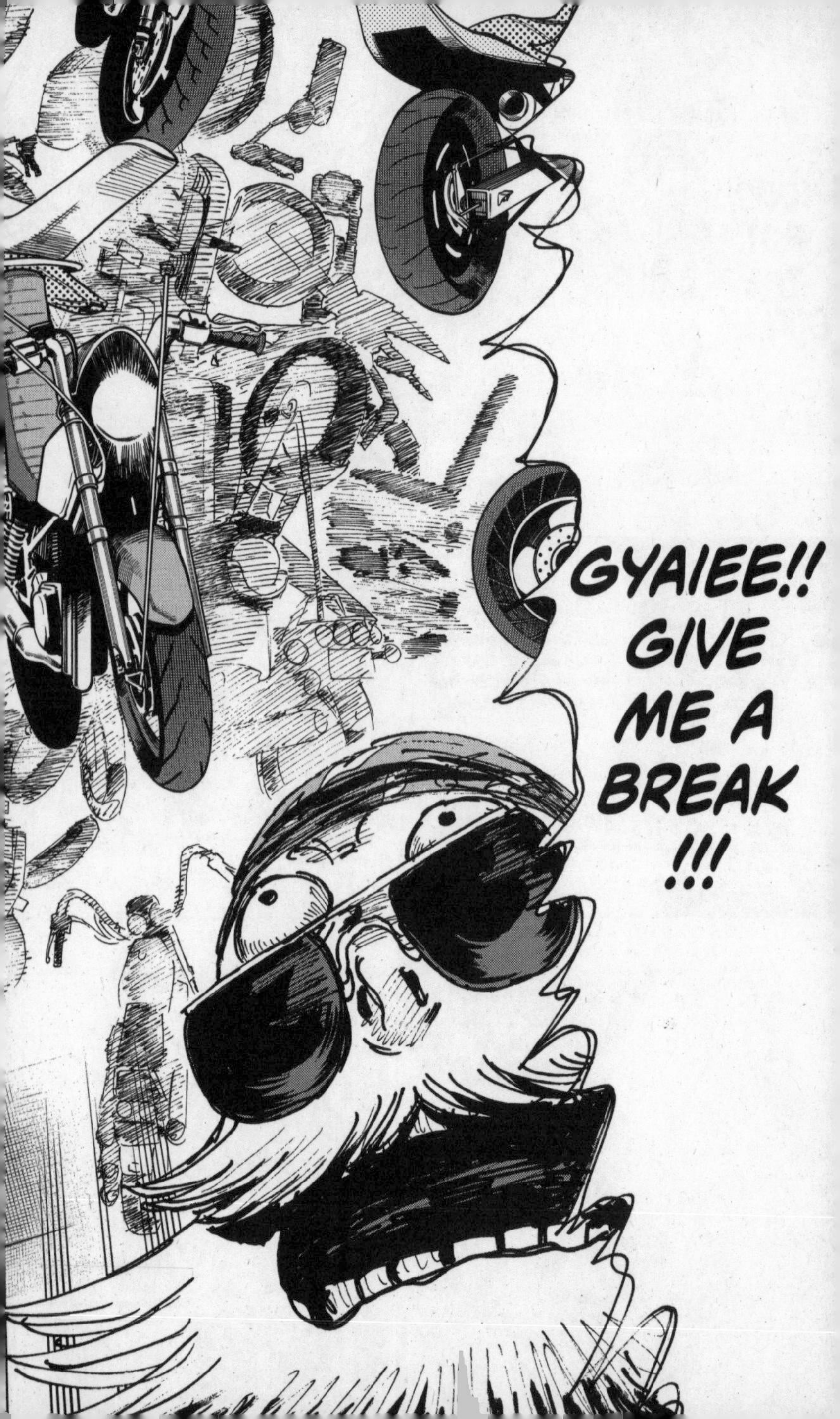
GYAIEE!! GIVE ME A BREAK !!!

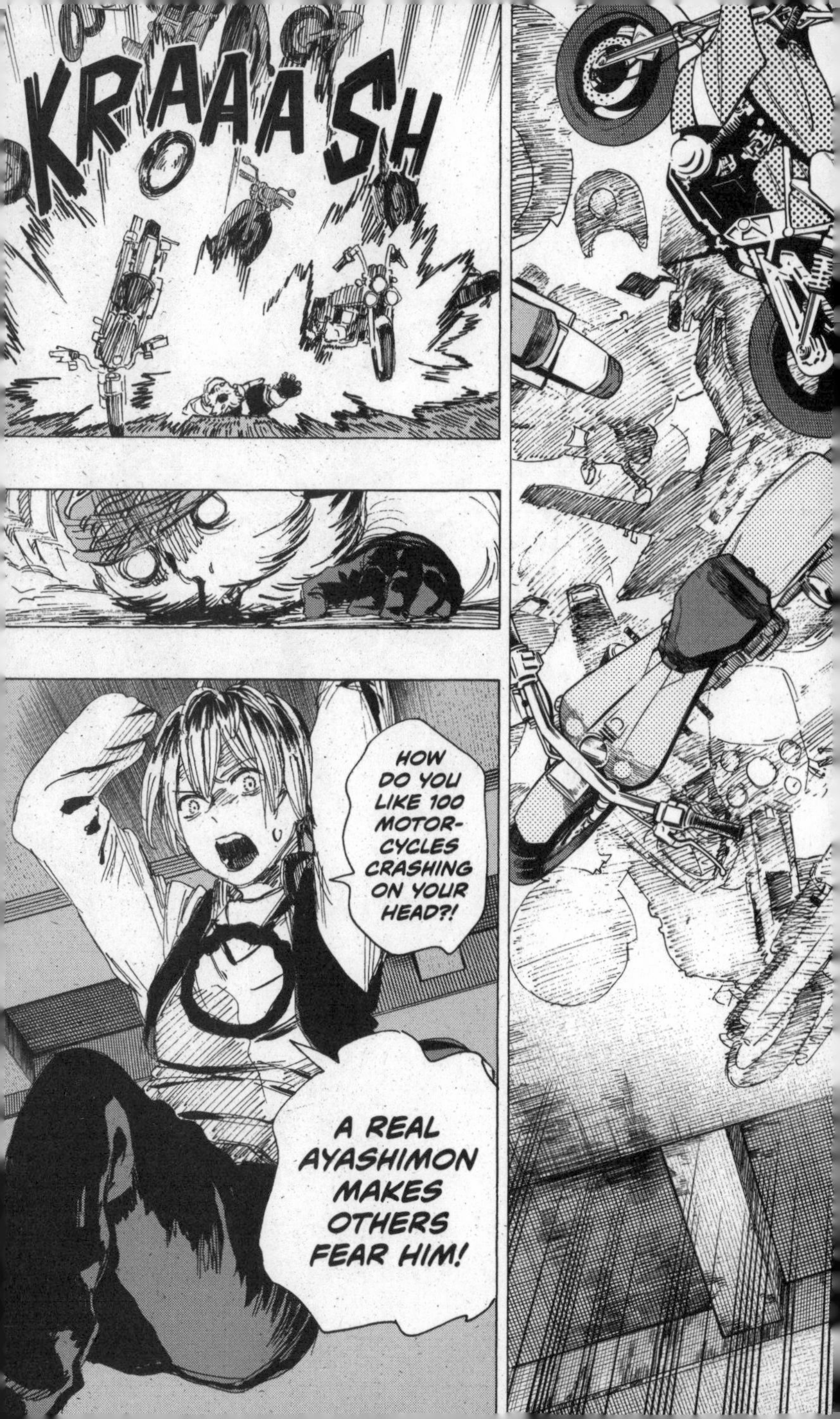
KRAAASH
HOW DO YOU LIKE 100 MOTOR-CYCLES CRASHING ON YOUR HEAD?!
A REAL AYASHIMON MAKES OTHERS FEAR HIM!

KABUKICHO MONSTER MANUAL

Wakku (Wanyudo)

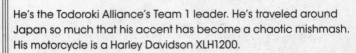

He's the Todoroki Alliance's Team 1 leader. He's traveled around Japan so much that his accent has become a chaotic mishmash. His motorcycle is a Harley Davidson XLH1200.

Chapter 16: Only You

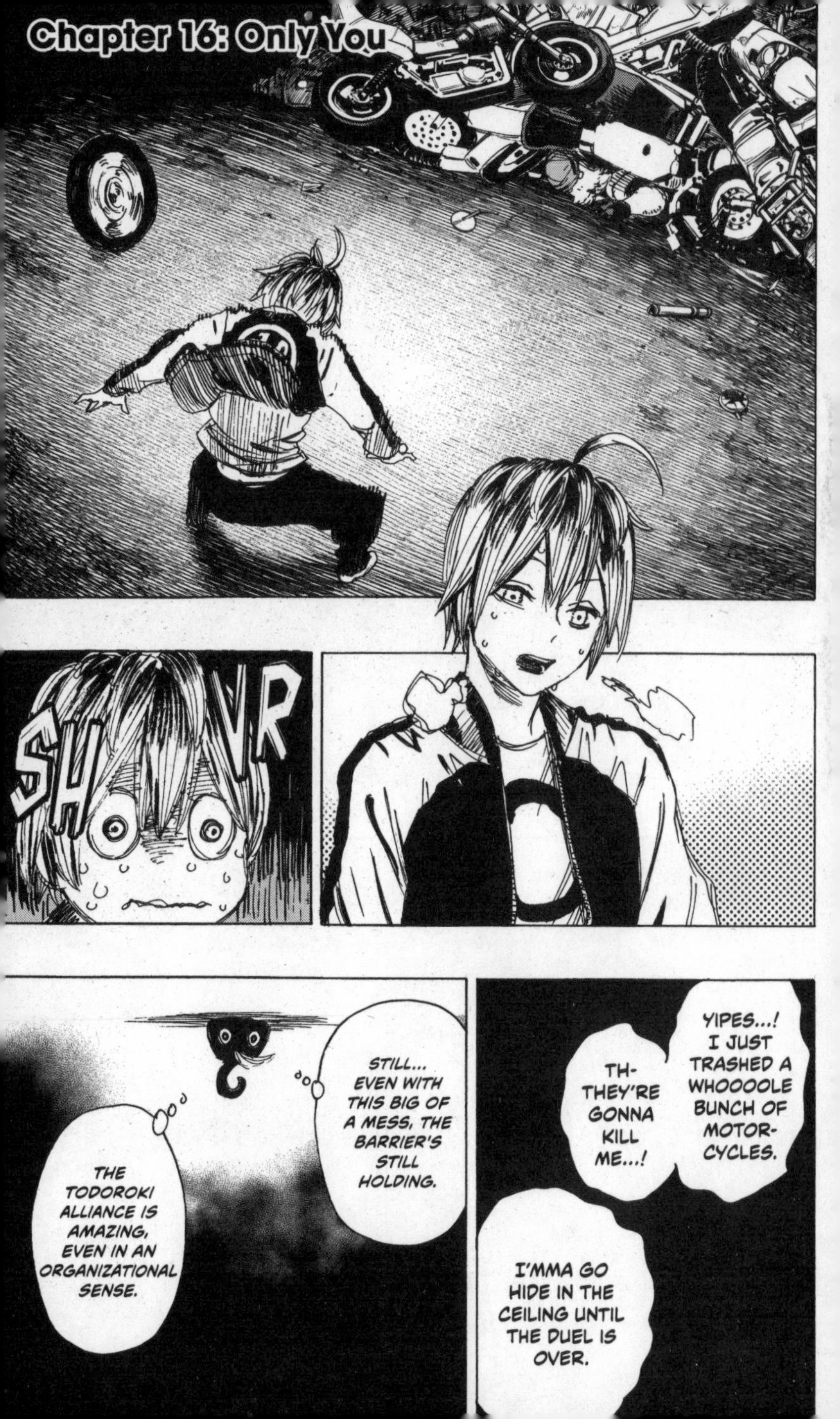
SH VR
YIPES...! I JUST TRASHED A WHOOOOLE BUNCH OF MOTOR-CYCLES.
TH-THEY'RE GONNA KILL ME...!
I'MMA GO HIDE IN THE CEILING UNTIL THE DUEL IS OVER.
STILL... EVEN WITH THIS BIG OF A MESS, THE BARRIER'S STILL HOLDING.
THE TODOROKI ALLIANCE IS AMAZING, EVEN IN AN ORGANIZATIONAL SENSE.

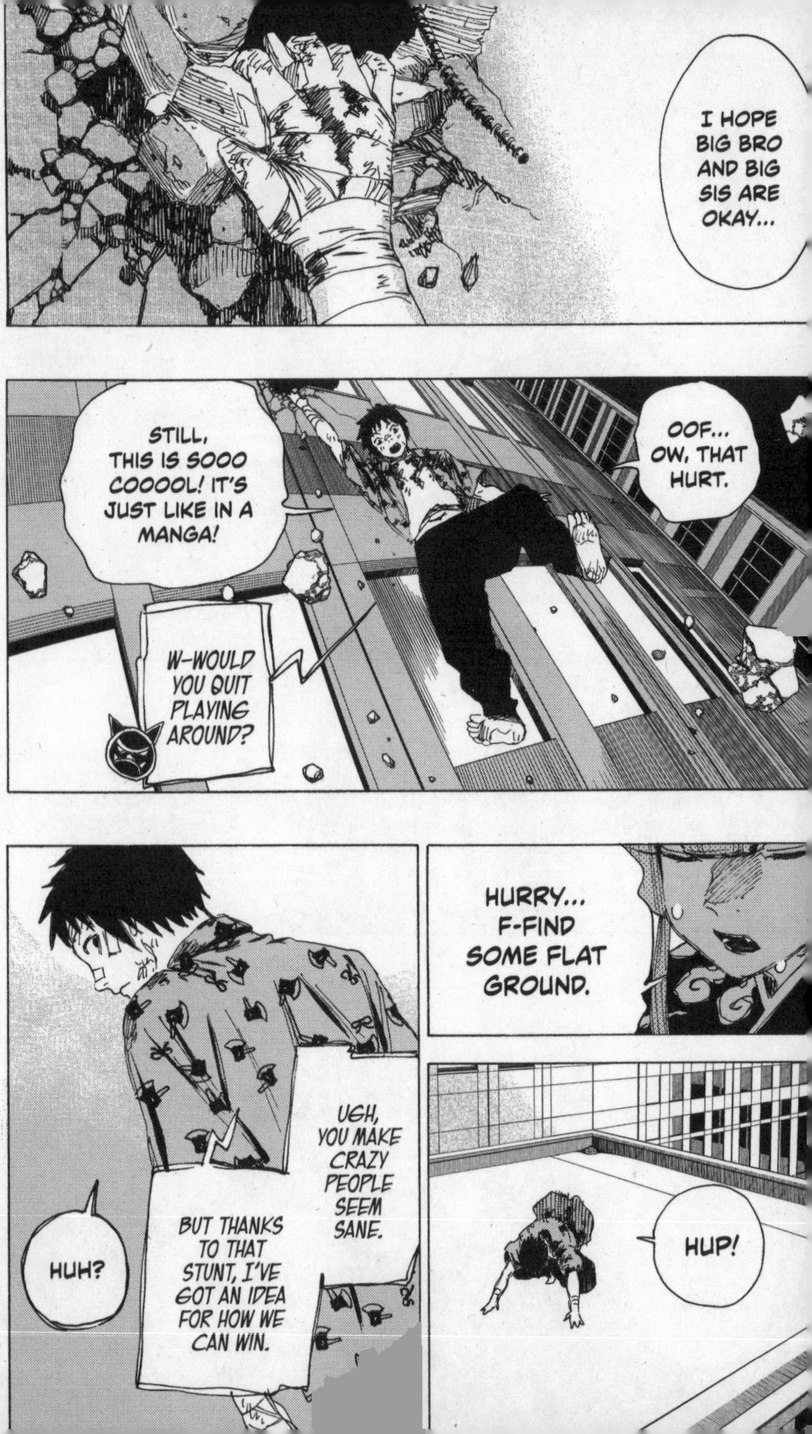
I HOPE BIG BRO AND BIG SIS ARE OKAY...
OOF... OW, THAT HURT.
STILL, THIS IS SOOO COOOOL! IT'S JUST LIKE IN A MANGA!
W-WOULD YOU QUIT PLAYING AROUND?
HURRY... F-FIND SOME FLAT GROUND.
HUP!
UGH, YOU MAKE CRAZY PEOPLE SEEM SANE.
BUT THANKS TO THAT STUNT, I'VE GOT AN IDEA FOR HOW WE CAN WIN.
HUH?

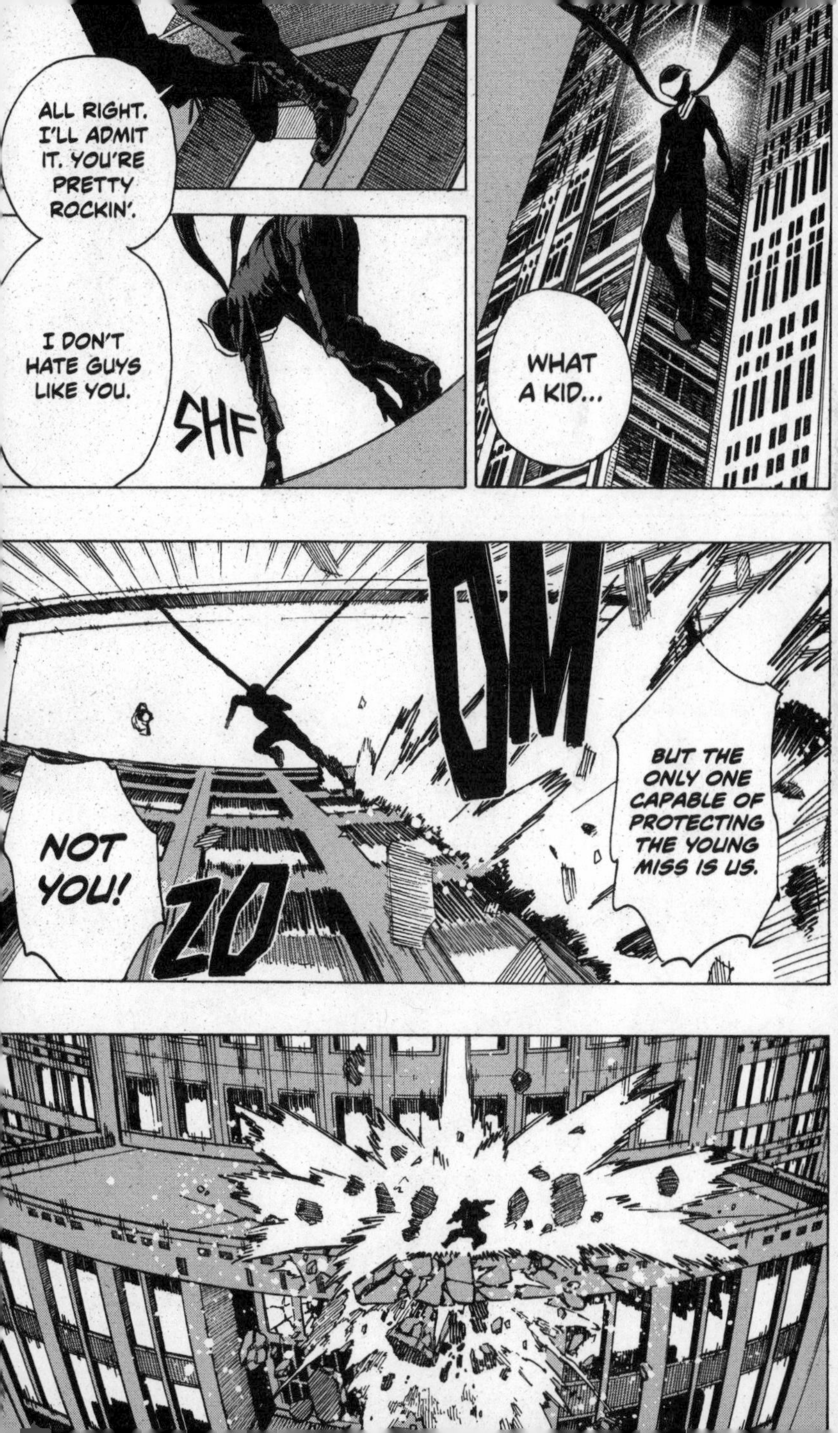
WHAT A KID...
ALL RIGHT. I'LL ADMIT IT. YOU'RE PRETTY ROCKIN'.
I DON'T HATE GUYS LIKE YOU.
SHF
BUT THE ONLY ONE CAPABLE OF PROTECTING THE YOUNG MISS IS US.
NOT YOU!
ZO

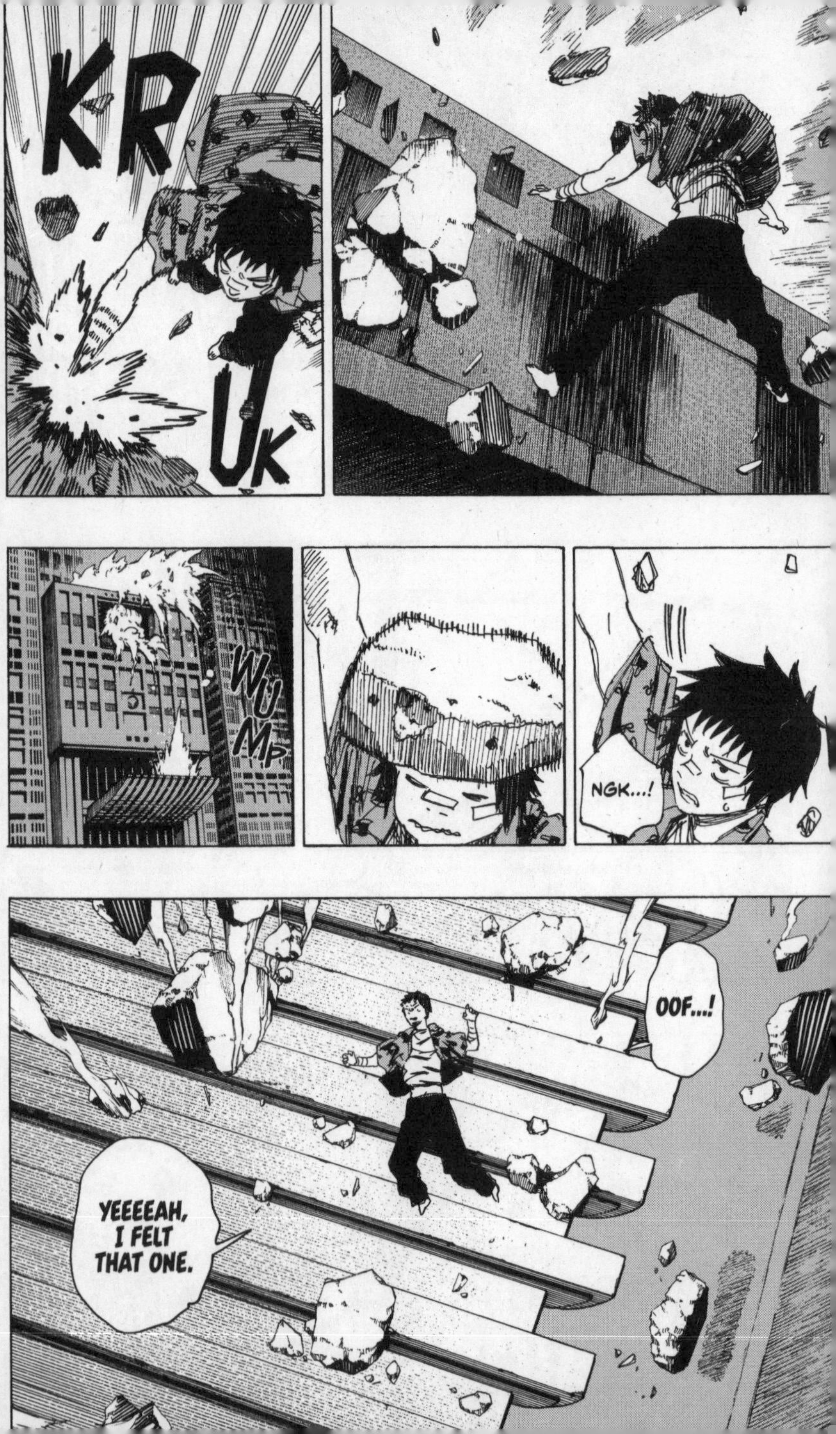
KRUK
NGK...!
WUMP
OOF...!
YEEEEAH, I FELT THAT ONE.

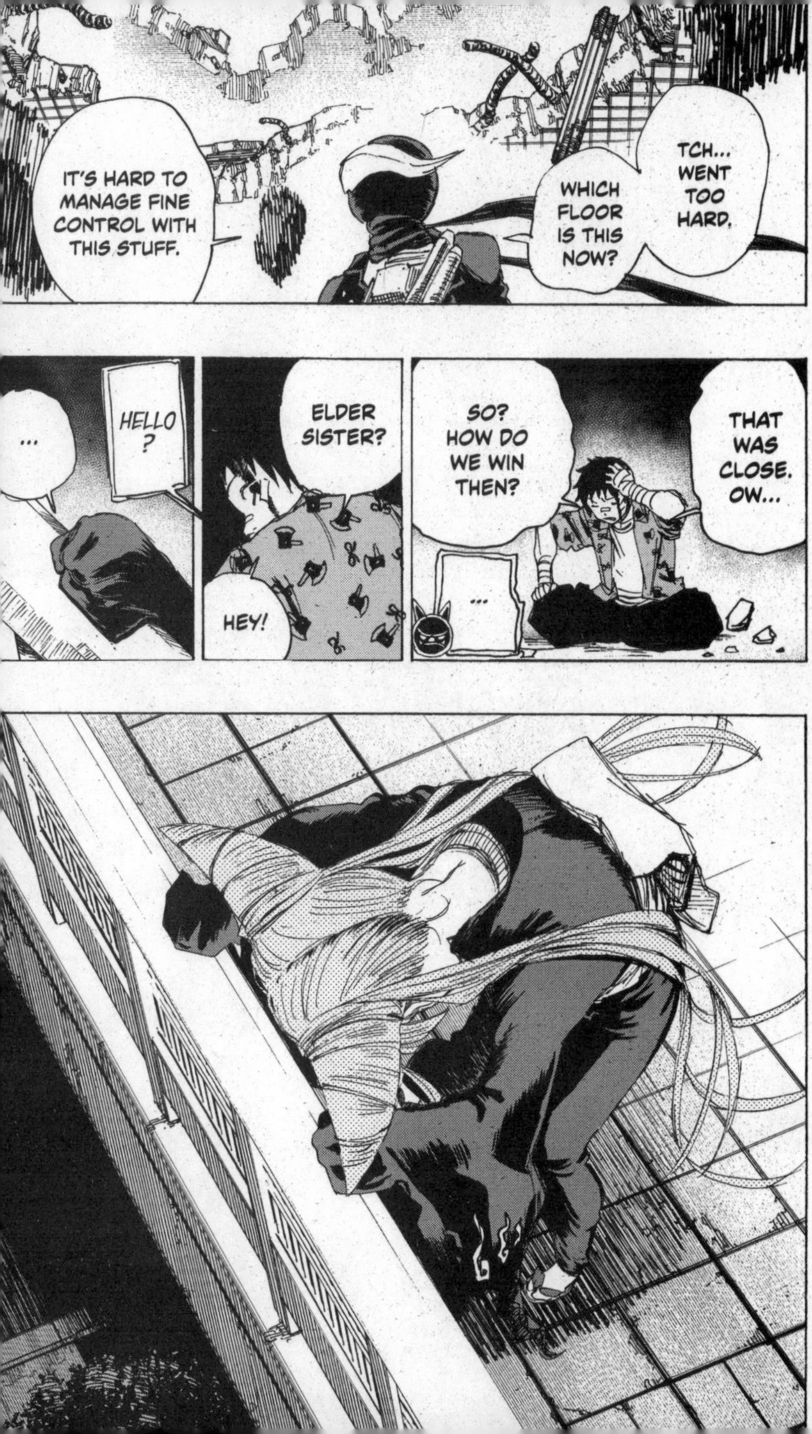
TCH... WENT TOO HARD.
WHICH FLOOR IS THIS NOW?
IT'S HARD TO MANAGE FINE CONTROL WITH THIS STUFF.
THAT WAS CLOSE. OW...
SO? HOW DO WE WIN THEN?
...
ELDER SISTER?
HEY!
HELLO ?
...

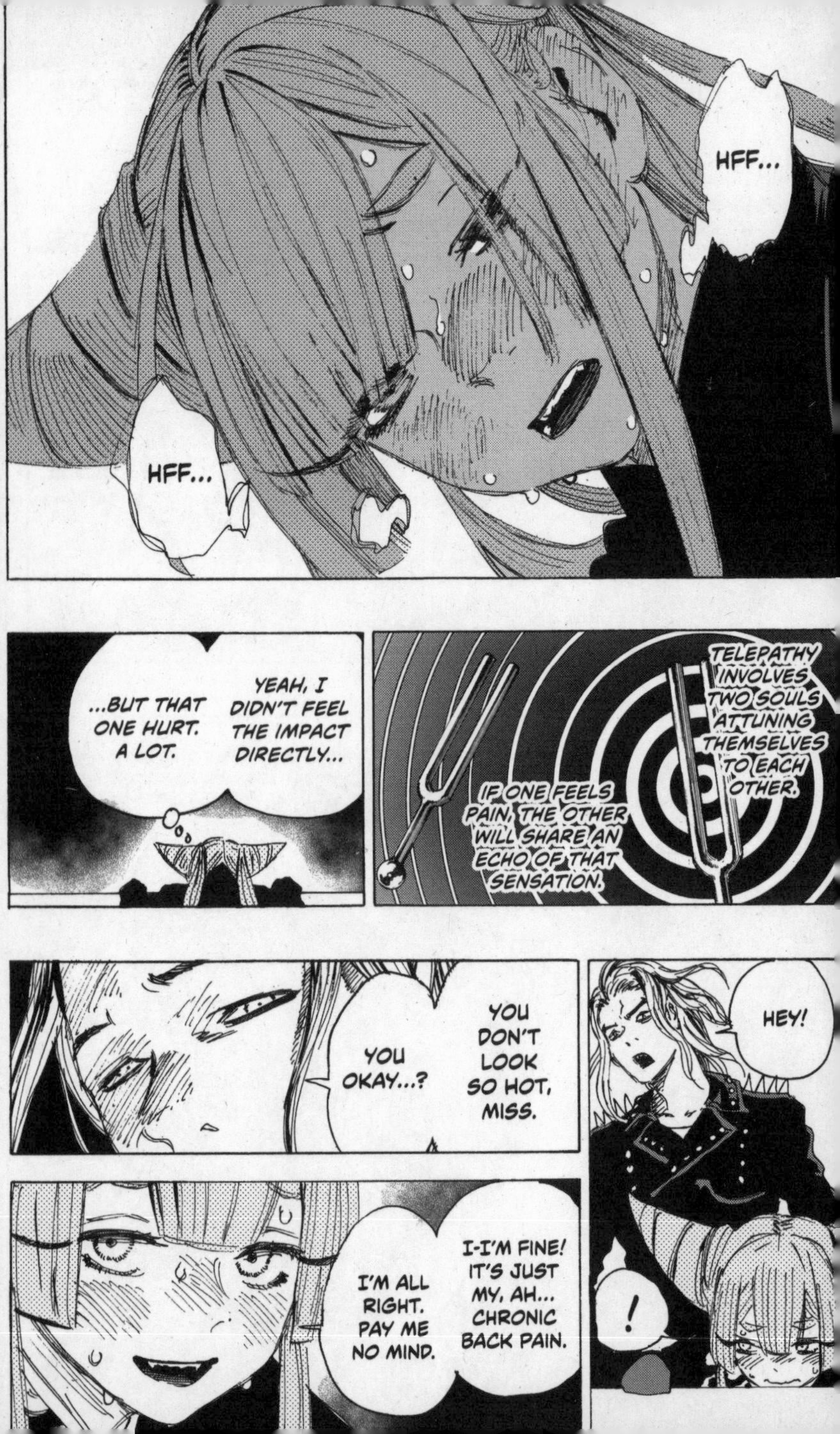
HFF...
HFF...
TELEPATHY INVOLVES TWO SOULS ATTUNING THEMSELVES TO EACH OTHER.
IF ONE FEELS PAIN, THE OTHER WILL SHARE AN ECHO OF THAT SENSATION.
YEAH, I DIDN'T FEEL THE IMPACT DIRECTLY...
...BUT THAT ONE HURT. A LOT.
HEY!
!
YOU DON'T LOOK SO HOT, MISS.
YOU OKAY...?
I-I'M FINE! IT'S JUST MY, AH... CHRONIC BACK PAIN.
I'M ALL RIGHT. PAY ME NO MIND.

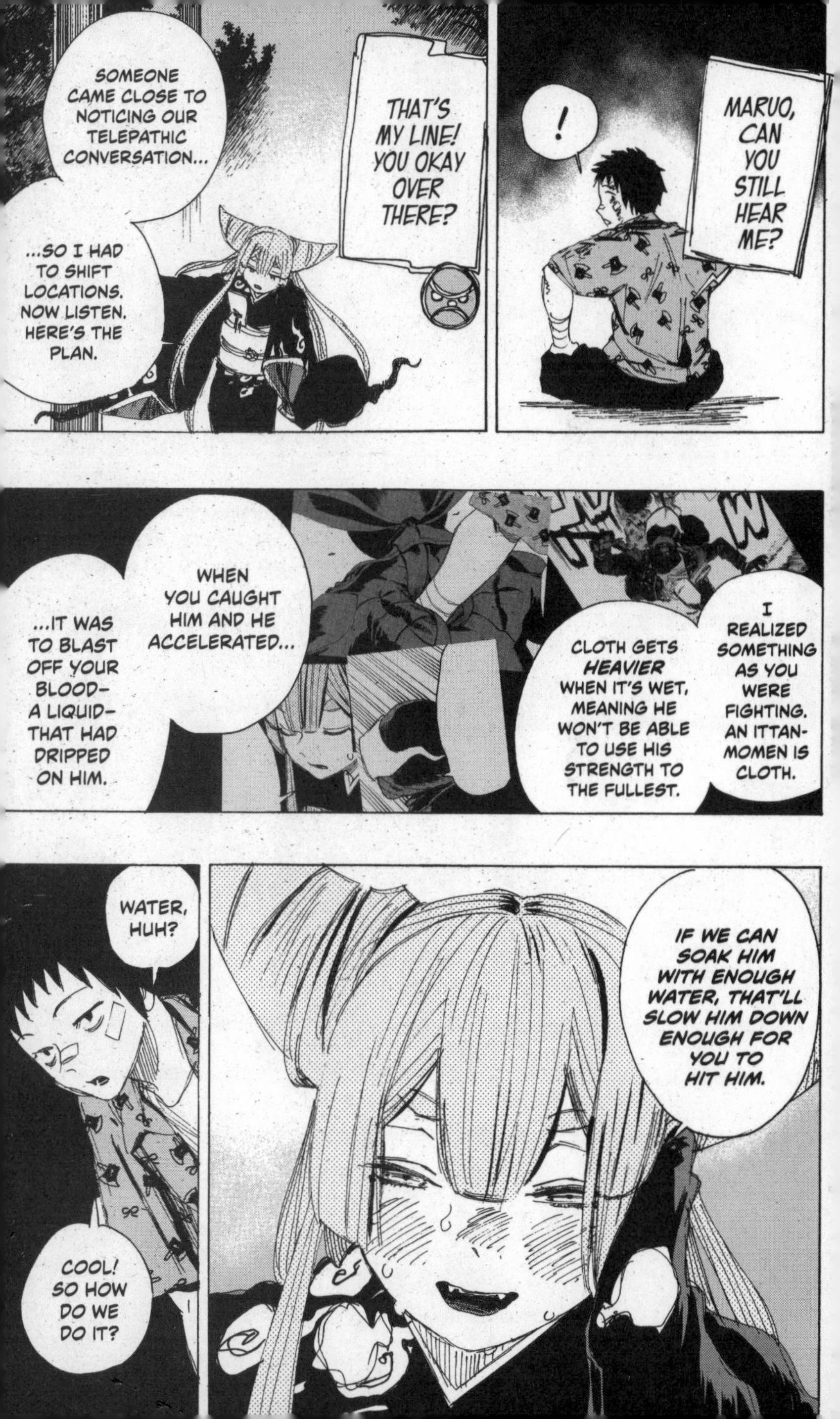
MARUO, CAN YOU STILL HEAR ME?
!
THAT'S MY LINE! YOU OKAY OVER THERE?
SOMEONE CAME CLOSE TO NOTICING OUR TELEPATHIC CONVERSATION...
...SO I HAD TO SHIFT LOCATIONS. NOW LISTEN. HERE'S THE PLAN.
I REALIZED SOMETHING AS YOU WERE FIGHTING. AN ITTAN-MOMEN IS CLOTH.
CLOTH GETS HEAVIER WHEN IT'S WET, MEANING HE WON'T BE ABLE TO USE HIS STRENGTH TO THE FULLEST.
WHEN YOU CAUGHT HIM AND HE ACCELERATED...
...IT WAS TO BLAST OFF YOUR BLOOD- A LIQUID- THAT HAD DRIPPED ON HIM.
IF WE CAN SOAK HIM WITH ENOUGH WATER, THAT'LL SLOW HIM DOWN ENOUGH FOR YOU TO HIT HIM.
WATER, HUH?
COOL! SO HOW DO WE DO IT?

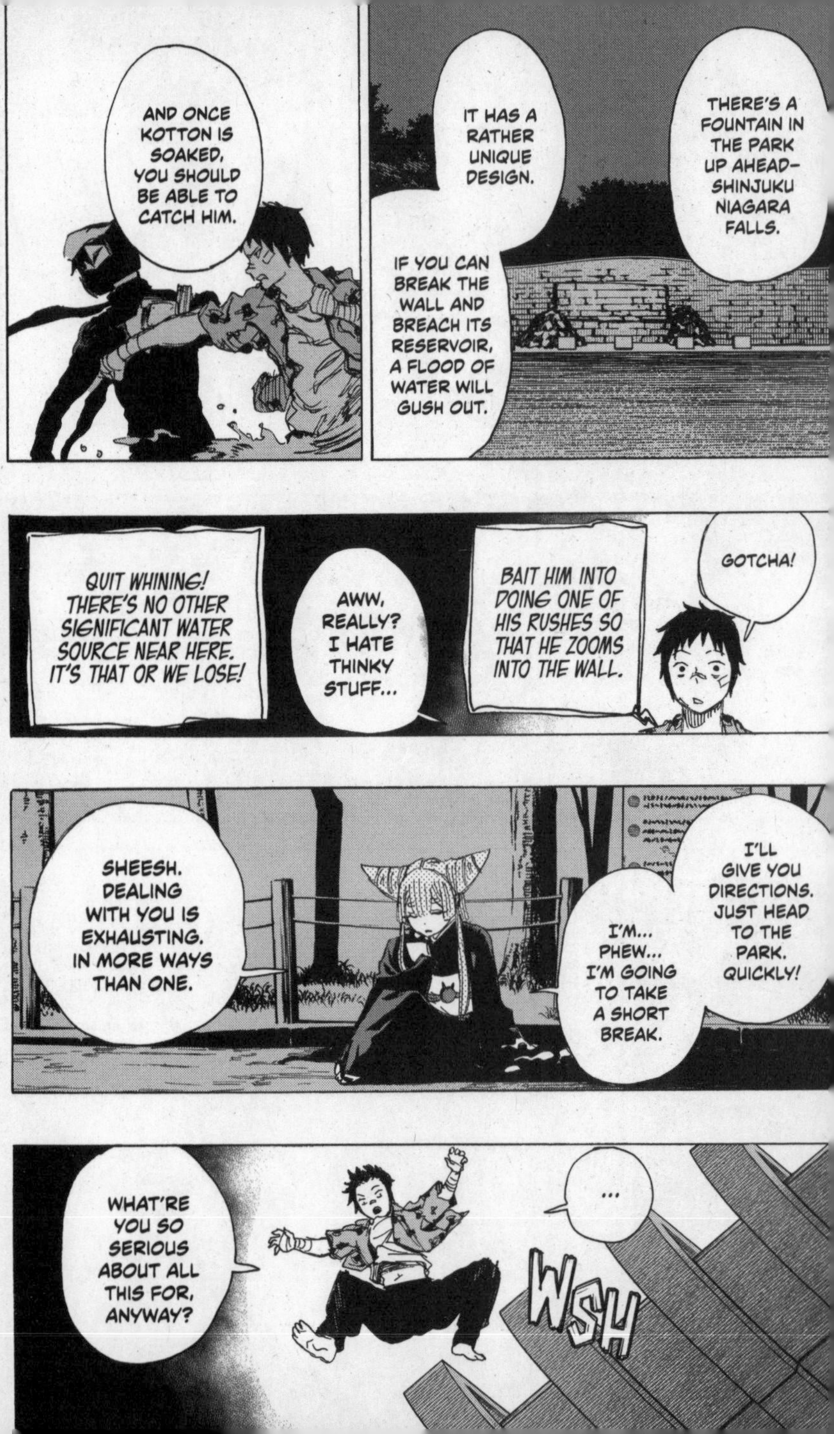
THERE'S A FOUNTAIN IN THE PARK UP AHEAD– SHINJUKU NIAGARA FALLS.
IT HAS A RATHER UNIQUE DESIGN.
IF YOU CAN BREAK THE WALL AND BREACH ITS RESERVOIR, A FLOOD OF WATER WILL GUSH OUT.
AND ONCE KOTTON IS SOAKED, YOU SHOULD BE ABLE TO CATCH HIM.
GOTCHA!
BAIT HIM INTO DOING ONE OF HIS RUSHES SO THAT HE ZOOMS INTO THE WALL.
AWW, REALLY? I HATE THINKY STUFF...
QUIT WHINING! THERE'S NO OTHER SIGNIFICANT WATER SOURCE NEAR HERE. IT'S THAT OR WE LOSE!
I'LL GIVE YOU DIRECTIONS. JUST HEAD TO THE PARK. QUICKLY!
I'M... PHEW... I'M GOING TO TAKE A SHORT BREAK.
SHEESH. DEALING WITH YOU IS EXHAUSTING. IN MORE WAYS THAN ONE.
...
WSH
WHAT'RE YOU SO SERIOUS ABOUT ALL THIS FOR, ANYWAY?

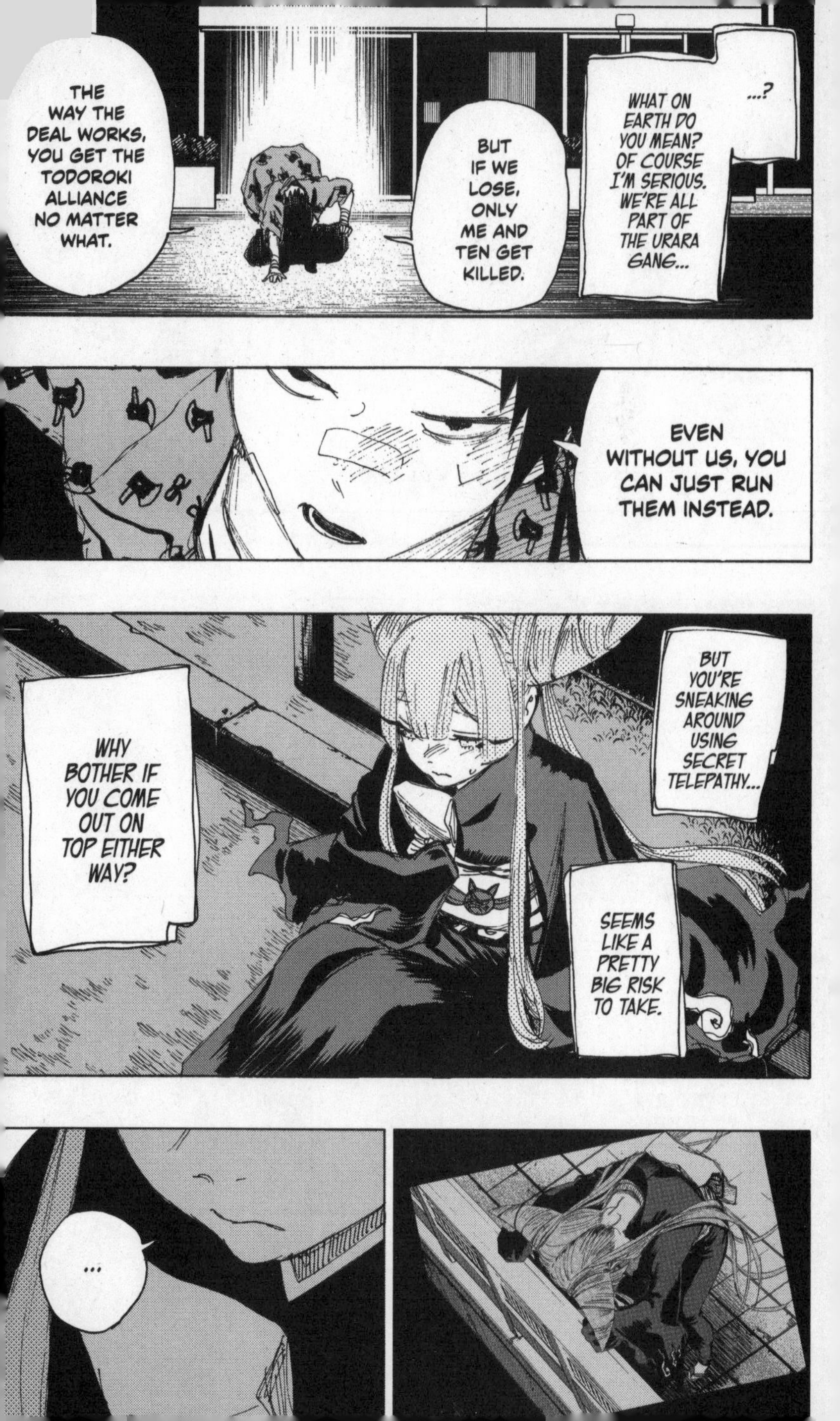
...?
WHAT ON EARTH DO YOU MEAN? OF COURSE I'M SERIOUS. WE'RE ALL PART OF THE URARA GANG...
BUT IF WE LOSE, ONLY ME AND TEN GET KILLED.
THE WAY THE DEAL WORKS, YOU GET THE TODOROKI ALLIANCE NO MATTER WHAT.
EVEN WITHOUT US, YOU CAN JUST RUN THEM INSTEAD.
BUT YOU'RE SNEAKING AROUND USING SECRET TELEPATHY...
SEEMS LIKE A PRETTY BIG RISK TO TAKE.
WHY BOTHER IF YOU COME OUT ON TOP EITHER WAY?
...

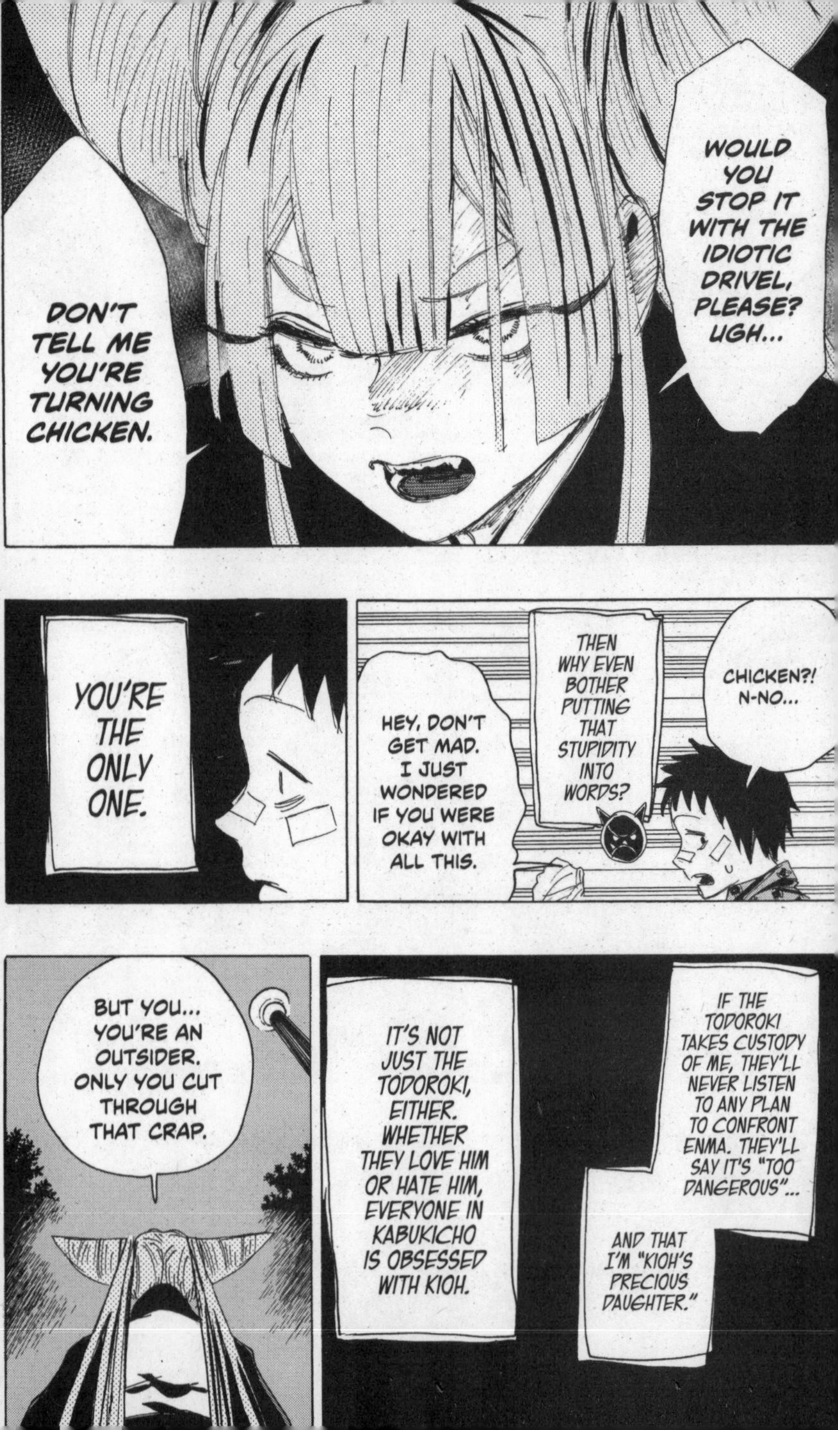

WOULD YOU STOP IT WITH THE IDIOTIC DRIVEL, PLEASE? UGH...
DON'T TELL ME YOU'RE TURNING CHICKEN.
CHICKEN?! N-NO...
THEN WHY EVEN BOTHER PUTTING THAT STUPIDITY INTO WORDS?
HEY, DON'T GET MAD. I JUST WONDERED IF YOU WERE OKAY WITH ALL THIS.
YOU'RE THE ONLY ONE.
IF THE TODOROKI TAKES CUSTODY OF ME, THEY'LL NEVER LISTEN TO ANY PLAN TO CONFRONT ENMA. THEY'LL SAY IT'S "TOO DANGEROUS"...
AND THAT I'M "KIOH'S PRECIOUS DAUGHTER."
IT'S NOT JUST THE TODOROKI, EITHER. WHETHER THEY LOVE HIM OR HATE HIM, EVERYONE IN KABUKICHO IS OBSESSED WITH KIOH.
BUT YOU... YOU'RE AN OUTSIDER. ONLY YOU CUT THROUGH THAT CRAP.

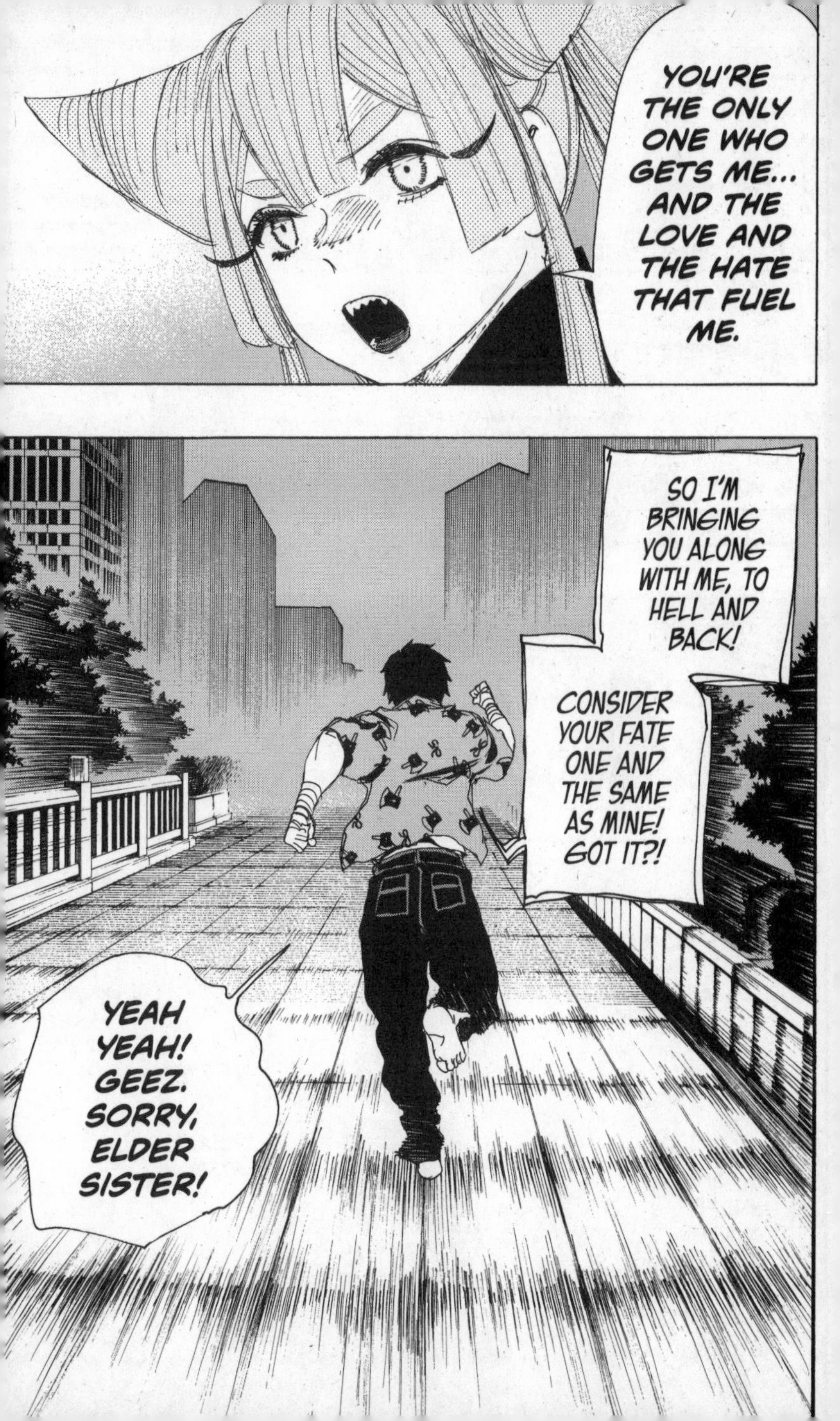
YOU'RE THE ONLY ONE WHO GETS ME... AND THE LOVE AND THE HATE THAT FUEL ME.
SO I'M BRINGING YOU ALONG WITH ME, TO HELL AND BACK!
CONSIDER YOUR FATE ONE AND THE SAME AS MINE! GOT IT?!
YEAH YEAH! GEEZ. SORRY, ELDER SISTER!

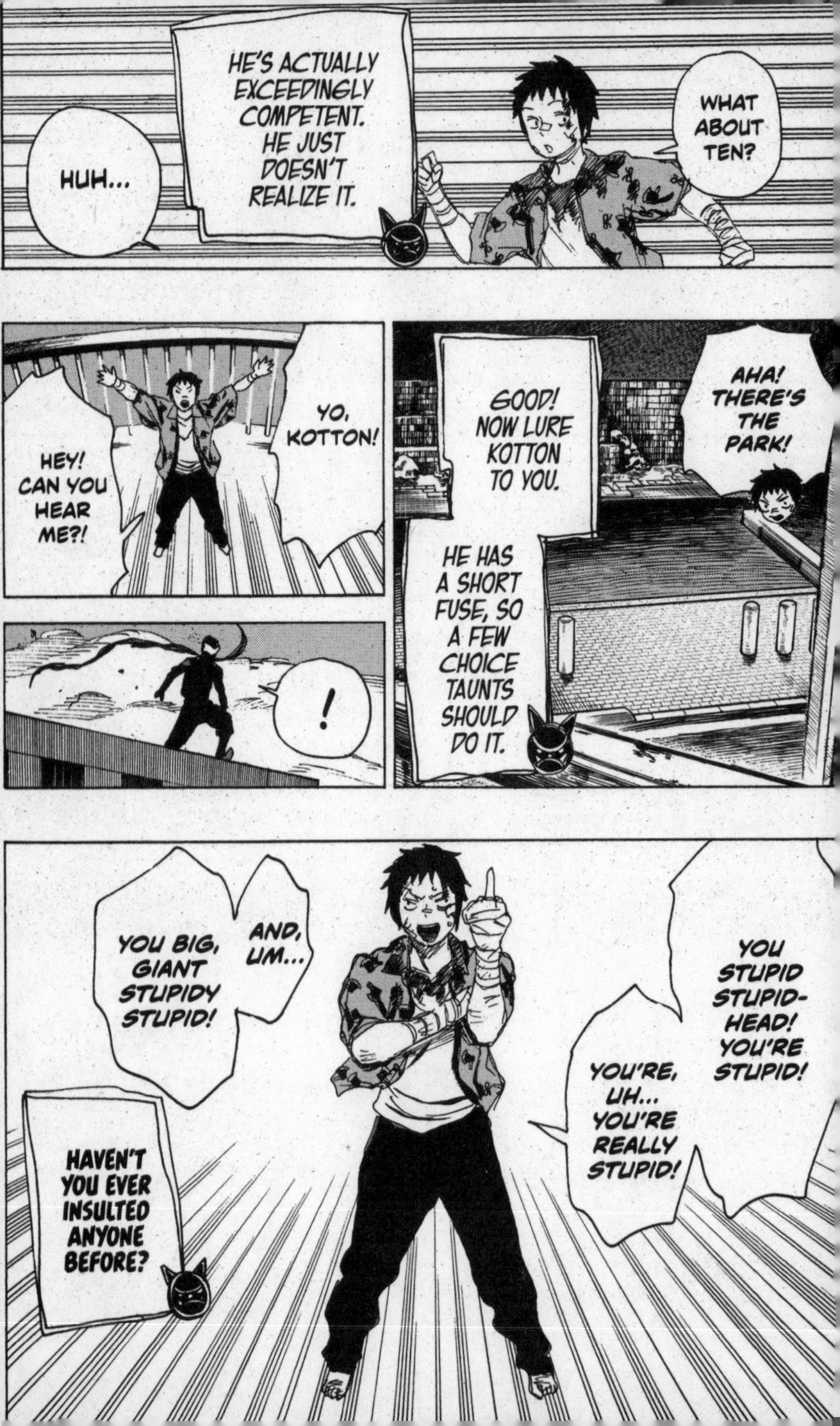
WHAT ABOUT TEN?
HE'S ACTUALLY EXCEEDINGLY COMPETENT. HE JUST DOESN'T REALIZE IT.
HUH...
AHA! THERE'S THE PARK!
GOOD! NOW LURE KOTTON TO YOU.
HE HAS A SHORT FUSE, SO A FEW CHOICE TAUNTS SHOULD DO IT.
YO, KOTTON!
HEY! CAN YOU HEAR ME?!
!
YOU STUPID STUPID-HEAD! YOU'RE STUPID!
YOU'RE, UH... YOU'RE REALLY STUPID!
AND, UM...
YOU BIG, GIANT STUPIDY STUPID!
HAVEN'T YOU EVER INSULTED ANYONE BEFORE?

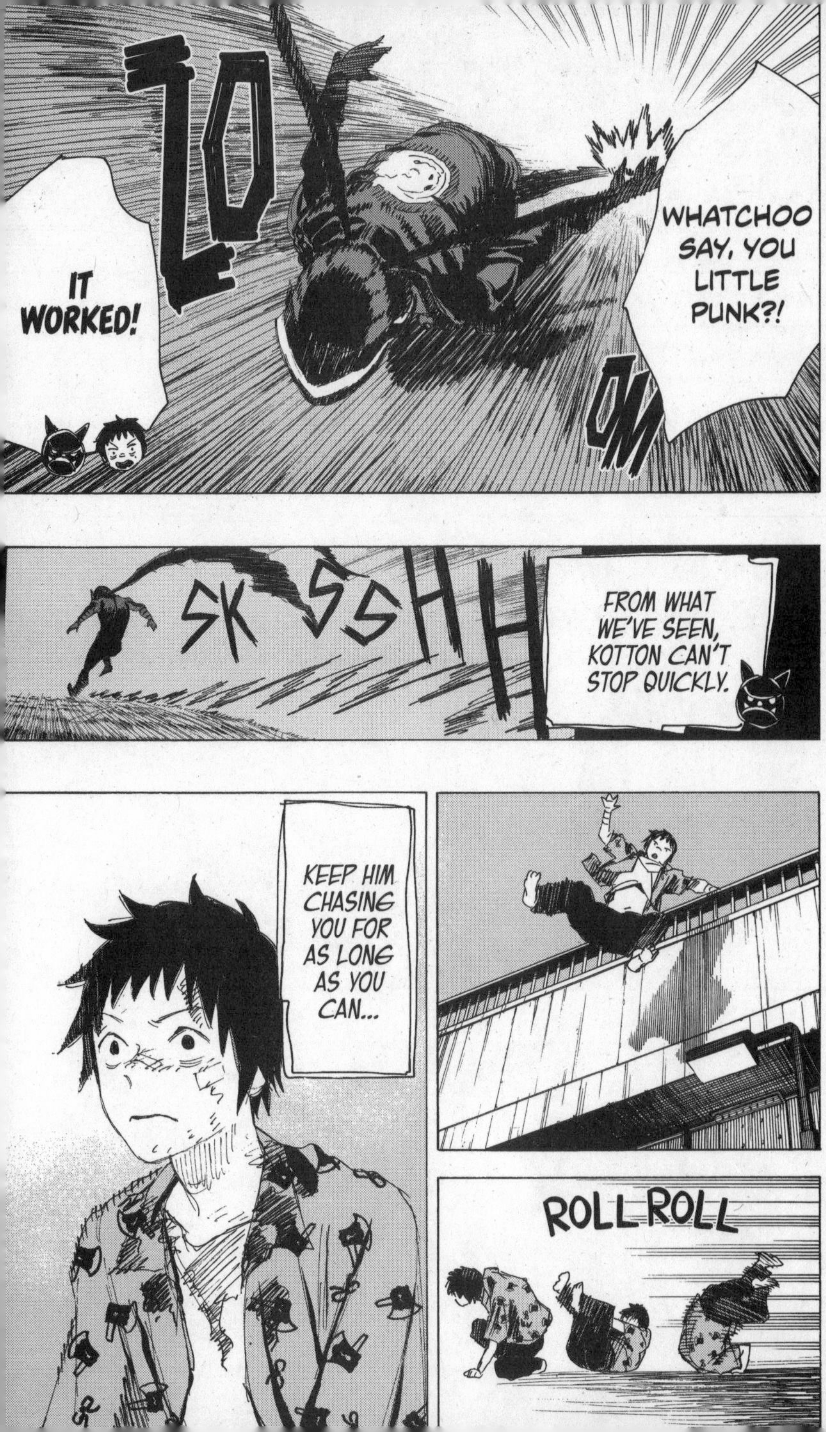
WHATCHOO SAY, YOU LITTLE PUNK?!
ZO
OM
IT WORKED!
FROM WHAT WE'VE SEEN, KOTTON CAN'T STOP QUICKLY.
SKSSHH
ROLL ROLL
KEEP HIM CHASING YOU FOR AS LONG AS YOU CAN...

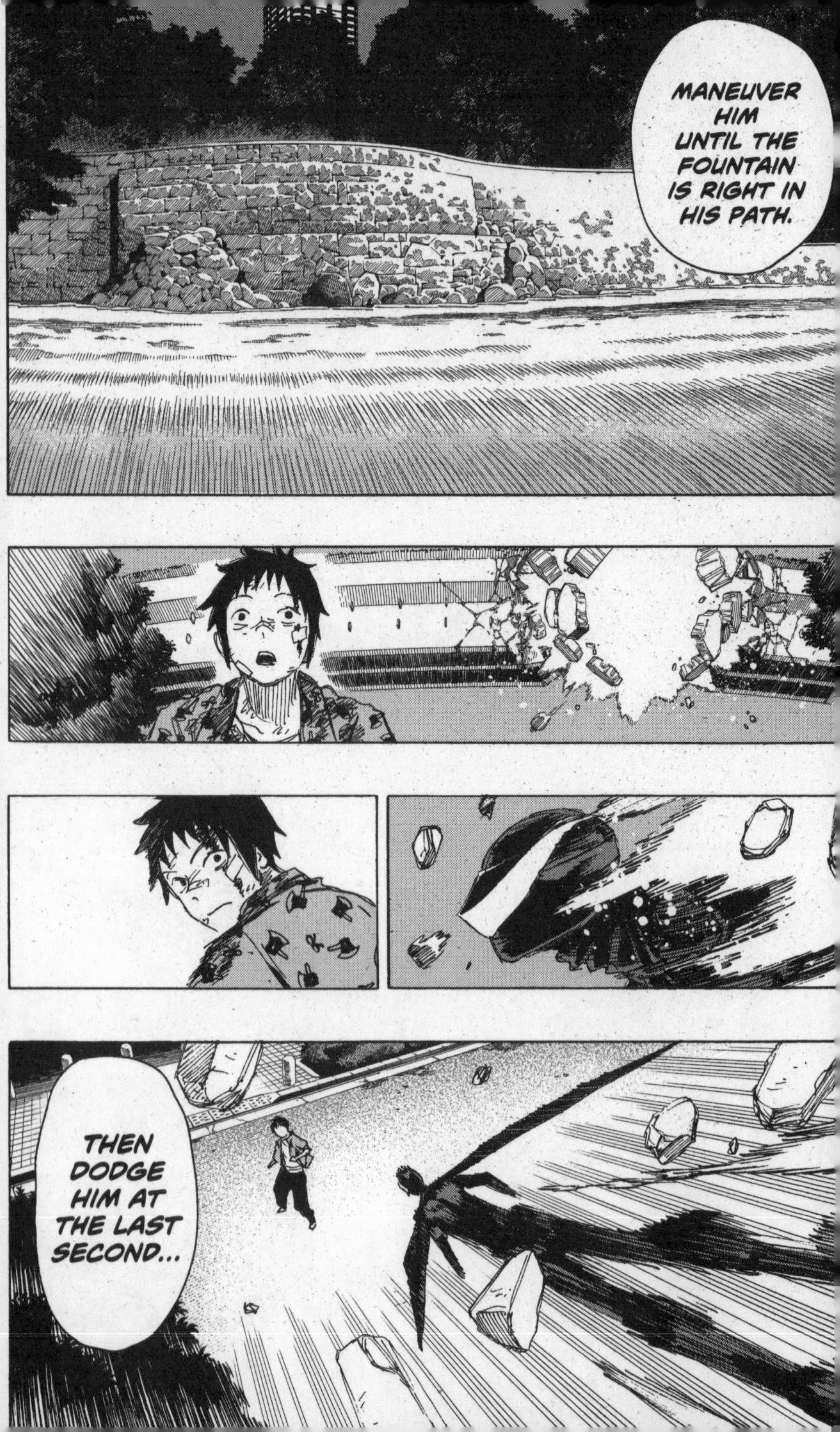
MANEUVER HIM UNTIL THE FOUNTAIN IS RIGHT IN HIS PATH.
THEN DODGE HIM AT THE LAST SECOND...

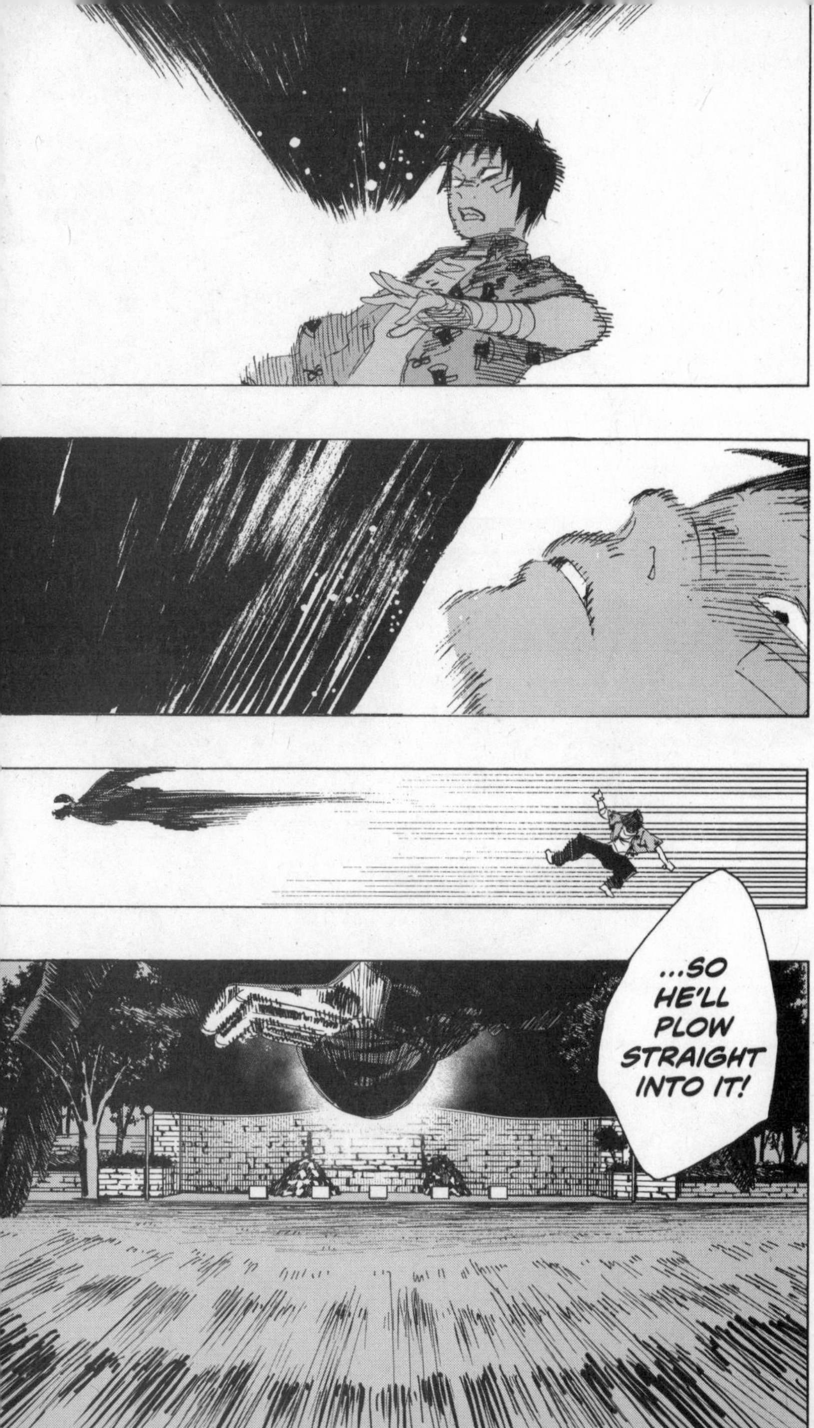
...SO HE'LL PLOW STRAIGHT INTO IT!

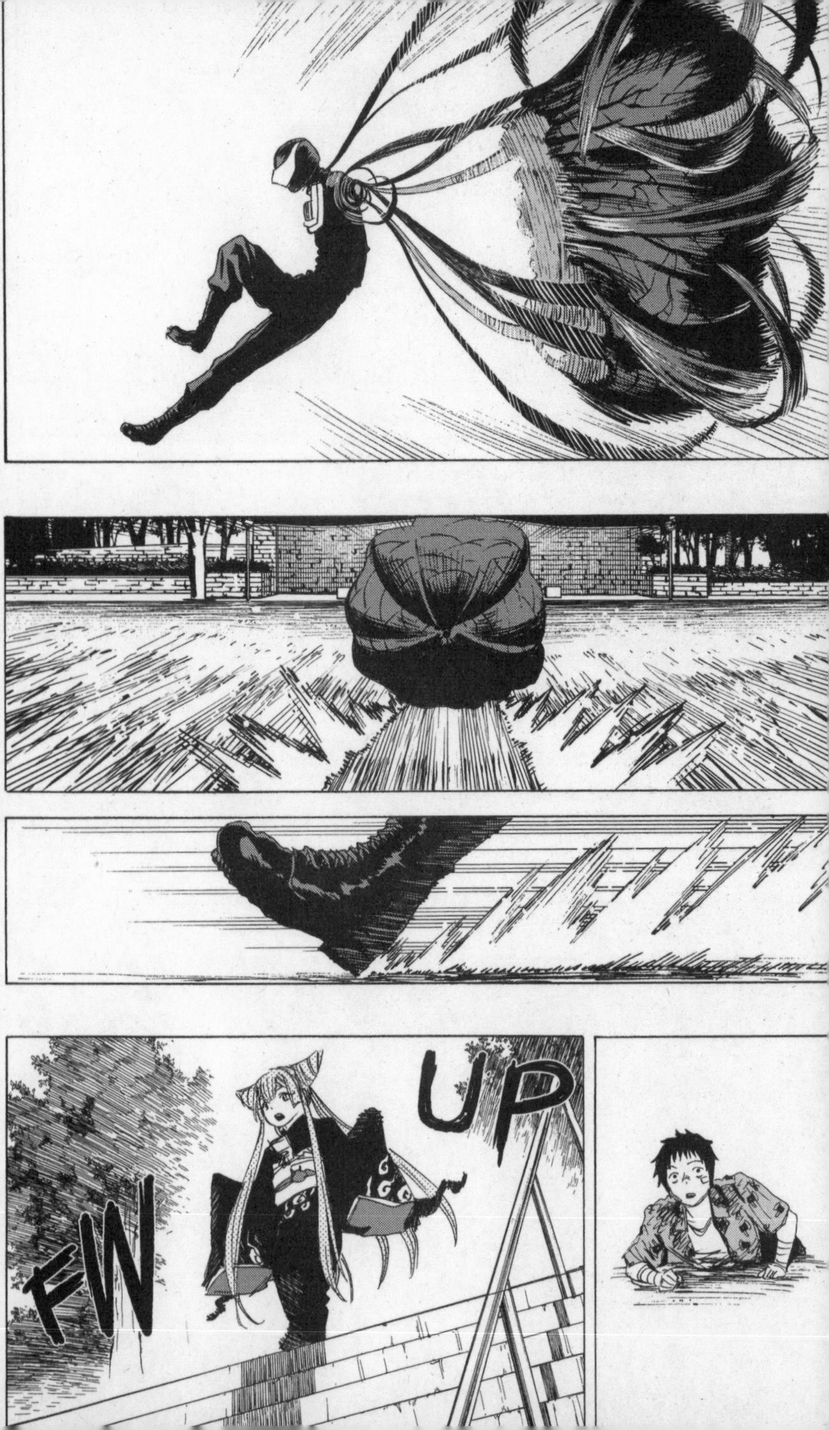
UP
FW

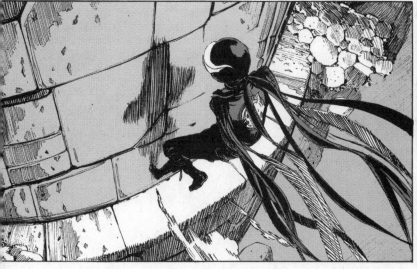

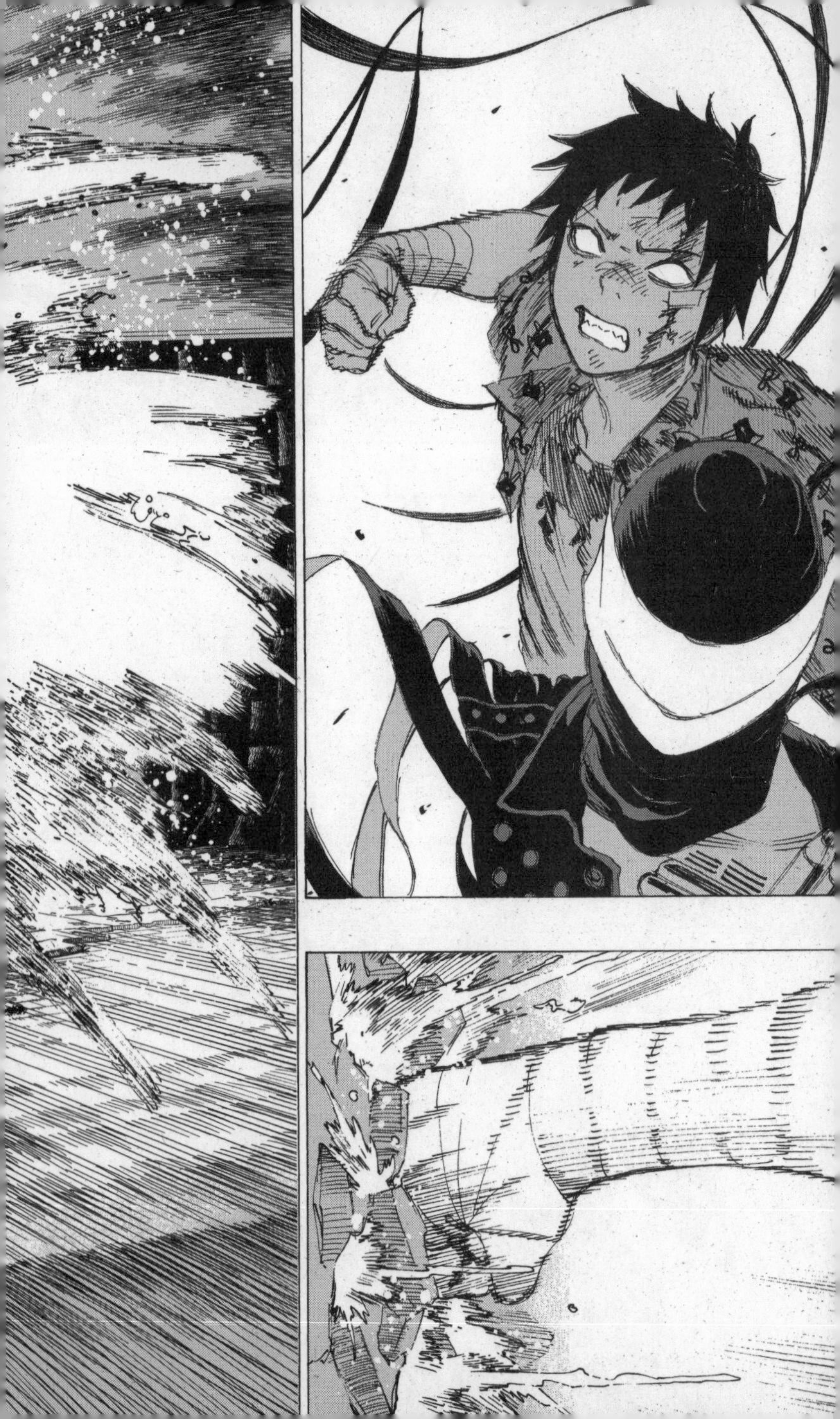

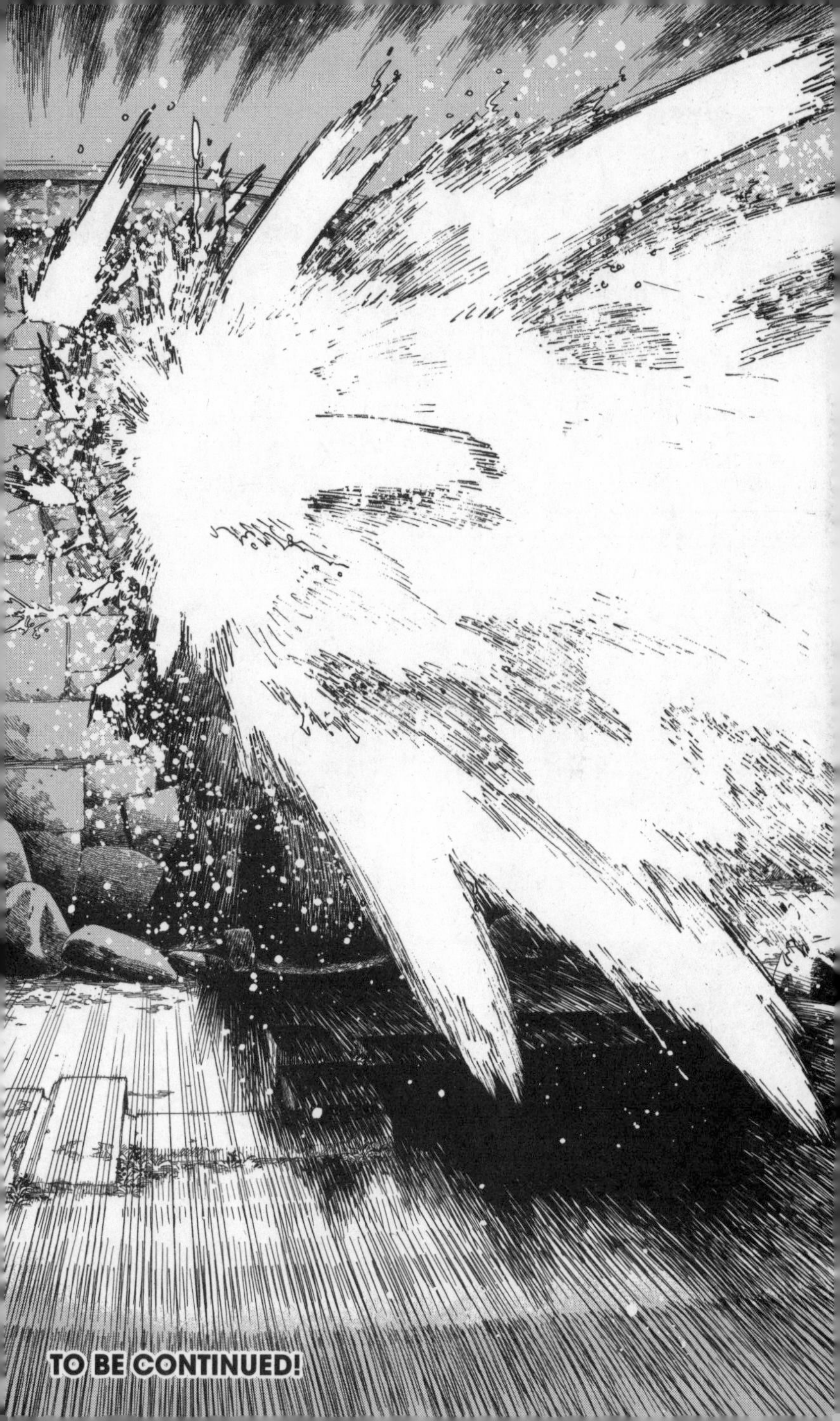
TO BE CONTINUED!

Bonus Story 1: New Year's

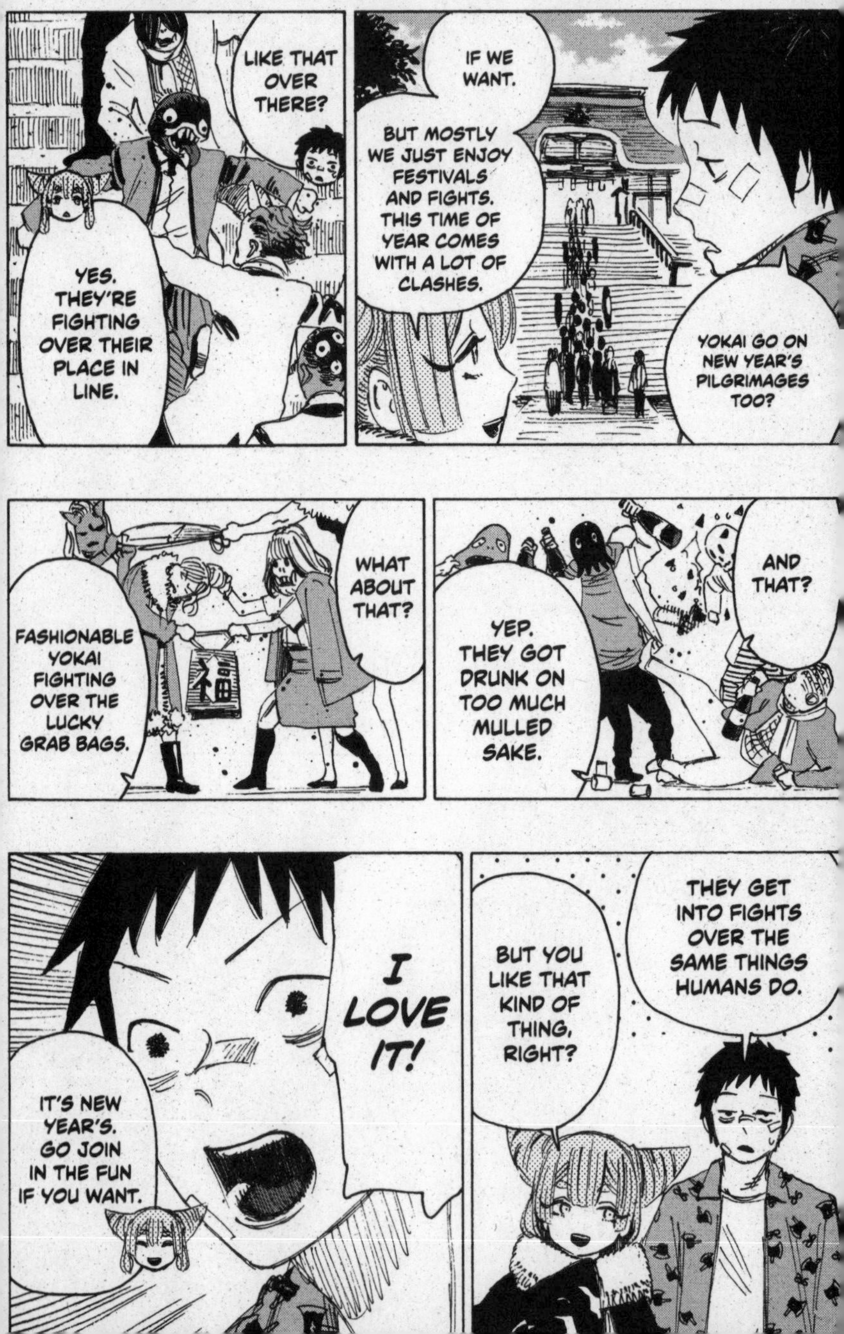
YOKAI GO ON NEW YEAR'S PILGRIMAGES TOO?
IF WE WANT.
BUT MOSTLY WE JUST ENJOY FESTIVALS AND FIGHTS. THIS TIME OF YEAR COMES WITH A LOT OF CLASHES.
LIKE THAT OVER THERE?
YES. THEY'RE FIGHTING OVER THEIR PLACE IN LINE.
AND THAT?
YEP. THEY GOT DRUNK ON TOO MUCH MULLED SAKE.
WHAT ABOUT THAT?
FASHIONABLE YOKAI FIGHTING OVER THE LUCKY GRAB BAGS.
福
THEY GET INTO FIGHTS OVER THE SAME THINGS HUMANS DO.
BUT YOU LIKE THAT KIND OF THING, RIGHT?
I LOVE IT!
IT'S NEW YEAR'S. GO JOIN IN THE FUN IF YOU WANT.

AYASHIMON

Bonus Story 2

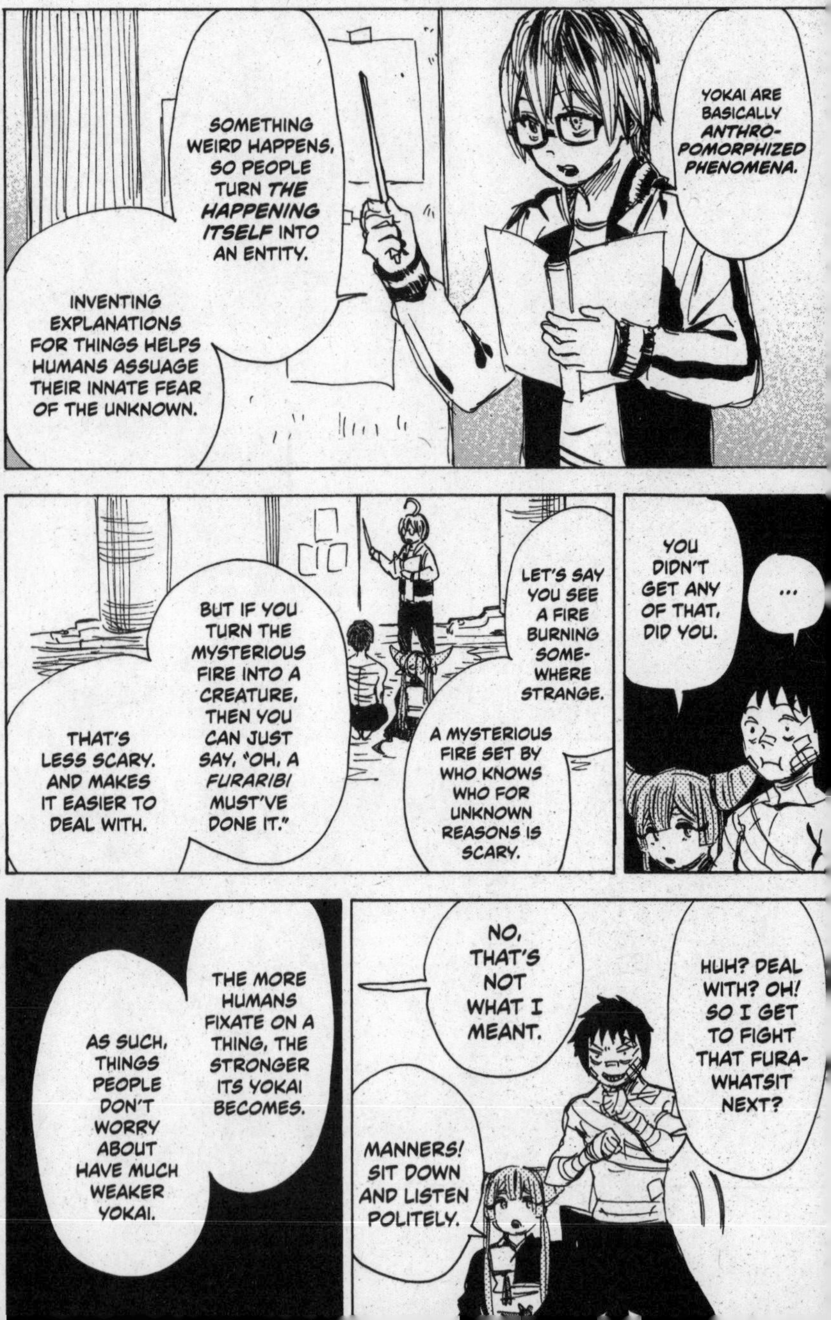
YOKAI ARE BASICALLY ANTHRO-POMORPHIZED PHENOMENA.
SOMETHING WEIRD HAPPENS, SO PEOPLE TURN THE HAPPENING ITSELF INTO AN ENTITY.
INVENTING EXPLANATIONS FOR THINGS HELPS HUMANS ASSUAGE THEIR INNATE FEAR OF THE UNKNOWN.
YOU DIDN'T GET ANY OF THAT, DID YOU.
...
LET'S SAY YOU SEE A FIRE BURNING SOME-WHERE STRANGE.
A MYSTERIOUS FIRE SET BY WHO KNOWS WHO FOR UNKNOWN REASONS IS SCARY.
BUT IF YOU TURN THE MYSTERIOUS FIRE INTO A CREATURE, THEN YOU CAN JUST SAY, "OH, A FURARIBI MUST'VE DONE IT."
THAT'S LESS SCARY. AND MAKES IT EASIER TO DEAL WITH.
HUH? DEAL WITH? OH! SO I GET TO FIGHT THAT FURA-WHATSIT NEXT?
NO, THAT'S NOT WHAT I MEANT.
MANNERS! SIT DOWN AND LISTEN POLITELY.
THE MORE HUMANS FIXATE ON A THING, THE STRONGER ITS YOKAI BECOMES.
AS SUCH, THINGS PEOPLE DON'T WORRY ABOUT HAVE MUCH WEAKER YOKAI.

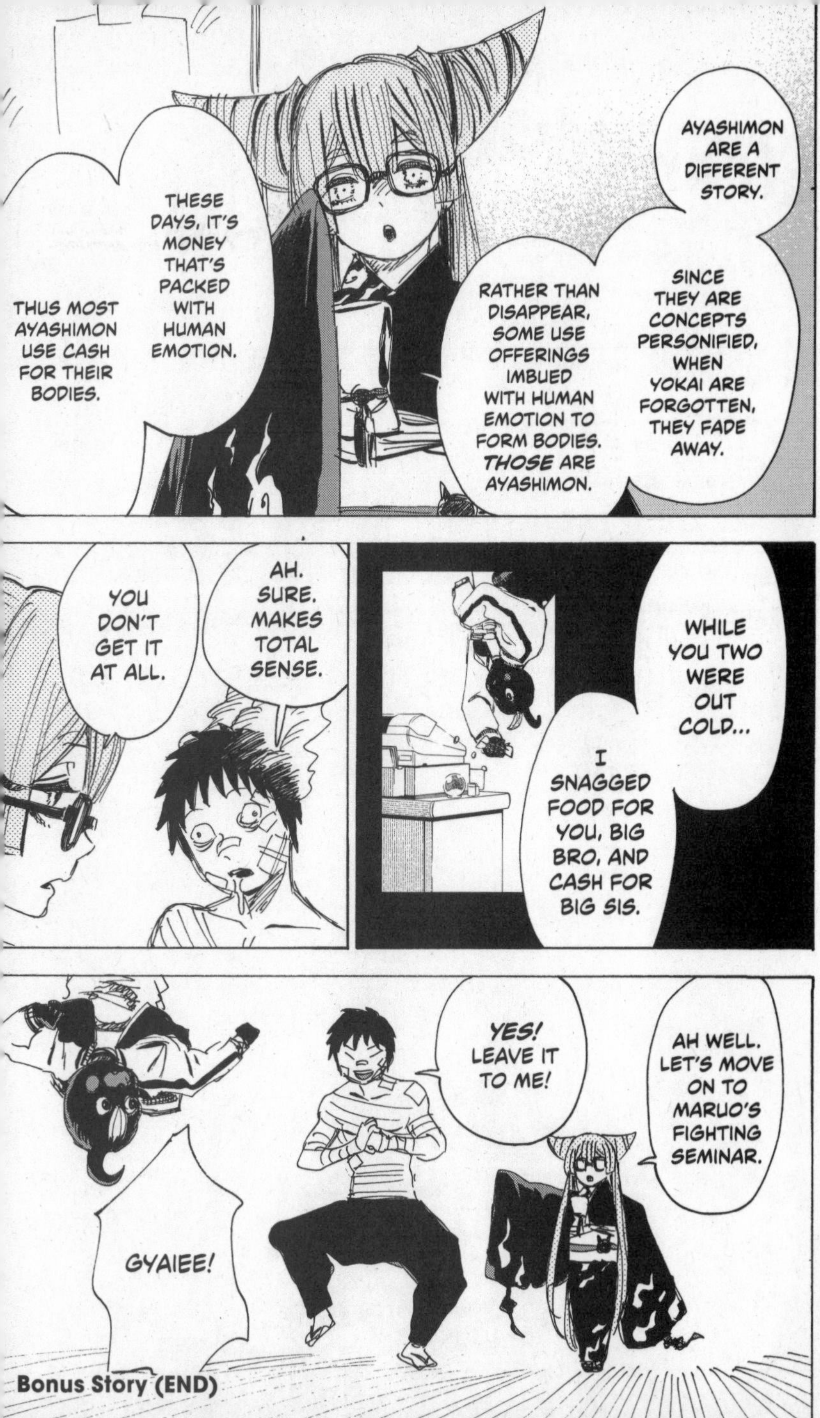
AYASHIMON ARE A DIFFERENT STORY.
SINCE THEY ARE CONCEPTS PERSONIFIED, WHEN YOKAI ARE FORGOTTEN, THEY FADE AWAY.
RATHER THAN DISAPPEAR, SOME USE OFFERINGS IMBUED WITH HUMAN EMOTION TO FORM BODIES. *THOSE* ARE AYASHIMON.
THESE DAYS, IT'S MONEY THAT'S PACKED WITH HUMAN EMOTION.
THUS MOST AYASHIMON USE CASH FOR THEIR BODIES.
WHILE YOU TWO WERE OUT COLD...
I SNAGGED FOOD FOR YOU, BIG BRO, AND CASH FOR BIG SIS.
AH. SURE. MAKES TOTAL SENSE.
YOU DON'T GET IT AT ALL.
AH WELL. LET'S MOVE ON TO MARUO'S FIGHTING SEMINAR.
YES! LEAVE IT TO ME!
GYAIEE!

Bonus Story (END)

AYASHIMON

reads from right to left, starting in the upper-right corner. Japanese is read from right to left, meaning that action, sound effects, and word-balloon order are completely reversed from English order.

Check out the diagram shown here to get the hang of things, and then turn to the other side of the book to get started!

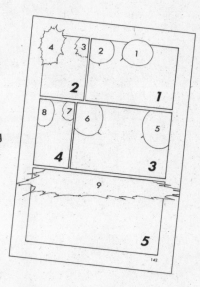